Other books by Susan Noyes Platt, Ph.D.

---

*Breaking Ground: Art Modernisms 1920-1950, Collected Writings Vol. 1*
(Susan Noyes Platt, 2020)

*Art and Politics Now: Cultural Activism in a Time of Crisis*
(Midmarch Arts Press, 2011)

*Art and Politics in the 1930s: Modernism, Marxism, Americanism*
*A History of Cultural Activism during the Depression Years*
(Midmarch Arts Press, 1999)

*Modernism in the 1920s: Interpretations of Modern Art in New*
*York from Expressionism to Constructivism*
(UMI Research Press, 1985)

# SETTING OUR HEARTS ON FIRE

Essays on Artists

from 1980 to the Present:

Addressing Inequities

and Inspiring a Future

BY

## SUSAN NOYES PLATT

Collected Writings Vol. 2

Book & cover design:
Vladimir Verano, VertVolta Design

Published in the United States by

Susan Noyes Platt
www.artandpoliticsnow.com

ISBN
Print: 978-1-7345043-2-3
ebook: 978-1-7345043-3-0

# Contents

## 6 Defying Clichés



## 7 Setting Our Hearts on Fire

# Acknowledgements

I would like to first of all thank all of the artists. It was my honor to have the opportunity to write about their inspiring work and seek to interpret and contextualize the many ideas they presented.

Second I thank my editor, Phoebe Bosché, whose wonderful work made this book so much better.

Third I thank Vladimir Verano for his inspired design and careful layout.

Last I thank my family. My husband Henry Matthews for his photographs and ideas, my daughter Jean Carmalt for her support and above all my grandchildren, Eleanor and Sky who inspired me to think about collecting these essays so they would have a record of what I was doing while they were growing up.

I dedicate this book to my grandchildren Eleanor and Sky.

# Preface

## Lighting up our collective conscience: writings by Susan Platt

A prolific and insightful author, Susan Platt is in the process of publishing a three-volume anthology of her writings from the past four decades. The first, "Breaking Ground: Art Modernisms 1920-1950" was published in 2020.

In this second volume of her collected writings, *Setting Our Hearts on Fire*, she turns to contemporary artists, primarily in the United States, whose work has been deeply engaged with activism for social and political change. The final volume will turn to global issues. A number of the reviews have been posted previously on her blog, "Art and Politics Now," (the title references her book, *Art and Politics Now: Cultural Activism in a Time of Crisis*, 2011).

*Setting Our Hearts on Fire* is not simply the title of this volume but of the last of its seven sections. The six artists reviewed there are representative of the diversity of the artists in the book as a whole: Lillian Pitt (WarmSprings/Wasco/Yakima), Joe Feddersen, (Confederated Tribes of the Colville Reservation), Barbara Earl Thomas, (African American), Alfredo Arrequín, (born in Mexico), Preston Singletary (Tlingit) and Robert Davidson (Haida). Many of the artists are based in the Pacific Northwest, and although they are well-known regionally because of exhibits at the Seattle Art Museum and elsewhere in the area, their works do not yet have the broader recognition they deserve. Another goal this volume achieves is to acknowledge the importance of the art of these artists and to increase our awareness and understanding of the strong northwest coast culture of indigenous and other artists of color.

Finally, Platt's lively writing brings vividly to the reader the urgency with which all of the artists in the book address crucial issues of today, as indicated by the titles of the sections: Homages, Uprooting History, Ecologies and Extinctions, Indigenous Resistances, Upending

Expectations, and Defying Clichés. Here are artists who are working against the norm, and certainly are not concerned with following trends. Rather, all of these artists are activists, and their art, like Platt's writing, is inseparable from their activism. Avoiding propaganda, the artists nonetheless motivate, even inspire the viewers to become activists, and to recognize that passivity is untenable in the current moment. The reader comes away from this volume with a respect for the artists' commitment and courage, and the innovative ways in which they have transformed their traditions.

In short, *Setting Our Hearts on Fire* not only provides new perspectives on contemporary art, but also an analysis of the many possibilities for intersections of an aesthetic practice and political activism. It opens the way for all of us to think creatively about facing the many problems that we face today.


~Pamela Allara, Ph.D. Professor Emeritus, Brandeis University

# Introduction

My title, *Setting Our Hearts on Fire,* comes from the title of my review of the stunning work of Haida artist Robert Davidson whose work concludes this book. But I feel it sets the tone for all the artists in this volume II of my collected writings. I have selected writings from 1982 to the present. Prior to the works included here I wrote for the *Austin American Statesman, Dallas Morning News,* and *Artforum.* I began my national career writing as the sole reviewer for *Artforum* in the entire state of Texas, from 1979-81. Texas was suddenly in vogue then, so as a mere graduate student I was hired! But I am not including any of those articles, because they were in the 1970s *Artforum* style (bland and impersonal) and type of artist (almost all White men).

When I moved to the Bay Area from Texas in 1981, I began writing for *Artweek,* a large format art newspaper. We were able to develop our ideas at length, and the 1982 article on Vito Acconci included here explored issues in his then-changing work. I believe it is the only review of this transitory work, and I was thrilled that the artist responded to it with a postcard commending my work.

But that is not the beginning of this book.

## 1 Homages

I begin with Jay DeFeo, in an homage from 1989 (one of very few articles included here that was not published in some format). Jay was a personal friend of mine during the three years I taught at Mills College from 1981–1984 and we stayed in touch until her death, so my homage is personal. Since her death in 1989 she has become exponentially better known including new perspectives from a new generation of art historians.

The second homage, to Selma Waldman, is also for a personal friend. We first met in person when she complained about my analysis of her work in my 1996 *Art Papers* article "Politically Incorrect, Outing the Political Artist" (not included here). On an icy day in 2007 I went with Selma to the last demonstration she attended—we were protesting waterboarding at Guantanamo—and held up her works about that. The animating force for her lifelong engagement with politics was the Holocaust. The politics of racism that created it are eerily similar to the current environment in the United States. Hopefully her work will soon become more prominent as it is ever more crucial.

The other homages are not to people that I knew personally with the exception of Mary Henry, whom I met near the end of her life at her home on Whidbey Island. I met Jacob Lawrence when he was receiving an award at Southern Methodist University. I have a special connection to James Washington as I worked for several years at his historic home. Most dramatically, in 2007 I rediscovered his six granite portraits of prominent African Americans behind a temporary wall in Philadelphia. They had not been seen since the day of their installation when they were targeted with attacks.

Anthony Caro, Antoni Tàpies, Jack Whitten and Charles White, the other artists to whom I offer homage, are all giants in their fields and need no introduction.

## 2 Uprooting History

This section features artists and curators who dramatically challenge accepted ideas about American art and art history in media, gender, and content. The essays cover the mood after 9/11, feminism, black performance art and dance, rethinking traditional positions and perspectives on Latinx and native art, and the most avid uprooter of history—Benny Andrews. I conclude with a review of a recent collection of the writings of Gloria Anzaldúa, the radical Latinx thinker.

## 3 Ecologies and Extinctions

Beginning with a longer essay I wrote in 1992, this section speaks to the current crises on the planet. These artists address crucial subjects as we face the excalating extinctions and disruptions caused by climate change. The essay begins with an historical perspective, then shifts to the contemporary art of rural Eastern Washington and its relationship to the specific landscape there, known as the Palouse. Next are the well-known artists Maya Lin and Buster Simpson. Other articles in this section range from reviews of exhibitions and cultural events in Greece (a place I have been fortunate to visit many times because my sister-in-law lived there), as well as other approaches to the theme of ecologies and extinctions—ranging from the mechanical to the painterly, concluding with the unique work of Olive Ayhens.

## 4 Indigenous Resistances

I am fortunate to be based in the Northwest with its many outstanding contemporary Native artists. While I resist categorizing by ethnicity, these artists create a strong presence when grouped together (although there are also Indigenous artists in other sections). Here I also include personal experiences, including a trip to Haida Gwaii (formerly Queen Charlotte Islands) and participation in some of the oil pipeline protests. During the years included here, we have seen the passing of the torch from one generation of contemporary Indigenous artists, many of them now retired professors, to a younger generation often supporting themselves with successful careers. All of these artists reveal deep roots in Indigenous perspectives as well as wide-ranging media and contemporary insights.

## 5 Upending Expectations

Here is the earliest essay in the book, my 1982 article on Vito Acconci. His experimental work sets the tone of this section, including many well-known artists such as Nancy Graves and Masami Teraoka. Also in this section is Tatiana Garmendia, an installation artist who addresses feminism, racism, and many other issues in highly original ways. I conclude with the internationally-known Kerry James Marshall, Kehinde Wiley, Titus Kaphar, Mickalene Thomas and Zanele Muholi.

## 6 Defying Clichés

This section focuses on women artists who may or may not be addressing feminism, but who move outside conventional ideas about art and women. I start with the 1996 stained glass windows of Dallas artist Jean Lacy. Short essays discuss nationally and internationally-known artists Betye Saar, Marilyn Waligore, Alice Neel, Carletta Carrington Wilson, Deborah Faye Lawrence, Imna Arroyo, Gloria Bornstein, Martha Rosler, LaToya Ruby Frazier, and Turkish feminist Tomur Atagök (there will be more on Turkish art in Volume 3 of my collected essays, focused on "Global Issues"). I conclude with radical installation artist Natalie Ball. These bold artists break rules in order to express themselves.

## 7 Setting Our Hearts on Fire

Although all of the artists in the book address urgent issues, the final essays return directly to my theme with a small group of artists who particularly inspired me: Lillian Pitt, Joe Feddersen, Barbara Earl Thomas, Alfredo Arreguín, and Preston Singletary. As the grand conclusion Robert Davidson's elegant paintings set my heart on fire and gave me the title for the book.

# 1 Homages

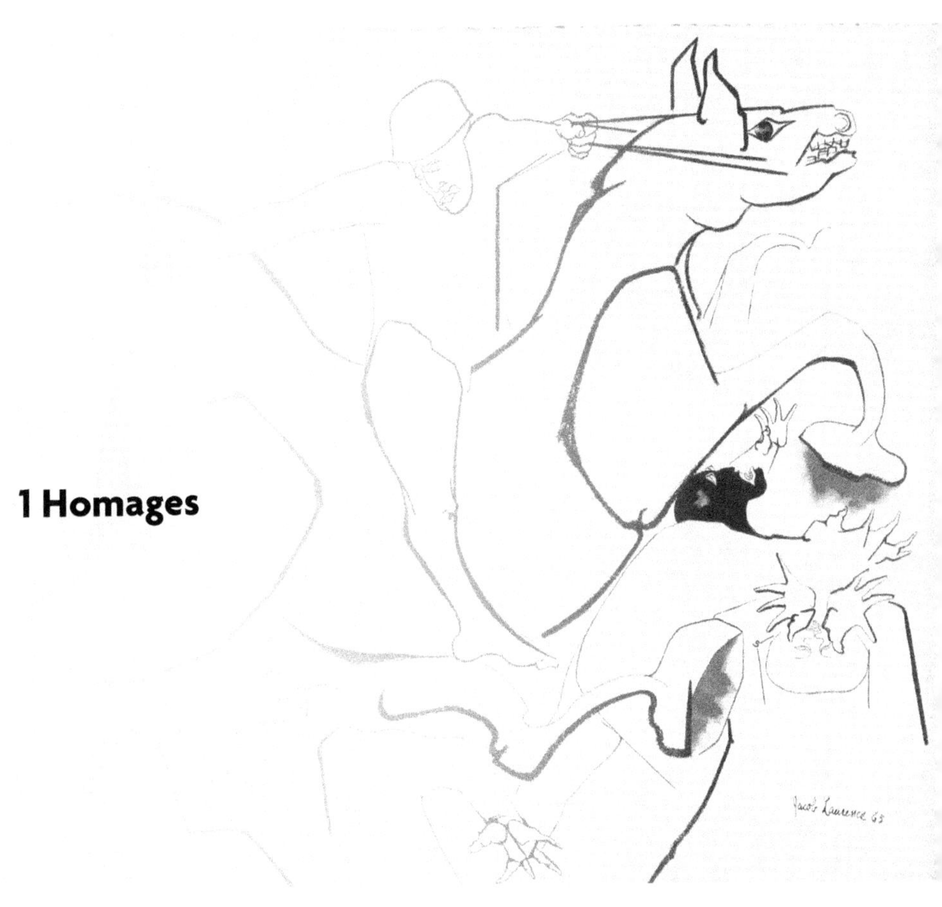

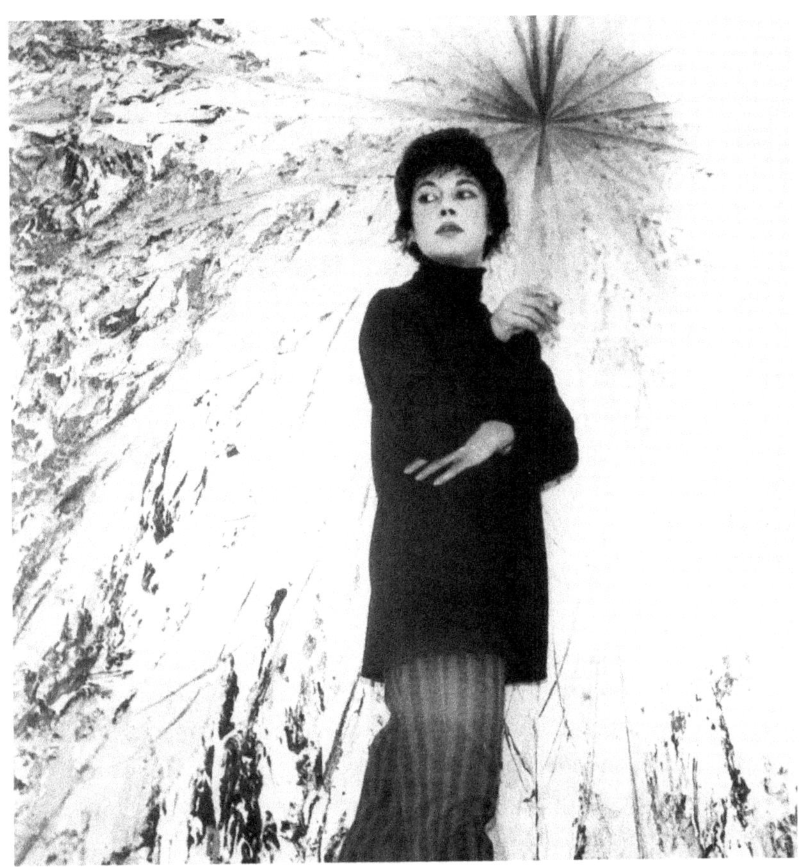

Jay DeFeo, in front of early stage of *The Rose,* 1961, ©2021 The Jay DeFeo Foundation, Photograph: Marty Sacco (*San Francisco Examiner*)

## In Memoriam Jay DeFeo 1929-1989

JAY DEFEO DIED NOVEMBER 11, 1989, the same weekend that the Berlin Wall fell. She was part of the earliest group of Beats in San Francisco, before revolution became an established attraction there and an outpouring across the nation. In the early 1950s, they opposed the complacency of Americans and the simplistic polarities of the Cold War. That historic group of poets, musicians, playwrights, and painters congregated on Fillmore Street and North Beach. They rejected the aesthetics of traditional art and the values of the materialistic, mainstream, culture.

She and her fellow artists, Wally Hedrick, Bruce Connor, George Herms and Wallace Berman, were concerned with throw-away art, anti-aesthetics and junk materials that wouldn't last—much in the same spirit as the Dada artists during and after World War I who expressed their horror at the war and their disgust with traditional bourgeois aesthetics by using rubbish in artwork and meaninglessness in poetry.

The "funk" artists of San Francisco, as they later came to be known, reacted against the glamorized utopianism of abstract expressionism around the same time that Jasper Johns and Robert Rauschenberg began making targets and all-black or all-white paintings. But the California attitude was more nihilistic, less staged for an audience; they were existential and in despair about the future; why make art that would last when there was no future. It was the era of Fall Out Shelters and above-ground nuclear testing; it was the time of impending, total annihilation paired with the marketing of the American Dream.

Jay DeFeo and Wally Hedrick, at that time her husband, were "discovered" by Dorothy Miller for an historic Museum of Modern Art exhibition of "Sixteen Americans" in 1959, that included such later-to-be-famous artists as Frank Stella, Robert Rauschenberg and Jasper Johns. Hedrick and DeFeo chose not to go to New York for the opening nor move to New York to be part of the mainstream art world. They stayed with their roots in California, a decision entirely consistent with their Beat philosophy.

One of the works illustrated in the catalogue of the Museum of Modern Art exhibition, because it was unfinished in 1959, was Jay's painting *The Rose,* sometimes titled *Death Rose.* Started in 1958, the painting was not completed until 1966. By then it weighed 2300 pounds, measured 128 by 92 inches, and the paint surface was up to 11 inches thick. Painted with lead white built up and scraped off over and over, the work became virtually a piece of sculpture. In addition to its staggering weight of paint, *The Rose* is also full of beads, wire, and junk. With lines radiating from a center point created by obsessive and repeated actions, *The Rose* contradicts, at its core, the spontaneity and cubist-based bravado of abstract expressionism. Instead it presents monumental, but futile, energy focused to a central point with so much power that it becomes an icon to the meaninglessness of the 1950s.

At the same time the painting is the deathbed for the dispersed heroics of abstract expressionism. Its title is frightening, suggesting an almost bewitching transformation of the harmless beauty of its namesake. *The Rose* was finally taken from DeFeo's studio to go on exhibit in 1965, its removal filmed by Bruce Conner as a massive hulk moving away from its diminutive creator. Eventually, DeFeo became very ill from the side effects of the lead in the paint.

She went into hibernation for almost ten years, following the dispersal of the original Beat group, and the break-up of her marriage. She supported herself by making jewelry and sharp, tiny, linear paintings with excruciatingly precise, but intentionally ordinary, images such as dental bridges.

In the 1980s DeFeo re-emerged with paintings that assumed a larger, but never huge, scale. Based on exquisite linear compositions that still moved between literal image and abstract metaphor as *The Rose* had done, her paintings now were accomplished studies in dark and light, with flashes of color. They suggest survival rather than despair. But, after almost another decade of assured work, DeFeo fell prey to the terminal illness she had resisted for over a year.

DeFeo overcame isolation, illness, and even abandonment, from her earliest years to adulthood, to persevere as an artist. In her last ten years, she was a professor of art at Mills College, the first secure teaching job of her career. The flowering of her career in the eighties was partially a product of that new base of support as well as the greater acknowledgement of women in the art world. The Beat group early in her career also had provided her with a base. The lack of support during the middle years of her life was at least partially because of the generation to which she belonged—ten years older than the active feminists of the 1970s. It can also be attributed to her geographical location in Northern California, an area given only sporadic and selective acknowledgement by national writers and museums.

Despite many years of tenuous outside affirmation, Jay DeFeo continued to work and ultimately emerged as an extraordinary and important painter with her own particular vision and fate. It is interesting to compare her career to those of the young artists of the 1980s who ardently pursued acknowledgment, but who often didn't ourvive immedlate exhaustion. DeFeo's *Rose* was begun when she was in her twenties and was, indeed, an exhausting and definitive statement. But DeFeo chose to withdraw rather than to surrender, and emerged again after a full decade.

In contrast, young artists today are under almost unbearable pressure from the distortions caused by money, politics, and overexposure, paired with the dissolution of clear-cut moral stances. They speak loudly and quickly, and, sometimes, as in the case of Jean-Michel Basquiat or Francesca Woodman, also surrender quickly.

Jay DeFeo belonged to a different generation, one that believed, like the avant-garde of the early twentieth century, that art's role was to oppose materialism-and to make a statement about the inner reaches of the human spirit. It seems appropriate that DeFeo, who created art shaped by the dawning of the Cold War, died in the same hours that the Berlin Wall crumbled.

Note: Since Jay DeFeo's death, the artist has become extremely famous nationally and internationally, due in part to the tireless efforts of Leah Levy, who has spent her life working on promoting Jay's work.

In 2021 Jay was the subject of a symposium at the Courtauld Institute in London. A young generation of art historians explored such new perspectives as the artist's use of photography and xeroxes).

(1989)

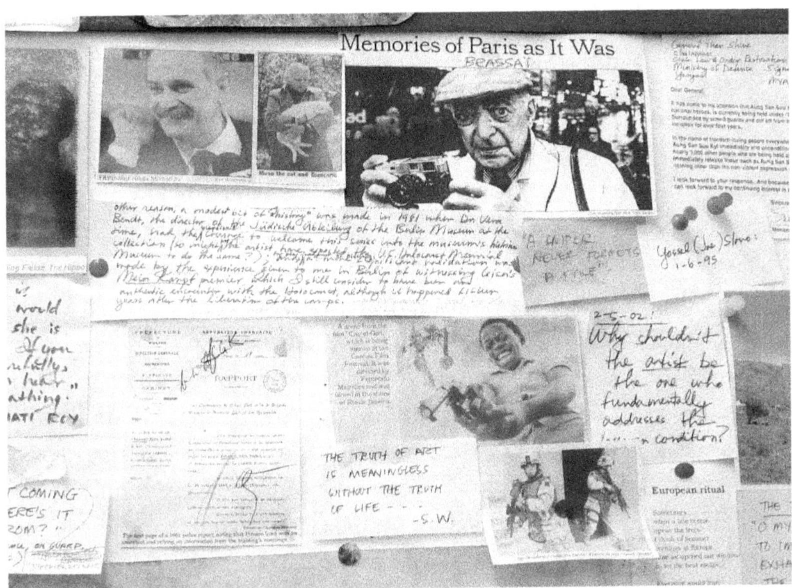

Selma Waldman's Desk, Photograph: Henry Matthews

# Selma Waldman: The Pornography of War

Lust for power and territory is the same lust that kills man, women, children and the land itself.

—Selma Waldman, 2002

Selma Waldman explores the relationship between war and sex. Two small three letter words that drive powerful forces in the world. When you put them together you have a lethal combination. Literally.

Waldman's drawings are seductive: they invite us in with their sensual lines. She often works in charcoal because she believes that the fragility of charcoal parallels the fragility of human life. It is strong and resilient, yet easily crushed. In her commitment to line and drawing as the basis for her art, she is consciously working in the tradition of the great German artist Käthe Kollwitz, whose career was also spent protesting the injustices of war in graphic form. Waldman's charcoal drawings unrelentingly confront the seductive power of war, the perpetrators of war, the addiction of war and its physical, sexual energy. In her sketchbook of combatants, each soldier is formed from a continuous web of lines, the phallic gun and the soldier's male organ forming a partnership, as they do in war.

She began a small-scale drawing series in October 1998 called *The Book of Combatants*: her combatants are naked below the waist; sometimes they carry a cigarette, sometimes they are overwhelmed by the size of their armament. Usually the works have a dominant red, associated with both passion and death. *The Book of Combatants* is part of the series "Naked/Aggression" that the artist began in 1989 during the First Intifada in Palestine. Many of the source images come from newspapers. For this exhibition she has framed the works individually to make a *Wall of Perpetrators*. "Naked/Aggression" is itself part of a larger series called "The Altars of Fear." Waldman enlarged some of the small drawings. She works in gesso on paper, with charcoal and colored pencils, sometimes adding acrylic on top. *Naked Child's Play* shows just the upper two thirds of the body, and half of that is naked. The vulnerability of the naked body is contrasted with the warrior's garb, even as the whole drawing is stitched together by the threads of violence which animate it.

The acid-green *Blow Your Head Off!* is based on an actual incident. A journalist in Kosovo was driving across a checkpoint from Zagreb to Kosovo. His companions were shot. He survived, after the guards played a game by putting a gun in his mouth and withdrawing it. Waldman has made the connection to the sexuality of this game obvious. The image is blatant, also unusual, as the male organ is the central focus of the drawing.

*Riot Man: Naked Cover* is a long, large painting of faceless riot police in front of a nameless city. They are dehumanized warriors, who advance toward us without any understanding of the humanity they are about to slaughter. Usually, as in Goya's *Disasters of War*, all the combatants in Waldman's drawings are equally violent. Waldman's all-encompassing theme, the "altars of fear," implies the presence of the victims of aggression in all its forms, but also the fears of the combatants who act out of their own fears to kill, rape, maim, and terrify.

Waldman has dedicated her life to exposing this dark world.

(1989)

❧

I am an artist who continues to be enamored of charcoal (the tool that does not lie) and the act of drawing . . . nothing more than the visceral release on paper of the most fragile, humble, and deceptively simple of media—in an age that despises fragility, humility, and simplicity.

Although both charcoal and pastel can be fragmented, crushed, and reduced to dust in a single arbitrary or careless moment of time, both of these media can project into visual art potent and sensuous powers of endurance that will resonate with the same epic, intimate, universal and demonic obstinacy as life itself.

The Wall concept generally has been to spare nothing and no one: the works will not stop with American perpetrators—from Gitmo to Abu Ghraib to Bagram to CIA "black sites"—but will reconfigure multiples of the infamous Goya *God of War* painting, to confront global contemporary "gods" who will be seen nakedly devouring both "the enemy" and their own people—in the gulags and combat zones wherever they have raged and continue to rage.

—Selma Waldman (letter to the author, 2006)

The centerpiece of this small exhibition is *Naked /Aggression: Wall of Perpetrators IV-V, The Black Book of Aggressors (I-IV)*, 2005-2006. These walls of drawings bear witness to the degradation of human beings and the systematic abuse of power in Abu Ghraib, Guantanamo, and elsewhere. Left unfinished at the time of the artist's death in April 2008, the *Black Book of Aggressors* would have included two hundred drawings and eight walls. The final wall would have reconfigured Goya's *Saturn Devouring His Son*, 1820-23, *The Colossus*, 1808-1812, and other Black Paintings, to address atrocities world-wide.

*Wall of Perpetrators IV* and *V* represent acts of torture: beating with chains, the use of dogs, cables, sexual abuse, jumping on prisoners, violation of women, electric shock to testicles, force feeding hunger strikers, extreme positions, prisoners immobilized in their own shit,

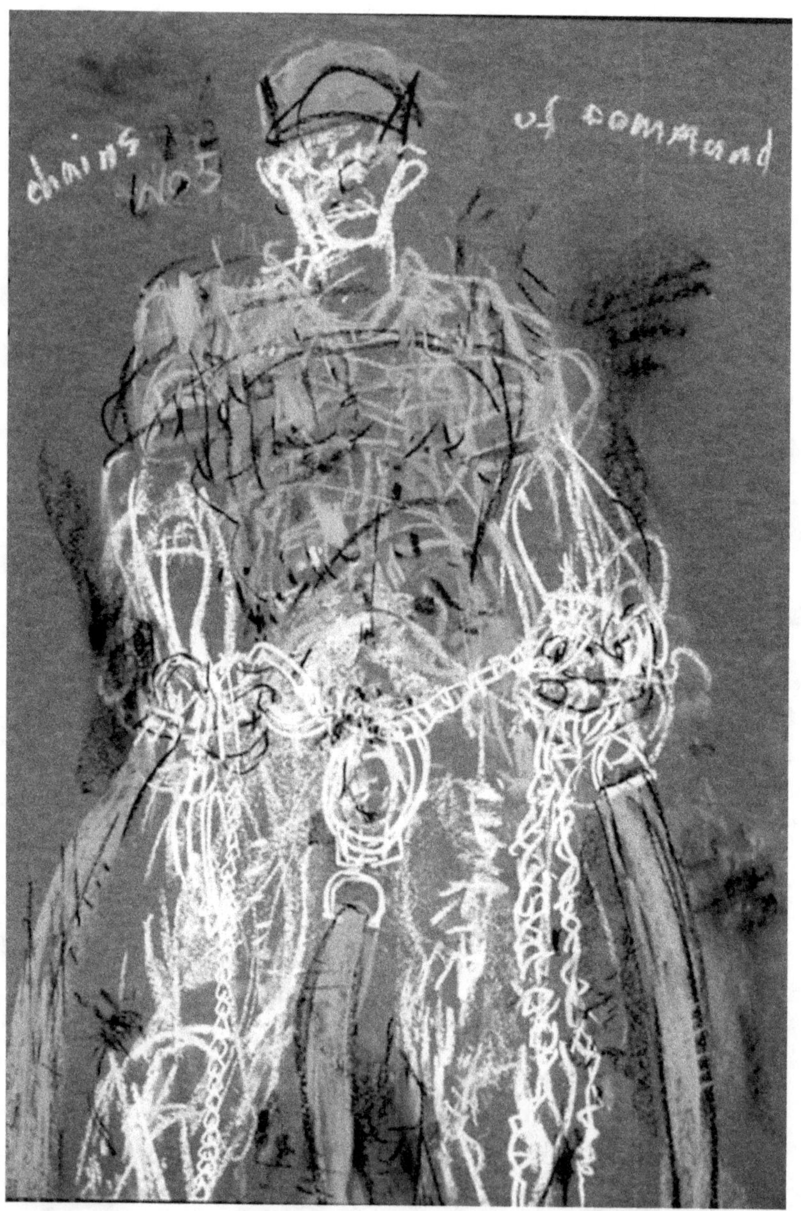


Selma Waldman, *Black Book of Aggressors / No 1 Chains of Command*, 2005, pastel and charcoal on black paper, 8 5/8" x 11 ¾," Estate of the Artist, Courtesy Rainer Waldman and the final six works on techniques of waterboarding. Drawn on 9 x 12" black paper taken from a spiral memory book, the works glow with brilliant colors of blue, orange, yellow, green. But these colors are not decorative, they correspond to aspects of the torture: yellow and orange relate to electrical torture, brown to excrement, red to blood.

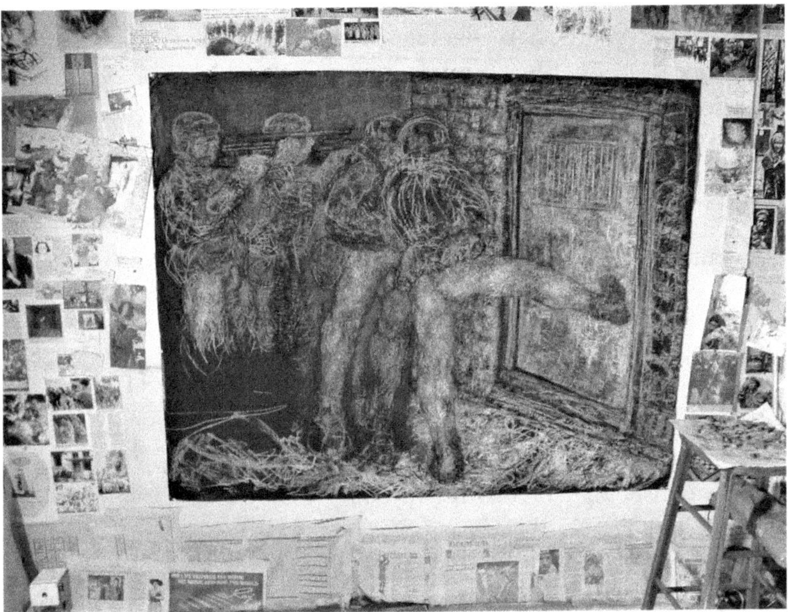

Selma Waldman's Studio with her final work, *House Raid,* 2008, work in progress, dimensions variable, Photograph: Henry Matthews

*Installation: House Raid* was created for this exhibition. Begun in the fall of 2007, Selma Waldman's final, large unfinished work, the *House Raid* started from specific photographs of soldiers raiding houses in Iraq, some of which are included here. Underlying it is a lifetime of study and confrontation with the forces of violence in our society. Other artists that Waldman admired included Francisco Goya, Käthe Kollwitz, and Rembrandt, but she studied many other artists for their command of drawing and line, her primary means of expression. She avidly read hundreds of books and drew from poetry, history and literature in her creative process. Even as her work bore witness to the violence of armed power and its victims, she joyfully celebrated the human spirit. The walls of her studio/home were covered with images of this celebration. This installation suggests her working environment where she combined handwritten notes, photographs and poetic quotes, as well as reproductions of her favorite art works.

## The WTO

Selma Waldman was deeply concerned about police brutality world wide. She collected hundreds of photographs of that subject, documenting the sameness of brutality in every country. *Thin Red Line,* 1999-2002, is related to press photographs of the Seattle riot police who attacked the anti-World Trade Organization demonstrators in 1999. But they represent mass police assault anywhere. They are dehumanized warriors who advance toward us as a group. They have lost their individual humanity.

## The Balkan War

Waldman began the "Naked/Aggression" series in 1998 with *Book of Combatant I and II* represented here by three drawings on brown paper, from a total of eighty. Also usually shown as "walls," these drawings, along with the larger *Invitation to the Dance,* are based on documented atrocities in Bosnia and Herzegovenia (former Yugoslavia), from 1992 to 1995. *Skelani Stalker (Hunter/Lust)* refers to a Serbian paramilitary on patrol in the Skelani area of Bosnia "who frequently gang raped their 'prey' as 'hunters.'" Typically Waldman included source materials documenting the actual incidents when she displayed these works. She insisted on both the realism of her work, as well as her witness to an actual atrocity. Her transformation of atrocity into art never lost sight of the injustice she was representing. The title unavoidably connects rape and war. The artist was particularly motivated by the novel *S* by Slavenka Drakulić—reporting on abuses by paramilitaries in "women's camps" in Bosnia.

## The Bread and Soup Series

The "Man and Bread" drawings are images of pain, fear, and anger turned inwards, or turned outwards, brother against brother, to show a fragment of the wretchedness inflicted on so many masses of people.

But the murdered, the insulted, and the martyred of yesterday and to-day must in time be reconciled with the earth. And the earth which buries the dead also promotes life and regeneration.

The two *Bread* drawings come from a group of more than 300 works (of which 25 are in the Collection of the Terezín Memorial Ghetto Museum). The point of departure was the writings of Elie Wiesel, particularly his descriptions in *Night* of the daily death struggle for bread.

*Soup III* represents an archetypal theme, the necessity of food in order to survive. As stated by Ori Z. Soltes, "much of (your work) can relate directly to Terezin or to the Holocaust, but it is far more universal than only that, and relates to the larger condition of human inhumanity of which the Holocaust is a (merely) particularly horrific subset..."

## Grief is The Gravity of the Earth

*Unearthly Grief* is an iconic image of grieving in response to incomprehensible suffering. A related work is in the collection of the Palestine Refugee Center in Amman, Jordan. This subject is also manifested in Waldman's "Messenger" performances inspired by the idea of the Russian village "wailer,"—a woman who weeps for other people to articulate their grief. In 1996, with another Jewish woman, Waldman first wore a weeping mask to demand peace with justice in Israel/Palestine. The group later became the "Sisters of Bat Shalom" and joined with Women in Black. The weeping masks appeared at demonstrations in Seattle, in Europe, and in Israel.

## Graphikos

Selma Waldman used this term to refer to "bonding the viscerally exposed archetypes of war, genocide, and violence to the demands of witness, the passion for justice, and the discipline of drawing."

Few artists succeed in both political engagement and aesthetic expression without one part of the equation overwhelming the other. Waldman balanced these two disparate worlds, both in her artwork and in her life. Even as she produced hundreds of drawings, she also made time to join demonstrations against war and in support of justice. She brought her aesthetics to demonstrations, and her political engagement to her art. It is that dual commitment that gives her work so much presence.

Day after day Waldman penetrated to the heart of darkness and returned with detailed, factual information. She embedded those facts in drawings that by their very nature speak of creativity as an alternative to depravity.

(2008)

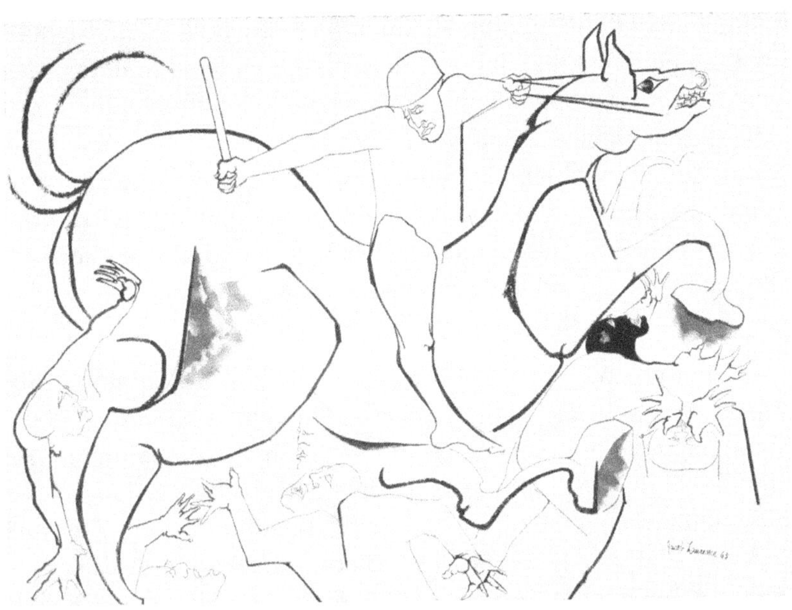

Jacob Lawrence, *Struggle II Man on Horseback,* 1965, brush and ink and gouache on paper, 22 ½" x 20¾," Collection of Seattle Art Museum (anonymous donors in honor of the museum's fiftieth year),©2020 The Jacob and Gwendolyn Knight Lawrence Foundation, Seattle / Artists Rights Society (ARS), New York

# Jacob Lawrence: History Painter from Harlem to Hiroshima

Jacob Lawrence came of age during the Harlem Renaissance. He was surrounded by a galaxy of brilliant people including W.E. B. Du Bois, founder of the NAACP, and outspoken writer on racism; Alain LeRoy Locke, who wrote *The New Negro*, a book that called on artists to construct positive images that rejected racist stereotypes; Langston Hughes, the poet who used jazz and blues rhythms in his poetry to celebrate being a Negro; blues singers Bessie Smith, jazz singer Ella Fitzgerald, anthropologist Zora Neale Hurston, and many more.

Lawrence had the opportunity to study art at federally-funded workshops during the 1930s with major artists like painter Charles Alston, and sculptor Augusta Savage. In Harlem he also met his future wife, the artist Gwen Knight. He would also have been inspired by the sweeping murals of the Mexican muralists, Diego Rivera and José Clemente Orozco, both of whom were working in New York City in the 1930s. Aaron Douglas completed his four-part mural, *Aspects of Negro Life* in 1934 at the Schomburg Library where Lawrence frequently did historical research. Douglas constructed narratives with modern principles: flattened space and bright colors combined with the symbolic abstractions of African art, a method which would contribute to Lawrence's own approach to art.

Lawrence made a rapid ascent as an artist. He began by painting "American scene" images of Harlem, like *Street Orator's Audience* (1936) that emphasized the real life of the streets of Harlem that he saw around him. By 1941 he had already completed five historical series, four of them about the life of heroes in African American history: *Toussaint L'Ouverture* (1938), *Frederick Douglass (*1939), *Harriet Tubman* (1940), and *John Brown*, 1941. His fifth and most famous series, *The Migration of the Negro* also from 1941 presented the economic and social forces that led thousands of ordinary people to migrate from South to North in the early twentieth century.

During the 1940s and 1950s Lawrence continued to depict Harlem, as well as adding new themes, the Navy, the War, and the South, based on his personal experiences and commissions. The next historical series, *Struggle . . . From the History of the American People* (1954-6), followed the Brown v. Board of Education 1954 desegregation ruling. Ten years later, *Struggle II, Man on Horseback*, 1965, depicts a brutal attack during the Civil Rights Movement: a baton wielding policeman rides on a horse with bloody feet that stomp on protestors. The electric energy of the black and white lines highlighted with red dramatizes the violence.

*Confrontation at the Bridge* (1975), documents a specific event when Civil Rights marchers from Selma to Birmingham, led by Martin Luther King, were brutally turned back by the police. Lawrence has indicated the tensions with the jagged shapes in the sky and under the bridge: the open jaw of a single dog confronts the dense group of marchers.

In 1971 Jacob Lawrence and Gwen Knight moved to Seattle, Washington, where he became a tenured professor at the University of

Washington. They bought a small house near the University with a studio upstairs, a location made possible by recent Civil Rights legislation that removed redlining. Soon after his arrival he was invited to create a new historical series based on the story of George Washington Bush, an African American pioneer. The five panels (originally intended to be larger works) detail the pioneering trek West by the wealthy Missouri farmer who funded six wagons on the Oregon Trail. The dominant image conveys the swirling river waters of the Continental Divide. An entirely new subject for Lawrence, the energy and complexity of the panels is an example of his willingness to transform his style in response to the demands of the subject Another unrealized commission is represented by two small maquettes, *Debate I and II*, 1987. Lawrence withdrew from the commission after the murals of his colleague, Michael Spafford, were censored by the Washington State Legislature.

During his years in Washington State, Lawrence was a celebrity artist who received many commissions for posters and murals. Best known is his Kingdome mural *Games* (1978), ten connected steel panels which celebrate huge-limbed sports players of many racial mixes in the foreground with their cheering fans surrounding them. Lawrence uses scale to highlight the drama while also subtly foregrounding integration in sports as another milestone of change. *The Games* mural builds on many representations of games in Lawrence's career.

Lawrence continued to work thematically with subjects from much earlier in his career, particularly *Libraries* and *Builders*. First represented as part of his series on the "Black Belt" commissioned by *Fortune Magazine* in 1947, the subject reappears often as a metaphor for positive action. *Builders* present kaleidoscope compositions with complex diagonals and intricate spatial relationships. They are also part of a long-term theme of African Americans actively pursuing various types of professions, such as *Lawyers* and *Clients*. The Supermarket was a theme that Lawrence pursued specifically during his years in Washington State, probably because they were rare in Harlem. A series from 1994 includes *Tools, Fishes, Meats, Used Books*, and *Celebration*. In combination they convey the specific spirit of Seattle at the end of the twentieth century.

Lawrence created imagery in response to John Hersey's book *Hiroshima* that vividly describing the dropping of the bomb on Hiroshima.

In Lawrence's paintings elongated figures, in the throes of extreme suffering indicated by strong pinks and reds, pursue everyday activities like flying a kite or sitting in a park.

Throughout his life, Jacob Lawrence constantly responded to new subjects, new challenges, and new circumstances. His commitment to representing both the realities and the successes of African Americans is paired with his extraordinary ability to constantly alter his expressive compositions in response to changing subjects and emotional situations. While he is best known for his early historical cycles, his entire career, with all of its variations, is honored in this small exhibition as a tribute to his full complexity as a major American artist.

(2009)

At this moment in time, as we are all struggling with so many challenges, Lawrence's *American Struggle: From the History of the American People* is both crucial and inspiring. Lawrence rethought American history and American struggle from the perspective of those on the margins of our established history. Although he includes some familiar figures, such as Paul Revere, or events such as the Boston Tea Party, his interpretation is so original, that we see these events entirely differently. In the case of Paul Revere he is shown almost in the dark, with a black cloak, suggesting the secret nature of his ride, a stark contrast to the moonlight aerial view by Grant Wood. The insurgents at the Boston Tea Party are dressed as Mohawk Indians, factually true, but not emphasized. In other words if they are caught the Indians get blamed. We see Sacajawea, the famous native who was the only woman on the Lewis and Clark expedition, reuniting with her brother in a stunning juxtaposition of the brown clothed explorers and the colorful robes of the natives. Throughout we see the meaninglessness of conflict, the sacrifice of those who fight, and the huge efforts of the ordinary workers, as in the building of the Erie Canal. The movement West is seen with two oxen weighted down almost to the ground, as a metaphor for the struggle of the pioneers.

Not only the subjects identify the concept of "struggle" in new ways. The compositions are dynamic. Most of us are familiar with Lawrence's *The Migration of the Negro*, 1940-41 which represents the many reasons why African Americans migrated from the South to the North. Although *American Struggle* still has a small format, the thrusting diagonals, and dramatic compressed spaces explode, immerse us, or confront us. Color is not simply filling in realistic details, but creating its own rhythms and relationships. Keep in mind that this series from the mid 1950s was created at the height of both the Civil Rights movement and the McCarthy Era. The FBI described Lawrence as "subversive" because he "propagandized alleged acts of racial discrimination of Negroes."

Abstract Expressionists dominated the art world, with their huge paintings of abstract form and color. In Jacob Lawrence, we also see abstraction in the dynamic thrusting diagonals. But they are wedded to his intense vision and the paintings shine as examples of courage, originality, and defiance.

As we witness contemporary struggles, this representation of the suffering that accompanies the effort for democracy echoes down the decades. Even as the Capitol insurrectionists declared they supported freedom and attempted to overthrow the election (and the government), they echoed the ideas of the Minutemen of our Revolution creating eerie parallels and twists of history.

The series of 30 paintings have not been shown together since 1958: they were scattered for decades among private collectors. But as the exhibition opened last year, two more missing panels were discovered, Panel 16 "there are combustibles in every state that a spark might set fire to – Washington 26 December 1786" and Panel 28 "Immigrants Admitted from All Countries: 1820 – 1840," both incredibly timely topics today.

Lawrence planned to have the series continue through the Civil War and the Industrial revolution up to 1908 when, as he specifies, "the American fleet sailed around the world." But he only created half of the planned sixty works, stopping in 1956 with the beginning of the movement west in 1817. He never completed the second thirty works, instead moving to the contemporary Civil Rights movement and other topics.

(2021)

# James W. Washington, Jr.:
# Painter, Activist, Sculptor

## Early Years

JAMES W. WASHINGTON, JR. WAS BORN in Gloster, Mississippi, in 1909, the fourth child of six. His father, The Reverend James W. Washington, was the local Baptist minister. Gloster is thirty miles south of Nachez, at that time a small town with a lumber company and a saw mill, which supplied most of the jobs for Blacks and Whites. It also had the Ku Klux Klan. As James Washington recounts in his unpublished autobiography:

> I remember living in fear most of the time. When I was very young my father had to get out of town. Suddenly. It was said that he had a dispute with a white man . . . (who) threatened to go to the Klan about it. A white friend of my father's hid him in the trunk of his car and drove him out of town. I never saw my father again.

His mother had five children and a baby on the way, with no means of supporting them. She had to send her children to live with relatives and friends. Washington was moved to his grandmother's house when he was seven or eight. There he got his first jobs, and already asserted himself as not willing to be insulted. He quit a delivery job because "I couldn't stand riding my bike to the back door of a white family's home and have the woman who answered the door act like I was there to rob her." He returned to live with his mother when she remarried. He had a deep bond with her until her death in 1944. When he was fourteen, she observed him taking apart an old shoe and found him a job as an apprentice at a shoe store. While working there, he figured out how to do jobs even his boss didn't understand, and, as he said, "From that day

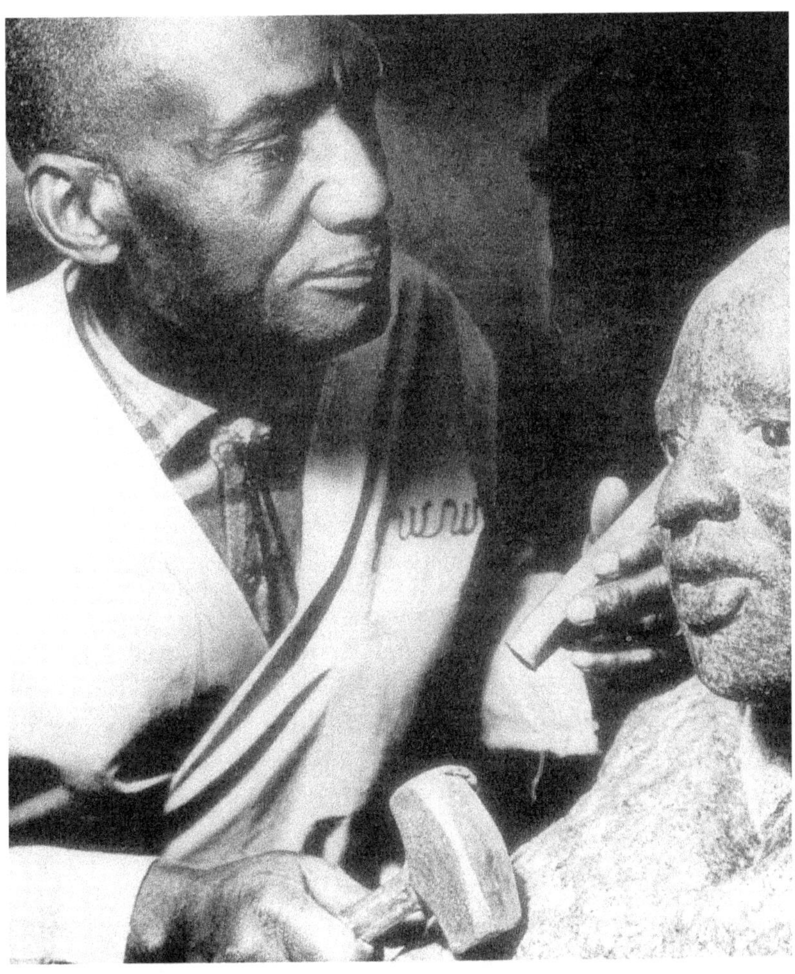

James W. Washington, Jr., carving the bust of Martin Luther King, one of six busts created for the *Rotunda of Achievement*, Freedom Plaza, Philadelphia, Pennsylvania, 1969

on I used my imagination to accomplish things other people assured me were 'impossible.' "

During the 1920s in Mississippi, he went from one job to another in order to survive—shoe repair, landscaping, lumber mills, assistant to itinerant fruit peddler. Starting in 1927, he also worked intermittently for the U.S. Government on naval ships on the Mississippi River as a "sounder," line splicer, and other short-term employment.

At the same time, he began teaching himself art. He studied the principles of color and perspective space from correspondence courses and self-instruction. By the mid 1930s, he began to make a name for himself in Vicksburg, Mississippi. As a result, his first major break came in 1938 when the Works Progress Administration (WPA) invited him to work as an artist and recreation assistant at the YMCA in Vicksburg. He later described his work for the New Deal program, "I would be asked to hang the paintings of the exhibition for the whites, but then they would remind me that I could not exhibit with them." In response, Washington created "the first Negro art exhibition sponsored by the WPA division of recreation in the state of Mississippi." This proactive response to discrimination would characterize Washington's entire career.

The WPA was a significant, but short-term professional boost. Following the WPA job in Vicksburg, he moved to Little Rock, Arkansas, in 1941, where his mother was living. After six months he was hired by the War Department at Camp Robinson in the orthopedic shoe repair department, with the elaborate official title Quartermaster Clothing Equipage.

In his art from 1938 to 1944, Washington subtly began to celebrate Black achievement and community. His small, intensely-colored pastel drawings of Baptist churches in Vicksburg, like *Travelers Rest* and *Little Rock*, still glow with his newly acquired skills with color and his exploration of linear perspective. His subjects were sites of Black community and achievement, like Baptist churches and Philander Smith College, one of the oldest traditionally Black colleges in the country.

While Washington was in Little Rock, the educated Black community was deeply involved in Civil Rights activism. As documented in a pamphlet in Washington's archives, the Urban League of Greater

Little Rock organized a program called "The Negro: Some Community Problems in Five Areas" in September 1942. Washington's early involvement with Civil Rights is also marked by a brochure he saved titled the "80th Anniversary of Negro Emancipation Celebration" which took place on January 1, 1943, at the First Baptist Church, Little Rock.

At the same time, in a life-long pattern, Washington paired activism with pursuing his art career. He befriended a White artist, Harry Louis Freund, who was painting murals with the Treasury Department in Arkansas, and took private lessons with him. In June 1943, he organized an exhibition with Freund at the 9th Street USO in Little Rock (a segregated USO). Washington showed his flare for self-promotion and his serious commitment to art by identifying himself in the brochure as the "James W. Washington School of Art." Freund gave a lecture as part of the exhibition and they remained friends after he moved to the Northwest.

## In the Northwest

James W. Washington, Jr. arrived in the Northwest from Little Rock, Arkansas, in August 1944. He came as a civil servant, one of thousands of African Americans who migrated to the Northwest during World War II as support personnel to the active military. His wife, Janie R. Washington, followed later in the fall. He and Janie lived in Sinclair Heights, a government housing development in Bremerton occupied only by African Americans. They moved to Seattle in August 1945, into the house that is today the James W. Washington Foundation and Studio. Washington experienced discrimination from both Whites and the "old timer" Blacks who were already established in a relatively unsegregated Seattle. They referred to the influx of Southern Blacks during the war as "newcomers" and "sharecroppers."

Washington wrote about the difficulty of joining unions and getting jobs in Seattle. Early on he emerged as a leader in resisting discrimination. In 1946 he chaired a discussion in Sinclair Heights as chair of the education committee for the Elks Olympic Lodge. The topic was "Is the Negro being permitted to fully participate in the special job opportunities in the Northwest?" Sinclair Heights was being disbanded following the war and the problem of further employment for African Americans was acute.

This experience would lead him to focus on job discrimination and labor negotiations in the 1950s and 1960s as part of the National Association for the Advancement of Colored People (NAACP) and Congress of Racial Equality (CORE) in Seattle.

But Washington always emphasizes the positive in his autobiography:

> Some Blacks leave the South with a chip on their shoulder. They assume, and many of them believe now, that all whites are dangerous. They think all whites are out to get them. I don't believe this because I accept everyone as an individual . . . Despite the inequities in society, I found it necessary to develop ideas about the potential for good in other people.

He never stopped pursuing his career as an artist. Only one short month after he moved to the Northwest, Washington took the ferry from the Bremerton Naval Base to visit the Gallery of Northwest Painters in the Frederick and Nelson Department Store in Seattle. He boldly approached the director, Theodora Lawrenson Harrison. Harrison gave him a two person show in January 1946 with Leo Kenney, later a well-known Northwest artist. His immediate success was the result of the strength of his art, the smallness of the Seattle art scene, and Harrison's own dynamic personality. She included him in a 1946 group exhibition in Chicago, "Northwest Paintings Go East," with Mark Tobey, Kenneth Callahan, and thirty-seven other Northwest artists, and encouraged Washington to meet Mark Tobey.

As lynchings multiplied for African American veterans, Washington made his first sculpture—*The Chaotic Half,* 1946, carved on a 4 x 4 inch block of found wood. In painted low relief, the hand of the Black voter reaches for the ballot box; behind a diagonal red line, indicating a wall, is a menacing Klansman, a swinging noose, a cross, and the all-seeing eye. In this simple work Washington incorporated his frightening childhood in the South where he felt perpetually under surveillance, his disgust with the continued lynching of Black veterans, and his hope for democracy.

In the second half of the 1940s, Washington spent several years in informal classes at Mark Tobey's studio. With Toby's encouragement, Washington enlarged his scale, included collaged newspaper clippings, changed his subject matter, and began to explore symbolism. While pasted newspapers had been included in modern art since 1910, Washington adapted it to his own purposes by selecting clippings about specific racist events that expanded the theme of his painting.

*The Making of the United Nations Charter,* completed in early August 1945, was focused on a particular political act of discrimination. He declared that the painting

> depicts the chaotic condition which existed when the [UN] charter was being formulated. Black men were dying in the wars (as symbolized by the skeletal hand), but were not represented in the formation of the charter. W.E.B. Du Bois was allowed to speak for a few minutes, but they would not let him pen an amendment, as symbolized by the safety pin in the hand.

The oil painting includes eight carefully selected clippings that refer to specific racist events such as violence at a Paul Robeson's concert.

*Democracy Challenged (Lynching),* 1949, the last of his works to directly address racism, is the most graphic. It is based, according to Washington, on Ezekiel 37:9—"breathe into these slain, that they may live." He represents the scales of justice with a lynched family on one side and the Statue of Liberty barely visible on the other. Seven newspaper clippings expand on the meaning of the work. The most prominent is the headline behind the Statue of Liberty in the upper left: "Fiery Cross KKK Note Found Near Home."

Still working as a civil servant, he transferred to Fort Lawton in 1948, where he was asked to set up and run a shoe shop on the military base. His brightly colored painting of the *Shoe Repair Shop (Fort Lawton, Washington)* includes all of the equipment that he assembled, as well as some of his paintings hanging on the walls. In an interview in 1989, he spoke of the racism he encountered at Fort Lawton and subsequent jobs for the civil service. At the same time, though, he managed to counter his problems with tactical maneuvers that made it possible for him to be continuously employed and even promoted at a time when many Blacks were unemployed after World War II.

Starting in 1949, Washington began to emphasize his belief in the interconnectedness of all people, the idea of universal spirituality. Motivated by this belief, he participated in interracial art and cultural organizations like Artists Equity, founded in Seattle in 1948. The roster lists almost 50 members, including University of Washington faculty, Glen Alps, Walter Isaacs, and George Tsutakawa, as well as Mark Tobey, and, of course, James Washington. Washington was appointed Secretary of the Seattle Chapter of Artists Equity in December 1951. He served as President from 1960 to 62. With other Artist Equity members, he pioneered Rental Art exhibitions and an annual exhibition in department store windows on Pine Street in Seattle. Through the national network of Artists Equity, he also gained opportunities to show his work in other states, and to travel as a representative of the organization to St. Louis and New York City.

In 1950 and 1951 Washington participated in two "international exhibitions" in the International District of Seattle with Japanese American and Chinese artists. These are landmark events since they included artists who had been interned during World War II, like Kenjiro Nomura; artists newly gaining recognition, like Paul Horiuchi; and artists who had been successful for many years, such as George Tsutakawa, Fay Chong and Andrew Chinn.

Also pursuing his hope for interracial harmony, Washington launched an annual multiracial art exhibition at the historically Black Mount Zion Baptist Church. He transformed the Baptist Training Union, an educational organization in the Baptist Church, into a means of displaying art. As he later explained:

> Back in the 1940s in Seattle there was an exceptional Black preacher, F. Benjamin Davis of the Mount Zion Missionary Baptist Church. After I found out that Blacks were not welcome in most of the city's White districts I told him the solution would be to put on an art exhibition and invite both Blacks and Whites to participate.

Thus began the Mount Zion Art Show in 1948, for which Washington drew in the major White artists of the city at that time, professors from the University of Washington, curators from the Seattle Art Museum, and others. Integration in Seattle was still far away, but in these shows Washington realized his idea that art is an international language. In 1950 Mark Tobey was a keynote speaker. Kenneth Callahan was a juror and participant for several years. The exhibition continued for thirteen years, until 1961.

After the art exhibitions ended, Washington organized Maundy Thursday Seder Suppers at Mt. Zion. He invited people from all spiritual backgrounds and professions. Jacob Lawrence and his wife Gwendolyn Knight, who moved to Seattle in 1971, participated in one of these Seders, as did Regina Hackett, at that time beginning her long career as art critic for the *Seattle Post-Intelligencer*.

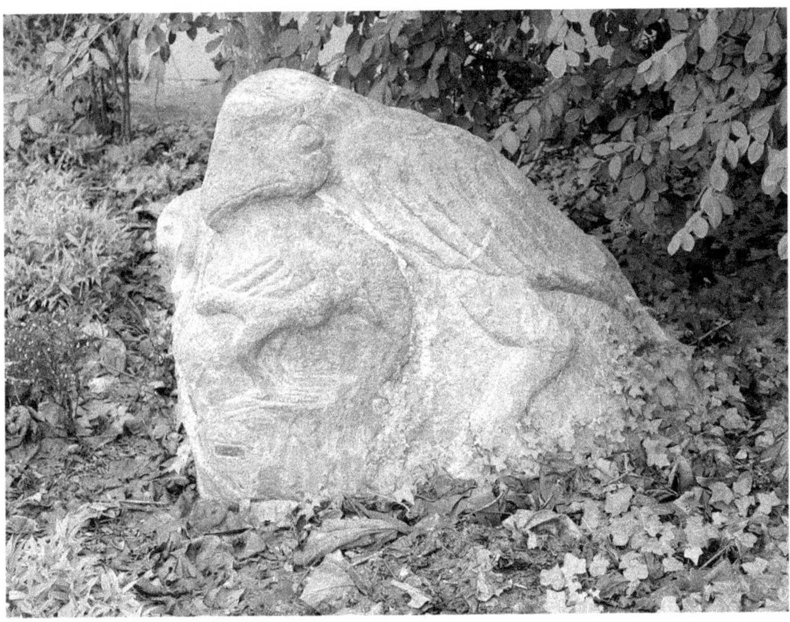

James W. Washington, Jr, *My Testimony in Stone*, 1981, Odessa Brown Children's Clinic, Seattle

## Washington Becomes a Sculptor

On a trip to Mexico in 1951, Washington met Diego Rivera and David Alfaro Siqueiros, the famous Mexican muralists. While visiting Teotihuacán, the ancient Meso-American site near Mexico City, he impulsively picked up a volcanic stone from the site. This stone inspired him to make the bold change to working primarily in carved stone. His first major sculpture, *Young Queen of Ethiopia* (1956), cut from a small block of limestone, connects to African American history and civil rights.

As a result of his wife's financial support through her work as a nurse, Washington was able to leave the civil service to be a full-time artist in 1960. In 1962, he traveled to seventeen countries, making appointments to meet artists everywhere he went through embassies and local art academies. One of the places that impressed him was Jerusalem, with its intersections of many different religions. Not long after his trip, he created a portrait in sandstone of Jomo Kenyatta. In 1962, as Washington was making his sculpture, Kenyatta had just been released from jail and by 1964 he would be President of newly-independent Kenya.

Throughout these years, Washington also actively participated in the civil rights struggle in Seattle. Active in the NAACP from the 1940s, he became Labor Chairman for the NAACP and CORE in the early 1960s. He and his committee received and evaluated claims of racist practices against Black employees. They also negotiated with employers based on statistical evidence to force hiring Blacks in positions other than janitors. He organized picket lines against stores who continued racist hiring practices, made banners for demonstrations, and much more.

In 1968, at the height of the Civil Rights Movement, Washington was invited by the Reverend Leon Sullivan of Philadelphia to create an installation of sculptures for a minority-owned shopping plaza in Philadelphia. Washington created six busts from granite for what he called *The Rotunda of Achievement*. They included *Frederick Douglass, George Washington Carver*, the great scientist of Tuskegee, *Martin Luther King, Jr., Benjamin Banneker, Nat Turner*, and *Crispus Attucks. The Rotunda of Achievement* was dedicated in October 1969. Sadly, because of racial tensions in Philadelphia, the sculptures were vandalized the day after they were installed. The violence of the defacement, painting the digni-fied Black portraits with whitewash, suggests how effectively Washing-ton's art presented African Americans. These portraits, lost to sight for many years, were rediscovered only in 2007, when I found them stored behind a wall in the office of the shopping plaza. Their fate is still in limbo. ("Missing Public Art Work Of Progress Plaza Uncovered, *Hidden City Philadelphia*, March 27, 2019 by Sherry Howard.)

From 1970 to the end of his life Washington did not depict indi-viduals in his sculpture, with one exception. In 1976, the year that Mark Tobey died, he honored him with a portrait. At the same time, he made a self- portrait. Toby's portrait on a slab of limestone set on a stunning wood burl includes a summation of many of his favorite symbols. In his *Self Portrait* the artist seems to commune with a small bird that symbolized freedom for him.

Washington's sculptures range from small enough to hold in your hand to monumental boulders for public spaces. In the smaller works, Washington carved a single animal or bird, with just a few chisel marks. But in those chisel marks he always respected the contours of the stone, and revealed the creature itself. In his largest works he used symbols drawn from the Masons, the Bible, science, and numerology with animals and birds. His large public art sculptures can be seen at public schools, libraries, churches, banks, and on the campus of the State Capitol in Olympia, Washington.

By the time of his death in 2000, Washington's work was collected by hundreds of people and his public art had become part of the fabric of the Northwest. The highly resistant granite and basalt that he chose to use for most of his sculpture was a metaphor, he said, of the difficulties of life. His early chalk drawings of African American churches, his 1940s sculpture and paintings about racism, and his stone sculptures, were all dedicated to celebrating creativity as an alternative to violence and as a means to universal harmony.

In that spirit, the James W. Washington Foundation sponsored a lively artist-in-residence program for several years, drawing artists from all over the state to work in the several studios that Washington built behind his house. Each of the artists responded in a different way to the spirit of James W. Washington, Jr.: some to the unused stones he left

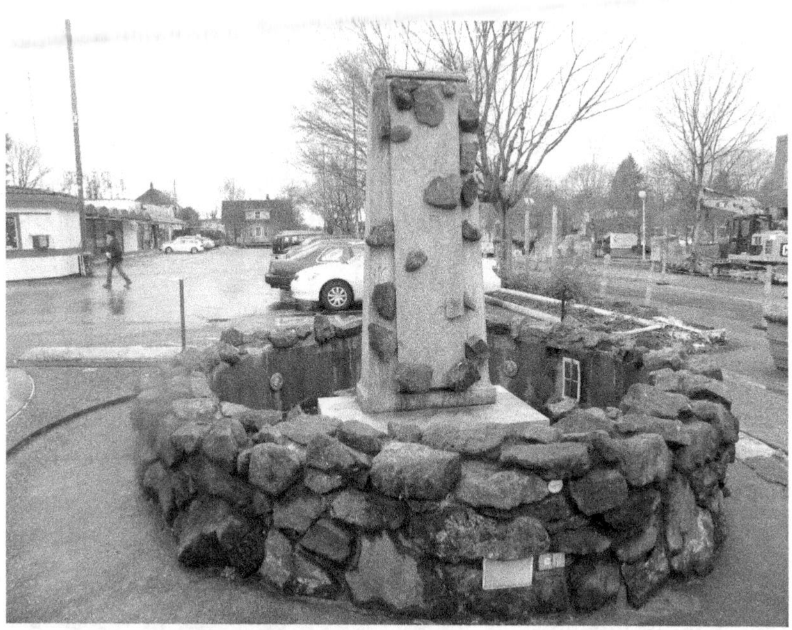

James W. Washington, Jr., *Fountain of Triumph,* 1997, public art sculpture, 23rd and Union, Seattle, currently being restored as original location undergoes redevelopment. The sculpture, the last public artwork by Washington, originally clearly showed salmon swimming upstream to spawn. Washington stated, "As the salmon starts back on its physical trend to complete the cycle where life began, so it is with Blacks of the racial trend on the American scene who have struggled like the salmon to reach his or her pinnacle of life and the free spirit again . . . This is the goal of the African-American women and men: To pass on to their offspring the energy in their body and recycle their physical remains in Mother Earth to be used again."

in the garden, some to his tools left in the studio, others listened to his recorded speeches or read his poetry. All of them experienced the spirit of the house itself.

The living room and dining room of his house, which through his foresight and efforts was designated as an historic landmark, is now an intimate installation of artifacts that document his and Janie R. Washington's life and achievements—from their roots in the South to their contributions to the cultural life of the Northwest.

(2011)

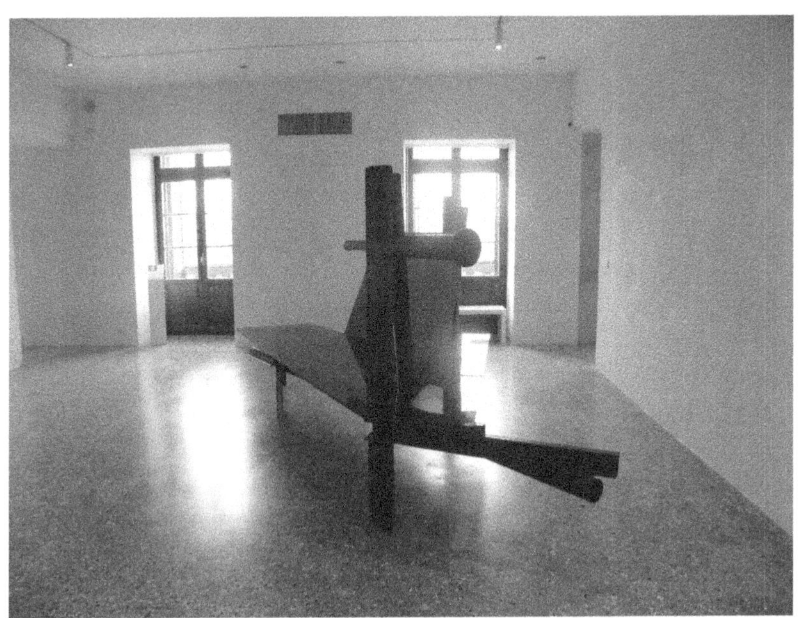

Anthony Caro, *Park Avenue Series: River Song,* 2011-2012,
Steel, rusted & varnished 93 x 193 x 85 ", © Barford Sculptures Ltd and Gagosian
Gallery,Photograph: Mike Bruce

# Anthony Caro:
# Offering Utopia while Facing Hell

I saw Anthony Caro's exhibition at the Museo Correr on the Piazza
San Marco in Venice on September 29th and he died on October 24th
in London. That means that this exhibition is one of the last for which
he supervised the installation (which he did with great precision.)

Caro, for me, is a reminder of my roots, in the 1960s, when I believed
in the idea that abstraction was an end in itself full of utopian meaning.

Caro was creating expressionist clay works under the influence of
Henry Moore, although reacting against his smooth surfaces, when he
came in contact with David Smith and Clement Greenberg in the early
1960s and entirely changed his vocabulary to abstract metal planes
painted in bright colors, as in the famous *Early One Morning* from 1962.

Clement Greenberg's ideas dominated my graduate studies in contemporary art in the early 1970s. I completely believed in Caro's spare metal planes and space-filling pieces as meaningful cerebral aesthetic statements.

Having given little new thought to Caro during my many years of teaching, I was shocked when, in 1999, I saw his *Last Judgment* in Venice. It changed my perspective on Caro entirely. It was the antithesis of everything I thought I knew about him. Content heavy, mixed materials, full of the horrors of war. The material is a combination of stoneware, steel, cement, ceramic bronze, brass. It was spiritual, rather than religious, but still abstract.

Now this spare exhibition in Venice. Nothing distracts from immersion in space and material. There is no explanation of metaphor, context, or significance. I am back to the early ideas of form in and of itself, and, surprisingly, because he is a consummate sculptor, I found it riveting.

I know from his intense *Last Judgement* installation that Caro feels deeply about the disasters in the world. Caro himself declared in the catalog that his *Last Judgement* could not "be fully appreciated in what might be called 'art' terms." I include here a diagram of the installation that identifies the themes and specific references. We enter through a "Door of Death" and proceed through deadly sins including references to contemporary acts of torture, imprisonment, and sacrifice. The catalog is full of quotations about the Last Judgement. Here is one example that is apt for today:

> Day of Judgement? It is a synonym for the present moment—
> it is eternally going on. It is not so much as a moment—it
> is just the line that has no breadth between past and future.
> There is not—cannot be, if you think it out—any other Day
> of Judgement.
>
> —Edward Burne-Jones

In spite of his *Last Judgment* though, if you look for metaphors or meaning on his website, you will not find them: all the work is organized by materials and size.

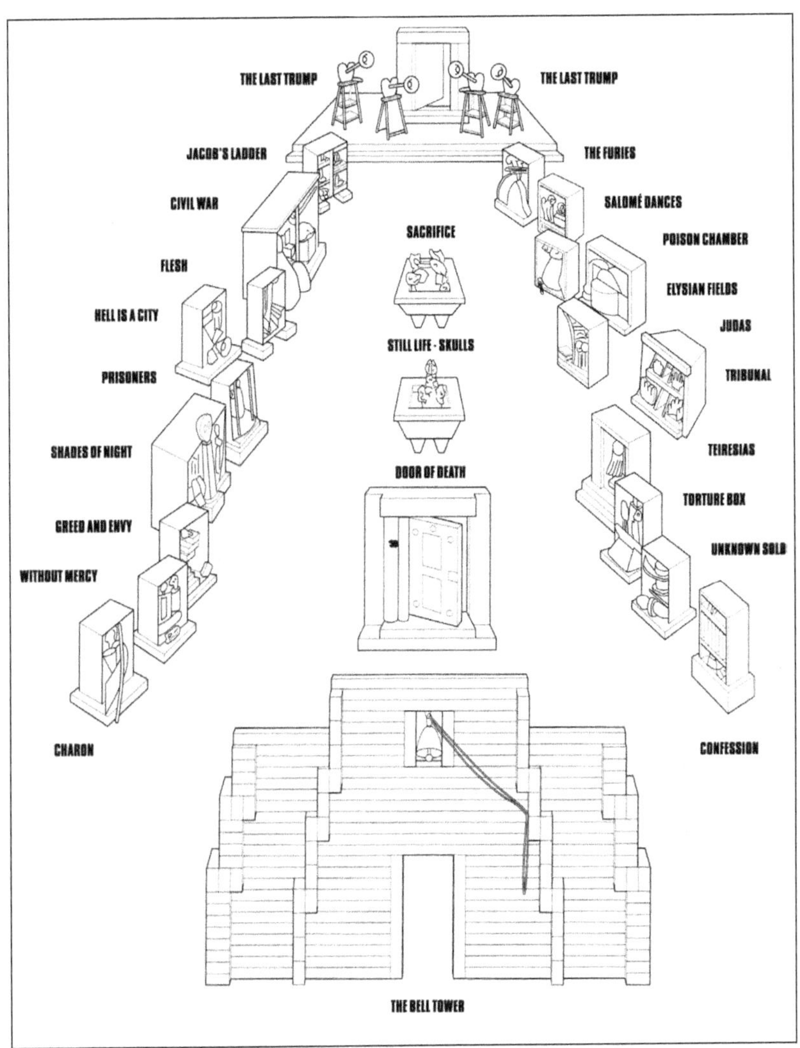


Anthony Caro, Diagram of "Last Judgement" installation, Venice, 1999

It seems Caro's choice in this 2013 Venetian exhibition is to create an experience that is outside of time and place. It is a utopian experience, we become absorbed entirely in the work, the use of industrial materials that create different textures, weights, directions, often overcoming gravity to float in the air. These issues become the only meaningful thing in the world. It is odd to go back to thinking this way and feel at the same time a strange sense of euphoria, as I realize that each sculpture is many sculptures, depending on where you stand to view it; that each sculpture is freeing us to think outside the here and now, into some sort of perfect world, where people don't kill each other.

At the Museo Correr, Caro sculpts space with his work. His work does not simply exist in space, it defines space. The early drawings show us his roots in Cubism, specifically Picasso, pulled apart. He sees figures in space as strong straight lines.

The exhibition touches on every decade of the artist's career. *Hopscotch* (1962), in corrugated aluminum, jumps up in steps like a pick-up sticks game, rising against gravity. *Red Splash*, 1966, is one deep red color, 4 tubes and a mesh, also during this 1960s period when he was definitively moving away from Henry Moore's bronze solids and toward open floating planes, under the inspiration of David Smith.

*Child's Tower Room* of 1983-84, has a different quality, perhaps because it is made of wood, actually a special wood, Japanese oak. It has more solids, a spiral inside to a platform, but no one can actually go up because it is a discontinuous stairway. It points to the future in a return to more solid forms.

*Dejeuner sur L'Herbe*, 1989, is rusted steel reaching out from a horizontal plane, the appearance of casting, but found shapes, and subtle patina: no color. Caro can build up density without clutter, he multiplies forms to a point where we can't take it all in in one viewing. In the *Triumph of Caesar*, 1987, waxed steel, the two sides go vertically up from the plane, creating an angle like a pediment.

Suddenly at the center of the exhibition, the artist presents a complete change of pace with subtle paper sculpture made in Obama, Japan in 1981, with Washi tissue.

*Duccio Variations*, 1990-2000, is an obvious choice for Venice with its examination of Duccio's space.

And in the last room, *Venetian*, 2011-12, with red plexiglass. It glows with the red of Venice and changes radically according to the light, as does the city itself. As my friend Pamela Allara said, she felt her eyes had been cleansed by the end of the show. I felt my brain had been cleansed as well and only my eyes remained.

The *Last Judgement* is exactly the opposite. It is heavy, weighted with the cares of humanity, its sins and suffering. The installation has 25 separate "episodes" beginning with Dante's boatman, Charon. It continues on the left with *Without Mercy, Greed and Envy, Shades of Night, Prisoners, Hell is a City, Flesh, Civil War, Jacob's Ladder*. On the left side are *Confessional, Unknown Soldier, Torture Box, Teiresias, Tribunal, Judas, Elysian Fields, Poison Chamber, Salome Dances*, and *The Furies*. In the middle is the Bell tower entrance, *Door of Death*, still life with skulls and sacrifice all culminating in the four last trump[et]s leading up to the final *Gate of Heaven*. The topics mix literary, classical, biblical, legal, and religious ideas.

The 1999 brochure accompanying the display links it to the artist's disgust and horror with the

> so called 'ethnic' cleansing in Bosnia, Rwanda, and most recently with the worsening conflict in Kosovo. As a Jew he has been asked more than once to make a sculpture commemorating the Holocaust, but has felt unable to undertake it as the subject is too terrible, too enormous to do justice to. However in 1992, working with the ceramicist Hans Spinner in the South of France, Caro made some ceramic pieces which resembled heads. When they were shipped back to his London studio they became the basis for his Trojan War sculptures, which were shown in the form of a battlefield. . . . In a sense the sculpture is nothing less than Caro's own *Guernica*. . . . It is fitting that with a century that began with the *Gates of Hell* of Auguste Rodin should now close with the *Last Judgment* of Anthony Caro.

This material appears nowhere online. These powerful, misshapen forms redefine all of his work: they bring together his deep sense of material and space with a specificity and direct sense of tragedy. Each sculpture is purposefully enclosed in a rectangular box, physically containing the tortured themes. The abstracted forms evoke direct associations with the history depicted. It is as though Caro, after a lifetime of efforts to create utopian spaces on earth, is now acknowledging here, as well as in his *Trojan War* series, that what we have is the opposite.

The 1999 installation in the spare industrial space of the Antique Granary in the Giudecca enhanced the overall sense of horror of the individual pieces. Collectively, all the pieces point toward *The Gate of Heaven,* as the climax of the path through the darkness of human actions. *The Gate* is an open door, as though it is enticing us to pass through, in spite of the sins behind us. But it is ambiguous as to whether anyone is actually going to be admitted: there is no judge, there is no Saint Peter, there is no sense of salvation. Only an open door surrounded by sculpture that make reference to four trumpets that play at the resurrection (one can't help but think of Handel's *Messiah*). So, in the end Caro's message is to offer the possibility of salvation, just as his abstract nature based sculptures offer the possibility of utopia. The choice is ours which way we choose to go.

We have lost one of the greatest sculptors of the twentieth century.


(2013)

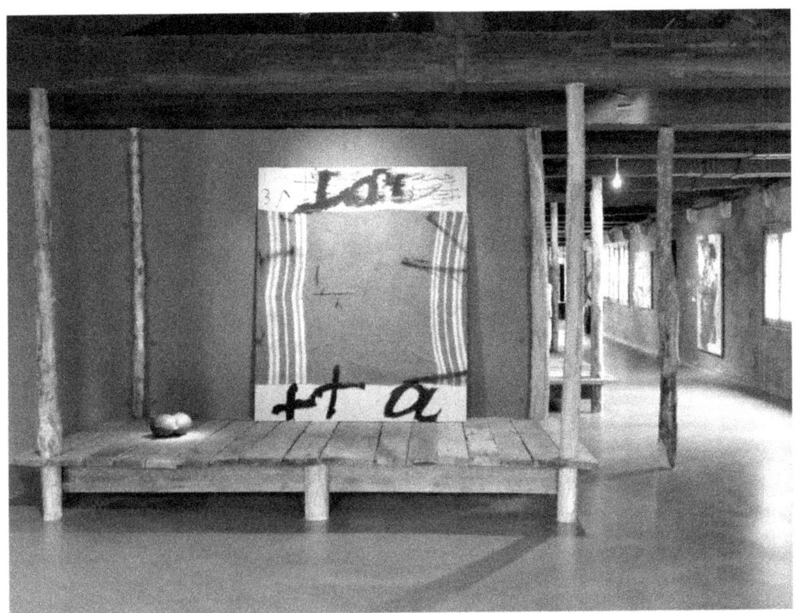

Antoni Tàpies, Installation view, "Lo Sguardo dell' Artista," Museo Fortuny, Venice, fall 2013

## Antoni Tàpies: Sweeper of Souls

IN HONOR OF THE NEW YEAR 2014, I give you Antoni Tàpies, one of the outstanding twentieth century artists who engaged both profound concerns about the state of the world, and corresponding boldness in exploring aesthetics and material as a way to connect to those concerns.

> Franco wanted to show Spain he was tolerant, so he allowed modern art—I had to walk a fine line to not allow myself to be used.

Thus speaks Antoni Tàpies in "Lo Sguardo dell'Artista" (The eye of the artist) at the Museo Fortuny in Venice. More than an exhibition, "Lo Sguardo" is an act of love from his friends to honor him in the year after his death. It includes two films, many major art works by the artist, selections from his wide-ranging personal art collection, never before exhibited, works by his friends, and even personal pieces of furniture.

Each floor of the large palazzo had a different mood. On the ground floor was a large simple space with one big work by Tàpies, as well as a single sculpture by Anthony Caro in an adjoining room.

The first landing had a rough wooden floor that changed the atmosphere from gallery to unpredictable exploration. We were confronted with an intense African sculpture from the Tàpies collection juxtaposed to a painting and a single sculpture. They spoke to each other across the room.

On the next floor the official Museo Fortuny displays the fashion and designs of Mariano Fortuny created in collaboration with his wife. Included in the collection are Chinese paintings and robes, stage sets, wooden dummies, and memorabilia. Inserted into this array, without labels, are such works as a painting by Picasso, a marble Gudea, Tàpies's *Book 1 Libre*. A small case arranged on successive shelves by the curators includes a coat hanger, copper pot, bronze cross, painting on concrete, screwdriver, spatula (for plaster), scrolls, shell, leather, cat/tiger emerging from granite, stone tied with leather. The mixture of dissimilar objects created a rough conversation, disrupting our equilibrium as viewers and opening off beat aesthetic connections.

Nearby is a heartfelt statement by Antone Ueng:

I urge viewers who struggle to understand Tàpies's art not to look for explanations. If they look carefully and that is all if they are open and allow themselves to be possessed by what refuses to be classified, the painting will find its way through, by stealth. And one day unexpectedly the core of our soul will be swept away like the walls of Jericho and a pleasure produced by the gaining of recognition will be obtained.

In a dark side room a dazzling red painting by Gutai artist Kahuo Shigako jumps off the wall, the paint so thick that it looks like smeared blood. Tàpies hung the Shigako painting at the entrance of his home, telling visitors exactly what to expect from him.

In another room is Tàpies's *llit* (*Bed*), a Chinese Buddha sculpture (Suei Dynasty, 6th century) that he had in his bedroom, an intimate

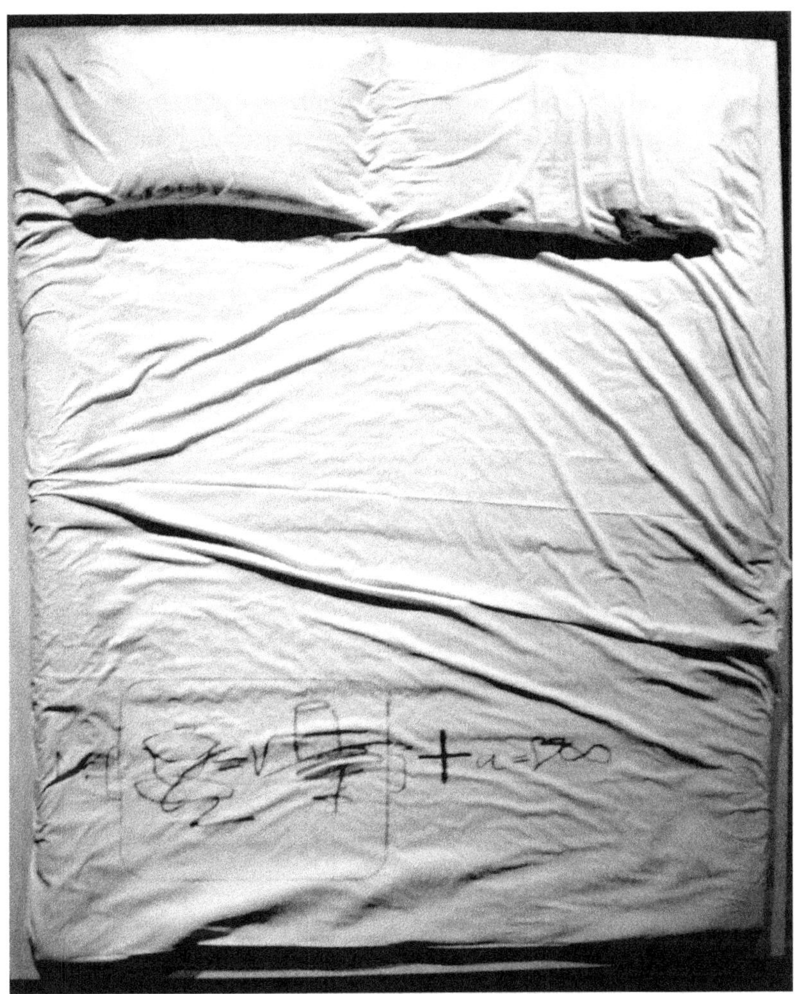

Antoni Tàpies, Installation view, "Lo Sguardo dell' Artista," (*Llit*, 2009), Museo Fortuny, Venice, fall 2013

Miro and Max Ernst's *Fort Bleu*. The music playing is by Giacinto Scelsi—"Xnoybis"—performed by Vincent Royer on two strings. James Turrell's glowing light installation, *Red Shift*, has another room to itself. These are meditative experiences. Tàpies' *Bed* makes an intriguing comparison to the famous Rauschenberg bed. Here we feel a restless sleep, a hidden anguish, a bed that invokes private moments for a man who felt the oppressions of the world so deeply.

The main rooms of this floor create a textured intersection of Fortuny and Tàpies, fashion and desire, juxtaposed to the deep material metaphors of Tàpies that speak of oppression. But in this display the textures, intimacy, and cross references foreground spirituality, an important dimension of Tàpies personal collections and private life.

On the second floor a large open room with walls bearing plaster *pentimenti* creates a desolate sensation, with the widely spaced *Despertar*

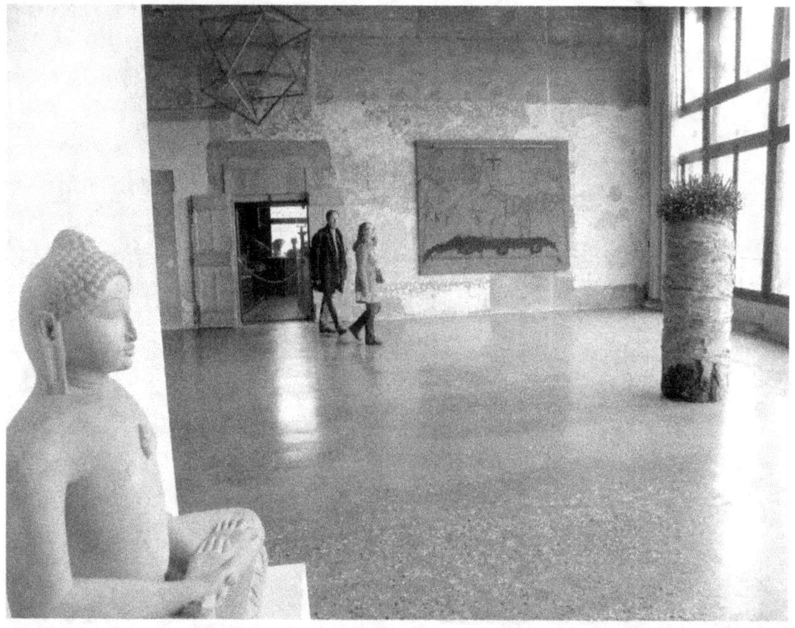

Antoni Tàpies, Installation view "Lo Sguardo dell' Artista," Museo Fortuny, Venice, fall 2013 (*Despertar Sobtat* 2006 near to Günther Uecker's *Trees and Nails a Tribute to Tàpies,* 2008–2013, center, and a Jain seated sculpture in the foreground

*Sobtat,* 2006, and *Gran Tors,* 1996, near to Günther Uecker's *Trees and Nails a Tribute to Tàpies,* 2008 – 2013 (center), and a Jain seated sculpture in the foreground. A film on this floor speaks of Catalans identifying with Tàpies in their religious and political resistance to Franco.

The entire top floor is devoted to an installation "Wabi Inspirations" conceived by architects Axel Vervoodt and Tasuro Mik, explained as follows:

Towards the end of his life Tàpies developed a heightened interest in Eastern culture, a concern which increasingly became a fundamental philosophical influence on his work because of its emphasis on what is material, the identity between man and nature and a rejection of the dualism of our society. In this 'labyrinth of silence' labyrinth of sacred proportions inspired by Eastern and Western culture are several "tokonomas" four outside and four inside. Toko means platform "ma" framed emptiness, made from humble materials as Venetian bricolet, cardboard, painted with earth from the lagoon. I tried to create a dialogue between the most silent and serene works by Tàpies related to the great masters of calligraphy and anonymous objects made by nature.

A small work by Kandinsky points to an interior labyrinth: in the semi-dark a score by John Cage appears, then in the deepest interior a Toraja Funerary door from Indonesia and *Grans Vertical*.

It was a temple.

As a way of coming back to reality, near the exit was access to Sadahoru Horio's *21 Meter Pole* resting on a water mattress that rose from the bottom to the top of the building in an inner courtyard. I stood on the water mattress without my shoes and felt the instability of the base as well as the cold of the water.

(2014)

# Jack Whitten's Odyssey

Jack Whitten emerged as an abstract painter in New York City in the 1970s and had a solo exhibition in 1974 at the Whitney Museum! He was friends with musicians, poets, writers, and other artists. It was a time of intersections among different creative fields, but he made a name for himself as a painter of large abstract canvases that were purchased by the likes of the Metropolitan Museum of Art and the Whitney Museum of American Art.

One publication stated at the time of his death "And as a black artist, he resisted the period's prevailing impulse of racial representation to explore the plastic and metaphorical possibilities of paint." I will return to this point later. Other artists honored Whitten with these words:

> Jack would preach that art was one of humanity's last bastions, and abstraction was where we as black artists could truly be free. —Shinique Smith, artist

> Whitten was always trying to find a celestial dimension in the most prosaic materials. —Massimiliano Gioni, curator

> To talk to Jack was to recognize the beauty and richness of existence, the possibility in even the dimmest times.
> —Adrianna Campbell-LaFleur, curator, *Artsy* Editors January 23, 2018

These comments about Jack Whitten as an abstract painter, and his experimentation with materials, give insight into his current exhibition "Odyssey: Jack Whitten Sculpture, 1963–2017" at the Met Breuer.

It is astonishing that these works have never before been shown except in small exhibitions in Greece. The sculptures reveal an intricate and layered mind, that brought together the cultures of Africa and

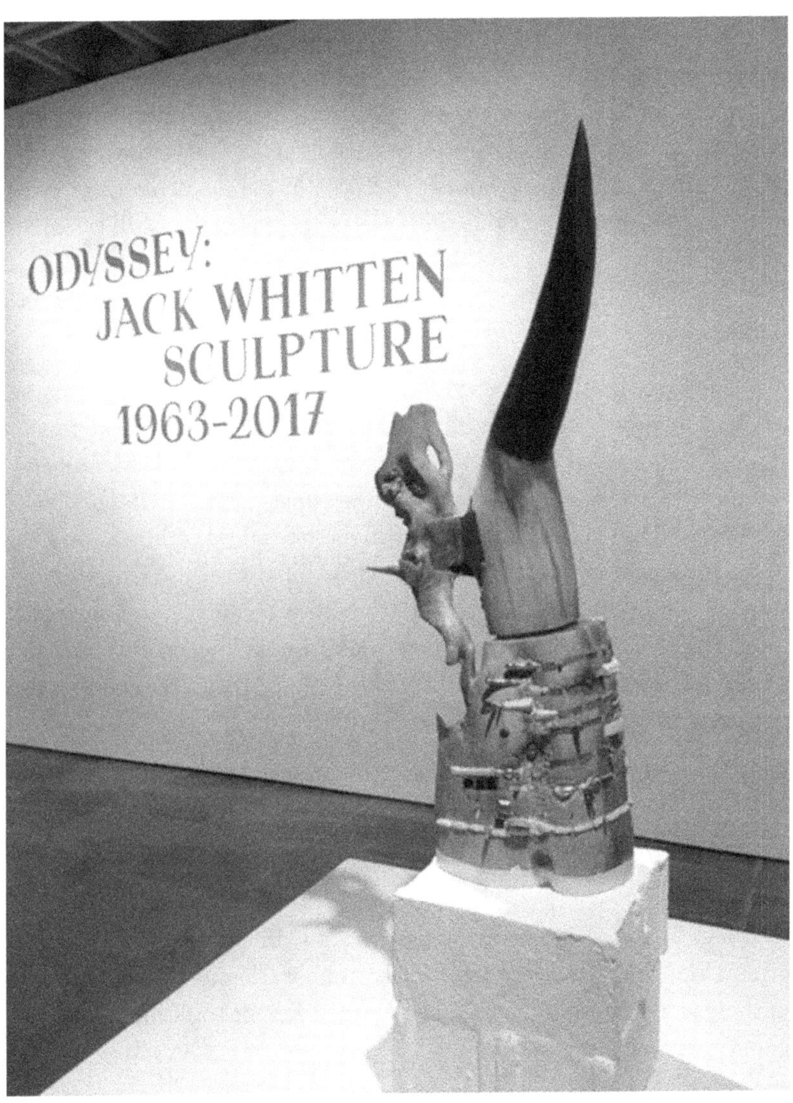


Jack Whitten, Entrance to the exhibition "Odyssey: Jack Whitten Sculpture, 1963–2017" with view of *Lichnos*, 2008, black mulberry, carob wood, whitewashed cinder block, mixed media, 63 3/4" x 19 5/8" x 15 ¾," The Met Breuer, 2018

Europe on the south coast of Crete, where he started to go with his wife beginning in 1969.

Because I have spent quite a bit of time in Greece, I loved these sculptures: their materials, their sense of lightness and space all spoke of Greece for me. They were lovingly created from various materials, both found detritus and beautifully-joined wood. The virtuosity of the joining these contrasting woods reflects Whitten's experience as a carpenter: he did not simply glue these pieces together. That skill is seen in the unusual woods that he chose as well as the eccentric compositions. They suggest a calm inner joy that is balanced and exuberant at the same time.

At the entrance to the exhibition stood *Lichnos*, 2008. The name refers to a "spiny bottom-dwelling fish," used in "a Greek Fisherman's stew." Composed of specific types of wood, carob and black mulberry, the piece is set on a pedestal of whitewashed concrete cinder blocks that immediately made me think of my sister-in-law whitewashing her home in Greece every year. It is the same lime wash used here. What stopped me in my tracks is the huge creative eccentricity of the piece, the juxtaposition of unlike parts to make an assymetrical whole. The stringy character of carob wood makes it hard to carve, echoing the challenge of catching the lichnos.

There are more references here embodied in the found materials, to Africa, to Alabama. And as we walk around the work it seems to be a strange beast seeking to escape confinement. The stunning polished red-colored carob wood is flame-like.

Jack Whitten is absolutely original, a word I rarely use (nor do I often write about abstract art). But I strongly felt the layers of content in these works bringing together so many different traditions, mythologies, types of knowledge.

*Phoenix for the Youth of Greece,* 1983, one of the earlier sculptures, includes mulberry wood, olive wood, bone, glass and a small piece of writing. The soft olive wood frames the hard shiny mulberry.

Underneath is an "ossuary," a cluster of bones made of jaws of small fish and above a mysterious parchment with the phrase "Using the bones from the past, we can understand the present and foresee the future."

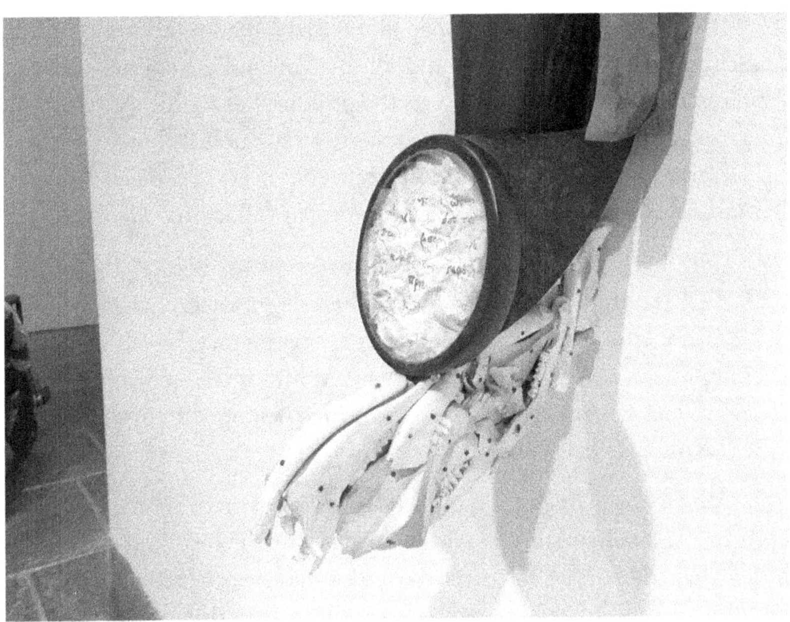

Jack Whitten, *Phoenix for the Youth of Greece* (detail), 1983, black mulberry, olive wood, bone, glass, handwritten text on paper, 39 3/8 x 7 7/8" x 15 3/8," Collection of the Estate of Jack Whitten, courtesy Hauser & Wirth

All of these materials suggest a larger story or myth, illusive, but still very present. (On Greek islands, where soil is scarce, ossuaries are commonly used. The bones of the dead are dug up in one year and placed in a container to conserve valuable cemetery space.)

In addition to the layers of mythology, the "monolith series" pays homage to great African Americans, in a medium that Whitten developed, handmade acrylic tiles: these stunning works, shimmer in the light, as the "portrait" emerges from its surfaces. Basically abstract works, they pay homage to such people as Chuck Berry, James Baldwin, Édouard Glissant, Terry Adkins and Muhammad Ali. The riveting complexity of the surface evokes music, another crucial reference point for Whitten.

How exciting to be confronted with a body of work by a well-known artist that has never been shown before. Each of these works is a revelation.

The *Tomb of Socrates* is shaped like a shield, made with wild cypress, black mulberry, marble, brass and all sorts of found materials. At the center is a black stone that suggests the philosopher's skull. As we know, Socrates died by drinking poison because a new political order ganged up on him and declared him dangerous. We need this piece today to remind us of what happens when governments reject knowledge.

Why have these sculptures never been shown before? I came up with the idea of logistics. They were all made in Greece, they are fragile, they are embedded in that landscape, that history, mythology, that geography, not far from Africa. Perhaps Whitten felt he wanted them to stay there, whereas his abstract paintings belonged in a post World War II American art world.

Whitten was one of a handful of African American artists to succeed in the mainstream art world throughout his life. Was he simply better than those who have less recognition, or was he less threatening because he did not pursue political content? Thinking about the tone of approval of his work in the quotes at the beginning of this article, abstraction was certainly more elusive as a means of speaking than the unavoidable imagery of a Charles White (who was also successful, but in a different arena).

Whitten did not adopt abstraction in order to be safe. Abstraction worked with his abstract way of understanding the world. His abstraction is not an empty gesture, it is an act based on wide-ranging exploration of ideas.

Based on the homages quoted above, it is clear that he was held in a certain amount of awe by his colleagues and fellow artists. He was deep, poetic, and incredibly willing to take chances.

He came from extreme poverty in Alabama in the 1940s. His father died when he was five, his mother left with seven children to raise alone. She must have been a remarkable woman. He went to segregated schools, but was already interested in shop and music. He was in the south during the bombing of the 16th Street Baptist Church and the murders of the four children at Sunday School as well as other less widely publicized atrocities. He joined civil rights protests as a student in Baton Rouge that were attacked by police. The violence propelled him to New York City where he went to then tuition-free Cooper

Union art school. But what a leap to end up as a major painter in New York City.

So the mystery of life and success remains: is it initiative, luck, mentoring, perseverance, charm, talent? We know that for a Black man in the art world of the 1970s in New York City, brains and talent were not enough. The fact that his experiment with materials fit with what was acceptable at that time is a conjunction of time, place, person, and inclination. He may also have been just lucky in his timing.

In the 1970s the art world was shifting from its exclusive focus on White men making abstract paintings, but diversity was not yet established as a crucial consideration (although as a result of Black Lives Matter, thinking is slowly shifting—2020). He slipped in then, and off he went.

But to return to the sculptures, which I can't help feeling are his greatest art. Why were they never shown? Because they didn't "fit" what the art world wanted? Or because he saw them as personal and informal studies. I want to believe that he saw them as an ongoing exploration, a synthesis of all his ideas. They were not ready for the world until after he died. Thank goodness we have them now.

(2018)

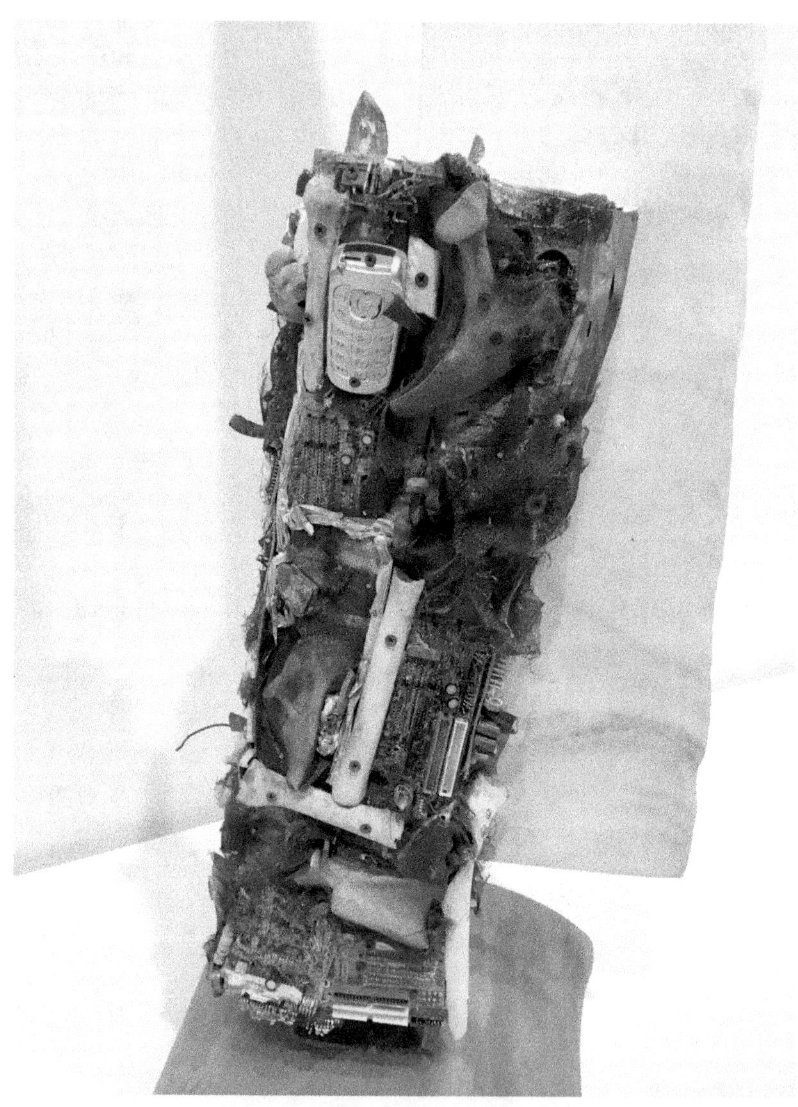

Jack Whitten, *Quantum Man (The Sixth Portal)*, detail, 2016, Marble, Cretan walnut, Serbian oak, lead, acrylic, mixed media, 62"x12"x16 ½", Collection of the Estate of Jack Whitten, courtesy Hauser and Wirth

# The Humanism of Charles White

THE HUGE MURAL BY CHARLES WHITE, *5 great American Negroes*, on loan from Howard University, overwhelms us before we even enter the Charles White Retrospective at the Museum of Modern Art in New York.

In this first mural that White created for the government-sponsored WPA mural program, Sojourner Truth leads a march of freed slaves that recedes into the background in a tapering curve on the left. In the center, Booker T. Washington promotes his famous Tuskagee College to potential benefactors, standing at a lectern with Frederick Douglass behind him holding a grieving slave. In the right foreground, George Washington Carver peers through a microscope and behind him Marion Anderson performs against a blue sky; the two are linked by a young man reading and a mentor pointing dramatically toward a future.

In the mural White has successfully juxtaposed carefully observed portraits of well-known African Americans by placing them in a succession of deep and shallow spaces. White would subsequently focus on portraiture and powerful Black bodies, with a particular emphasis on hands and gestures, throughout his career. Four other murals from these years are represented in the exhibition by studies and sketches such as the vividly-detailed carbon pencil over charcoal portrait of Paul Robeson. We see Robeson as a powerful but troubled person, a brilliant talent and a political activist who paid a heavy penalty for his activism during the McCarthy era.

The Charles White Retrospective at the Museum of Modern Art foregrounds the artist's deep commitment to presenting the humanity and dignity of African Americans. He died young at age sixty-one, and saw profound changes in the U.S. and in his own life, but he always followed his own vision:

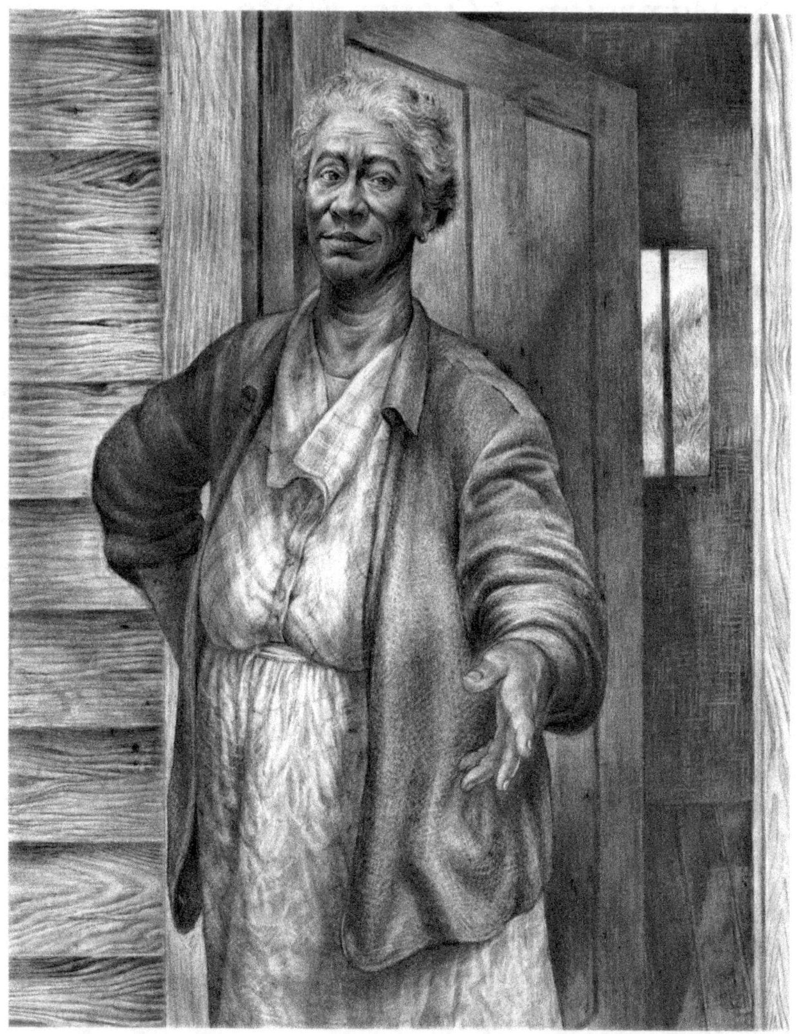

Charles White, *I've Been 'Buked and I've Been Scorned,* 1956, compressed and vine charcoal with carbon pencil and charcoal wash splatter over traces of graphite pencil on illustration board, 44 5/8" x 35 3/8," Blanton Museum of Art, The University of Texas at Austin, Gift of Susan G. and Edmund W. Gordon to the units of Black Studies and the Blanton Museum of Art at The University of Texas at Austin, The Charles White Archives

For me, the thing that matters most is not the form per se, but the depth of the content. I may experiment with new compositional forms, but my chief concern is always with expressing a particular feeling or emotion.

In his earliest years as an artist in the 1930s, as with many African American artists who became prominent after World War II, the WPA programs provided professional acknowledgement, the support to make art, and a sense of community. African American artists who joined the federal programs were often self-educated in art at public libraries and classes, also sponsored by the WPA. The artists in Harlem and Chicago had a community of supportive musicians, poets, writers and visual artists which proved invaluable in their early development.

Rural Black artists, especially in the South, were isolated before the government programs began, excluded from White public libraries and access to any art training. The community centers and art schools the government sponsored provided both jobs and a sense of personal support. I am thinking here of the less famous, but also extraordinary James W. Washington, Jr., who joined the WPA program in Mississippi, based entirely on his own study and survival skills in the Jim Crow South. He went on to have a successful career as a sculptor in the Northwest.

As I looked at White's portraits, as well as his anonymous individual figures, I could feel the challenges that these people overcame; I could feel their anger, and their hopes, their poignancy and power, resilience and resistance, strength and dignity.

White declared:

I like to think that my work has a universality to it, I deal with love, hope, courage, freedom, dignity—the full gamut of human spirit. When I work, though, I think of my own people. That's only natural. However, my philosophy doesn't exclude any nation or race of people.

During the 1960s White's work altered dramatically. His drawings became much larger, dominated by a single figure. *General Moses* (Harriet Tubman) (1965), sits legs apart, with arms on her knees, hands crossed in front, her expression one of anger. She sits in front of a wall of massive rocks cut unevenly (and brilliantly rendered by White). This work, created at the height of the obsession with abstraction in American art, defies us in every way and the large figure defies the world.

In 1966, White created several large figure drawings with the title *J'Accuse,* based on the anti-semitic Émile Zola drama in 19th century France. Each of the five works suggest different emotions. In this drawing we have the enigmatic African mask carried on a woman's head covered with grass and swathed in a voluminous robe. We see her immense strength and determined expression, even as the African sculpture gives her spiritual power that seems to lift her up.

White stayed with the figure, increasingly embedding it in a large textured surface. The complex drawing awes us with his mastery. The figures engage the interior lives of people challenged by life. They honor resistance to oppression through strength and love.

In his series *Wanted Posters* he conveys the injustice of the system through subtle facial expressions and deep compassion.

Just a few years before he died, he was still experimenting with new formats, media and content, as in *Sound of Silence,* a black man with a large conch shell at his center, suggests symbolism, but ambiguously. Is the shell protecting him? Empowering him? We don't know.

Indeed with Charles White, it is easy to make glib comparisons with White mainstream references, that are often completely inadequate. The most glaring example of this type of comparison is with *Our Land,* 1951. A powerful and defiant woman holds a pitchfork as she looks out from her doorway. In the catalog she is repeatedly compared to Grant Wood's *American Gothic* (which White would have seen in the Art Institute of Chicago). She could not be more different from the pale, insipid farmer and his daughter. White's woman with her giant hands and assertive posture is clearly saying don't come here or this fork will be a weapon. I immediately thought of the artist Clarissa Sligh's story of her uncle who was killed and left on her mother's doorstep when she was ten years old and he was twelve. This pitchfork-holding woman protects her family with her working woman's hands and her very sharp pronged fork.

Kellie Jones's essay in the catalog "Charles White, Feminist at Midcentury," provides a much needed new perspective on activist African American feminists in California. We all know that the history of feminism in the art world has long overemphasized a group of White women in California. Jones's essay gives us a fresh perspective.

Another great insight from the exhibition is White's life-long close friendship with Harry Belafonte. Indeed, Belafonte narrates parts of the audio in the exhibition. They inspired and encouraged each other. Music played a major role in White's life and many of his portraits are of famous singers such as Mahalia Jackson and Bessie Smith.

Every one of these paintings and drawings rivet us with their aesthetics as well as confronting us with their perseverance. We feel these people from the inside, rather than passing over them from the outside because of the color of their skin.

I watched a discussion online between one of the (White) curators of the exhibition, and the (White) director of the Museum of Modern Art. A question from the audience came as to why White was so neglected after he died. In the answer there was no reference to racism in the art world (nor did that word occur at any point in the discussion). But it is obvious that White art history still practices tokenism when it comes to artists of color. Happily, the three museums showing this major exhibition are finally giving one of the great twentieth century artists his due.

(2018)

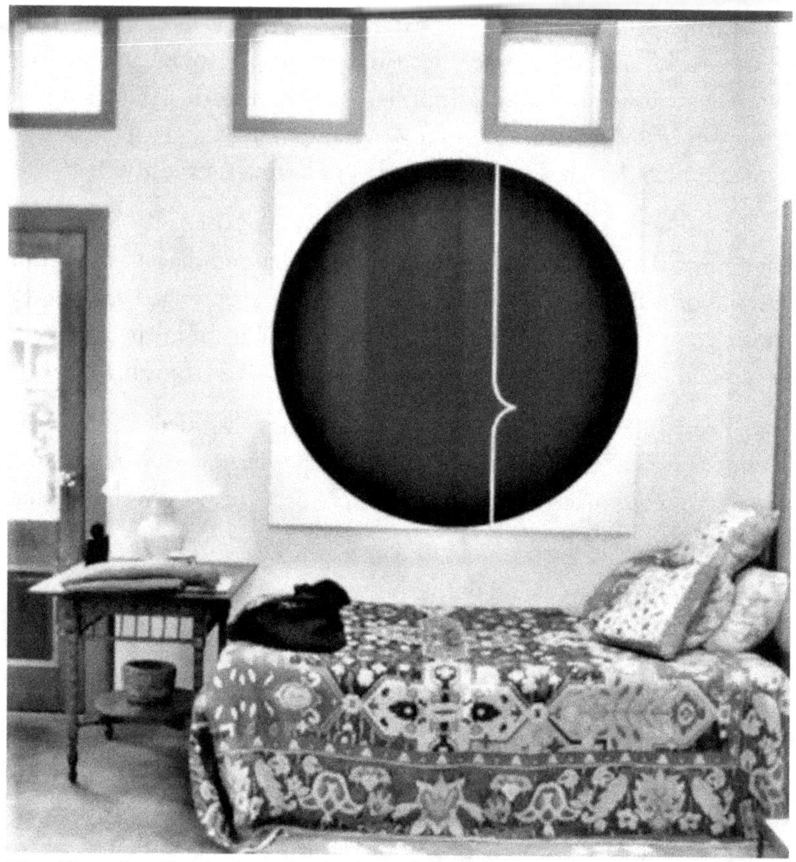

Mary Henry, Installation view in her home, Whidbey Island, 2002

# Bauhaus in the Northwest:
# The Art of Mary Henry

ROOTED IN A DIRECT KNOWLEDGE OF Bauhaus and Constructivist principles, Mary Henry studied with László Moholy-Nagy at the Institute of Design in Chicago in 1945-1946, the last year of his life. She was the only student during that year with an art background (and she had studied industrial drawing, which fit well with Moholy-Nagy's principles on combining art and life). At the end of the year, with the program rapidly expanding through the GI bill, Moholy-Nagy even invited Henry to join the faculty. Unfortunately, she was not able to stay in Chicago, and Moholy-Nagy died of leukemia only a few months later.

A photograph of Henry's own light-space modulator, made from wire rods, string and wood, with complex interconnections of space, hangs in her current home and provides a direct link to those student days as well as a demonstration of her knowledge of Bauhaus principles. It moves beyond layered planarity into a multidimensional world defined by light.

Her grasp of Moholy-Nagy's concept of "vision in motion" gives her work a spatial complexity that contrasts with that of artists who work with the low relief space of cubism or the grids of Mondrian. Many American painters (and Clement Greenberg himself) picked up an understanding of abstraction in the late thirties and early forties from Hans Hofmann, whose concept of "Push and Pull" was based on cubism with a dash of expressionism, the result of Hofmann's brief early contact with Kandinsky. But Moholy-Nagy believed:

> Abstract art creates new types of spatial relationships, new inventions of forms, new visual laws—basic and simple as the visual counterpart to a more purposeful, cooperative human society.

Painted in acrylic on a two-dimensional surface, Henry's *Company I, II* and *III,* 1998, give the viewer a visceral experience of color moving in space. Their structure holds us in a parallel universe. *Company I* centers on a large white irregular polygon tracked by a few black lines held by a square of blue with a yellow, orange and purple polygon against a grey background. *Company II* features a larger white area, with a more dynamic line, deeper orange, blue and red. *Company III* is denser, with large circles of white partly overlaid with gray areas and framed in intense yellow with just a little red in the center. The three paintings carry on an increasingly complex conversation.

Other paintings in the exhibition included *Still and All* (1997), *The Tagus* (1992), and *Red Fracture* (2001), each with different geometric and color relationships. *The Tagus* has yellow, red and blue squares with a lot of black; *Still and All* has more diagonals and long verticals and more grays; *Red Fracture* is black and white with a large circle in red, broken by a stepped white.

Paired with these bright works was a second room with more subdued colors and playful geometry. *She Bang*, 2000, is a diptych with bluish gray and white panels that seem to be juggling circles painted in black and white stripes, blue or white. The black and white-striped circles recall Henry's op work from the sixties, when she occasionally extended into three dimensions.

The *North Slope* series at the Bellevue Arts Museum (June 30 – September 23, 2001) has a more ascetic, less playful quality. The eleven works (there are a total of twenty-two paintings and fifty drawings in the whole series) are based on the artist's trip to Alaska in 1975, when she visited a tiny village on the North Slope that was barely accessible to the outside world. (Not surprisingly, it was an oil company that had only recently built a road penetrating this pristine world.)

The *North Slope* paintings are all grays and whites with some black. An emphasis on diagonals abstractly invoke the top of mammoth submerged glaciers or impassable mountains. Sometimes there is a pinkish tone inspired by a hardy lichen that survives in the far North. In the delicate drawings (not exhibited) the spare geometry and color variables play out on a smaller scale like a highly disciplined musical composition. These somber, meditative works invoke the clarity and purity of a place barely touched by human life and the loneliness of those who dare to live there.

This summer, in an entirely different spirit, Henry designed an exuberant two story 360 degree mural, *No Limits*, in a special projects gallery in the new Bellevue Arts Museum. The commission was the inspiration of Brian Wallace, curator at the Museum. Allyn Behr did the actual painting from Henry's small model. Henry's ability to organize abstract color in an irregular five-sided, 360 degree space drew on both her practical experiences as a mural painter in the 1950s and her confident grasp of abstract space and its relationship to real space. The mural has ten colors: yellow, green, violet, three variations on orange, sky blue, crimson, black, white and a lemony yellow. Anchored by just a few floor-to-ceiling verticals, with large punctuating circles, the composition moves around the room and across corners flawlessly. (You can see it on the Bellevue Arts Museum website). Since the actual walls did not correspond to the architect's measurement, Henry had to adjust it several inches without throwing off the proportional relationships of the whole. The mural was dedicated on September 20, with an avant-garde electronic musical composition by her son-in-law, John Rahn. Henry's mural and her son-in-law's avant-garde electronic music perfectly suit the new museum's constructivist inspired architecture by Steven Holl.

In addition to these three shows, twenty-eight of Henry's paintings are on exhibit in the Museum of Northwest Art in La Conner ("In the Garden of Myth and Logic") Museum of Northwest Art, October 12, 2001 to January 6, 2002, and another exhibition at Lorinda Knight's Gallery, Spokane, February 2 – 27, 2002.

While each exhibition features a different aspect of the artist's work, every painting conveys the complexity and flexibility of a purely abstract vocabulary when it is handled by an artist who has studied its theoretical underpinnings rather than simply its formal devices. As Henry has said, "I can't invent things I don't understand." While affiliated with the utopianism of early twentieth century abstraction, Henry does not directly speak of a social agenda. Yet there is a feeling of exuberance in viewing these paintings that distinguishes them from abstraction by younger artists whose ironic or postmodern perspectives foreclose any sense of hope. They seem closed and opaque, while Henry's paintings are full of a transparent joy, a quality in notably short supply these days.

(2002)

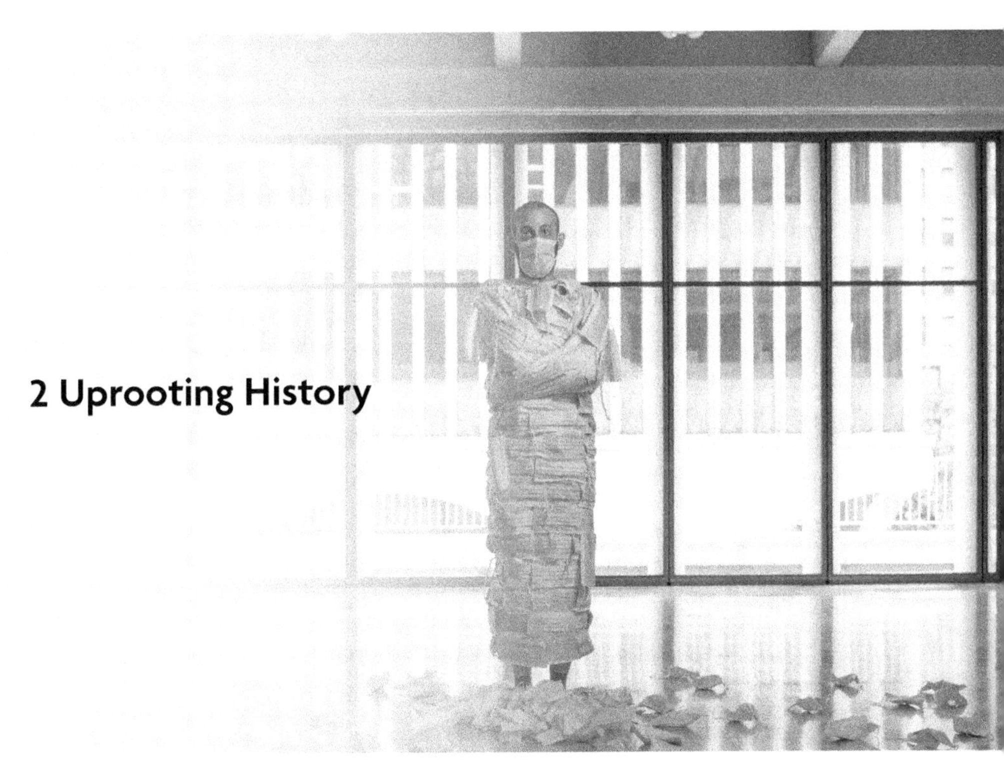

# 2 Uprooting History

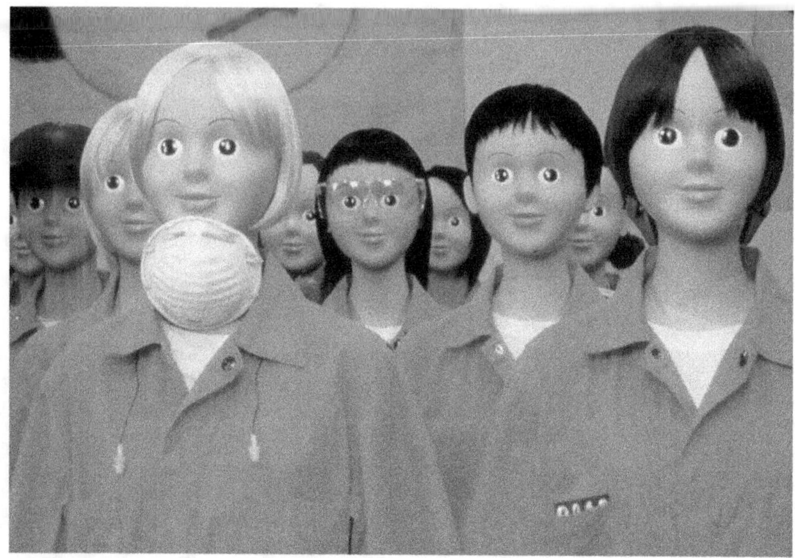

Tokyo design studio Groovisions' "Superflat," *Chappie*, 2001, detail of installation, Henry Art Gallery, safety orange jumpsuit, dust mask, knee-pads

# Where are We Since 9/11?

WHERE ARE WE SINCE 9/11? How has the position of culture changed, how has our perception of culture produced before 9/11 been altered?

We see art differently. Everything has taken on new layers of meaning. So, for example, in "Superflat" at the Henry Art Gallery, University of Washington, thirty-three life size Chappies (pubescent teenage girl dolls with identical faces) are lined up wearing bright orange work suits as well as assorted helmets, earphones, facemasks and goggles. What else do we think of but rescue workers, something that would not have crossed our minds two months ago. These dolls were originally created as a comment on conformity in Japanese society, now they can also suggest community and solidarity and the challenges and difficulties of alternative paths. But this doll army has no feelings, they are automatons who work without thinking. That is the gulf that separates us from them. Deep, searing feelings are back.

Likewise, Katsushige Nakahashi's photographic replica of a crashed Japanese Zero plane (constructed with 25,000 enlarged Polaroid photos of every millimeter of a model), takes on a new significance. We now think of those Kamikaze pilots not as an historical event from long ago, but as a current phenomenon. Kamikaze, like Nakahashi's tiny model replica, has been blown up to new proportions as civilian suicide flyers target symbolic buildings with thousands of civilians inside.

At the entrance to the "Superflat" exhibition is a wall covered with red-eyed nymphets dressed in Issey Miyake clothing, wanly standing in a wispy fantasy landscape. They are facing a wall of stills and laser-disc excerpts from Yoshinori Kanada's classic animé, *Galaxy Express 999*,1979 and *Goodbye Galaxy Express 999*,1981. Cities are bombed, people run for their lives, everything is going up in flames on one wall, while the larger-than-life-size nymphets gaze in a stupor from some other dimension, somewhat the way we felt (if we weren't in New York) watching the terrorist attack on television. Obviously the mass destruction in the film still recalls Hiroshima and the fireballs of that dreadful bomb, even as they also make us think of the current bombing and terror in Afghanistan.

The rest of the show can also be read as a layered interpretation of the contemporary moment as much as a carefully-curated manifestation of Japanese pop culture.

"Superflat" refers, according to the exhibition's curator, Takashi Murakami, to the space of the Japanese animé, its flatness and flexibility, its linearity and its illusion of multiple dimensions, its instability and its artificiality; even this can be read metaphorically: before 9/11, much like the world before Galileo, we had a two-dimensional grasp of a multi-dimensional world.

(2001)

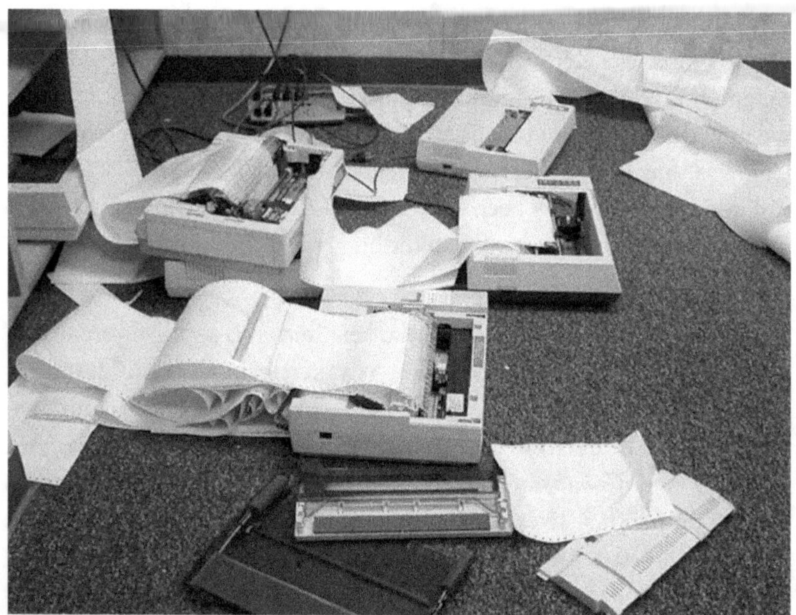

"Designed Obsolescence/Third Floor," detail of installation, anonymous downtown office building, Lubbock, Tx, 2005

# Designed Obsolescence

In December 2004, an architect (Szu-Han Ho), a musician (Zachary Watkins), a photographer (Robert Mears) and a painter (Chad Dawkins) got together in a nondescript building in downtown Lubbock to think about staging an art show. On the third floor of the seven-story building, they found a room overflowing with obsolete office equipment, some of it dating back decades. It was like a time capsule—1983 Apple computers, Portafaxes, Scantron machines, Krown phones, modems and printers, reel-to-reel projectors, microfiche readers, Polaroid ID equipment, dot-matrix printers, perforated paper and so on. Built in the 1920s, the building served as the West Texas Hospital until 1974. Sometime in the late 1970s, South Plains Community College remodeled the interior. Accordingly, the group also found medical and educational detritus—motivational posters, tapes, medical illustrations, cooking show videos, training manuals for remedial skills—that referenced the space's varied history. It was a view into out-of-date concepts, as well as out-of-date technology.

This found mix of obsolescence led to a couple of months of brainstorming sessions. Somewhere along the line, two more artists joined the group: Shreepad Joglekar—a photographer from Mumbai currently in the process of shifting from commercial to fine art—and Piotr Chizinski, a business sector dropout who loves regurgitated machinery. The result was an installation that took up fifteen rooms. Even in its excess, there was a prevailing wit and unity to the show— an understated absurdity based on the conjunction of machines, light, sound and visuals. Although some of the pieces could be attributed to individuals, the installation was really the result of a creative partnership between the machines and learning props, the artists, and the space itself.

In the elevator, a trio played serious classical music, setting up a witty tone and aesthetic that ran throughout the exhibit. As soon as the elevator doors opened, the sound of multiple machines amplified by contact microphones displaced their music, creating an accidental symphony. Humming, screeching, clicking, whirring, whining, vibrating and chugging, these noises also merged with voices coming from instructional videos and audiotapes. In the stairwell, a sound piece by Watkins also scrambled the sounds of rainstorms and people walking through the space.

The first room held one of several collaborations by Chizinski and Dawkins. The pair set up five old monitors, offering interactive programs obviously intended as remedial aids. The room was dark; the monitors glowed with green letters and everyone over twenty felt a flash of nostalgia. The machines seemed animate—benevolent old friends that spoke to us when we touched their keyboards.

In the next two rooms, the pair piled a half-dozen dot-matrix printers on shelves with paper churning back and forth in an endless loop, followed by a boneyard of broken monitors and keyboards, as well as printers issuing high-pitched whirring noises and low-pitched clacking sounds. Ho's row of glowing trash cans led down a hall to another room with a sound and light collaboration with Watkins, in which an oscillator circuit board responded to fluorescent light. As bulbs flickered on and off, their amplified sound shifted from a high-pitched whine to a low-frequency vibration.

Joglekar printed texts from Kafka's *Metamorphosis* and Marguerite Duras' *The Malady of Death* on an antique modem. Fifteen feet of paper trailed out of the room and into a microfiche reader, where fragments popped up in huge letters. Words jumped off the screen, forming random and incomprehensible messages. Computer paper under foot turned into medical illustrations in Mears' installation. Mears covered the entire floor in one area, creating the opportunity to work out any hostilities one might harbor toward Western medicine right there on the spot. His main contribution, though, was a lens from a slide projector placed in a dark room to create a sort of camera obscura. It projected images from outside the room, creating a shadowy performance out of the movements of anyone who happened to pass by.

In the largest room, Ho and Watkins staged an improvised concert with Ho on violin and Watkins on an assembly of electronic toys—a kid's keyboard, a Simon Says game, an ET walkie-talkie set—as well as AM radios and contact microphones.

"Designed Obsolescence" spoke as a metaphor for the breakdown of the dream of technology and the myth of our society's permanence. Everything will end up like the equipment found in this building—a heap of unusable, out-of-date ideas as toxic as the mercury in old computers. Yet the show also spoke of the crucial necessity for play, creativity, absurdity and incongruity in the face of inevitable disintegration.

Collaboration and its potential creative freefall are often neglected in the uptight, self-conscious art world. Perhaps this type of risk-taking synergy can only happen in a place like Lubbock, where no one has anything to lose. Szu-Han Ho, whose family foundation bought the building with the hope of jumpstarting revitalization in downtown Lubbock, succeeded in bringing renewed energy to a desolate corner. This may just be the start of an avant-garde community on the High Plains.

(2005)

# Women Artists Take on the World

In Paris the huge feminist exhibition "Elles: Women Artists from the Centre Pompidou, Paris" made a big splash and awakened a debate and discussion about feminism. In Seattle we have had a city-wide extravaganza of exhibitions of women's art, symposia, concerts, lectures, performances and special events. It is impossible to assess, though, if this really penetrated already-held perspectives, changed any minds, or even expanded thinking. We have some great creative people here, and some brilliant curators, but the critical discourse and analysis tends to be self-congratulatory. People did get worked up about the marketing of the show that used a photograph of a bikini-clad bimbo. But it reminds us why we need to give more thought to what these women are saying in their art. The issues they present are still with us.

Less than 20 percent of the Pompidou Center's exhibition crossed the sea, but because the show came from France, we first of all had a great opportunity to see some extraordinary modern and contemporary art by women working in France and the rest of Europe. For me, it was extremely refreshing to have that emphasis. Finally, an exhibition of women's art that isn't based on our "canonical" history, i.e. the book by Norma Broude, Mary D. Garrard and Judith K. Brodsky, *The Power of Feminist Art: The American Movement in the 1970s, History and Impact* (Abrams 1994).

"Elles" is not a systematic history, more of a series of unpredictable snapshots. I offer here a look at a few of those snapshots, emphasizing work that surprised or excited me.

In the very first room a stunning early painting by Sonia Delaunay jumps off the wall with its highly saturated reds, along with examples of her pioneering abstract color painting. Nearby are two works by the dynamic Russian futurist, Natalia Goncharova, a stage set from the

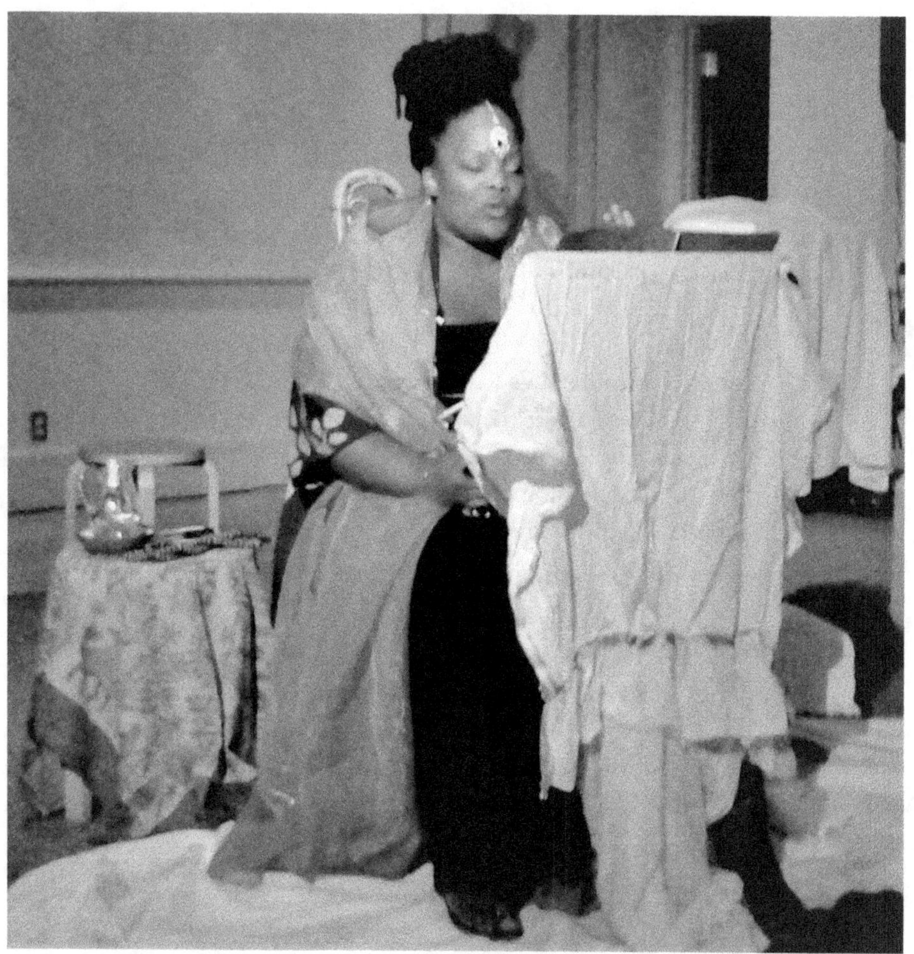

Christa Bell performing "1001 Holy Names," in "Elles: Women Artists from the Centre Pompidou, Paris," Seattle Art Museum, November 2012

Russian constructivist designer, Alexandra Exter, and a subtle Cubist painting by the lesser-known María Blanchard.

While these women often had male partners and collaborators, Suzanne Valadon's *The Blue Room*,1923, launches defiance. Reclining on a bed with a luscious blue patterned spread (an accomplished homage to Matisse), a tough, real life woman poses in the way of traditional male paintings of nudes, but she is a subject not an object of male desire. With her cigarette in the center of her mouth, she assertively supports herself on one elbow. She wears loose-fitting striped pants and her pendulous breasts are covered in a pink top.

Paris in the 1920s, that hotbed of cross-dressing and sexual freedom by later-to-be outstandingly famous women and men, comes to us in the photographs of Gisèle Freund, Dora Maar, and Berenice Abbott, who photographed celebrities such as Virginia Woolf, Vita Sackville-West, Sylvia Beach, Nusch Éluard, James Joyce and Jean Cocteau.

Another segment of photographs includes two photographers from that bastion of male domination, the Bauhaus—Lucia Moholy and Florence Henri. Henri confronts us in a close-up self-portrait with her intelligence and sense of her own strength.

Familiar and still formidable work by sculptors like Lee Bontecou, Louise Nevelson and Louise Bourgeois, are followed by a room of abstract paintings, and then by what the Seattle Art Museum calls "Genital Panic." In one famous performance called "Action Pants Genital Panic," made in 1969, Valie Export walked around movie theaters with the crotch of her pants cut out, directly confronting people with a counter narrative to the passivity of women in film. She is way out there.

Sanja Iveković, a Croatian artist, continues the theme of cutting the body, as does Orlan's painful surgeries commenting on the cult of beauty. (I wondered why Yoko Ono, the pioneer on cutting, wasn't included here).

Hannah Wilke invited people to chew gum which became like vulva that she stuck on her body, then posed in various pin up postures in "Starification Object Series."

Hanging high over our heads on one wall, Niki de Saint-Phalle's enormous woman made of junk materials includes hundreds of pieces of dolls and old underwear.

The second half of the show had fewer surprises, although Atsuko Tanaka's electric dress jumped out. But it is a reconstruction and should have had at least a photograph of the artist in the 1950s wearing her garment constructed of hundreds of colored light bulbs that followed her nervous and circulatory system.

Particularly timely to see again are the videos by Mona Hatoum and Sigalet Landau, both presenting metaphors of the Palestine/Israeli conflict. They address the body: Hatoum's video gives us endoscopic surgery-penetrating orifices, and Sigalet painfully swings a barbed wire hula hoop.

The inimitable curator Sandra Jackson-Dumont invited Christa Bell to perform "1001 Holy Names" for guess what, and included Adrian Piper's work "Cornered." Piper confronts us with our own racism in a particularly effective way. Watch and be cornered. Needless to say, both "Elles" and SAM have a skimpy representation of women of color.

So it is a delight that Yayoi Kusama steals the show on the third floor, (all works on loan from the Gagosian Gallery). Her wriggling erotic forms crawl everywhere on shoes, hats, furniture, walls, floors. She takes the sterility of minimal grids and crosses it with organic shapes that seem to crowd together like underwater coral. The boat in the show constructed of stuffed work gloves, as well as the snake-like yellow and black eruptions on the floor, take over. Her painstaking, obsessive compulsive patterns cover acres of canvas, but the three-dimensional forms are much more evocative for me in their physical presence. Kusama lives in a mental hospital in Japan by choice. We should all be so self-aware.

From the perspective of global feminism, other exhibitions in Seattle took it further. At the Asian Art Museum, "Women's Paintings from the Land of Sita" featured artists who formerly decorated houses, and now make paintings on canvas. That museum is also showing "Touba" by Iranian artist Shirin Neshat, the two-screen video that takes its title and its sacred tree from *Touba and the Meaning of Night* by Shahnush Parsipur.

So where are we so far? Seattle is a city that can be really cosmopolitan. We are fortunate in our curators and their innovative approaches. As far as women artists are concerned, to immerse ourselves in these art works is to provoke us to think about women's place in yesterday's and today's world.

(2012)

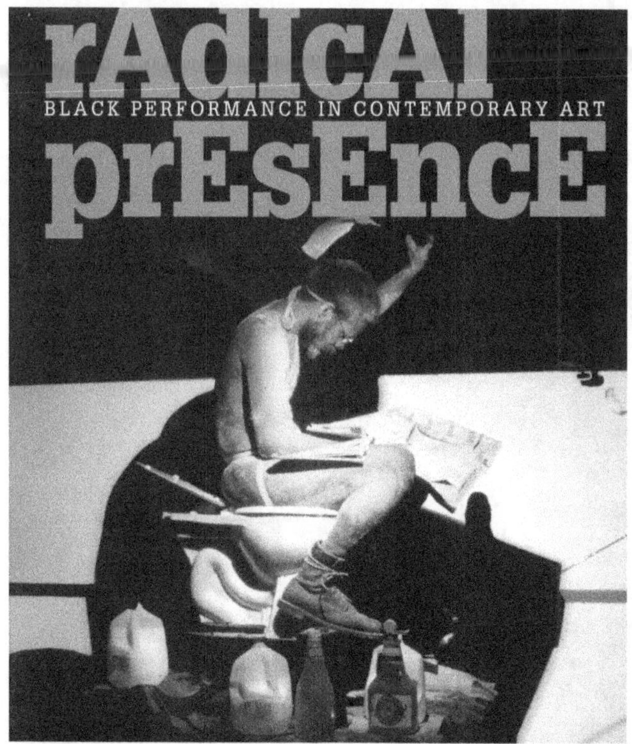

Valerie Cassel Oliver *et al.*, *rAdIcAl prEsEncE Black Performance in Contemporary Art*, Contemporary Arts Museum, Houston 2013, cover art: Pope.L., *Eating the Wall Street Journal*, 2000

## rAdIcAl prEsEncE

Yes, that's exactly how it is spelled. All the vowels are capitalized. The vowels are calling attention to themselves as active letters that make meaning. We usually don't even notice their crucial contribution. Likewise, Valerie Cassel Oliver, in her book *rAdIcAl prEsEncE Black Performance in Contemporary Art*, wants to make Black performance stand out. At first she was only planning a book, but the project became an exhibition at the Contemporary Arts Museum in Houston, Texas, in late 2012, and is now a two venue exhibition in New York City.

Cassel Oliver began this project with a study of Benjamin Patterson, a founding member of the pioneering performance group Fluxus in the late 1950s. As she states "Patterson… [is] a touchstone for questioning the visibility of foundational figures within the canon of performance art." That is a polite way of saying that racism in the writing of art history means that all but a few token Black people are left out. Just to make the point clear, let us imagine a book with the title "White Performance in Contemporary Art."

But there is much more to think about. Cassel Oliver examines three generations of Black performance artists over a period of forty years. She also documents, in her text and in a chronology at the end of the book, the unique history of the performing Black body in American culture from slavery onwards. The fact is that performance has always been part of the experience of African Americans in this country.

Black artists who choose public performance as their medium are boldly contradicting the sale of Black bodies at slave auctions, the stereotypes of minstrelsy, and current abuses such as the police practice of "stop and frisk," as well as mass incarceration. They also are calling out the perpetual stereotypes their bodies must carry in public through the media, sports, and entertainment industry.

They purposefully disrupt public space through fearless and extreme actions.

William Pope.L, wearing only a jock strap, covered himself in flour and sat on a toilet on top of a rickety structure. He ate the *Wall Street Journal* with ketchup and milk and then regurgitated it. The artist declared: "My focus is to politicize disenfranchisement … to reinvent what's beneath us, to remind us where we all come from."

Pope.L's *Eating the Wall Street Journal* while sitting on a toilet is on the cover of the book.

Papo Colo ran down the West Side Highway with a huge pile of sticks dragging behind him. Sherman Fleming stood in a doorway as lumber was wedged all around him, then walked away, leaving the wood to collapse. Dressed as El Conquistador, Shaun El C. Leonardo engaged in a brutal boxing match. Taneka Norris, a young MFA Yale graduate, pushes borders with hip hop lyrics and a minimalist painting created with her own blood. Finally, Jacolby Satterwhite wears an iPod, iPad touch, and iPad. His marathon performance "turns his body into a shamanistic pathway toward the future . . . in which the corporeal self is neither male nor female but rather an amalgamation of the sexes."

In addition to Cassel Oliver's overview and provocative chronology, there are five other all too brief essays, Yona Backer's "Performance Trace: Staged Actions, Live Art, and Performance Made for the Camera," explores the difficulty of creating a record of performance art and the act of performance for cameras; Tavia Nyong'o's "Between the Body and the Flesh: Sex and Gender in Black Performance Art," explores the connections of recent performance to the slave body and what she calls a "subversive self-fashioning" by artists like Dread Scott. Naomi Beckwith's "Dark Mirrors: Performance Documents as Bodily Evidence" explains how three women, Adrian Piper, Senga Nengudi and Coco Fusco, chose to create a permanent record of their performances.

Franklin Sirmans's "No Safety Net: Lorraine O'Grady and Performing in Public without Sanction," explains O'Grady's bold challenge to African American artists at an opening when she bellows at them as Mlle Bourgeoise Noire, "THAT"S ENOUGH, No more boot-licking. No more ass kissing . . . BLACK ART MUST TAKE MORE RISKS."

Finally, Clifford Owens, who is a performance artist himself, has a two-part essay. Part I "Notes on the Crisis of Black American Performance Art" (2003) celebrates politicized performance artists like William Pope.L . "Part II" (2012) explains his own project "Anthology," which invited twenty-six artists to give him a score for a live performance. As a result he is "a conduit for transmitting profoundly powerful messages from a group of enormously talented artists."

The book has stunning color photographs of all the artists, although detailed descriptions of the work is confined to selected live performances at the end. My favorite aspect of this project is that it suggests continuity with the present and future. The generation of artists who matured just after the Civil Rights Movement have dominated our perceptions of African American artists for several decades. It is a joy to see the work of those legacy artists as a touchstone for young artists today. Valerie Cassel Oliver intentionally is writing a history that opens up a path to the future.

(2013)

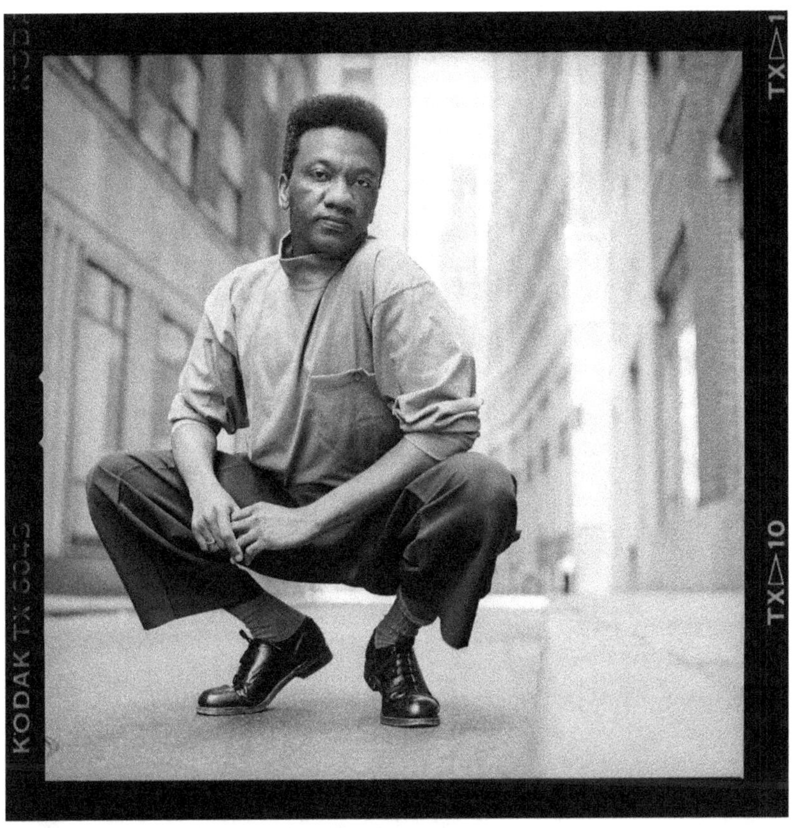

Donald Byrd, 1989, Photograph: Jeffrey S. Kane

## Donald Byrd: Dance as Provocation

Donald Byrd transforms movement into resonant art. The world-renowned choreographer has been based here in Seattle since 2002. I have previously written about his humble base in the Madrona Beach Bathhouse on Lake Washington.

Now, a groundbreaking retrospective at the Frye Art Museum, "Donald Byrd: The America That Is To Be," curated by Thomas F. DeFrantz, Professor of Dance, Duke University, successfully overcomes the challenge of exhibiting dance in a venue designed for visual art.

Videos from the 1970s to the present (from tiny to huge), as well as photographs from throughout Bryd's astonishing career, mesmerize us as we witness his extraordinary creativity. In addition, on a low stage inside the gallery, Spectrum Dance Theater presents intimate performances several days a week.

Donald Byrd has been radical from his first performances in Los Angeles as early as 1978, when he challenged racism, gender, and bourgeois sensibilities with a classical pas de deux that paired a "disaffected" Black man and "blasé cigarette smoking" White woman. His choreography has deep classical roots, but he has consistently expanded the ways that he can confront us with deep social issues through music, movement, gesture, and settings. He deeply believes that dance can trigger social transformation.

His main inspirations are the giants of twentieth century dance, George Balanchine, Merce Cunningham and Alvin Ailey, but he also

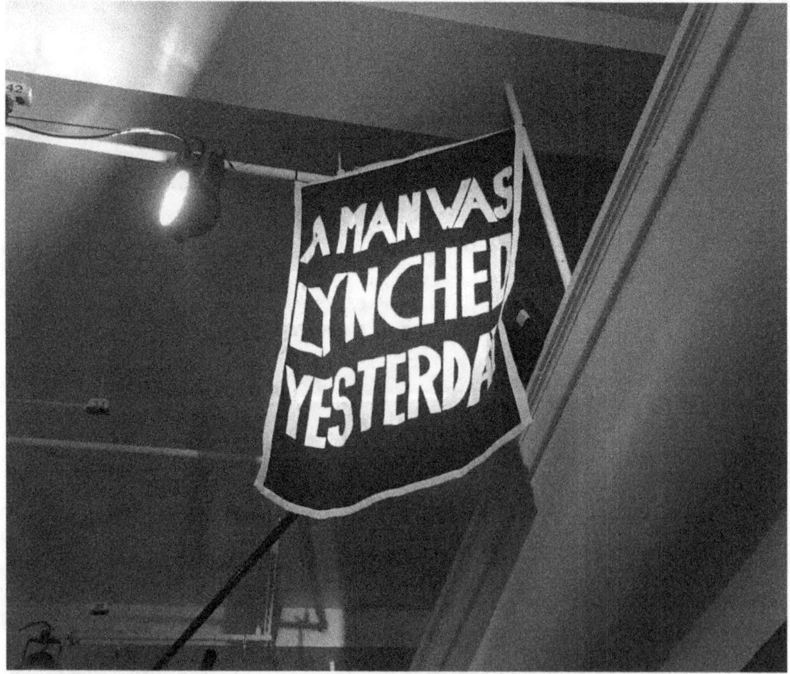


Spectrum Dance Theater Company, "A Man Was Lynched Yesterday," Performance banner from "Wokeness Festival," April 2019, "A series of dance and non-dance events intended to push against assumptions around race, equity, gender, and justice, while creating an environment for examining the presumptions around being 'woke.' "

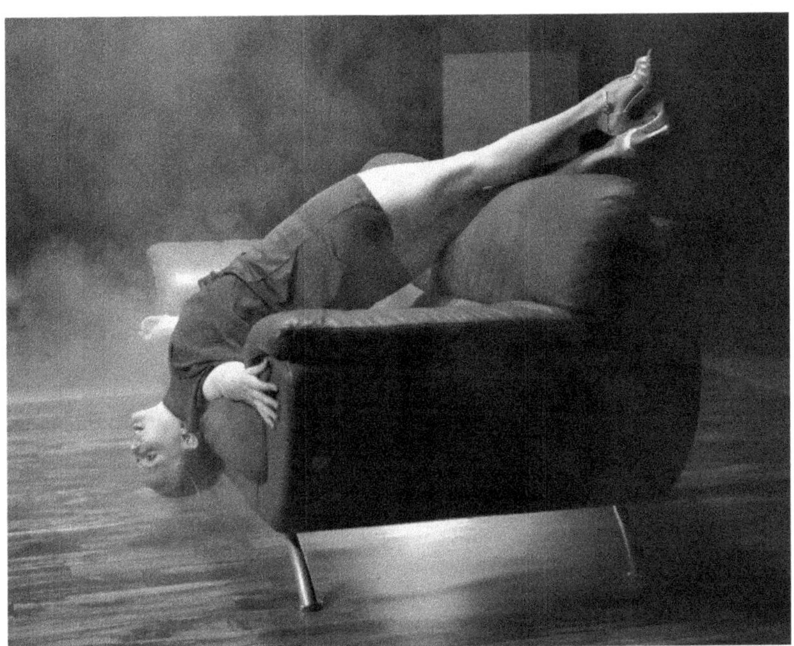

Spectrum Dance Theater Company, dancer Emily Pihlaja performs Donald Byrd's "Lyric Suite," Photograph: Marcia Davis. "A 12 solo film dance work of a Kafkaesque world that explores the mental and emotional impact of extended isolation in a time of plague and social protest on 12 individuals told in 11 vignettes," November 13-15, 2020

explores popular traditions ranging from punk and funk to Irish jigs. His encyclopedic vocabulary of movement (as well as music) becomes his own as he embodies challenging social issues.

Earlier in his career he aimed to shock: we see him in beauty pageant drag, singing an exaggerated "God Bless America" in "American Dream," 1995, a performance that includes "a phantasmagoric patchwork of terror and display." You will have to see it to know what this means!

In addition to confronting bourgeois race and gender clichés, Byrd rewrites classics. In his "Harlem Nutcracker," 1997, Clara, now an African American matriarch, welcomes her well-to-do family for Kwanzaa and Christmas in Harlem. The choreography both honors and parodies traditional ballet while it also celebrates African American dance traditions. Another even bolder retelling is "The Minstrel Show, Revisited," 2016: it confronts us with the ongoing existence of the racist blackface.

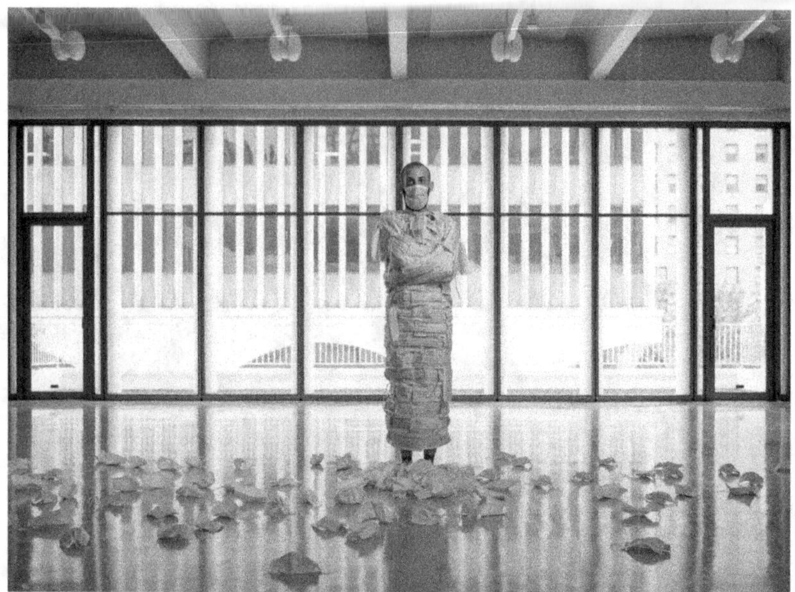

Spectrum Dance Theater Company, dancer Nathanaël Santiago performs Donald Byrd's "Lyric Suite," November 13-15, 2020, Photograph: Marcia Davis

At the center of the exhibition at the Frye, videos project on four walls the performance "A CRUEL NEW WORLD/the new normal," 2013. The dancers, wearing the orange jump suits worn by prisoners and detainees, from inside a hurricane fence with an American flag falling on the ground. The performance explores, through extreme movements, the anguish of being trapped with no way out.

(2019)

**Addendum:** During the pandemic Spectrum dancers presented the ironically named "Lyric Suite." It included single dancers performing themes of "homelessness," "death," "protective gear," and other themes related to the year of horrors, 2020. Each performer either danced in isolation, separated by a partition, or danced outside, so the company adapted to the restrictions of the Coronavirus pandemic. Each piece was excruciating to watch, as the dancers conveyed confinement, desperation, staggering loss, and isolation.

"The Race and Climate Change Festival" in June 2021 included "POOL/after, a powerful, two-part danced ritual developed by humans in an adapted climate-disaster future." The ritual dances set in 2090 honor the deification of Greta Thunberg and a mysterious black woman "she who sees."

In addition to the dance rituals, this extraordinary program projected us into the future based on science, science fiction, philosophy and much more.

Afro futurist writer Octavia Butler's *The Parable of the Sower* published in 1993, imagines a future society of humans basically returning to herds of hunter/gatherers as all systems collapse. It provides a point of departure for the vision of the future presented by the Spectrum Dancers. Spectrum included youth perspectives, who also helped inspire the theme and its format, as well as community participants such as well known writers and poets.

As Donald Byrd succinctly states: "People of color are already experiencing the climate emergency, and the future is already here in terms of the disasters on the planet."

(2021)

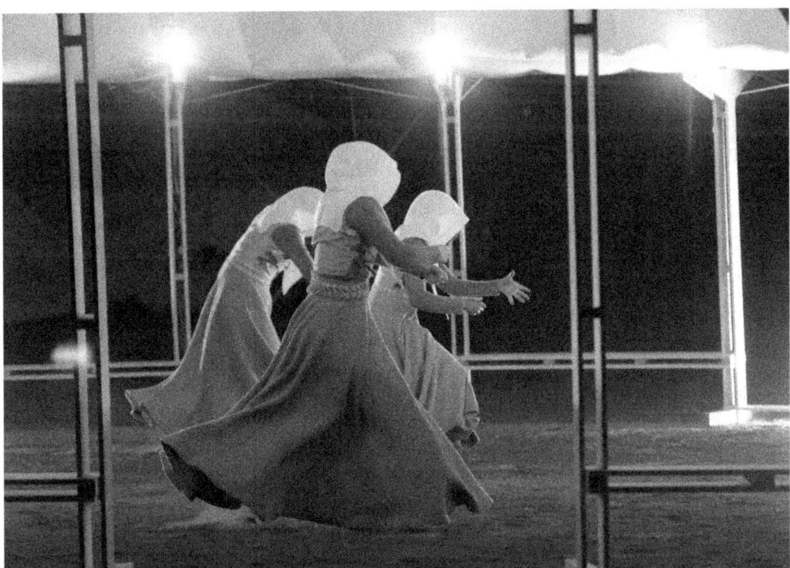

Spectrum Dance Theater, POOL/After, Ritual Dance 2090, detail, performed as part of "The Race and Climate Change Festival," June 2021, Photograph: Marcia Davis

# Joan Jones and Gina Pane: Process and Pain

"Parallel Practices: Joan Jonas & Gina Pane," on view at the Henry Art Gallery until June 18, is a rare opportunity to see two groundbreaking artists working with performance in entirely different ways.

Joan Jonas was deeply inspired by the East Coast avant-garde interdisciplinary Judson Dance Theater of the 1960s. It was based, in part, on the ideas of John Cage with a focus on re-thinking process, movement, body, space, and gesture as an exploration in itself. Pane emerged in Europe at the peak of the Situationist Movement based in a Marxist critique of capitalism. They believed that emphasis on commodity consumption instead of lived experience was leading to passivity and alienation. Situationists stated that this "spectacle" could be countered by "the construction of situations, moments of life deliberately constructed for the purpose of reawakening and pursuing authentic desires." But those desires are political, not simply aesthetic.

There is a direct connection to Seattle with the Judson Theater Group, in that John Cage taught at the Cornish College of the Arts and developed some of his formative concepts there.

Both Joan Jonas and Gina Pane were included in the 2007 feminist exhibition "WACK! Art and The Feminist Revolution" and the subject of my very first blog post! "Parallel Practices" was curated by Dean Daderko, Curator at the Contemporary Arts Museum in Houston. I am going to focus here mainly on Gina Pane, as this is her first exhibition in the United States. Jonas is still working, while Pane died in 1990.

So, as a starting point, let us return to those profound differences as a result of their context: Jonas is more involved with process and experimentation with media, Pane with content and presentation. I went to the show with two artists both of whom were mesmerized by Jonas's work, particularly the recent "Reading Dante III," 2010, a multimedia immersive environment that makes oblique reference to Dante with a drawing of woods that also appears in a video. The reference is clearly to the first sentence of Dante's *Divine Comedy*: "Nel mezzo del cammin di nostra vita, mi ritrovai per una selva oscura, ché la diritta via era smarrita"—"Midway through the journey of my life, I found myself in a dark wood, the straightforward path being lost." There are also video animations of the artist (whom we don't see) drawing spirals that may suggest the circles of hell. The installation plays on our sense of reality and fantasy through games with photography, video, and animation.

What captured my friends was the immediacy of the act of drawing represented in the videos. In another work, "Double Lunar Dogs," 1984, a video using 1984 state of the art techniques, engages with science fiction in an imaginary space trip in which the participants lose their way (it co-stars Spalding Gray!), but it is mainly funny and full of visual tricks. It was accompanied by a performance by the artist and some huge drawings she did as part of a performance.

Pane, in contrast, is not at all amusing or tricky. Her work is bloody, as a result of purposeful self-mutilation. She is best known in the U.S. for the single work, *L' Escalade Non-Anesthésiée (Climb Action non-anaestheticized)*, April 1971. It consists of a series of 69 photographs that document her increasingly excruciating climb up a specially fabricated "ladder" with steel razor blades on the widely spaced rungs. Beside it is the actual ladder which she climbed. We can see the projecting blades on the rungs which cut her feet and hands as she climbed, we feel her pain viscerally as we look at this physical artifact. The work was originally accompanied by a small typewritten statement by the artist which clearly states her meaning and purpose:

> Stratégie qui consiste à gravir les "échelons". L'escalade américaine au Vietnam./Artiste—Les artistes aussi grimpent. Douleur—douleur physique á un point ou plusieurs points du "corps". Douleur interne, profounde, souffrance. Douleur (morale) le contraire d'une escalade anesthésiée.

> The strategy consists in climbing a ladder.

> The American escalation in Vietnam

> Artist —the artists also are climbing

Pain—physical pain in one or many points of the body

Pain internal, profound, suffering. Pain (moral)

The opposite of an anesthesized climb.

Pane has a deep political intent: she is responding to the apathy of the public by arousing them to the reality of pain and injury. But, the only way that we are witness to her performance is through the photographs, arranged as a rectangle exactly corresponding in size to the ladder, and the ladder itself. She scrupulously orchestrated her actions and controlled how they were experienced. In doing that, she chose to remove the immediacy of her own pain, to make it a document of suffering, much as we experienced the war in Vietnam.

I can remember at that time feeling the same way: how can people sit and watch this terrible killing on television while they eat crackers and cheese. It horrified me and radicalized me. Gina Pane felt the same way, and, in the spirit of the Situationists, she tried to break through to people who are numb to violence. But why did she often choose to perform without an audience and give us only her highly-controlled document of it?

In contrast to other artists who have used bodily damage, most famously Chris Burden, who was very carefully shot in his right arm by a friend in a studio with a small audience in November 1971, Pane represents something which seems more radical and, to me, specifically feminist: she slashes her hands and feet with razors. She actively hurts herself. Razors appear in several of her other performances as well, most notably, *Azione Sentimentale (Sentimental Action)*, 1973, and *Action Little Journey I, 1977.*

We associate cutting ourselves with razors with suicide or attempted suicide, particularly for women. Shooting guns is more male (and Burden carefully chose where to be shot, although likely his work was also a response to the Vietnam War). The extreme of sexual violence, domestic violence, or anguished isolation, have all driven women to attempt suicide, and this form of suicide is always enacted alone (and often unsuccessfully). The topic is only rarely addressed in feminist performance art at this time.

The profoundly important Yoko Ono explored cutting as early as 1964 with the first performance of her extraordinary "Cut Piece." Each time Yoko Ono performed the work, the context gave it a new meaning. In the "Destruction in Art" Symposium in 1966 in London it was part of a manifesto that declared destruction of art is linked to the "cataclysmic increase in world destructive power. "Cut Piece" was one of a series of works she performed in 1966 that included "Bag Piece, Strip Tease for Three, Question Piece, Wall Piece, Wind Piece, Toilet Piece," etc. She most recently performed "Cut Piece" after 9/11 in Paris, calling it an "offering for world peace."

Looking at an early anthology of feminist performance art, *Amazing Decade: Women and Performance Art, 1970-1980,* we see goddesses, we see mid-life crisis, we see body issues. Most related, we see works about rape. But blood is not the result of self-mutilation, but of menstruation.

Peggy Phelan, in "The Return of Touch: Feminist Performances 1960 – 1980," emphasizes Pane's influence on Marina Abramović and Orlan, both artists who took body performance to extremes of damage to themselves in later decades, but with different dynamics. Abramović has the audience choose how to hurt her; Orlan underwent painful plastic surgery.

One artist who uses blood as a direct reference to political nightmares is Regina José Galindo of Guatemala. In her performance, "Who Can Erase the Traces," 2003, which is about the violent dictatorships in her country, she carries a bowl of blood (not her own) into which she dips her feet, leaving bloody tracks on the street.

So Pane is unusual in her willingness to take self-mutilation as a subject of her work and use it as a metaphor for political violence. She really goes beyond any performance by later artists in her willingness to not only hurt herself, but knowingly deal with that self-inflicted pain as a protest of violence. This is what she said:

[The wound] is a sign of the state of extreme fragility of the body, a sign of suffering, a sign which indicates the external situation of aggression, of violence to which we are always exposed. It introduces the vaster phenomenon of the relationship between the external world and the psychological world.

At the same time, her actions are personal. *Azione Sentimentale*, 1973, as described in a handwritten narrative that accompanies the photographs, was a tribute to her mother. The narrative recalls a bitter sweet moment of both beauty and sadness, as she visits a cemetery with her mother. As a recording played of two women reading intimate letters, Pane carefully pierced her arm with eight thorns from a bouquet of red roses, then cut her palm with razor blades. She repeated the action with a bouquet of white roses, "then offered herself as a supplicant to the audience." In this case there was an all-woman audience.

The "supplicant" aspect is key to another dimension of Pane's work, her identification with the martyrdom of Catholic saints. A few years later she created *Partition,* 1986, consisting of three circles which had tangible, but highly abstracted, icons referring to the martyrdom of the three saints (San Sebastian, San Pietro, San Lorenzo). She identified with them, who "like her, had voluntarily accepted suffering, hoping to transform their contemporaries and make them better people."

But, my favorite piece in the exhibition predates all of these: *Enfoncement d'un rayon de soleil (Burial of a Ray of Sunlight),* 1969, is a simple action: the artist digs a hole, reflects the sun into it with a mirror, then strolls away. The principle of burying the sun seems so pertinent to our current state of the world. Her environmental work is barely referenced here, and this early work does not include the debilitating physical exertion of the *Actions,* nor the heavy philosophical significance of martyrdom, but in its simplicity, it demonstrates a profoundly creative mind and deep love of nature.

Perhaps it was this work with mirrors that led the curator to pair Pane with Joan Jonas, who frequently uses mirrors in her work. Likewise both were pioneers in the use of video. But unlike Pane, the mirroring and video is an end in itself and self-referential for Jonas. She is interesting, even poetic at times, but I was more emotionally affected by Pane's extreme actions.

Pane, who would have benefited from a lot more explanation in the gallery, is a major contributor to early feminist performance art. It is amazing that this small display is her first in the United States. It also has an odd conclusion which seems to be the antithesis of her highly controlled early work: a large, scrawled drawing sent to Franklin

Furnace for a performance in 1979-81. *Action de chasse, C'est la nuit Chérie (Hunting Action, It's the Cherished Night)* is a giant messy sketch, that again seems to superficially connect the artist to Joan Jonas, whose big rough outlines of drawings for *Lunar Dogs* are in the next room. But this work, remotely assigned to others to perform, seems the antithesis of Pane's principles, as well as demonstrating how much her art changed.

Pane's pairing of performance involving extreme pain with carefully controlled aesthetic presentation has failed to resonate for audiences in the U.S. because, for all our ability to spread damage and pain around the world, as well as at home, we still have our utopian illusions and a low tolerance for witnessing actual pain inside of an art venue, even in Pane's carefully orchestrated presentation. Pane failed to wake us up from our numb state, but she certainly succeeded in creating a ground-breaking art form that demonstrates her own deep concern about the world.

(2014)

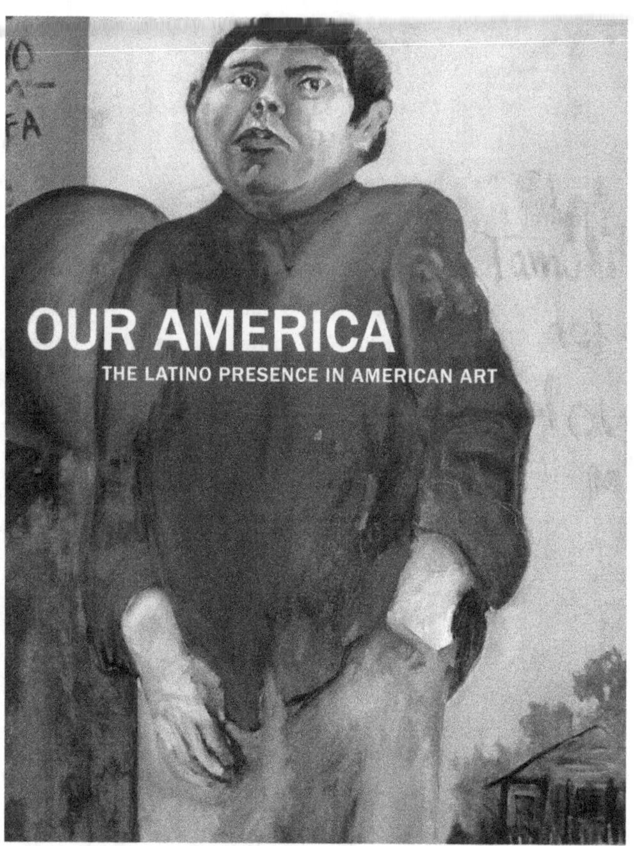

E. Carmen Ramos, *Our America: The Latino Presence in American Art*, Smithsonian American Art Museum, 2014, cover art: Roberto Chavez, *El Tamalito del Hoyo* (detail), 1959

# Embedding Latinx Art in American Art History

THE FIRST JUXTAPOSITION, in the lecture by E. Carmen Ramos that introduced "Our America," an exhibition at the Smithsonian American Art Museum, foreshadowed the story she wanted to tell: Frank Romero's 1986 painting *Death of Rubén Salazar*, of the police shooting of Rubén Salazar in 1970, placed next to Emanuel Leutze's *Washington Crossing the Delaware*: two significant historical events of equal value.

*Washington Crossing* we are all familiar with. The shooting of Rubén Salazar, the pioneering journalist, originally from Mexico, who worked for the *Los Angeles Times* for many years as an investigative journalist, is much less well known. Placing these two historical events side by side declares that our perspectives are still exclusive and limited, when it comes to American art and its partner, American history.

E. Carmen Ramos, Curator of Latinx Art at the Smithsonian American Art Museum, is building a new narrative for the history of American art. We are accustomed to the oft-repeated lineage from colonial portraits to revolutionary history painting, to genre painting in the nineteenth century, still life; then in the twentieth century we have Alfred Stieglitz and modernism, the art of the New Deal, after World War II, Abstract Expressionism, then Pop, minimalism, conceptual art, Feminism, Postmodernism, up to the present uncategorized moment.

We know that in the 1960s and 1970s the Civil Rights Movement and the Feminist Movement sparked new narratives and new inclusions in that traditional trajectory. Gay rights and AIDS added more dimensions. But today, we still don't have an integrated history of American Art. We have mainly White men, with extras, a few women, a few African Americans, a few gay artists.

Latinx artists sometimes are acknowledged, in the midst of the Civil Rights Movement, when the Chicano movement emerged full force.

But Ramos has another idea about the way to write an inclusive history of American art: Latinx art is not an add on, it is embedded in all of the art that we have, all of the styles, directions, and politics.

By integrating Latinx art into the mainstream, we get a different perspective. Ramos's exhibition, "Our America," based on a selection from the permanent collection at the Smithsonian American Art Museum, emphasizes artists from Mexico, Puerto Rico, Cuba and the Dominican Republic. Artists from Central America, with one exception, are not included. Nor are artists from Latin America. They will have to wait for the next installment.

This exhibition is a first step in the process of inclusion of Latinx artists in the mainstream. It is going to travel all over the United States and hopefully change our conversation. Its timing is perfect. Just as our culture is demonizing immigrants forced to come here by our trade policies which are wiping out their means of making a living in their own countries, we are offered these sophisticated works of art by immigrants, and descendants of immigrants, that declare that Latinx are immeasurably enriching our country. As they assimilate U.S. culture, they are also changing it, in exciting directions.

These art works address specific moments in Latinx, U.S. history or current conditions. They are all from the last half century. Ramos has divided the exhibition into categories that underscore her purpose: "Reframing Past and Present," "Migrating Through History," "Everyday People," "We Interrupt this Message," "Signs of the Popular," "Turning Point," "Street Life, "Defying Categories."

In "Reframing Past and Present" she has included the most specific art about immigration and violent acts of racism.

For example, a tree photographed by Ken Gonzales-Day is just one work from his project *Searching for California Hang Trees*, a groundbreaking book and photographic project on the lynching of Latinos in California in the 19th and early 20th century. In the book he describes going to the trees he has located and trying to experience the moment of lynching. One of the trees is in the center of downtown Los Angeles.

Another section of the exhibition, "Migrating Through History," includes what is described as "dreamlike" imagery and a reflection of the conditions that cause migration. María Magdalena Campos-Pons's *Constellation* uses hair as a metaphor for the middle passage as well as the passage from Cuba to the U.S. It creates an evocative and frightening reference to migration and its threats.

"Everyday People" includes such classics as paintings by John Valadez, Jesse Treviño and Mel Casas. So the question is: why is Mel Casas excluded from mainstream discussions of Pop Art? Why not include Jesse Treviño and John Valadez in Realism?

The artist ADÁL's footage on the small tv inserted in a suitcase projected romantic scenes from the *West Side Story* film, alternating with the realities of Puerto Rican life in 1960s New York City including "documentary footage of Puerto Ricans in New York, readings of Nuyorican poetry by Pedro Pietri, and the music of Tito Puente and Brenda Feliciano."

"We Interrupt This Message" featured radical groups like ASCO, who pioneered street performance art and public interventions that subverted and upended media and art world stereotypes about Latinos.

"Signs of the Popular" included Carmen Lomas Garza's genre scenes, and other artists depicting aspects of everyday life. This is, of course, a standard theme in American Art History, the connection of popular art and the mainstream in genre scenes. Garza remembers her own childhood in Kingsville, Texas.

Political posters by famous artists filled an entire wall. The strong Latinx graphic arts traditions became even more confrontational in the

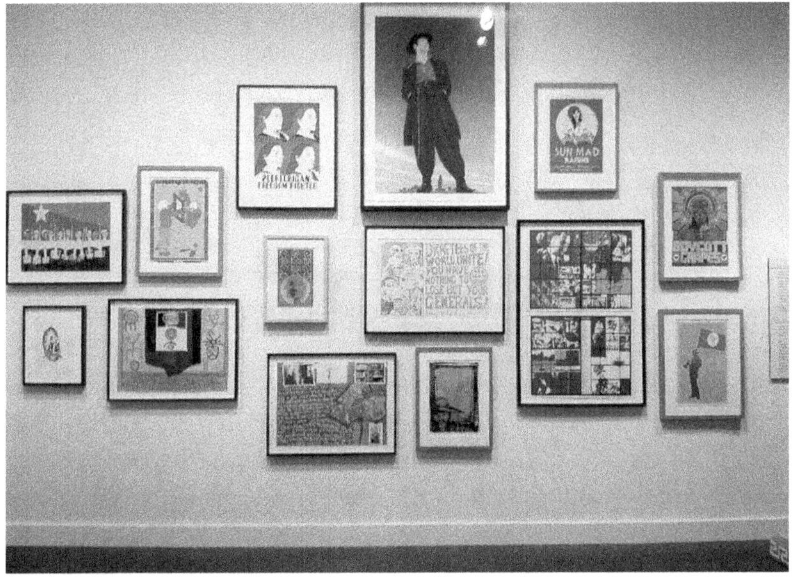

Wall of posters in "Our America"

1960s. Here we see the heart of the Chicano political graphics movement. Ignacio Gomez's *Zoot Suit*, 2002 commemorates the central character in Luis Valdez's eponymous and famous 1978 play, *Zoot Suit*. As Ramos explains:

> During the early 1940s, young and stylish Mexican Americans or *pachucos* wore zoot suits as a rebellious stance against

their elders and against a racist environment that often dismissed them as criminal gang members.

Just to the right is the famous work by Ester Hernandez, *Sun Mad Raisins (The Virgin of Guadalupe Defending the Rights of the Chicanos)*, that needs no explanation. It could have been done yesterday.

Malaquias Montoya, a crucial figure in printmaking and political action over the last fifty years, is included in the wall of posters. As Ter-ezita Romo states, "Montoya did not accept any division between the political and the artistic; instead his artwork forged a tight relationship in which each was intrinsic to the other."

Another political section was "Turning Point: Civil Rights Era," that included the famous altar by Amalia Mesa-Bains, *Ofrenda for Dolores del Rio,* 1984. Mesa-Bains herself is another revolutionary, still today, speaking up about the need to be proactive and resist oppression.

"Street Life" included the powerful work of Luis Cruz Azaceta, an artist I first encountered and wrote about in a review for *New Art Examiner* in 1987. He is now an old master, but still raw and compelling.

But the real surprise of the exhibition came in the last room, a room full of elegant abstraction. Here was Curator Ramos's most clear-cut stand for mainstreaming Latinx art. The artists in this gallery were working within the abstract traditions, so beloved of art historians and art critics, particularly on the East Coast. Why are these artists never mentioned outside of Latinx publications? Because they are immedi-ately perceived, as in the review of "Our America" by the *Washington Post*, as imitating well known artists. The abstract artists are all tossed off as "derivative," a tired cliché.

Freddy Rodriguez was, as he has said, inspired by early Stella, but it is obvious that he has found his own way to include jazz-like rhythms and rich colors, with a spiritual heat that clearly speak of the Caribbean.

He responded to the *Washington Post* review:

When White artists engage the history of art, critics speak of influence and dialogue. When Latino or African Ameri-can artists do so, it's derivative. This is both an antiquated way of thinking and simply historically inaccurate. Asco's

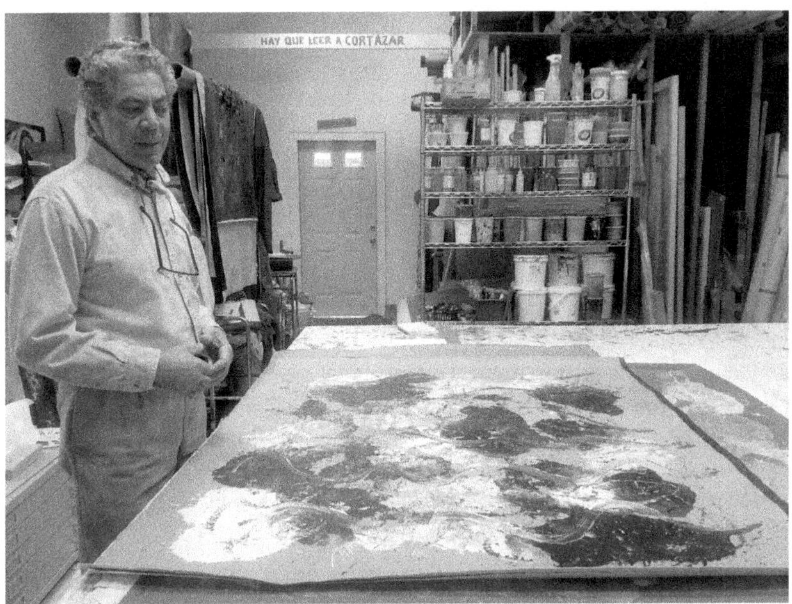


Freddy Rodriguez' studio, Washington, D.C., 2013

*No Movies* predate Cindy Sherman's film stills. Raphael Montañez Ortiz's recycled films remain the most avant-garde works in the history of that approach to appropriated film. Carmen Herrera was in Paris at the same time when Ellsworth Kelly was there. They were both influenced by the City of Light's abstract art scene.

Rodriquez own work has many aspects. His intense series from 2000, titled *En esta Casa Trujillo es el Jefe / In this House Trujillo is Chief,* combines sumptuous surfaces, intense content and writing.

But the reality of this exhibition is that all of these artists do fit exactly into what is going on in mainstream U.S. art history even as they distinctly make their own contribution.

Every category corresponds. I quickly perused a half dozen new histories of American Art to see if that was true (admittedly there may be a 21st century survey I have not yet seen). But the reality is that African Americans are still tokens, and Latinx artists are barely mentioned.

The title of "Our America" is taken from an essay by the famous Cuban intellectual José Martí who spent a good deal of time thinking about the solutions to imperialism and the independence of Cuba. America, in his writing, is a term that refers to the entire hemisphere, not just to the U.S., a fact people in this country frequently forget.

Martí wanted a revolution in Cuba to come from people who understood the inner nature of Cuba, who were not conditioned by European perspectives. He believed in the U.S. model of cultural blending. Using this title for the exhibition points to the thesis that the artists in the exhibition are both distinctly themselves as well as part of a larger culture to which they contribute.

To underscore that idea, the exhibition concludes with Luis Jiménez's fiberglass *Man on Fire,* 1969—Jiménez's homage to Orozco's painting *Man of Fire,* a reference to Cuauhtémoc, the valiant Aztec ruler tortured by fire during the Spanish conquest. Jiménez's dark brown figure cast in slick hot-rod fiberglass, also references Native Americans as part of Chicano history. In this work we see the heritage of the great Mexican mural artists once again flow North as it did in the 1930s, when Rivera, Orozco and Siqueiros all created art in the U.S. under various patrons.

(2014)

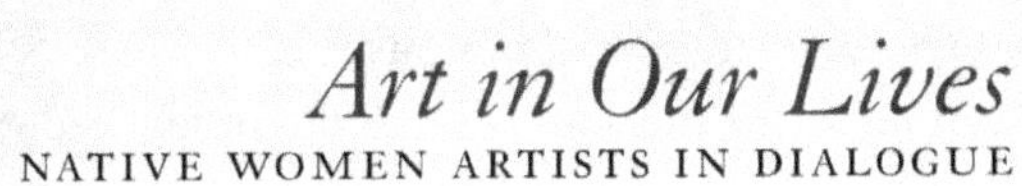


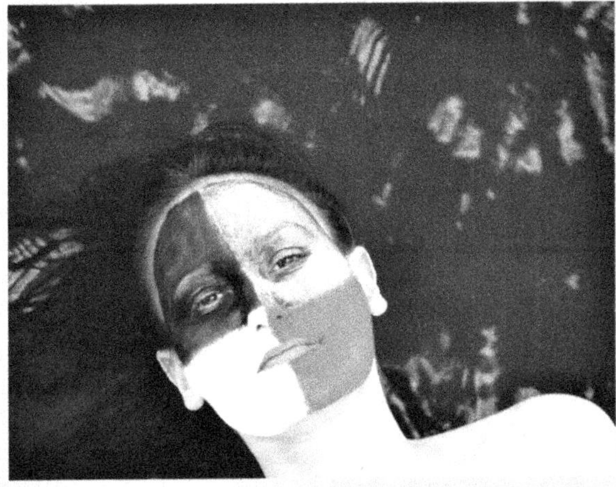


*Art in Our Lives, Native Women Artists in Dialog,* edited by Cynthia Chavez Lamar and Sherry Farrell Racette with Lara Evans, School for Advanced Research Press, 2010, cover art: Lara Evans "Water Keeps Moving," from the *Directions for Home* series, 2008

# Working Outside Norms:
# Contemporary Art by Native Women

LARA EVANS, ART HISTORIAN AND ARTIST at The Evergreen State College, just published, with other authors, a new book called *Art in Our Lives, Native Women Artists in Dialog.* It creates a partner to her recently curated exhibition "It's Complicated—Art About Home."

The two together give us new perspectives on contemporary Native art, voices of a new generation. In the book, there are actually several generations, but the book is based on a seminar among the artists.

The essays are overviews of various themes, "Art as Healing, Art as Struggle" by Gloria J. Emerson; "Gender Women and Art Making" by Sherry Farrell Racette; "Space Memory, Landscape Women in Native Art History" by Elysia Poon; and "Crossing the Boundaries of Home and Art" by Lara Evans. The dialogue among these artists and others spans the personal and historical.

Sherry Farrell Racette provides provocative references to the history of tribal gender roles. I was a little surprised, though, that unmentioned was what I understood as a fact (perhaps it is not)—that settlers declared they had to deal with a male chief in negotiations with tribes that had been matriarchal, and that caused a major shift in the gender power relations in many tribes. Also, in the Northeast, it was the rights of Native women that inspired the suffragette movement to demand more rights for White women.

But certainly, gender roles vary from tribe to tribe and era to era. Also the value associated to various activities has been arbitrarily assigned perhaps by outsiders. Why is it necessarily less significant to cure and cook fish than to catch them? Why is bead work or basketry less significant than sand painting?

These women moved outside expectations and norms in order to be artists. Their work is intriguing and complex.

In the exhibition, Maria Hupfield's *Flap Flap Flap*, 2003, addresses ecological crisis with her dead birds, but they are so beautifully laid out on the floor of the gallery that it is possible to almost forget the actual subject. That edge of aesthetics and politics is crucial to this entire exhibition.

The artists often address the intersections of Native world views and mainstream (White) ideas. For example in one piece by Merritt Johnson, the animals patch the Sky Dome: they give up their lives in order to keep the world going, A bear stands on top of a ladder offering his skin. We, on the other hand, just go on with our same bad habits. In another work by Johnson, an injured turkey is protecting the sky. In a third she makes a reference to the BP oil spill.

One of the themes of the art exhibition, and the book, is the changing relationship to the land for contemporary Native artists. But,

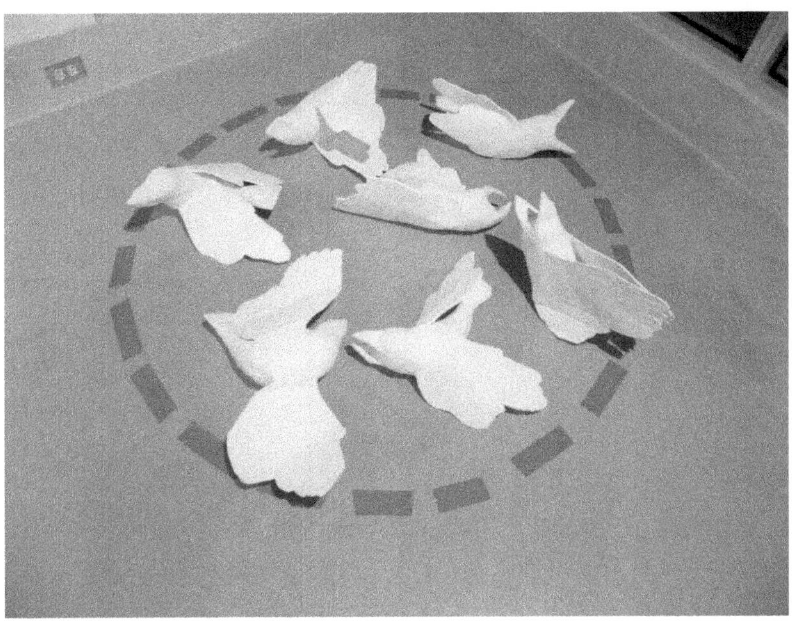

Maria Hupfield, *Flap,Flap,Flap,* 2003, floor-based sculpture, paper mache, installation in the exhibition, "It's Complicated, Art About Home," 2011, Courtesy of the Artist

in spite of that, the urban/reservation split is not absolute in any of these artists' works. They all move back and forth, between different realities, as does their art. That is the reason for the title of the exhibition: "It's complicated, Art About Home."

Perhaps the most compelling work in the exhibition was by Kimowan Metchewais. *Goodwill, 118 Avenue, Edmonton*, 2010, is an innocuous image of the place where people drop off, get rid of, furniture for Goodwill. But Lara explained that many Native people furnish their homes from this drop off. In addition, this detailed and extraordinarily beautiful artwork was done by an artist who had lost the use of one whole side of his body.

The exhibition also includes YouTube videos of Phoenix, Arizona (other peoples' idea of home), a creation myth, and a stunning pair of photographs by Sarah Sense with an overlay of woven photographic imagery based on traditional weaving from the Chitimacha tribe who have a long tradition of basketry.

Each of these artists, both in the book and in the exhibition, were previously unknown to me. How enriching to have this opportunity to expand my knowledge.


(2011)

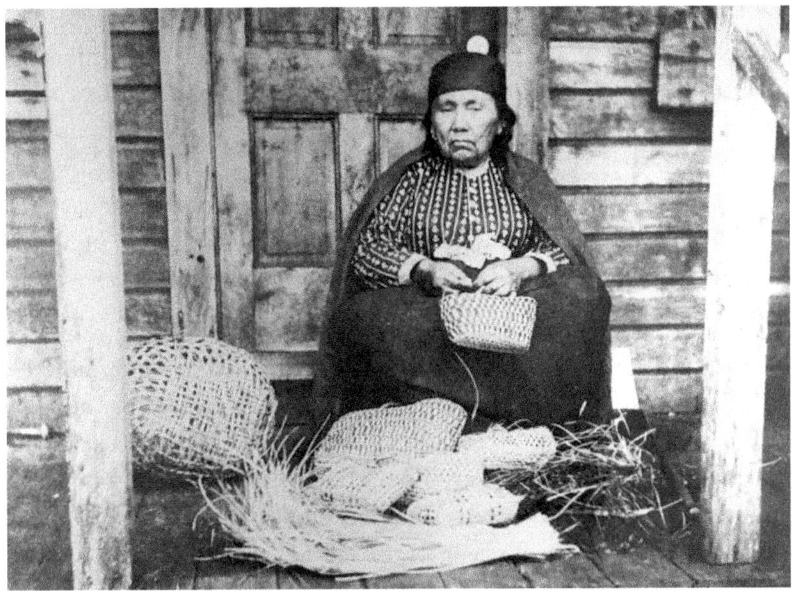

*Basket Maker*, Suquamish archival photograph

# Reworking the Legacy: Edward Curtis

ON THE 150TH BIRTHDAY OF PERHAPS our most famous local photographer, Edward S. Curtis, you will not be able to escape him this summer! In addition to exhibitions at the Tacoma Art Museum and the Seattle Art Museum, twenty other institutions are exploring Curtis and his legacy in a collaboration called "Beyond the Frame: to be Native." Contemporary native artists contradict, correct, and caricature Curtis and the cliché of the "vanishing race." His monumental work, *The North American Indian*, a staggering 20 volumes of text and images, tries to "preserve" Indians in a pristine past that was already a myth when he worked between 1907 and 1930.

The Tacoma Art Museum's "Native Portraiture Power and Perception," part of their ongoing redefining of "western art," includes only two iconic Edward Curtis photographs, as well as a few traditional "western" artists, then jumps to provocative contemporary Native art.

At the entrance "This is a Stereotype: Misconceptions of the Native American," a video by Cannupa Hanska Luger, Dylan McLaughlin and Ginger Dunnill is based on archival footage and interviews. It exposes popular culture stereotypes forced on Native people. For example, a Native man dresses up as a "chief" to be photographed at a festival. Wendy Red Star caricatures clichés with her self-portraits in hokey settings. Stephen Foster creates 3D sepia photographs using toy figurines. And there is a lot more.

The Seattle Art Museum's "Double Exposure: Edward S. Curtis, Marianne Nicolson, Tracy Rector, and Will Wilson" opens on June 14, with 150 works by Edward S. Curtis, paired with three contemporary Native artists, Nicolson, Rector and Wilson. Barbara Brotherton, curator of Native American Art at SAM, presents Curtis's great project as almost an accident of fate: he saved some climbers on Mt. Rainier who turned out to be eminent scientists. In 1899, when they went to Alaska on the Harriman expedition to study Native culture, they invited him to join them as the photographer. He was established in Seattle as a successful portrait photographer and had photographed local Natives, particularly "Princess Angeline," who posed for him in the abandoned "winter villages" in the mid 1890s, just forty years after the arrival of White settlers and the Treaty of Point No Point, 1855. But this trip and his subsequent trip to Montana with George Bird Grinell where they witnessed the sacred Sundance of the Piegan and Blackfoot tribes led him to his great work.

On a smaller scale, The Seattle Public Library opens an exhibition on June 8, focusing on the Salish Sea and Indigenous Stewardship. It crucially focuses on the environment, in this case, the sea. Since contemporary tribes are leading the resistance to resource extraction, pipelines, and the expansion of coastal ports for shipping coal or processing natural gas, I was surprised not to see that as a focus of any of these exhibitions.

The Suquamish Museum, with the exhibition "Deconstructing Curtis: Romanticism vs. Reality," places the Curtis photographs in the context of the stories "behind the photographs." If you haven't been to this fascinating museum, just past the Agate Pass Bridge connecting Bainbridge Island to the Kitsap Peninsula, I recommend it. Another tribal museum participating in this project, starting on June 1, is the

Tulalip Hibulb Cultural Center which combines a museum with a nature reserve, a good summer destination.

The Wenatchee Valley Museum & Cultural Center focuses on how the bond between Native Americans and their environment has changed over time. Accompanying their exhibition are lectures that focus on the Wapato, Wanapum and Wanatchi tribes.

This is just a sample of the Curtis legacy-reworking extravaganza that includes lectures, music, performances and other exhibitions.

(2018)

# The Nightmares of Ordinary People in the Paintings of Benny Andrews

IN ONE OF THE MOST POTENT IMAGES in Benny Andrews' "The Bicentennial Series" from the 1970s, the Statue of Liberty sucks a lollipop as she sits on top of the stump of a dead tree. Naked men wearing only army helmets and boots support the stump on a wagon.

In a final full-scale mural, *Liberty* leads a succession of carts, one carrying a "war bitch," as the artist describes her, and another, a giant penis topped by flowers. Several men, one of them a convict in chains, strain to carry everything off to the garbage dump. *Trash* is one in a series of murals by Andrews painted during the years leading up to the Bicentennial in the early 1970s. His dark vision could have been painted yesterday.

On seeing excerpts from his "The Bicentennial Series," 1970-75, at the Michael Rosenfeld Gallery in January, I was stunned with the forcefulness of his comments on the abuses of our American institutions. Today, as we struggle against the escalating wave of White supremacist policies from Washington, D.C., they speak to us directly.

During the early 1970s Benny Andrews created BIG paintings, as he put it, to provide his own perspective on the 200th anniversary of the Nation. BIG because the mainstream White artists at that time were working big, and he believed his work would stand beside them. He saw that preparations for the Bicentennial were devolving into clichés like slave cabins and great people; he knew there was more to the story than that.

He himself had grown up in a sharecropping family, picking cotton. With the support of his family, he followed an incredible journey to become a trained artist based in New York City. But he never forgot his roots in Georgia, the people he knew from his childhood, the strength of the people around him, their creativity, and their perseverance.

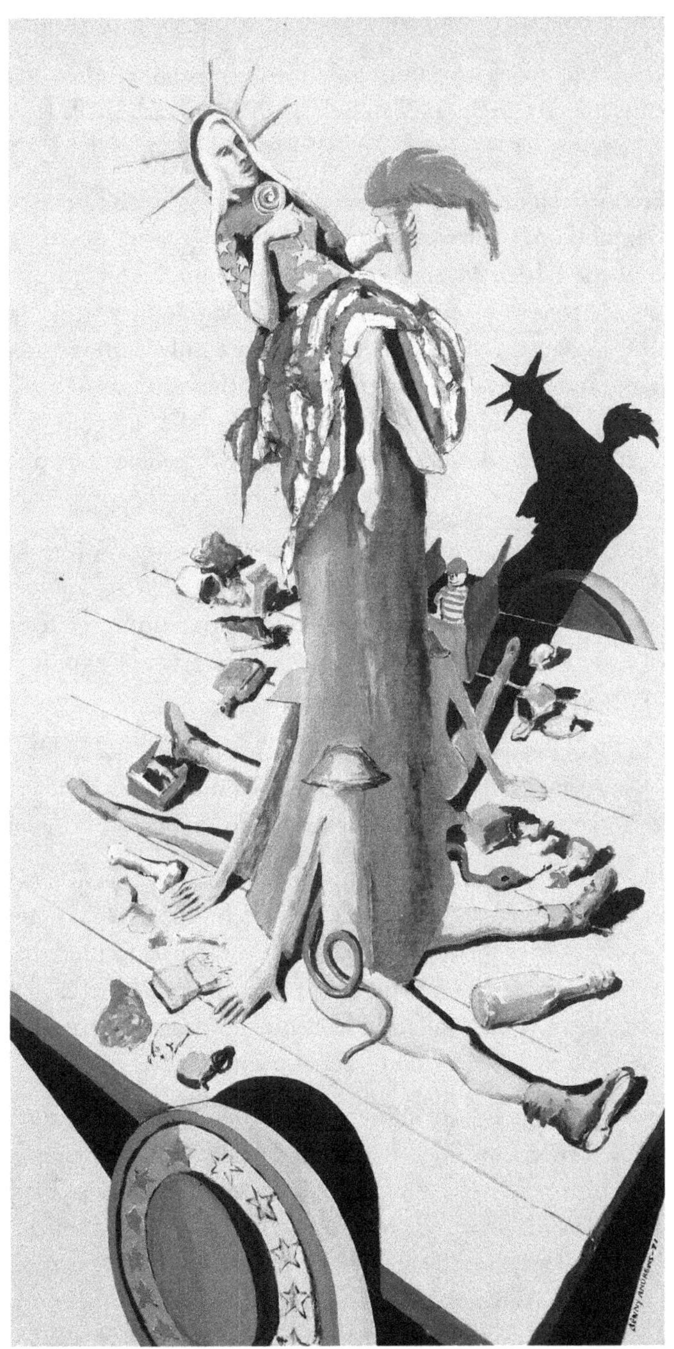

Benny Andrews, *Liberty #6 (Study for Trash)*, 1971, oil on canvas with painted fabric collage, 78" x 39 3/4" x¼", ©Benny Andrews Estate, Courtesy of Michael Rosenfeld Gallery LLC, New York, NY

The vivid series of paintings, drawings, small studies and large works include six themes: "Symbols" (1971), "Trash" (1971), "Circle" (1972), "Sexism" (1973-74), "War" (1974), and "Utopia" (1975).

His first large work, *Symbols*, paid homage to his roots. In the recent exhibition, we saw drawings for the large work now in the collection of the Ulrich Museum of Art at Wichita State University. His spare linear style is as elegant as Ingres. For this first work, he went back to Georgia and sketched his home, his family, a bride and groom, musicians, and in the center a "tree of life." There appear to be children playing in the tree, but it also seems to be people "hanging" from the tree, clearly a reference to lynching. Nearby two people carry off a dead child.

Since Andrews' family is of mixed Black and White heritage, though all were considered African American, he frequently suggests racial mixing. Even people who are White in his paintings reference his African American community in Georgia. The artist pairs ordinary life, ordinary people, and nightmarish events.

On the right, a man, his face split between Black and White, seems to sit in judgement in the *Symbols* mural. Andrews may be referring to an overseer, or a mixed-race businessman, his ambiguity is intentional.

He created dozens of separate sketches then put them together in a larger composition based on multiple panels. The space is complex as the imagery pushes forward or recedes into the background, based on strong diagonals that terminate at a tree in the center. In later murals his figures seem to float in an indeterminate space, sometimes framed by viewers, or encircled by odd faceless people.

*Trash* (1971) is full of anger and sarcasm. He painted it during the Attica State Prison Uprising. By this time Andrews had already founded the Black Emergency Cultural Coalition, demanding more Black curators and artists in New York Museums, but more important than that, he founded the first prison art program in the country. He was outraged at the failure of American institutions and *Trash* hauls them off to the junkheap, pulled by both a prisoner and another Black man.

Two studies present the *Statue of Liberty*, as she is disintegrating. In *Study No 2* for *Trash* she sits on top of a globe with the USA facing out, Black and White people reaching out to encircle it. The naked military, wearing only hats and boots, prop it up. In the *Puller*, the man hauling the trash wagon carrying the Statue of Liberty braces against the weight. Behind him a black shadow echoes his silhouette.

Use of shadows is a crucial device in Andrews' work, they reinforce his imagery, creating a shadow layer, perhaps evoking how Blacks experience their lives in a White world.

The mural *Circle*, the only complete mural included in the exhibition, fills one wall, with sketches and smaller paintings nearby. *Circle* focuses on a bed on which a Black/White person sits impaled, his heart is a watermelon rising above him lifted by an odd pipe-like shape (in earlier sketches it was a stove).

Around this tragic figure stand a circle of people both Black and White who shake their fists, look horrified, or sit passively in chairs, as the torture unfolds before their eyes.

Tied and helpless, the man on the bed reminds us today of torture inflicted on prisoners in detention, but here the reference is certainly to the tortures of simply living in the US as a dark-skinned man. Andrews is the visual partner to James Baldwin, whose words lay bare the torture and injustice of living in the U.S. for people of African descent.

In addition to painting, Andrews glues fabrics directly on the canvas. An old cloth creates the stained bed cover, a sheet bandages the head, a dirty cloth wraps around the figure's genitals like a diaper. That physicality paired with the personal surrealism of Andrew's fantastic imagery relies on the grotesque to warn us of dark realities. He penetrates our hearts; the physical additions to the canvas, assembled from found objects and discarded dirty materials, strike us visually and in our souls; they speak of poverty, of suffering.

The cycle "Sexism" includes several large works. At the entrance to the exhibition we are immediately confronted by a figure covered in a tent-like sheet. She appears to be rising from a bed, but she is still caught in the strings held down by odd detritus.

*Sexism Study No 8* appears to be a penis man holding an instrument of torture and wearing strange claw-like shoes. He looks like a rapist with primitive tools. This particular image did not appear in the final large mural.

"War" for which the artist never completed a large version, is featured in two poignant collage paintings: a young man dragging a dead body and a man with a pink bag tied over his head that refers to torture and the impossibility of escape.

Finally, Andrews created "Utopia," but because he could not see any redeeming features in humans, he created a fantasy landscape without people.

Along with his mural-scale works, and his smaller collage paintings, Andrews draws, and draws and draws. These delicate linear studies, populated by strange creatures or bizarre settings, create a constant dialogue with the final murals, giving us insight into his thinking. Frequently, he includes shadows for his outlined figures, suggesting even in the briefest encounter with paper, that the shadow world still haunts his every move and that of every person of color.

> Surrealism can get out of hand real fast, but then the Black experience is so ridiculous that surrealism is the best way to express it. I've seen the same kind of work coming from prison artists. To get through an oppressive real life, the artists have to live a fantasy life.

> —Benny Andrews

(2017)

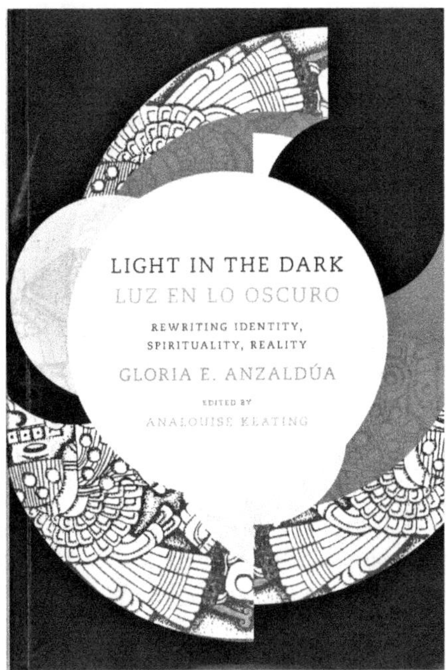

Gloria Anzaldúa, *Light in the Dark/Luz en Lo Oscuro: Rewriting Identity, Spirituality, Reality,* edited by AnaLouise Keating, Duke University Press, 2015, cover design Natalie F. Smith (detail of Coyolxauhqui)

## Gloria Anzaldúa: Beyond Binaries

I pick the ground from which to speak a reality into existence.
I have chosen to struggle against unnatural boundaries.

—Gloria Anzaldúa

FOR THOSE OF US WHO BELIEVE that Gloria Anzaldúa's concepts, first published in *Borderlands/La Frontera: The New Mestiza* [1987], broke new ground, philosophically, spiritually, and linguistically, the publication of a new book of her writing provides a glorious new opportunity to revel in her brilliant mind. All the more miraculous (and miracles certainly suit Anzaldúa), the book appears twelve years after her death, thanks to her dedicated editor AnaLouise Keating.

Hardly the dull academic book its tiny typeface suggests, *Light in the Dark / Luz en lo Oscuro* constantly shifts between original philosophical insights, Mexican mythology, and Anzaldúa's personal life/spirit. Impromptu image/text sketches periodically interrupt the intense text.

Anzaldúa's perceptions resonate with our world today, with contemporary realities, even with our nightmares. While her early writings focus on La Llorona, the weeping woman, a central reference point in *Light in the Dark* is Coyolxauhqui, the goddess of the moon. Coyolxauhqui, together with her four hundred brothers and sisters, tried to kill their mother Coatlicue (the earth goddess) because she was impregnated by a ball of feathers. As punishment she was killed and dismembered into a thousand pieces by her brother (hummingbird god of war/change) Huitzilopochtli. We here in Seattle have recently been horrified by a contemporary dismemberment of a young woman, in a resurrection of the Aztec myth.

The goddess prominently emerges in Anzaldúa's writing in the immediate aftermath of the September 11 bombings. She represents many ideas. In the first chapter of the book (written last), Anzaldúa emphasizes healing from the violent destruction with what she calls the Coyolxauhqui Imperative, which metaphorically stands for creativity itself, the act of creating wholeness from chaos.

In addition to the Coyolxauhqui Imperative ("Healing of the wound"), which she returns to in the last chapter, Anzaldúa writes of *flights of the imagination* (la curandera, shamanic journeys), *nepantla* (transition/transformation, the border), *nos/otros* (geography of self, reimagining identity, the new tribalism), and *conocimiento* (consciousness, mapping the soul's journey). *Conocimiento* includes seven stages: *arrebato* (earthquake), *nepantla* (transition), *Coatlicue* (the depths of despair), *breaking free, ordering your life, telling your story,* and, finally, "an ethical compassionate strategy with which to negotiate conflict and difference within self and between others." These stages recapitulate the sections of the book.

AnaLouise Keating painstakingly edited the book based on Anzaldúa's numerous drafts and notes, itself a vast *nepantla* between Anzaldúa's mind and *Light in the Dark*. She meticulously documented the basis of each chapter from dated drafts on Anzaldúa's computer and added appendixes of additional incomplete fragments.

With her intimate knowledge of Anzaldúa's entire career, Keating helpfully describes the arc of the book:

> From the late 1980s, Anzaldúa aspired to write a book-length exploration of aesthetics and knowledge production as they are inflected through, and shaped by, issues of social justice, identity (trans)formation, and healing. In *Light in the Dark/ Luz en lo oscuro* Gloria Anzaldúa excavates her creative process (her 'gestures of the body') and uses this excavation to develop an aesthetics of transformation, grounded in her metaphysics of interconnectedness.

Thanks to Keating's careful work, Anzaldúa's voice clearly emerges: the book flows in a poetic river of multiple languages, invented words and concepts, repeated passages, and a rhythmic return to sacred places, such as the "arbol de la vita" on a beach near where she lives. In one chapter, she confronts the inner demons that prevent her from writing (one of which is illness). But we experience a slow expansion, like a spiral, accumulating ideas, feelings, spirits, realities, along the way. At the same time, philosophically, Anzaldúa explores ideas that occupy the mainstream of theoretical thinking today, the fluid borders of gender and identity, fact and fiction, myth and reality.

> I'm guided by the spirit of the image. My *naguala* (daiman or guiding spirit) is an inner sensibility that directs my life—an image, an action, or an internal experience. . . . Often my *naguala* draws to me things that are contrary to my will and purpose . . . resulting in an anguished impasse. Overcoming these impasses becomes part of the process.

Interweaving such rational analysis of her own writing process with intuition and the spiritual, Anzaldúa easily transitions through multiple visions and realities. Most important of all though, she calls for "spiritual activism." She asks us to move to a "metaphysics of interconnections." In our contemporary world of intense binary thinking and wall building, Gloria Anzaldúa's insights provide an inspiring way forward.

(2016)

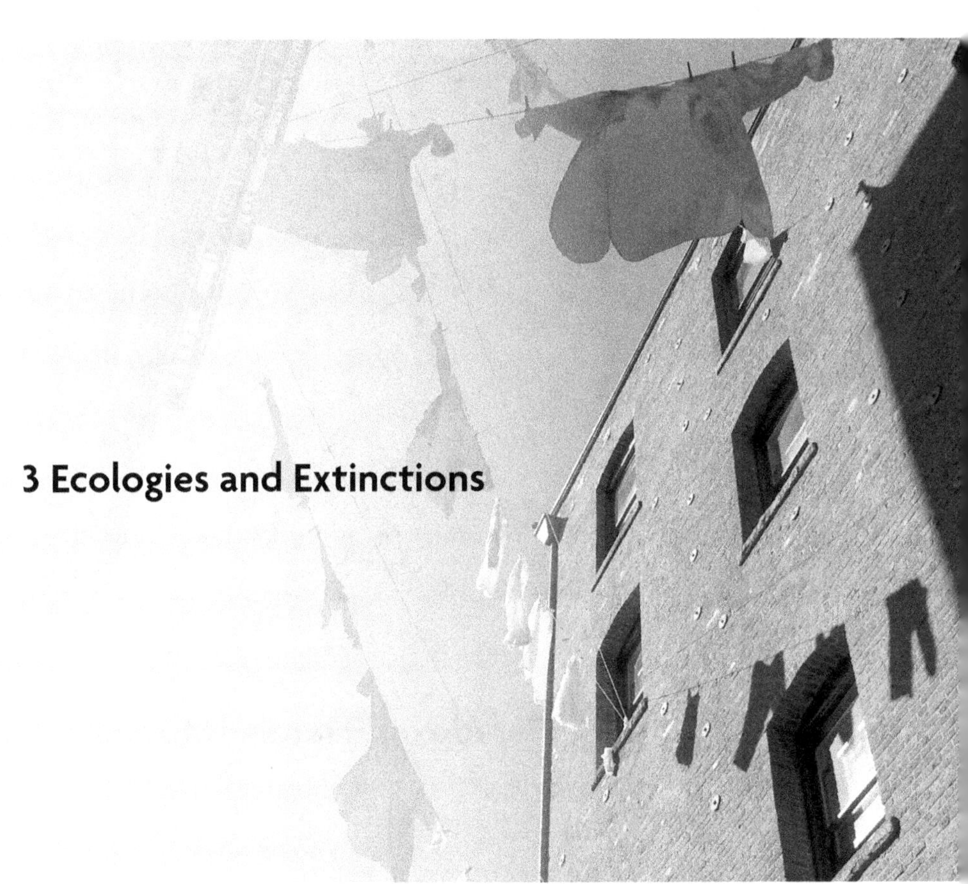

# 3 Ecologies and Extinctions

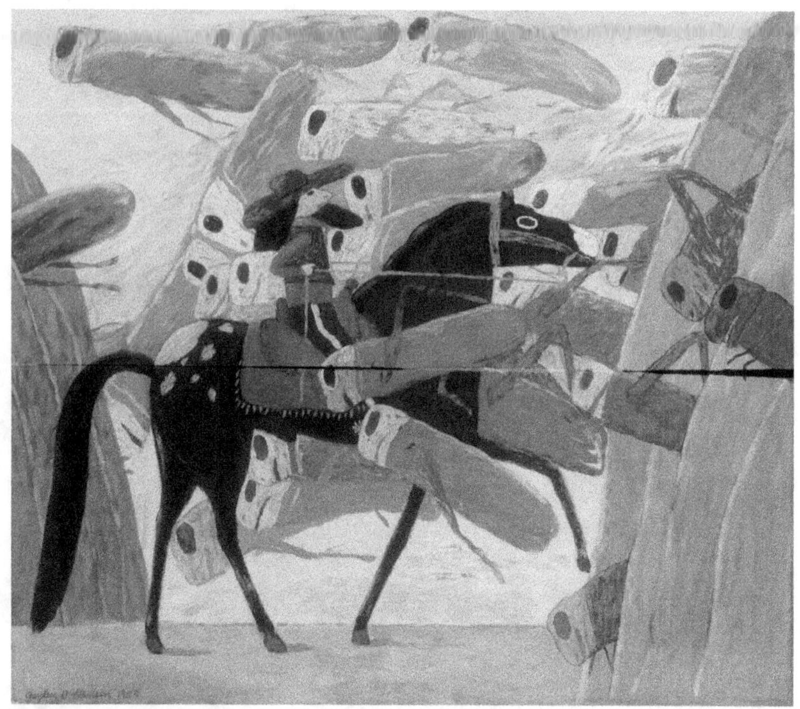

Gaylen Hansen, *The Kernal Encounters a Swarm of Crickets,* 1983, Oil on canvas, 71 ½ x 83, " Margaret E. Fuller Purchase Fund and gift of Byron W. Todd in memory of his wife Patricia Todd, Courtesy Seattle Art Museum (Note: currently Gaylen Hansen is 100 years old and still creating and exhibiting new art works)

# Paradigms and Paradoxes: Nature, Morality, and Art in America

To see clearly is poetry, prophecy and religion—all in one.

—John Ruskin, *Modern Painters*

THIS ARTICLE IS DEDICATED TO the memory my father, Rutherford Platt, who wrote about nature in order to inspire the ordinary person to realize its wonder, in award-winning books such as *This Green World*, 1942, and *The River of Life*, 1956.

In the late eighteenth and early nineteenth centuries, as nature began to be regarded as a positive presence, rather than an alien force, landscape art in England and America was based on several well-established aesthetic concepts.

The beautiful was seen as the tranquility of "smooth" nature that led the viewer to a meditative state, removed from the complexities of life. The Sublime, as articulated by Edmund Burke, referred to the spiritual uplift beyond rational understanding that came from untamed nature and its overwhelming forces, such as thunderstorms or waterfalls. The Picturesque, a category developed by Thomas Gilpin, pertained to the "satisfaction of viewing the complexity and continuous change of nature." Gilpin celebrated "roughness" or "variety." Another term, the Pastoral, applied mainly to subject matter; it could be either picturesque or beautiful, but the subject matter included shepherds and flocks in a gently-settled landscape.

In America in the 1820s Thomas Cole's paintings adopted all of these conventions, paired with his own commitment to the spiritual and moral role of the specifically American wilderness. Cole's theory of landscape suggested that, lacking the cathedrals and Greek temples that endowed the more settled European landscape with so many associations, the uncultivated "wildness" of our scenery gave it meaning in contrast to the homogeneity of more domesticated nature:

> Those scenes of solitude from which the hand of nature has
> never been lifted, affect the mind with a more deep toned
> emotion than aught which the hand of man has touched. . . .
> We are still in Eden; the wall that shuts us out of the garden
> is our own ignorance and folly.

At the same time he already mourned the destruction of the land by the advances of civilization:

> The beauty of such landscapes are quickly passing away—
> the ravages of the axe are daily increasing—the most noble
> scenes are made desolate, and oftentimes with a wantonness
> and barbarism scarcely credible in a civilized nation. (*Essay
> on American Scenery* 109, 1836.)

Cole used the imagery of identifiable monuments of the American wilderness, such as Mount Chocorua, to suggest Eden, as in the recently rediscovered 1828 painting of that subject at the Amon Carter Museum of American Art in Fort Worth. With obvious reference to both the Sublime and the Picturesque, this painting, along with its companion, *Expulsion from the Garden of Eden*, 1827 (Museum of Fine Arts, Boston), uses the paradigms of landscape imagery to speak to the idea of the moral role of unspoiled nature (Eden) as well as our punishment for not respecting it. Later in his career, Cole elaborated this theme in *The Course of Empire*, 1833-36 (New-York Historical Society), with its five states of human presence in the land: *Savage, Pastoral, Consummation, Destruction, Desolation*. Cole's message in this astonishing five-part sequence is the domination of nature by civilization and nature's eventual overthrow and destruction of humanity for its immoral act. (Exactly what is happening today with climate change in 2020!)

Cole was profoundly concerned that the artist not create "mere dead imitations of things—without the power to impress a Sentiment or enforce a moral or religious truth."

Contemporary with Cole, James Fenimore Cooper, Ralph Waldo Emerson, and Henry David Thoreau also responded to the American wilderness. For Cooper the wilderness represented a threat, for Emerson and Thoreau, a refuge. In Cooper's novels, such as *The Last of the Mohicans*, the still-rugged wilderness is an active and changing character that is partner to the conflicts that occur within it. In Emerson and Thoreau, the wilderness is a place of recuperation for the spirit. Emerson extolled nature, albeit somewhat abstractly, from his solidly civilized home in Concord. For him nature symbolized spiritual presence and the possibility of renewal. Thoreau more intimately and specifically engaged the wildness of nature from his cabin on Walden Pond and anxiously bemoaned its invasion by civilization. He decried the insensitivity of the townspeople of Concord in running waterpipes from Walden Pond to use for washing their dishes:

> Now the trunks of trees on the bottom and the old log canoe,
> and the dark surrounding woods, are gone and the villagers,
> who scarcely know where it lies, instead of going to the pond
> to bathe or drink, are thinking to bring its water, which

should be as sacred as the Ganges at least, to the village in a pipe, to wash their dishes with!—to earn their Walden by the turning of a cock or drawing of a plug! (*Walden and Civil Disobedience*, 144)

The widely-read criticism by John Ruskin reinforced the association of landscape with moral and spiritual qualities for Americans, as well as Europeans, during the middle of the nineteenth century. Nature was the "footprint" of God. Nature in art was the product of sensitivity to the incredible complexity of the work of the divine. But for Ruskin, examining and presenting nature in art engaged the entire moral person. Indeed, art and the depiction of nature in art were part of a larger moral activity: art was meaningful only in its connection to and inspiration toward larger social, political, and economic issues—and those issues were the economic exploitation of the land. In fact, by the 1850s Ruskin spoke despairingly of the "failure of nature" caused by the actions of man, a situation that was leading to the annihilation of life. As nature was being destroyed by the Industrial Revolution and the increased cultivation of land for farming in England and America, so was human life being diminished and so would it ultimately be destroyed.

Ruskin's despair forecasts prophetically the contemporary ecological crises of land and spirit in America.

In the same years of Ruskin's despair, American landscape painters were inspired by his writing, but not by his call to action. Alfred Bierstadt's paintings virtually illustrate, with their glowing backlighting as a symbol of the spiritual, the concept of Manifest Destiny, or the Christian mission to subdue the wilderness. The powerful western light draws the pioneer wagons forward. No sense of the threat that civilization poses to nature sullies these blissful prospects. Native inhabitants are diminutive. The paintings stand as testimony to American artists' wedding of morality with development, rather than preservation. Artists often accompanied surveyors for railroads and geological expeditions that determined the economic value of the land, and later profited from its development. Thomas Moran contributed to the creation of the first national park, with his grandiose *The Grand Canyon of the Yellowstone*, 1893-1901 (Smithsonian Museum of American Art). Linked to the Sublime, the painting speaks not of protection, but of celebration. The park, established in 1874, was created because the area was believed to have no minerals valuable for development, rather than for purely nature-loving reasons. Once a national park, the landscape itself became a consumer product—one that is currently under siege by millions of nature worshipers each year. (Note in 2021 David Treuer's article "Return of the National Parks to the Tribes," outlines the displacements of Native tribes on land that would become the National Parks. He stated bluntly: "Viewed from the perspective of history, Yellowstone is a crime scene." *The Atlantic Monthly,* May, 2021).

In the late nineteenth and early twentieth centuries artists began to reject the restraints of the decadent materialism of bourgeois society. They turned from what they saw as a meaningless realism to a purified art of color, line, and shape. As part of the dismissal of the tired conventions of the nineteenth century, modernists also began to celebrate modern technology, rather than nature. At the same time, the immensely influential modernist theory of Roger Fry dismissed Ruskin's nature-based criticism and relegated aesthetic experience to a separate sphere of life in order to purge it of what he saw as the pedestrian moralizing of Victorian painting.

By the 1930s, however, Utopian beliefs and pure aesthetic experiences no longer seemed very important, as people starved to death and artists were imprisoned for creating modern art. Artists felt a need, above all else, to express their social and political concerns. In this context, the landscape and its moral role reentered art as a major theme and subject. In literary and architectural theory, interest in the land was inspired directly by Ruskin's ideas. The Southern Agrarians, among them John Crowe Ransom and Allen Tate, at Vanderbilt University, proposed that life and art based in a rural environment were morally superior to the dehumanizing of industrialization and capitalism in cities. A profound emotional connection to a particular place led easily, by extension, to their rejection of an urban-based modernist art.

In painting, Thomas Hart Benton, Grant Wood, and John Steuart Curry consciously opposed the abstract style and subjects of European modernism and presented a nostalgic and stereotyped iconography of life on the land. This romanticized imagery was frequently connected to specific events of local American history in the "American Scene" agenda of government art programs.

While landscape painting by the Regionalists came to be denigrated as provincial nationalism in the highly politicized art world of the mid-1930s, in film and theater landscape imagery had a profound effect. Hallie Flanagan, head of the Federal Theater Project, created a statement of outrage about the agricultural crisis in "Triple A. Plowed Under," a "Living Newspaper" that combined theater, vaudeville, and other avant-garde techniques to engage the audience. Filmmakers used direct moral references that even recall the paintings of Thomas Cole. In the film *The Plow That Broke the Plains*, 1936, the force of wind and blowing sand during the Dust Bowl recalls the final scene of Cole's *Course of Empire, Desolation*, in which the ruins of empire are buried by the powers of nature. The film paired the sublime power of the landscape with Russian avant-garde film techniques. It explained to the urban citizen the problems of the farmers in the Dust Bowl caused by overgrazing, overproduction, and mechanized farming. Editing, cut to match the score by Virgil Thomson, cast "the grass as heroine, the sun and wind as villains." The government hoped to gain support for its Rural Resettlement Program with the film.

Yet, paired with these romantic and moral purposes in painting, film, and theater, other aspects of the economic turmoil of the 1930s generated the on-going domination of the urban and technological agendas through the construction of massive dams, such as the Grand Coulee in Washington state. The dam itself was a herculean effort that was likened to the construction of the Pyramids of Egypt. Its sanctified moral purpose was to rejuvenate the entire center of the state by attracting homesteads. Today that land is irrigated and farmed—not, indeed, by homesteaders, but by enormous corporations who reap their profits in absentia. (And the enormous devastation to salmon breeding is recognized, as dams are being removed. 1722 dams were demolished nationwide in 2019. —Lynda Mapes, *Seattle Times,* November 8, 2020.)

During the revival of modernism, particularly abstraction, following World War II, landscape imagery, as well as social and political concerns, were dismissed by critics. Regionalism was seen as provincial, chauvinist, and, at its nadir, fascist. American landscape paintings of the nineteenth century were interpreted as virtual abstractions. The critical concept of Luminism, developed in the 1950s and 1960s, almost entirely eliminated the image. Writers such as Barbara Novak depicted the artist as standing in a self-abnegating state before the abstract light of America. Cole's commitment to the moral content of his art, as well as his use of landscape as an opportunity to comment on the destruction of nature by American civilization, was, in these same years, dismissed as a violation of what was seen as his more important contribution—the depiction of landscape unencumbered by meaning.

In the late twentieth century many artists have turned once again to nature and the land as central themes in their work. Since artists are, in the majority, urban, and only visit rural environments, they often seize upon one aspect of the land to exploit for picturesque or even sublime images that can be marketed by urban galleries. Conversely, artists who move out of the city often simply bring their urban-based aesthetic with them. Decades of formalism and a lack of political engagement in the United States in general still prove daunting obstacles for many artists who have strong political feelings.

Some artists, such as Robert Smithson, made form into new paradigms, as in his earthwork *Spiral Jetty*, 1970, a metaphor for the spiral of evolution and the principles of entropy. The work has been consumed by the salt and water of the Great Salt Lake. Other artists working in the land—Nancy Holt, for example—have sought a social role by reclaiming industrial-waste sites. Still others collaborate with landscape architects to create an environment, somewhat in the tradition of Frederick Law Olmsted, that enhances and expands our awareness as we move through it. Yet the pressure of our devastation of nature still rarely appears in art, just as the devastation caused by Manifest Destiny in both human and natural terms was rarely seen in nineteenth century art after the time of Thomas Cole. Ruskin's absolute despair with industrialization rarely finds resonance in the work of contemporary artists concerned with the land. The paradox is now, as in the nineteenth century, between art as a moral statement and art as a marketable aesthetic object.

A group of artists located in a remote area of eastern Washington state, known as the Palouse, provide a case study of the difficulties and contradictions of making aesthetic objects and engaging political issues within a single artistic practice. These artists are linked to a land-grant research institution, Washington State University, that is providing scientific data for both the assault on the land by agricultural technology and some of the new alternatives to that traditional approach to agriculture. The Palouse initially seems a gentle place, when compared to the harsh expanse of irrigated farmlands of the central desert. In contrast to the agribusiness farms of central Washington, watered by the Grand Coulee Dam, with their irrigation devices scaled like huge, metamorphosed insects preying on the land, the rolling, lush hills of golden wheat on the farms of the Palouse seem intimate and friendly. Living in this land, the artists, as well as the farmers, of the Palouse are profoundly aware that the opposite is the case.

The Palouse is a land ravaged by modern technology and chemical fertilizers on a scale far more exaggerated than the conditions that led to the Dust Bowl of the 1930s. This has created massive erosion of the rich volcanic soil, now flying into the air at the rate of fifty tons per acre per year. For every bushel of wheat produced, fifteen hundred pounds of soil are lost.

The rivers and forests, too, have been robbed. Dams have created a "water desert" on the banks of rivers in place of orchards; native habitats of plants and wildlife have been destroyed. Logging has filled the streams with debris. Erosion has filled the dammed streams with sedimentation. The natural cycles of fish and birds are disrupted, their normal paths obliterated or decimated. The last remaining 5 percent of virgin forest is currently being clear-cut.

In this lightly populated region, the Department of Defense placed a lethal plutonium production plant on 570 square miles in the south central area of the state. Between 1944 and 1957 the plant at Hanford produced over five hundred thousand curies of radioactive iodine and created a massive toxic-waste problem. The nine reactors along the Columbia River used its water to cool the cores and then passed it directly back to the source, making it the most radioactive river in the United States.

Earth, air, and water are all in trouble. This rugged land of farms and small towns is far from simply picturesque. The isolated residents of the region intensely experience nature as a transcendental presence, as well as both oppressor and oppressed. The tiny communities form a haunting counterpoint to the massive presence of late-twentieth-century technology in the surrounding farmlands. They are usually kept alive by a single chemical-fertilizer manufacturer, which arrays massive machines in military ranks, awaiting the appropriate moment for their assault on the land.

Confronted with these disasters, as well as the still transcendent presence of the earth and sky itself, artists are faced with a dilemma. Do they respond to and interpret such horrific ecological conditions or do they create an alternative imagery that virtually preserves or re-creates nature as beautiful? Such artists as Robert Helm pursue an imagery that appears to be transcendently calm, but often contains a tense, unexplained melodrama lurking in its midst. Jack Dollhausen uses electronics as a metaphor for the extended natural time and space of the region. His complex light sculptures sometimes take an entire year to complete a single cycle, demanding that the viewer exist in nature's time, not the instant time-bite of contemporary life.

George Trakas addresses the balance between the individual and the environment. As part of a ten-year commitment to rework the center of the campus of Washington State University, Trakas is working with Catherine Howett to open the school and its residents to the extraordinary setting of the Palouse. They have so far created an open gathering place, embraced by slabs of granite, that provides a horizontal pause at the center of the narrow, linear campus axis.

Other artists, such as Gaylen Hansen, address the imbalance of animal and human interactions. He presents humans confronting huge animals, birds, insects, fish, and reptiles. The theme of enormous insects, for example, is psychically realistic, since grasshoppers actually can devour an entire garden within hours. Jo Hockenhull's work also addresses the interactions of humans and nature, but from a perspective of the structural bonds that connect us. Hockenhull uses x-ray images in complex, composite print media to explore ecological issues both historically and scientifically. Her iconography, as well as that of another printmaker, Rita Robillard, at times intersects with the concerns of deep ecologists and ecofeminists, who see humans as part of nature, rather than its dominator and exploiter. In these potent philosophies, the earth is "intrinsically feminine," and the primary problem is our androcentric institutions that value the earth only economically, not spiritually.

A few artists in the Palouse focus on political activism, rather than object making, as a primary commitment. Although interfacing with a formidable system itself, these artists actually attempt to restore the balance in nature. Victor Moore, a sculptor, founded the Palouse Preservation League, a group that attempts to reestablish ecological balance through sustainable agriculture, in cooperation with local farmers. The league advocates protecting habitats for wildlife, opposes the use of pesticides, particularly near schools, and tries to delay clear-cutting of the last few virgin growth forests. Moore even ran for the state legislature from Eastern Washington, on a platform of respect for the environment.

Crystal Dollhausen, a painter turned political activist, focuses on the virtually invisible problem of the Hanford nuclear production complex's toxic emissions. She has filled an entire small house with literature on nuclear health-hazard and pesticide issues. In her own immediate environment, she rejects the concept of the carpet of green lawn so institutionalized in our culture, and yet so ruthless in its arbitrary selections from nature's balance. In her home she has tried to reestablish the full complexity of the original plants in the Palouse:

> I feel as though we are hanging on by our fingernails against the juggernaut that reduces everything to a pesticide-dependent monoculture. I approach my little plot of earth feeling a great responsibility to protect the few species, pitiful remnants of the native Palouse, that have survived here. I live by the tenet that the diversity of species offers protection from infestations. It wards off the plague. . . The greater the variety, the more stable the community. . . . [Gardening]is an unraveling of the mysteries of the universe, the enterprise I assume humans are meant to engage in, in order to survive. (Letter to the author November 1990)

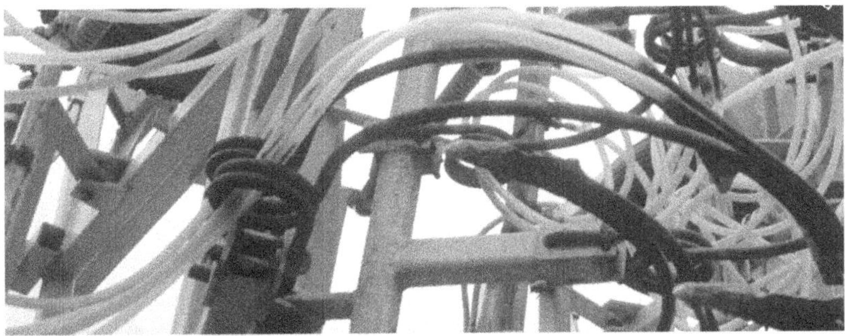

Agricultural Equipment, Eastern Washington State, 1991

From 1984 to 1989, I spent five years teaching at Washington State University and experienced the various paradigms outlined in this article. From an initial sense of the Pastoral, Picturesque, and Sublime, I have now come to see the environment as victim of a violent rape. I turn to that paradigm, dismissing more tranquil scholarly analysis, as I now see the earth dying under the assault of scientific objectivity.

On a recent return visit to the Palouse, I saw a poplar tree that had been chain-sawed during "routine maintenance," deeply scored and treated with a powerful, illegal poison: a violent death for a simple tree, in the name of efficiency. The poplar was, in fact, ten feet from the "utility" line it supposedly threatened. But the tree had, at least temporarily, the last word. Within a few months four saplings had already sprung up directly under the line. Although the main tree had been destroyed, its deep roots had survived and come back. Perhaps it is not yet too late for the Earth.

(1992)

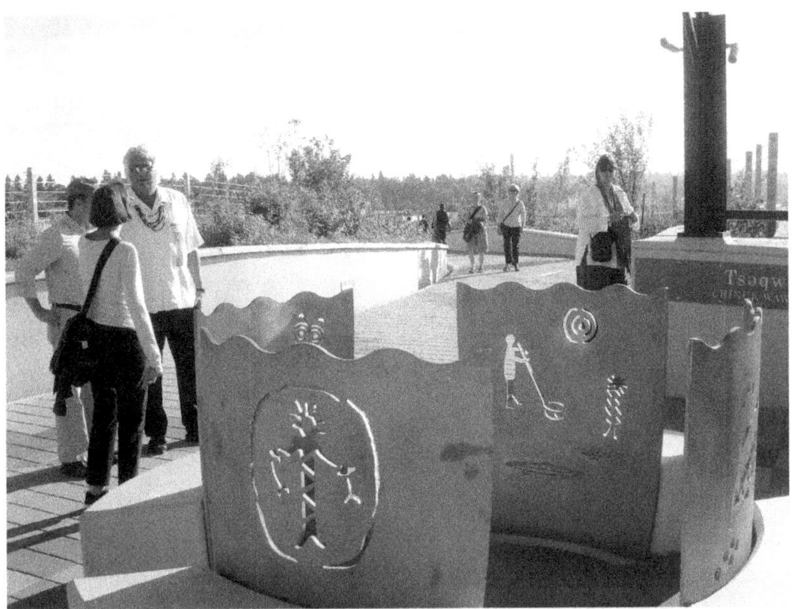

Maya Lin, The Confluence Project, on the *Vancouver Land Bridge* with Johnpaul Jones at the Dedication, 2008

# Maya Lin: Extinctions and Confluences

"WHAT IS MISSING?" MAYA LIN's "last monument," is an extraordinary online project that sounds an alarm for the planet in the midst of escalating mass extinction of species and their habitats. She refers to our current situation as the sixth mass extinction in geologic time, but the only one triggered by a single species, the human race, rather than a natural disaster.

Her website is comprehensive, including connections to information about extinctions, as well as success stories in saving species from all over the world. It includes history as well, going back to the earliest actions of humans on the environment.

As she stated in 1996, "We are the one species that has rapidly caused the extinction of so many other species. . . . We have to stop. We have to begin to understand that we cannot continue to overuse. I don't know how it will manifest itself, but this is my dream."

As competition grows for the last fossil fuels, resource extraction has become even more aggressive in such places as Alberta, Canada—where the entire surface of the land, what is called the "overburden" by energy companies, but which is, in fact, a crucial Boreal forest and carbon storehouse—is removed in pursuit of tar sands. (One good book on this topic is *Global Warming and the Sweetness of Life: A Tar Sands Tale* by Matt Hern and Am Johal, with Joe Sacco, MIT Press, 2018.)

In Pennsylvania and New York State natural gas extraction by fracking poisons ground water; mountain top removal in Appalachia blows up entire mountains; overfishing in the seas is leading to mass declines; and ocean acidification from carbon dioxide is destroying many organisms.

Sound is also a major reference point for destruction of species as massive ships disrupt the sonar wavelengths that whales and other sea creatures require to communicate. Planned new dams in Quebec will destroy the habitat of 97,000 pairs of songbirds. "What is Missing?" speaks to absence, like the sounds of those songbirds and all the other species lost, or about to be lost, by habitat destruction. Collaborating with scientists and environmental groups from around the world, Maya Lin honors the already lost and wants to inspire us to take action to prevent future losses. With vivid videos and sound archives from the Cornell Ornithology Lab, and imagery from BBC World and *National Geographic*, "What is Missing?" makes it possible for us to see giant fish and turtles swimming in the sea, and hear the extraordinary sounds of threatened frogs, birds and crickets.

"What is Missing?" includes multiple formats: a website, a Listening Cone, seventy videos, and the Empty Room, a space with projectors in the floor that let visitors "catch" a projected image of a species. Other formats are a sound ring with embedded speakers, a print book, a downloadable digital book and an interactive website. In addition to the connections to troubled sites all over the world it has links to environmental groups who are trying to counter the damage. The public can also contribute stories. Lin is redefining the idea of a monument from a single fixed work, to a constantly changing multimedia event. That sense of change parallels the constant losses in biodiversity ongoing throughout the planet.

In 2009, the California Academy of Sciences, in collaboration with the San Francisco Arts Commission, unveiled the first permanent *Listening Cone*—a megaphone shaped sculpture large enough for people to walk inside. In its narrow end a video screen projects twenty minutes of video and sound recordings of extinct, threatened and endangered species and their habitats. The exterior of the cone is bronze, the interior is a highly polished recycled redwood. People are asked to take off their shoes before going inside. Once inside, the curved inner space forces awareness of your footing, and the space narrows quickly. The physical dynamic of the Cone echoes the condition of the earth: we are increasingly treading on unstable ground and our planet's options narrow as species and habitat loss escalates. Slightly de-stabilizing our footing is part of Maya Lin's strategy to stimulate the public to think more about what the current crisis means now, and for the near future.

Changing contexts for the videos also destabilize our expectations, as in the Earth Day 2010 Project in Times Square, sponsored by Creative Time. Lin projected videos onto a billboard in the midst of one of the loudest cacophonies of man-made sounds and aggressive advertising imagery in the world. Three five-minute videos played every hour for two weeks: an image of a giant blue stingray or sea turtle swimming in the sea was paired with Lin's succinct texts: "What is Missing? Sea Turtles." The sounds of birds, crickets and frogs can be heard over the sounds of traffic. The visual impact of juxtaposing these images of magnificent endangered species, like the stingray, to the commercial promotions of Times Square makes the point that our commodity-based economy and thirst for energy drives destruction of habitats.

The final text was "With human alterations of their habitat the single biggest cause."

Capitalization of nature by corporations is of course the force that must be countered. As one CEO stated, "the largest corporation in the world is not Ford or Walmart. The largest corporation in the world is nature."

Note: May 2021 Maya Lin's latest iteration of "What is Missing?" is "Ghost Forest" installed in the middle of Madison Square Park in New York City. Lin transported 49 Atlantic white cedars from the Pine Barrens of New Jersey. They had died as a result of Hurricane Sandy which had deposited too much salt in the soil. In other words climate change killed the trees. She was inspired to create the work by looking at the dead trees outside her window in Colorado that had been killed by pine bark beetles as a result of climate change.

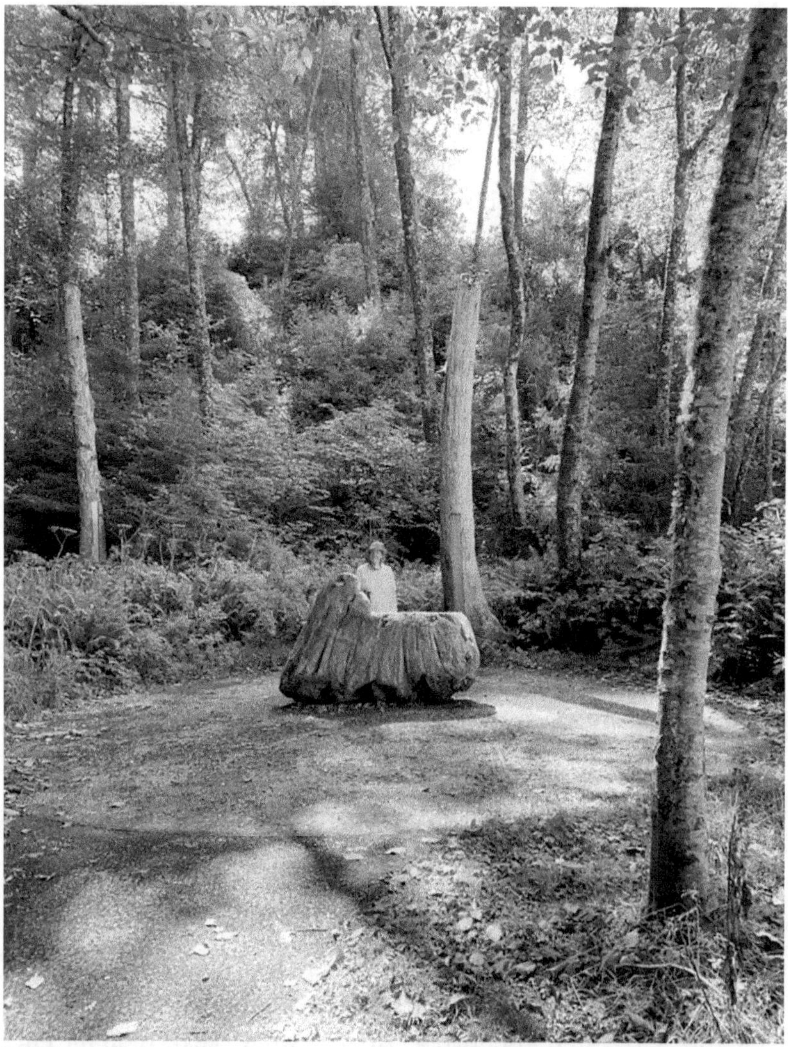

Maya Lin, The Confluence Project, Cape Disappointment, *Sacred Circle*, (detail), Dedicated 2006, Photograph: Henry Matthews, 2020

## The Confluence Project (2002- ongoing)

As it marks the lost and endangered species, ecosystems, and peoples along the Columbia River, based on a comparison to the present with the meticulous journals of the 1804-6 Lewis and Clark Corps of Discovery, Maya Lin's Confluence Project is also a manifestation of "What is Missing?" Spread over 438 miles at six sites, the project documents losses, marks survival, and initiates ecological restoration. Native groups mourn massive cultural losses since the Expedition opened the door to fraudulent treaties, devastation of natural resources driven by greed, and widespread illness of both people and the environment.

As Lewis and Clark went west from St. Louis, they mapped, counted, identified, and enumerated everything that they saw. They documented flora, fauna, Native villages and tribes, weather and daily life. They called their record "a summary statement of the rivers, creeks, and most remarkable places from the mouth of the Missouri as high up the river as was explored in the year 1804 by Captains Lewis and Clark." Near the place where the Columbia River joins the Pacific Ocean, the end of their journey, and the first site of the Confluence Project to be completed, a walkway lays out their summary on cast concrete planks.

Our relationship to those planks is quite different from that of the Vietnam Memorial, where the surfaces are vertical and we can easily approach them and touch them. At Cape Disappointment, we have to bend over to read them, and reading the texts interrupt our progress toward the beach and the sea. That physical sense of interruption, as in the destabilizing of our footing in *The Listening Cone*, parallels the point Lin is making: as White explorers charted these lands they interrupted the course of history and nature.

The Confluence Project began as part of the 200th anniversary commemoration of the Meriwether Lewis and William Clark 1804-6 Corps of Discovery, a topic in which Lin was completely uninterested. Antone Minthorn of the Confederated Tribes of the Umatilla Indian Reservation was one person who was instrumental in Lin's change of heart. He had seen a documentary in which she discusses the commemorations of the Vietnam War and the Civil Rights Movement. In her sensitivity to those two charged events, he suddenly saw a solution to the problem of the Lewis and Clark anniversary.

His own perspective on Lewis and Clark was, as for most Native Americans, that they brought conquest, greed, illness, and destruction. He and another elder, Chief Cliff Snider, retired member of the Tribal Council of the Chinook Indian Nation, went to New York City to tell Maya Lin about the ecological changes to the Columbia River since the Corps of Discovery, the huge loss of species, and the current efforts at restoration.

Dramatic ecological changes and losses coincided with Lin's long term interests in creating a monument to extinction. In the Confluence Project she brought together ecological restoration, Native voices, and Lewis and Clark's detailed observations of flora and fauna. Lin refers to those texts as an ecological "lens" that provide one marker of the changes in the environment between then and now.

As the first walkway of concrete planks was being dedicated by the Chinook Indian Nation, their beautiful prayer inspired Lin to redesign the project to incise their words in the planks of an oyster walkway. That walkway marks the original shoreline of the sea, before the huge jetties built to protect sailors and shipping were added.

Today (August 2020), that prayer can still be easily read, while the journal inscriptions from Lewis and Clark on the more exposed walkway have almost entirely been worn away. It seems so appropriate.

In addition, the restoration that Lin imagined here has taken place throughout the site, the trees have grown up, the grass has returned to fill fields.

In another part of the Cape Disappointment site, Lin inscribed the Chinook Creation Myth on a fish cutting table made of a huge piece of basalt that she selected.

At the Sandy River Delta in Troutdale, Oregon, Lewis and Clark thought the intersection of the Sandy River with the Columbia River was a major passageway and spent several days exploring it. Today, that main channel of the river is blocked by a dam that was installed in the 1930s, supposedly to improve fish flow, severely altering the ecosystem. The Forest Service collaborated with the Confluence Project to restore ecological balance with Native plants, as well as for the removal of the dam (which occurred in 2007).

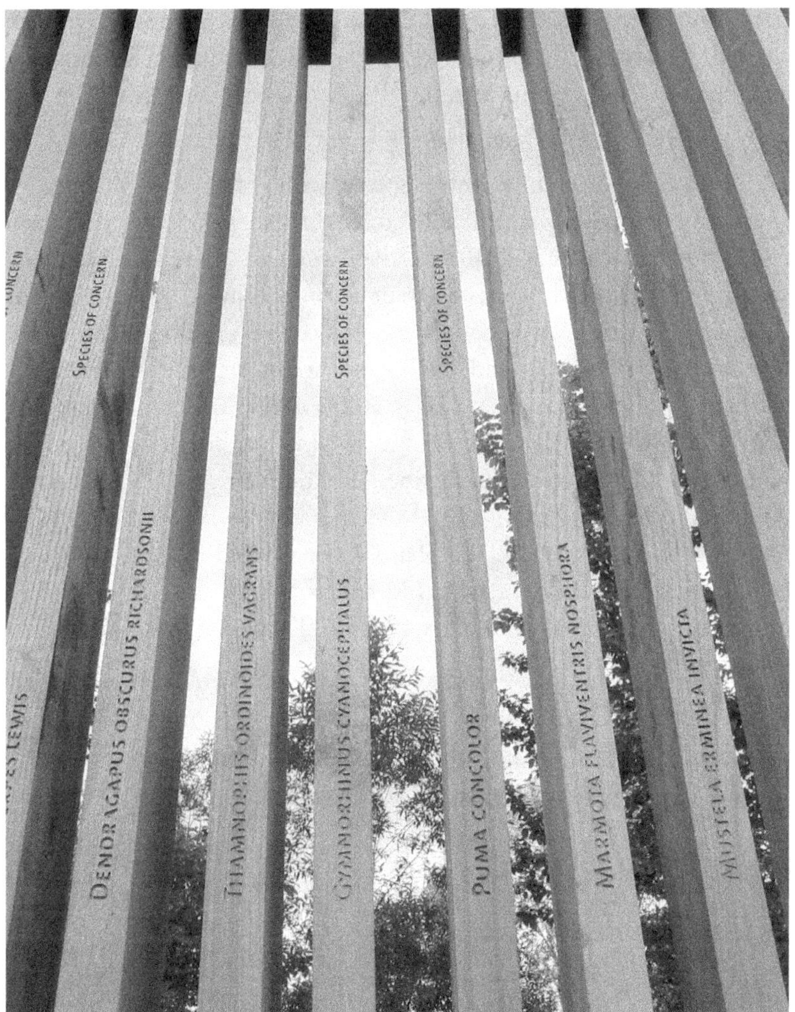

Maya Lin *Sandy River, Bird Blind,* Troutdale Oregon, detail 2008 Photograph: Henry Matthews

The *Bird Blind,* as Maya Lin calls the structure at the Sandy River Delta, is set in a large tract of land, what will be the Confluence of the Sandy River and the Columbia River, once the original delta of the river is restored. The *Bird Blind* is the opposite of its name. Rather than a site to enable us to look at birds without being seen, Lin has designed it so that we can barely see out between the almost twelve-foot high wooden slats because they are too close together. Instead we are confronted by texts on the slats: precise observations from entries in the Lewis and

Clark journal name species, and the date and place where they were sighted. Lin has added whether the same species today is currently endangered, threatened or extinct. The *Bird Blind* pays tribute to lost species and birds, as well as marking their survival.

The *Vancouver Land Bridge* speaks of a different confluence: it spans a six lane highway and train tracks in order to recreate the connection of the Klickitat Trail and the Columbia River. The trail was used by inland tribal groups to trade with Columbia River tribes for thousands of years. The *Land Bridge* was realized by Jones and Jones, Seattle-based Architects and Landscape Architects. Native American architect, Johnpaul Jones, worked in collaboration with ideas from Lin. The overall profile of the Land Bridge is an implied circle, a form important to both plateau and coastal tribes, evoking a circle of life, gathering, communication, and exchanging. On the bridge, the wide borders of native plants refer to both the plants in Lewis and Clark's notes and those used by Indians: Oregon grape, camas, Nootka rose, salmonberry, huckleberry, white oak, red cedar, and red alder.

There are plans for a "Treaty Table" on the Columbia River, funded by the percent-for-art program, on a planned bridge for I-5. The Treaty Table will reference the Isaac Smith treaties of 1854 which "legalized" the taking of indigenous lands.

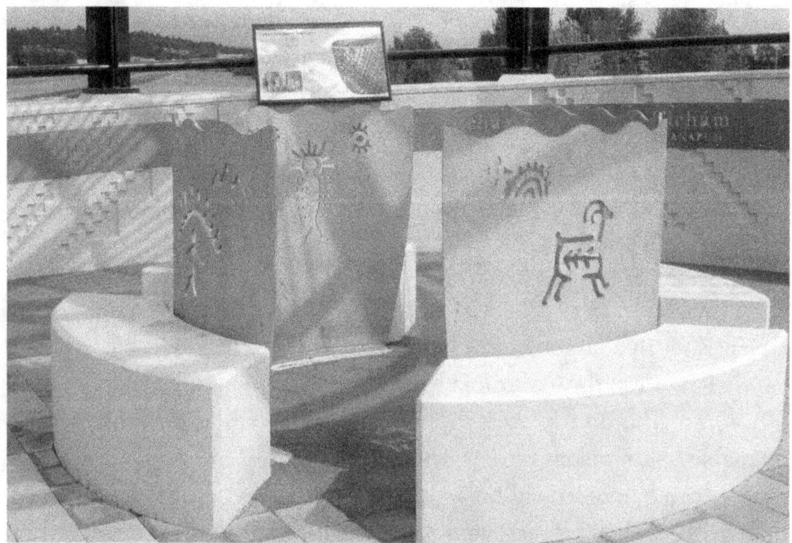

Lillian Pitt, *Stainless Steel Spirit Baskets* on *Vancouver Land Bridge*, 2008, Photograph: Henry Matthews

Native American artist Lillian Pitt created a *Welcome Gate* composed of two cedar paddles, crossed at the top, supported by cedar columns asymmetrically flanked by basalt columns. On the bridge, two seating areas with cutouts of abstracted petroglyphs, also by Pitt, refer to the 12,000-year-old cultures of the Columbia Gorge.

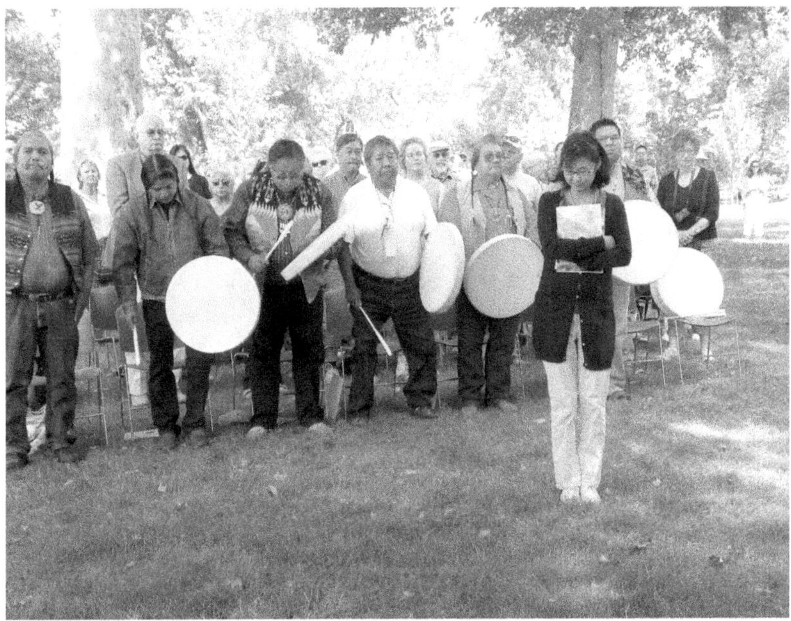

Maya Lin, The Confluence Project with Native leaders and musicians at Sacajawea State Park, *Story Circles,* Dedication 2010, Photograph: Henry Matthews

The *Story Circles at Sacajawea State Park,* set at the confluence of the Snake and the Columbia River, includes seven basalt circles incised with texts and images. A major gathering site for Native tribes for thousands of years, the circles mark species of salmon, plants, animals, and goods traded by the Indians, a tribal long house, and the dams that destroyed the natural abundance on which the cultures had thrived. Finally, one circle marks the mythic history and future of the cultures with a Coyote Myth about the return of the salmon. As we randomly access the circles rather than follow a fixed path, we move beyond linear thinking and open our minds to multiple dimensions of history, language, nature, and time.

The not yet completed Confluence site *Celilo Park (Wyam),* "Place of Echoing Water upon Rocks" or "Sound of Water upon the Rocks," commemorates a collision rather than a confluence. Prior to the arrival of settlers, Wyam Indians lived here for over 12,000 years, perhaps the longest continuously inhabited community in North America. Indians caught salmon in nets from complex platforms suspended over Celilo Falls.

Nineteen hydroelectric dams, and nuclear, agricultural and industrial waste pollution, and the erosion from clear-cut mountainsides have devastated the Columbia River. As a result, the salmon harvest declined precipitously from fourteen million in 1855, to fewer than seventy-five thousand today.

The John Day Dam, built between 1959 and 1968, turned the thundering falls into a silent lake.

On the weekend before the dedication, hundreds of Indians from all over the Northwest converged to grieve the loss of this cultural confluence. At the dedication itself, Maya Lin played a minor role, as spiritual leaders, dancers and singers invoked the sad history of the place. Lin humbly accepted the burden of their expectations.

Her model for the Celilo Falls site is a cantilevered ramp. The steel ramp will rise 300 feet, and hang twenty feet above the surface of the lake, where the falls used to be. The railings of woven wood evoke traditional basket weaving. Narratives texts on the ramp will tell the geological, historical, mythical, and political history of the site. Sounds will also be part of the experience, including descriptions of the sound of the falls and the silence that followed. Wyam Indians, who have never left the site and today live in what is called Celilo Village, declared that the "falls have never left . . . they still echo in our heart."

The Wyam never joined a tribal reservation and therefore have the status of an independent nation today. Recently, and in collaboration with efforts by nearby tribal groups, they have finally gotten new housing, sewage, streets, and a long house, promised many years ago. Their fishing rights have never changed. Their leaders personally invited Maya Lin to talk with them about what texts will be inscribed on the Celilo ramp. (Note: as of 2020 this site is not yet constructed.)

In 2005, a Native blessing ceremony dedicated a Listening Circle at Chief Timothy Park near the confluence of the Clearwater and the Snake Rivers. Consisting of a natural amphitheater made of basalt and incised with texts, it integrates with the dramatic, unspoiled landscape of the site. The site was completed in 2015. (This is the only site that I have not yet visited).

The Confluence Project and "What is Missing?" bear witness to Maya Lin's deep concern for the state of the planet. Spanning from ancient myths and rituals to the intimate imagery and sounds of digital technology, these projects are not only intended to be memorials; they are asking us to take action to save what is left. The Confluence Project continues with programming for children, and educational videos with Native Americans (www.confluenceproject.org).

(2011)

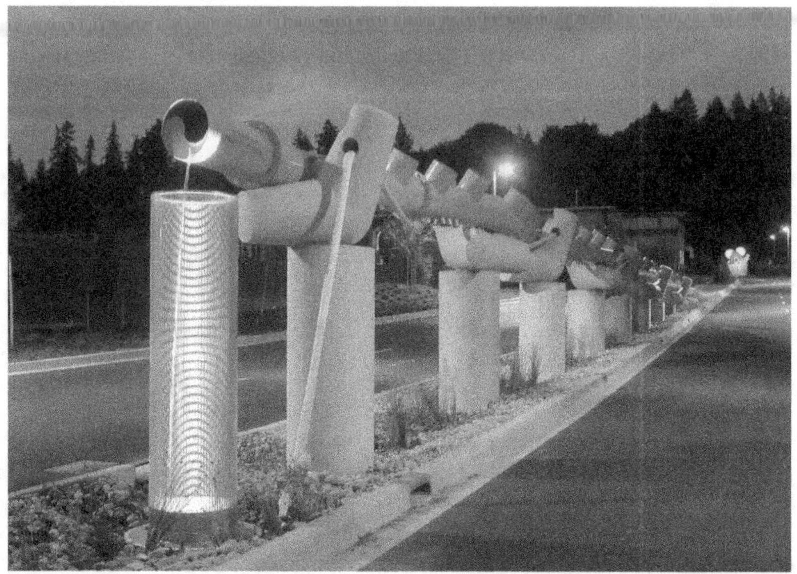

Buster Simpson, *Bio Boulevard and Water Molecule,* 2011, Brightwater Treatment Facility, Woodinville, Washington, concrete, stainless steel, plants, reclaimed water, 15' x 20' x 600', Photograph: Buster Simpson. "The sculpture receives water after the final stages of processing. The open ports facing to the south along the entryway into the plant provide a "value added "function of aeration to the processed water. In addition, there are irrigation nozzles that offer water to sedge bioswale beneath the sculpture that augments street rain water to maintain a healthy wetlands landscape. The sculpture is designed to direct a larger volume of water to adjacent wetlands when permitting is in place."

# Water Cycles and Water Treatment

BRIGHTWATER TREATMENT SYSTEM in Northern King County, Washington, is a massive sewage treatment plant with mechanical, biological, and electrical systems for cleaning water, a system of pipes running through deep-bored tunnels to Puget Sound, an Educational Center, and forty acres of reclaimed land on a salmon-spawning creek. The pipes not only carry wastewater to the plant and treated wastewater to the Sound, but also distribute thousands of gallons of treated water for reuse.

In 2002, Buster Simpson, Jann Rosen-Queralt, and Ellen Sollod, in collaboration with Cath Brunner, Director of Public Art for King

County, developed an "Art Concept Workbook" for Brightwater. The final art master plan, inspired in part by Lorna Jordan's innovative ecological project *Waterworks Gardens* (1996) at a water reclamation plant, called for participating artists to create a "vision of sustainability." The artists, like Jordan, make visible both active treatment and natural cleaning processes, such as detention pools and constructed wetlands. The Brightwater Art Master Plan stands as an inspiring document of what artists can do when full imaginative potential is wedded to the creation of a green world. But the realized projects also document how they adjust their ideas to engineering regulations and economics.

Simpson addresses reclaimed stormwater in a monumental sculpture at the main entrance to the plant. *Bio Boulevard and Water Molecule* suggests a heroic enterprise with a semi-Pop Art aesthetic. At one end, an enlarged red (hydrogen) and white (oxygen) "water molecule," an icon of the treatment plant itself, passes treated water through a "bubble tea straw" into an underground pipe that emerges in the arms of "heroic plumbers," really concrete tetrapods that evoke the muscled laborers of WPA public art. They "carry" the treated water through a purple pipe (plumbing code for treated water) pierced with holes that expose the water to the sun and allow it to off gas. At the end of the pipe, the water pours into a six-foot-high coil. The "plumbers" suggest communal collaboration as they collectively support the long purple pipe. The entire 600-foot long sculpture is a metaphor for the function of the plant.

Near the main entry point for sewage entering and treated water leaving the building, Rosen-Queralt's *Confluence* represents the speed and volume of water moving through the plant. Water rushes loudly across a constructed pool, an open pipe reminding us of the enormous amounts of water that we expend in sewage disposal. At the center of the pool is a cone-shaped sculpture that Rosen-Queralt refers to as a breathing "gill." Made of flexible strands of coiled wire, it rises, falls, and twists on its side, evoking the movement of a tidal pool, in and out. A third element comments on waste, slow drips leaking from holes in the sides. When the water accumulates to twelve inches, it automatically flushes out—the water in the sculpture is already processed, and it uses no energy to function. The well is set in a plaza that includes a concentric tile pattern evoking rings of water. A grove of willow trees, once they reach 10 feet, will represent one percent of the volume of water that moves through the plant. *Confluence* reflects Rosen-Queralt's philosophy of water as part of a system of exchanges and intersections. As she wrote in a proposal for an urbanized watershed at the Baltimore Water Resources Department (September 2010): "Understanding the connection between nature and technology is a reminder of the symbiotic relationships inherent in an ecosystem."

Ellen Sollod, Brightwater's third lead artist, also gives much thought to the crucial importance of water in our lives. *Collection and Transformation,* her window display in the Environmental Education and Community Center, features seventeen large glass sculptures that evoke aquatic micro-organisms.

The forms were made in a residency at the Tacoma Museum of Glass's hot shop, based on sketches and clay models. The glass micro-organisms are set into a stainless steel honeycomb structure and are incased in a blue mirrored glass, lighted from above. An adjacent window consists of modified, recycled laboratory glass, an increasingly obsolete tool as computers replace hands-on testing.

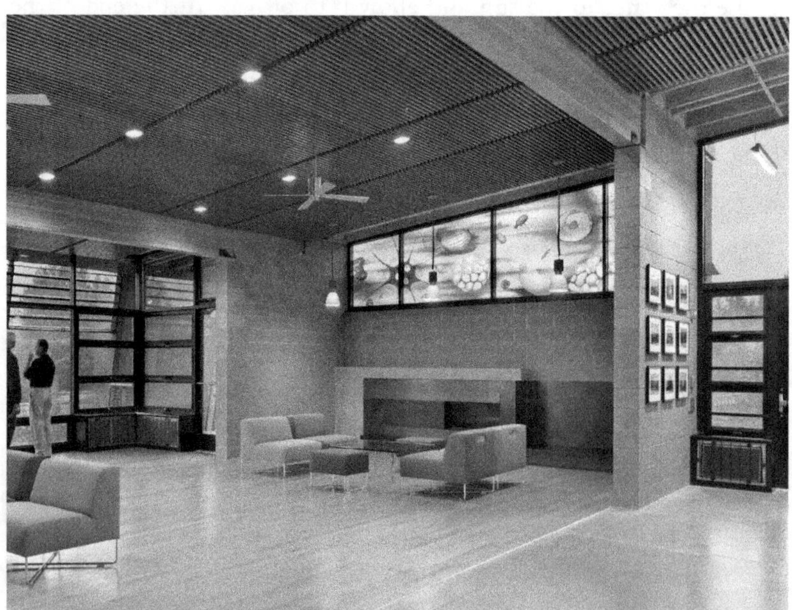

Ellen Sollod, *It's All About the Water,* hand-painted float glass, etched antique glass, on float glass, King County Public Art Collection.. ©Ellen Sollod, Photograph: Ned Ahrens

As part of the largest water treatment plant ever built, these three projects and many others (including works by Andrea Wilbur-Sigo, Christian Moeller, Jane Tsong, Jim Blashfield, Cris Bruch, and Claude Zervas) honor the importance of water and give visual form to treatment processes. With plans for temporary projects in the restored wetlands, Brightwater is intended to be a destination for recreation and education, as well as a model for returning wastewater to nature. Water as a fixed resource is here returned to the cycle of nature.

(2011)

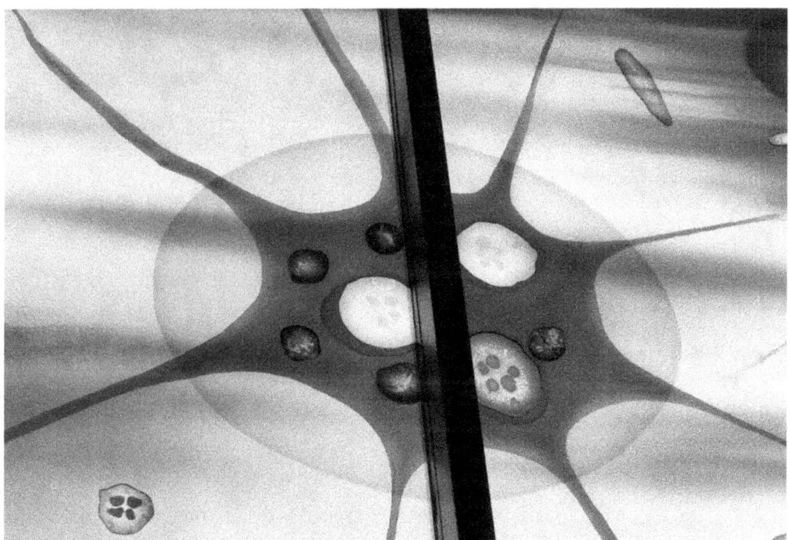

*It's All About the Water* (detail), hand-painted float glass, etched antique glass on float glass, King County Public Art Collection. ©Ellen Sollod, Photograph: Ellen Sollod

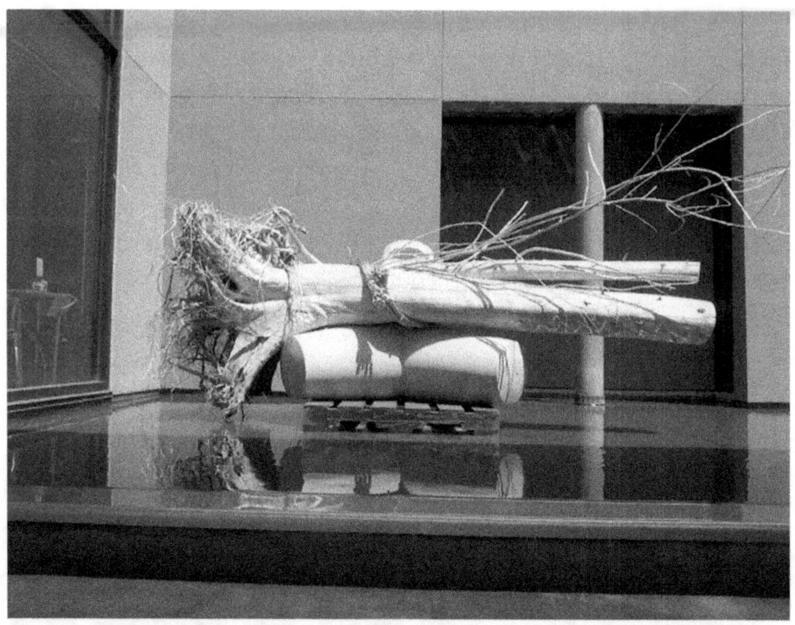

Buster Simpson *Secured Embrace*, 2013 concrete dolos, Western Red Cedar root-wad, stainless steel cable, 116" x 42" x 54", Installation, Frye Art Museum

# Buster Simpson:
# Court Jester of Eco-Urban Art

BUSTER SIMPSON ARRIVED IN downtown Seattle in 1973, only four years after Lucy Lippard came here to create what is now known as the first ever exhibition of conceptual art. The catalog for that exhibition, a stack of index cards, is part of the Seattle Art Museum's permanent collection. and on exhibit at the moment in "Minimal Art and its Legacy." Conceptual artists opposed the marketing of art and the separation of art from life. That led them to explore everyday life, and to use found materials as art; they also believed in calling attention to the abstract systems and structures of art.

Liberated by the open-ended ideas of conceptual art, Simpson, in collaboration with other artists and community activists living in downtown Seattle, began to intervene in the fabric of the city. The work of these early activists eventually transformed thinking in the city. Today we have urban gardens everywhere; we have a variety of trees; we have bus shelters with seats (sometimes); all of these were unknown in the Seattle of the early 1970s. Simpson himself has gone from guerrilla street artist to highly respected participant in major projects. Currently that project is the new waterfront that will emerge after the viaduct is gone (and the tunnel is completed, keep your fingers crossed that we SURVIVE that insanely gigantic drill going underneath Pioneer Square at this very moment).

Simpson's major retrospective at the Frye Art Museum allows us to see some of the ephemera of his earliest street work; remakes of some pieces in museum-sized scale; and materials and new work following in the spirit of some of his primary preoccupations.

In 1969 Simpson was in Woodstock, Vermont, creating what he calls "earthworks projects," actually, as Jen Graves jauntily describes in her article, an improvised farm for people to visit as an alternative to music. But it got overrun by the masses and he became a security guard, and then a janitor cleaning up after everyone. This experience was formative: he is still picking up junk and letting people mess with his art. Simpson moved west in the early 1970s to be part of the founding of Pilchuk, then conceived of as an experimental multimedia retreat.

He started living in downtown Seattle in 1973, when it was grimy and gritty, impoverished and unassuming, when poor people (and he was one of them) were part of the fabric of the city. From his point of view as a public interventionist, he began to pioneer absurdly simple solutions to the complex issues of urban ecology, or, in other words, how people and nature intersect with bureaucracies in a city.

He assumed a persona of "woodman" picking up cast off pieces of wood from the street (there is a great video of him impossibly loaded up and reaching for one more piece that he repeatedly drops). He worked with (and still works with) detritus, recycled industrial materials, and found objects in the spirit of Marcel Duchamp, but approaches them with a sense of compassionate humor and practical purpose, rather than deadpan irony. We can compare it to Lawrence Weiner's "Declaration of Intent" of 1968, in which he is trying to pick up driftwood. But

Weiner didn't do anything with it. It was the act itself that was his art. For Simpson there is always another step, a problem to solve.

Duchamp took a urinal and put it in an art exhibition. Simpson put a composting commode on the street for use in an area that had no public toilet. Furthermore, the toilet was going to provide fertilizer for an urban tree planted in the same spot. The difference is exact: in the first case a useful object was declared to be aesthetic, and consequently useless; in the second a basic need was met by creative thinking.

For Simpson, there has been no giving up, no sense of the futility of working with systems. He even included his videos of meetings in his retrospective, a wonderfully humorous nod to the hours he has spent in them. He has worked inside and outside of systems (bureaucratic, public art, political) throughout his career and pioneered, with other artists in Seattle, the idea of joining a design team for a major project at the beginning of the process, rather than as an art add on at the end. His ideas are often unrealized, altered, or reworked as a result of his interaction with systems. This of course is the case with all public art. When a brilliant idea that he has developed carefully over months is dismissed entirely (as in Southeast False Creek Master Plan for Vancouver, BC's Olympic Village), he still sees it as a model of what might be possible.

He continues to pursue an idealistic, even utopian, practice, but a practice that is also humble: he begins with a problem at hand. But he brings to that problem a sense of poetry that transforms it into a work of art. He likes to call his process "poetic utility." His work is never only an art object. It is placed within systems that shaped it, whether it is a city street, a salmon stream, a storm drain, or a crow's nest.

Early on, when he was hired at a minimum wage to clear a loft, he created an "exhibition" which he called "Selective Disposal Project" out of the dirt and rubbish. Again this is a contrast to Duchamp's "dust breeding experiment, in which he allowed dust to accumulate on *The Large Glass* for a year.

Simpson suggested working with youth corps and skilled craftspeople to make a park with rubble from the freeway construction that had been dumped on the waterfront, instead of what he describes as "lots of clean and green."

He made a "crow's nest" out of some rubble in a very old cherry tree about to be bulldozed, sat in it and then, by referring to the "legal rights" of trees, called on the city council to declare it in the public domain,

Although the Frye exhibition has an emphasis on the remainders of these early works—tiny photographs, plans, super 8 videos—the artist has also created sculptures specifically for the show: recreations of earlier street art and newly-made works. Some of these sculptural re-creations are pedantic compared to their original playful sources, such as the man knocking beer bottles off a table, originally conceived of as a peep show. *Crow Bars with Electromagnet Bottles* completely loses its point: the original piece was a target for throwing beer bottles in an alley which then fell into a recycling bin.

Another example of a new work is *Double Header Finial*, a massive piece of gilded anodized aluminum, steel (found parts, finials and a Boeing nose cone), set on a triangular black flag. It provides ample perching for crows. In the original, seen in an old video, we see crows competing for a perch on a flagpole; now it is a send up of the new Seattle, its gilded lifestyle and ornate housing—why shouldn't the crows join in? The black flag warns of the current risks of urban wealth.

One of Simpson's constant themes though has been waterfront and water restoration. He has thrown limestone into polluted rivers, as a way of neutralizing acid, most famously in "Hudson River Headwaters Purge", from 1990. The exhibition has a retrieved limestone disc from that project, a video of his original action, as well as its partner, "Projecting Limestone Purge," in which a naked Simpson slings limestones marked with "purge" at the World Trade Center as a protest against capitalism's destruction of the environment. The exhibition includes the re-created sling shot and rocks from that action. (These re-creations are also Duchampian: he was always making replicas of his work.)

Habitat restoration of the waterfront is also referred to in *Gabionne di Marble Venus*, in the foyer of the museum, which creates a classical Venus figure from chicken wire filled with marble, planned as a way to prevent erosion in a city. *Secured Embrace* comprised of what Simpson calls a "breakwater armor unit," a tetrapod, supporting a tree root. The tetrapod becomes a heroic figure trying to prevent erosion, and the piece is a model for a means of both stopping erosion and encouraging healthy tidal life. Simpson's *Tides Out/Tables Set* also refers to pollution. It initially looks like a somewhat elegant table with interesting plates. Actually, he placed these unglazed plates into polluted streams and then baked them, so the "solid waste" became a brown glaze. We are eating off a glaze of our own pollution. (This is also an ironic comment taken from Native historical perspectives on the rich marine life in the Duwamish, sufficient to amply feed them before White men arrived.)

The exhibition includes some of Simpson's "master plans" of which there are many: these plans basically follow the same principles of "poetic utility" but apply them to large scale projects. Collaboration is another major aspect of Simpson's work that runs through his entire career: teamwork with artists, with urban homeless, with the general public.

In many ways, a museum exhibition of Buster Simpson's work inevitably stretches his principles in the wrong direction: toward objects, toward scale, toward permanence. Museums are not adept at capturing ephemeral conditions, urban detritus, simple solutions to water pollution. The museum could have made a messier show. Simpson did tear out a few pieces of the walls, in an effort to counter the formality and impersonality of the spaces, but in the end Simpson still belongs in the street working with castoff materials.

To see a little more of his early work go to "When Buster Lived Next Door," at the Virginia Inn in Belltown, which has archival plans and photographs, and right outside the door are some surviving trees, benches, and tree guards from the early 90s' "First Avenue Project" and the "Urban Arboretum."

Go to Post Alley and see the recreation of his *Solar clothesline* (note the oxymoron), one of those simple and obvious acts to meet a need, save energy, and protest against condominium clothesline restrictions.

In every respect, Simpson is hard to capture as an artist: his work transforms before our eyes from one object to another, from one idea to another; puns and metaphors are rife. Perhaps that is the main characteristic to take away from this Simpson moment in Seattle: disarming

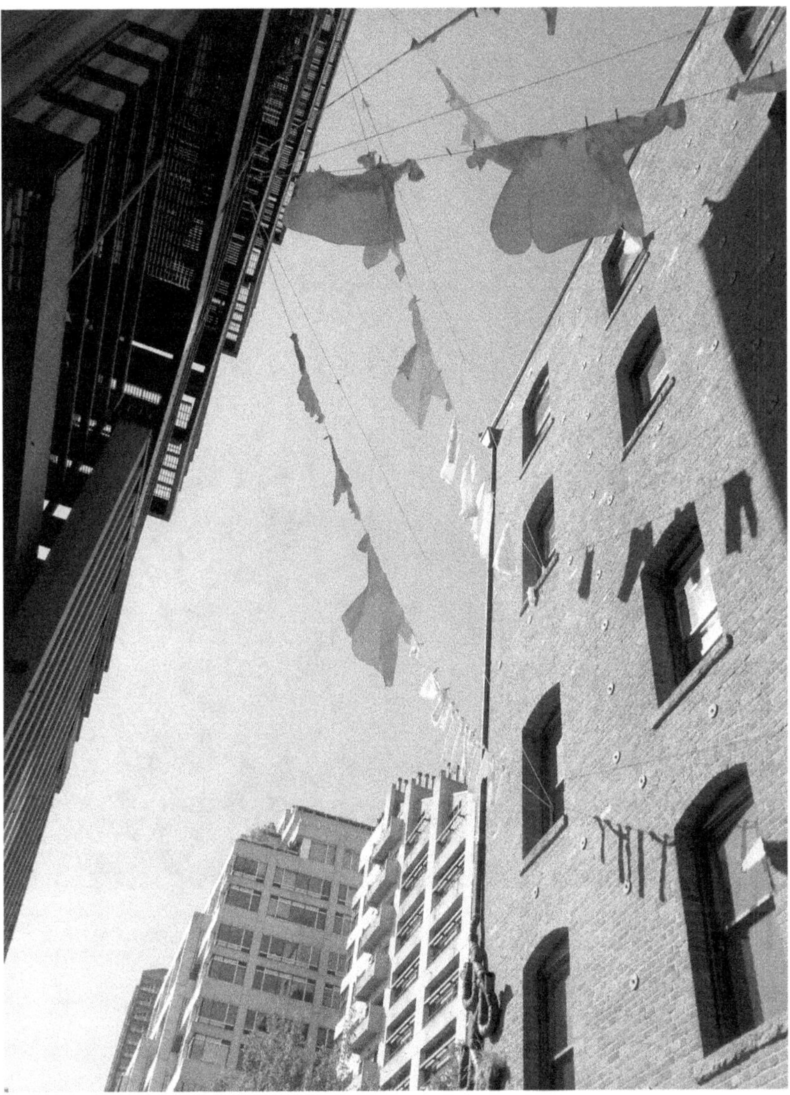

Buster Simpson, *Solar clothesline*, July 2013

humor can win you a place at the table and then you can subversively introduce unacceptable ideas, somewhat like a court jester. Of course, Simpson is never really jesting, and today he is regarded as a major figure in ecological art.

(2013)

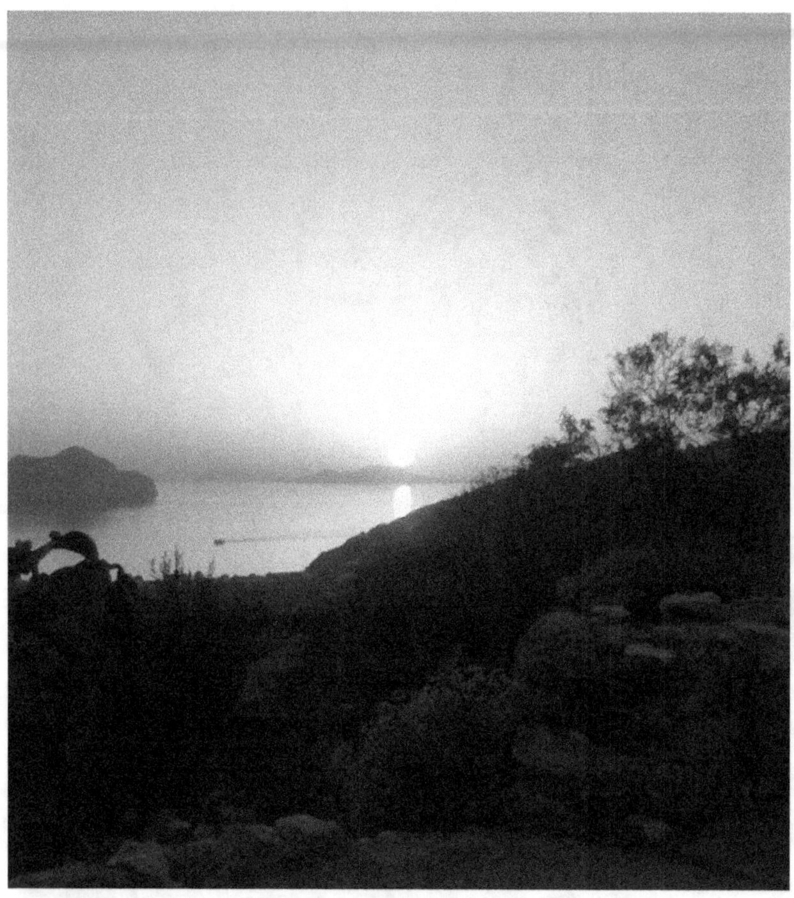

Sunset, Island of Amorgos, Cyclades, Greece

## Conceptualism and Climate Change in Contemporary Greek Art

WHILE PROTESTS WERE RAGING in the streets in Athens, the National Museum of Contemporary Art was holding a retrospective from its permanent collection of cerebral conceptual art since the late 1960s. It was beautifully curated by Anna Kafetsi.

I arrived in Athens after the protests against austerity ended and I had just spent ten days on a remote Greek Island, so I decided it was time for an injection of contemporary art.

At first I thought how can I possibly be interested in this, but then I surrendered to a John Cage work, lay down on the floor for thirty minutes of blissful emptiness listening to his extraordinary composition and watching light and dark patterns changing in the room. I left with a new feeling of receptiveness to conceptual art. The 1992 Cage piece is long, a total of ninety-four minutes, and I heard just one part. *Feature Film One and 103* is a "Film without subject." Cage writes: "*103* is an orchestral work. It is divided into seventeen parts. The lengths of the seventeen parts are the same for all the strings and the percussion. The woodwinds and the brass follow another plan... Following chance operations, the number of wind instruments changes for each of the seventeen parts." At any rate, it was beautiful in its randomness with an underlying sense of classicism.

After observing sunrises and sunsets, experiencing the burning midday sun and the rapid descent of darkness in Greece, I was really tuned into light and dark. Light is really what Greece is about in an aesthetic sense and random is what life is like if we give it a chance.

So then I went back to three early works: Sol LeWitt's *Sentences on Conceptual Art*, 1969, John Baldessari singing LeWitt's sentences to popular tunes, 1972, and Lawrence Weiner's *Declaration of Intent* from 1969. LeWitt's sentences are still resonant today and many artists would benefit from thinking about them. So here are these three "old masters" of conceptual art in the Greek National Museum, as protests against austerity rage in the country.

Let us think about that. These artists were fed up with capitalism, they were looking for the underlying structure and purpose of art outside the physical aesthetic object. The protesters are also fed up with capitalism and its dictates. They want the underlying significance of the state to survive; that is the obvious idea that the government is meant to provide certain basic supports for its citizens. What the conceptual artists and the Greek protesters share is disgust with the corruption of capitalism and its corrosive effect on the spirit.

In his 1969 work, Weiner is really young, bearded, lanky. He is wading into a storm-tossed sea to get random pieces of driftwood (drift logs I should say) that can or cannot be made into a sculpture if desired. It is a lovely open-ended statement—"I don't care about the thing, I care about the act and the act is determined by wind, sea, rain, water, and my own strength or ingenuity in lifting these logs."

Gary Hill was represented with a virtual mini retrospective. One of the most intriguing was *Thomas the Obscure,* based on a 1987 book of that name, in which Hill is telling a story (sort of). Looking at this piece, it was easy to see why he gave up on that direction and turned to the components of video, light, movement, space, sound, and psychological experiences.

The exhibition included many major Greek contemporary artists, for example, there was Bia Davou, with tiny drawings with Greek letters on graph paper called *Serial Structures: Odyssey,* and Chryssa with an amazing *Cycladic book* from 1957. Having just come from the Cyclades, it was easy to connect to this all-white piece.

I particularly enjoyed the 2012 sound and video installation with a surprise ending by Makis Faros. "They Have Departed" suggests a collapse of expectations.

Greek art intersected easily with U.S. conceptual art: sound and light are basic components of both conceptual art, the Greek environment, and Greek art.

The high point of the show for me was the accidental overlap and juxtaposition of two pieces: Bruce Nauman's *Playing A Note on the Violin While I Walk Around the Studio,* from 1967-68, and, so close that his violin could be heard, Danae Stratou's *Ice Songs 2.* Stratou's work caught the sounds of icebergs in the Antarctic forming, colliding, squeezing together, and falling into the open sea. Stratou based the sound on scientists' monitoring of the breakup of Antarctica with water microphones on the seabed of a defunct U.S. naval base. The project began as part of a massive monitoring effort to track Soviet submarines.

Stratou collaborated with Vassilis Koutouris on imagery to accompany the sounds. Changing waves of blue and white projected on the floor of a large gallery provided accents to the changing sounds of the ice bergs. So Nauman's violin note (actually two close together), by an artist rejecting aesthetics and consumption, combined here with an accidental sound "concert" by icebergs cracking up.

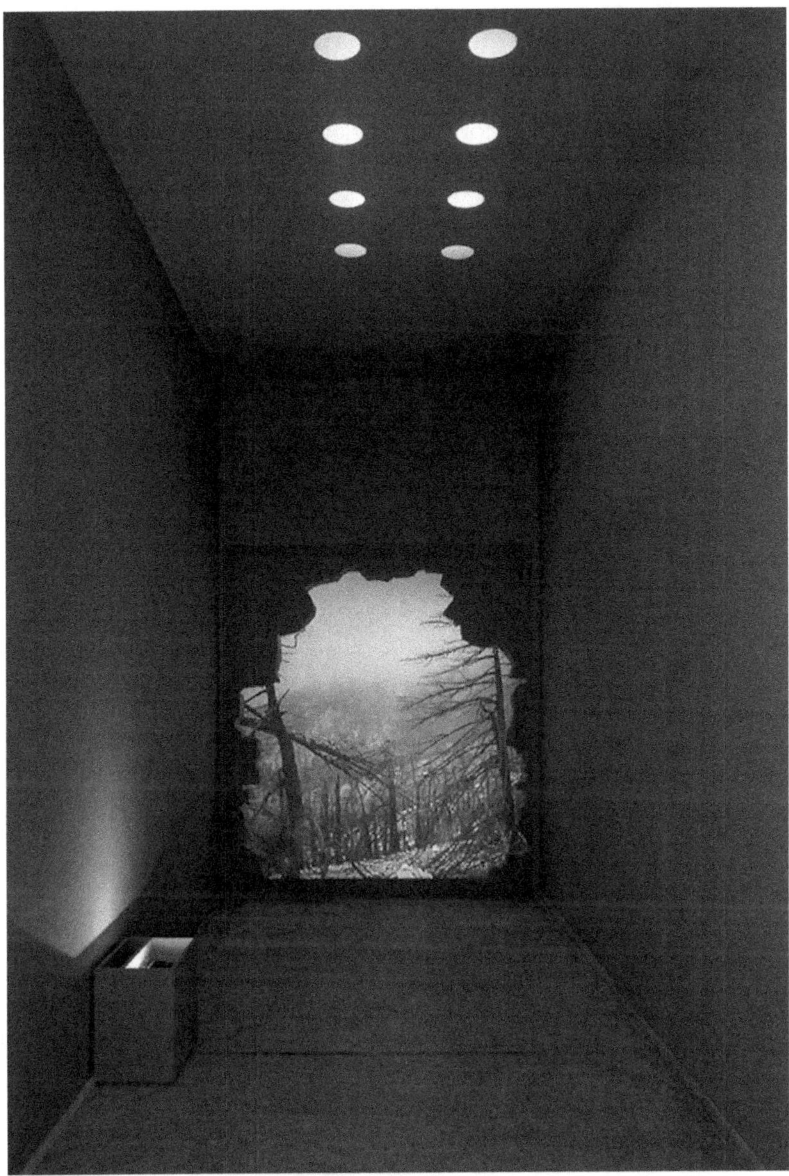

Makis Faros, "They Have Departed," installation detail in "Sonic Time," Museum of Contemporary Art Greece, 2012. "The installation uses the already intense nature of the space. With two video projections, the first on the wall with arc at the top, and the other one on the auditorium ceiling. In both cases small, white lighted circles appear. The atmosphere suggests a neglected temple illuminated by external light—the circles. This atmosphere of calmness will exist for quite some time when suddenly the large wall will break with deafening noise and at the back will appear a deserted landscape This landscape will be darkened to come slowly–slowly at the very first condition."

But in contrast to the 1960s works that sought to escape from the clutter and corruption of the world, *Ice Songs 2* calls attention to the disintegration of the world. Beyond the sound itself, the piece speaks of the invisible and powerful forces at work as our climate warms.

If we don't actually pay attention to these particular random sounds and what they signify, we are looking at an end of the world, a forecast of which we had this week with the Super Storm Sandy, itself a coming together of various powerful forces and fronts. Global climate change is with us. The extraordinary power of nature is going to win the day in the end. That is getting more evident every day. The conceptualist artists definitely had the right idea about rejecting capitalism and the "art" world and embracing nature on its own terms.

(2013)

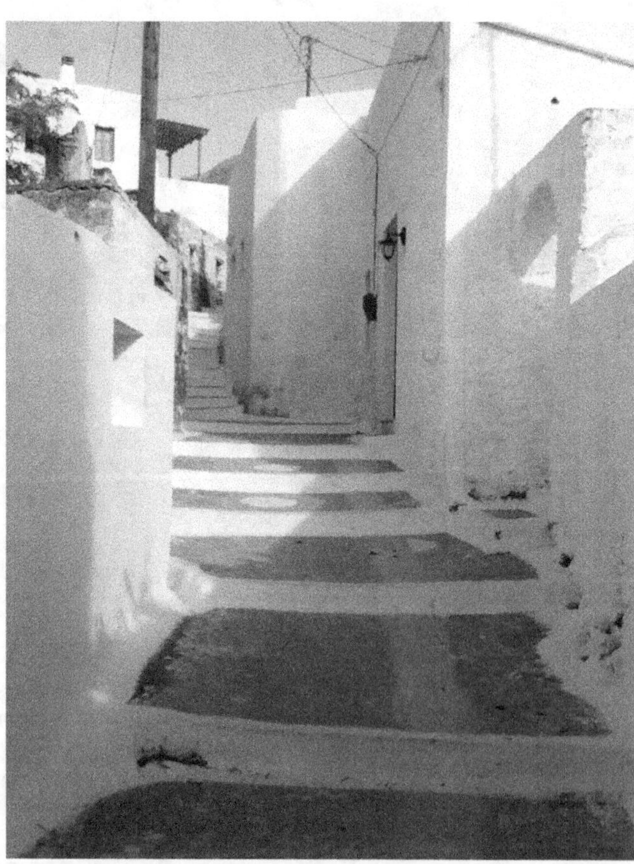

Street in the town of Langada, Amorgos, Cyclades, Greece

# Constellations on a Cycladic Island

*ASTERISMOS,* THE CREATIVE ARTISTIC FESTIVAL on the Aegean island of Amorgos, is in its fourth year, organized by a group of ten volunteers who live on Amorgos, two of them originally from the island. Amorgos is one of the Cyclades. Its more famous islands are Mykonos, Santorini, Naxos, Paros and Syros. Amorgos is less well known partly because it has no airport. You have to take a ferry there (eight hours from Athens, three hours from Naxos).

The festival celebrates the island and its amazing out-of-the-way villages, churches, and landscapes. The island is rugged, formed of hard metamorphic and volcanic rock. It used to have forests and a lot more terraced hillsides. Today it has goats, donkeys, mules, olive trees, wild herbs (we always come back with oregano and sage,) and religious festivals. There are some beaches, great hiking, and good food. You can do yoga at Iris Studio by the beach, you can get acupuncture and herbal tea from Vangelis in Langada. But, above all, it is a beautiful friendly island with amazing landscapes, houses, rustic churches and stunning villages without any cars. There is one road for cars from one end of the island to the other.

According to the organizers, the idea of the festival celebrates:

A diverse, beautiful place bursting with history and emotion. A circle of friends loving and living on an Aegean island. This is Amorgos, and this is us. For the past three years talented artists from all over Greece have showcased their creative work, honoring us and our guests with their presence, and bringing life to the island. Our goal for the 4th year of the festival is to encourage more artists to participate.

All performances take place next to ancient monuments, surrounded by landscapes of rare natural beauty without any complex stage settings.

No one involved in *Asterismos* is profiting financially in any way. Everything in this festival is created and offered out of love for the arts and the island. From Wednesday June 15 to Sunday July 3, they had events all over the island. We saw three events while we were there.

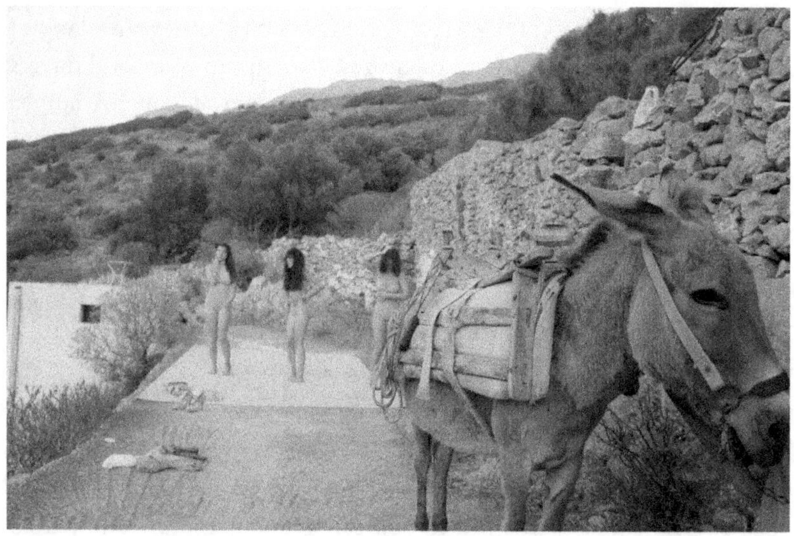

*Asterimos:* SaGyni Dance Theater by Fizz Dance group

SaGyni Dance Theater by Fizz Dance group took place in the last rays of the sun on a path to the famous Church of the Panagia Epanocholini. The path was just wide enough to provide a space for performing. The group began with a dance that for me evoked a connection to the most archaic kore and goddesses.

Amorgos is famous for the largest Cycladic figure ever found, which is now in the Archeological Museum in Athens. As these woman danced in their nude stocking costumes they appeared to be part of the earth, joined to a mythic past. They were like the kore of the archaic era coming to life.

The three dancers evoked contemporary feminist issues such as a scene of seduction between two women or a competition among three women. They were sometimes accompanied by recitations in Greek, so I couldn't understand the words, but I could sense musings on the theme of women.

The connection of the landscape and the dance/theater was perfect, they blended gently with the setting of the ancient stone walls, reddish bushes, and soft pink flowers, the setting sun, the cooling wind.

Then up the path came a man with his donkey! In Amorgos, donkeys are still very much the only transportation once away from the single paved road. They are working donkeys that help to carry an incredible variety of loads.

The Greek farmer leading the donkey could not pass, as we were seated on steps and blocked the road. He stayed and watched, although the donkey showed no interest and went to sleep.

It was a thrilling partnership to the avant-garde artistic performance, two worlds, two lives, respecting each other, and part of the spirit of the Constellations festival on the island.

The next night we went to a performance for children called "Concerto for Double Bass and Wolves." A dramatized narration by Mary Terzaki with Dimitris Sandalis on the bass cello, the Concerto retold fairy tales with wolves, recasting the wolf as a hero instead of as a scary character. At the end all of the children got up and danced along with Mary as they exchanged masks.

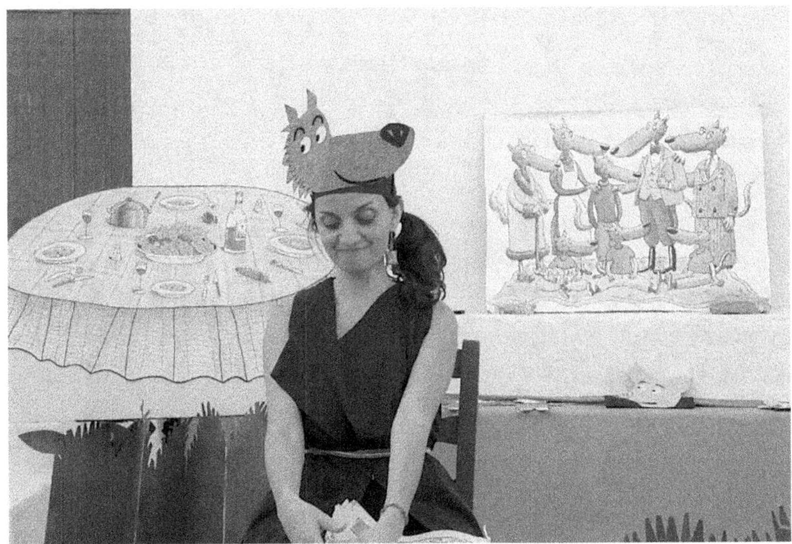

*Asterimos:* Concerto for Double Bass and Wolves, Mary Terzaki and Dimitris Sandalis

The last event that we went to was the theater performance, "It's been a year," by the Eos theater group from Athens.

"It was performed by seven actors at twilight on the top of a hill crowned by the famous Panagia church of Amorgos. The acting was so good that I could sense what was happening even without understanding what they were saying. The story is told through the eyes of a young man, exploring his family home and thinking about his ancestors at different times in twentieth century Greek history: World War I, Greco-Turkish Conflict early 1920s, World War II, the Civil War of the 1940s, the Dictatorship of 1967 – 1974, the 1980s economic crisis, and finally the contemporary world.

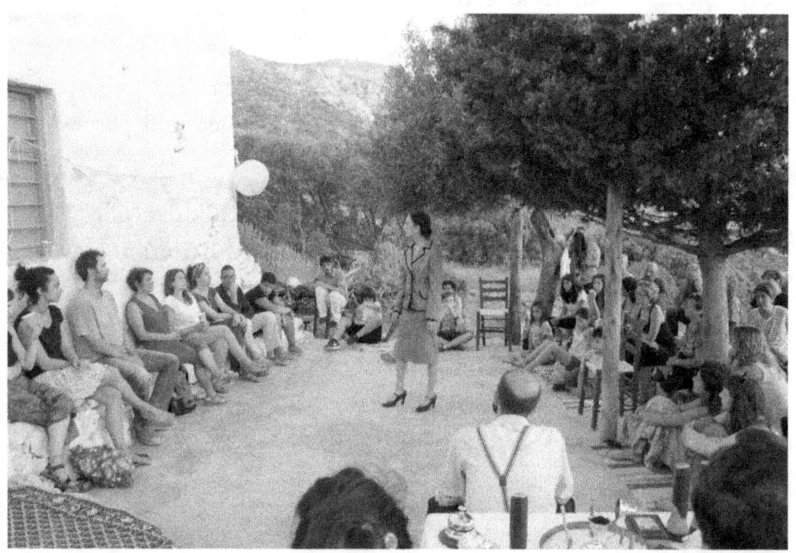

*Asterimos:* Eos Theater group, "It's Been a Year," Chap 1, Thalis Politis (First World War 1914 – 1918)

The Eos theater group is special. It emphasizes engagement with the audience. As they describe themselves "EOS was founded in 2012 with the vision for an accessible expression and research in all forms of art, culture and social affairs. EOS runs several theatre training programs for young people, including programs for the training of young immigrant children . . . ."

(2016)

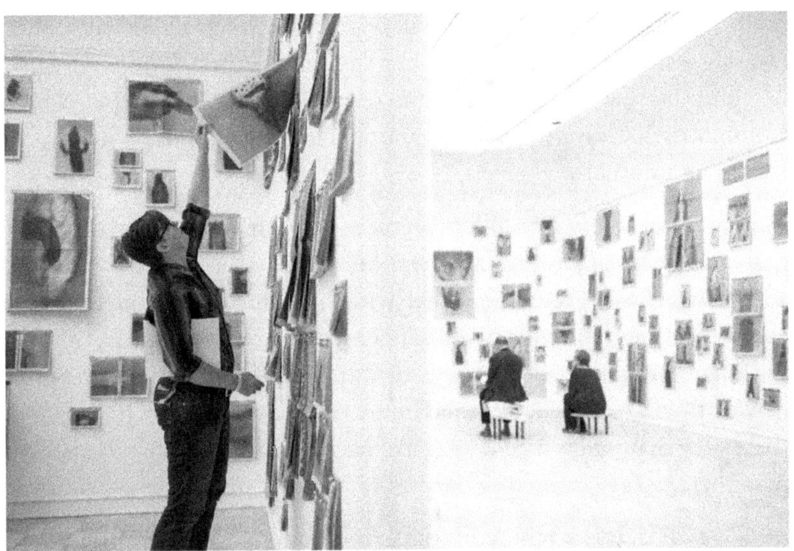

Ann Hamilton, *the common S E N S E,* installation view. 2014-2015, commissioned by the Henry Art Gallery, University of Washington, Seattle. Photograph: Jonathan Vanderweit

# Common Sense Can Save Our Planet: Ann Hamilton

I LIKE THE MULTIPLE PUNS IN the title of this exhibition. "The Common SENSE" is a term we use for what works on the most basic level. It helps us through a lot of situations that might otherwise be difficult. (We should, in fact, think of it more often these days, when everything seems so convoluted.) Another meaning is suggested by capitalizing SENSE. Ann Hamilton is fascinated by our senses: this exhibition emphasizes the sense of touch, but seeing and hearing are part of that idea for Hamilton.

A third meaning is that everything on the planet shares the common sense of touch. According to Jainism, the world is divided by the number of senses we have. The only sense that every class of life on the planet has is touch, some have only that (the pay-off is that some one-sensed vegetable bodies, like the turnip, have numerous souls). One might say that touch is what we will be left with when all else fails. That idea suggests another reference (not a pun) in this title. Common sense is telling us that climate change is deeply altering life on the planet. Common sense says we must change. The exhibition leads us to this idea in an unusual way.

In each gallery a shelf has been set up with pairs of metal prongs that hold stacks of a single passage of text on newsprint. We could read, and, if we chose, even take a text with us. During the course of the exhibition, then, the texts will disappear (they are taken from a Tumblr site where we can all add passages that are selected for inclusion). Some new texts will be added, but even in my two visits separated by ten days, there were many gaps where texts had been before. Gaps: that is another point here.

We are actively removing the exhibition content, the opposite of the usual museum visit, when we are allowed only to look, never to touch, and certainly not to take away the work. But here, the artworks are these texts on newsprint. They have no value except as an exchange of ideas. Although they are supposed to be on the theme of touch, I found most of them spoke of seeing, writing, creating. We can say that our creative lives are dependent on the primal touch: we touch the keyboard, poetry touches our ears, a play touches our eyes, and there is the touch of emotion on our hearts.

In the first gallery we immerse ourselves in brief passages from well known writers, like Elizabeth Bishop or John Berger or T.S. Eliot and, oddly, "Cock Robin" children's books. In the same gallery is a case full of scissors and copies of "commonplace" books, an accumulation of favorite texts copied down together.

We are invited to make our own "commonplace book" with the texts in the gallery and place them in a folder labelled "A Common Place" that we were given as we entered. Since I love to read, that seems like a great idea. There is a bit of a readymade quality, compared to actually copying quotes, the texts are readymade, preselected, and typed. But they are resonant quotes. And the pleasure of reading them is partly from the need to slow our pace, and think about what they say. We cannot rush through this space. That is one of Hamilton's trademarks: expanding time and space in a meditative way.

But suddenly the exhibition changes its direction as we turn the corner into the next set of galleries. First, we see dead animals in cases. We recoil and wonder why they are here. We had warning (the story of the murder of Cock Robin), but we didn't know it, until it was too late. But more copies of children's books with the story of Cock Robin's murder and funeral await us across the hall.

Then comes another shock: almost unbearably the next four large galleries have eerie, blurry images of dead birds and small mammals. They are reproduced as multiple copies: the dead creatures were laid on a flatbed scanner (we don't know that right away), printed on newsprint and then hung in stacks on the wall. Apparently, only the parts that touched the scanner are sharp (the claws, the heads).

What are they? Why are they there? I am invited to "take" an image. I can't make myself take anything. It is too horrifying to take an image of a dead bird. So the gallery facilitator rips one off and hands it to me. I feel sick to my stomach. As I pass the blurry photographs of dead birds and animals (dead at the hands of scientists who preserved them and studied them, I learn later) I feel increasingly oppressed. At first they are like shadows, then it is death captured in a copy, hanging on a wall.

Then, it comes to me. Of course, this is about extinctions, climate change, what we are doing to the planet. Our acts of early classification and taxidermy, our urge to extract species from their natural life cycle and habitat and categorize them, has led inexorably to our present accelerated slaughter of the planet. We are just killing on a larger and larger scale with each new extraction, by fracking, mountaintop removal, tar sands, as well as climate change itself which is altering the seas, the seasons, the cycles of life from the microscopic to the huge. For example, pine bark beetles have longer breeding seasons in warmer winters and are killing many more trees now.

In one gallery a young woman reads from a book. It is *The Peregrine* by J. A. Baker. She reads a passage and then copies it into a notebook. In another gallery, a young man sings a dirge, "We remember the elephant, we remember the polar bear, we remember the camel, we remember the shrew, we remember the armadillo, we remember the leopard, etc."

Downstairs we go to the next gallery which is filled with large, old-fashioned glass museum cases, all enveloped in curtains. When we open the curtain, we see a new set of specimens, not animals or birds, but fur coats, animal skin clothes, various examples from the Burke and Henry collections, each with a tag that identifies the donor. (Can you imagine donating your fox skin wrap to a museum today?)

After the claustrophobia of the specimens in cases, the final very large gallery opens up into an entirely different sensory experience. On one wall are the familiar shelves with texts, but filling the space are what appeared to be wind-operated fans; initially, I thought it was a reference to the millions of birds killed by wind power (perhaps it was indirectly). Scattered around on the floor are stools.

On closer inspection, though, the "fans" were complex devices: the artist identified them as "bull roarers," traditionally a simple shape with a string attached to it, that is swung around the head to make a vibrato sound that can be heard over great distances. Ann Hamilton's idea here appears to be to gather us together on the stools in this gallery to listen to the sound and meditate on it as well as the state of the world. But I am not sure of that. These bull roarers are extremely complicated in their design, one side is a blade, the other is a constructed device that makes a sound as it moves up the pole by friction and down the pole by gravity (like a breathing cycle the artist explained). They have little relationship to the simplicity of historical bull roarers (which we usually identify as part of a sacred indigenous ritual such as burial, perhaps another reference the artist had in mind). The exhibition needed a sense of resolution, but I think the mechanical "bull roarers" did not create a space for spiritual gathering.

In spite of my reservation about the last gallery, "the common SENSE" exhibition by Ann Hamilton at the Henry Art Gallery is a landmark event. First, the artist created unusual networks on the University of Washington Campus by reaching out to the Burke Museum, the Special Collections at the Library, and even the choral music program. Second, she invited our participation, in both the removal of texts from the exhibition to start our own "Commonplace Book" and the addition of texts at the Tumblr site (readers-reading-readers.tumblr. com), as well as, if we chose to, reading in the gallery.

Finally, at the exit of the exhibition, we are invited to have our own photograph taken behind a white screen, with only our shoulder touching. We become specimens like the birds in the galleries, except of course, we are not dead, and can walk out of the building.

But perhaps as we walk out, we bring with us a new common sense of the results of the actions of humans with five senses on the planet, and the responsibility we bear to make sure that the planet will continue to survive. We cannot continue in the line that Ann Hamilton has drawn from the medieval murder story of Cock Robin to the present rapid rate of extinctions. Ann Hamilton has embraced the present state of the planet and our responsibility for it in this emotionally complex exhibition.

(2014)

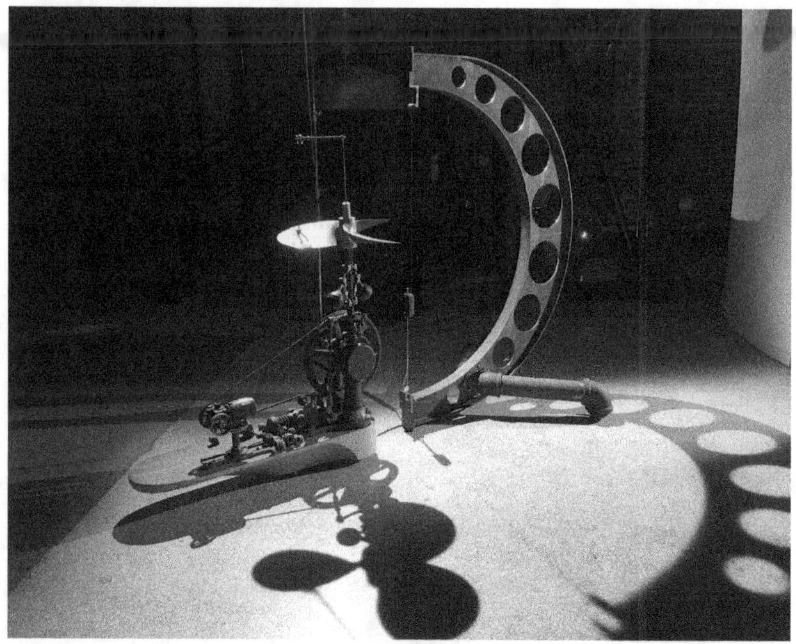

Amie McNeel, Mark Zirpel and Sam Stubblefield, "Portfolio of Possibilities," Caliper with amplified string and propeller apparatus, at MadArt, Seattle, 2016, Courtesy of the artists

# A Cautionary Tale of Nature's Forces: Amie McNeel, Mark Zirpel and Sam Stubblefield

MAD ART STUDIO SPONSORS ARTISTS to imagine and create work in a massive 4000-square-foot space with 23-foot high ceilings. Founder Allison Milliman wants to demystify the process of creating art and bring it into the community. The artists work in full view of the street through large sliding glass doors that encourage obsessed techies (this is the Amazon zone of Seattle), and other members of the public, to observe or participate in the artistic process.

Never has the MadArt mission been more realized than in the "Portfolio of Possibilities," a collaborative installation created by Amie McNeel, Mark Zirpel (both multimedia sculptors) and Sam Stubblefield (a technology architect).

Amie McNeel has a background in marine science and Mark Zirpel is fascinated by celestial science and astronomy. Stubblefield connects us to these realms through computer programs that tap into various surprising locations in cyberspace.

The artists describe "Portfolio of Possibilities" as revealing phenomena such as motion, gravity, sound, resonance, momentum, rotation, currents, and turbulence. To do that, they experimented with objects such as old buoys, ropes, inner tubes, anvils, propellers—to make them shake, glow, rotate, and sing in playful disharmony. They blew up the scale of small tools, such as calipers and magnets. They disrupted expectations at every opportunity. For six months, they dreamed, played, failed, discarded and rethought.

Outside the gallery, an oddball mound of intertwined inner tubes, programmed to connect to a bus app, vibrated when a streetcar approached the stop. Just inside the entrance a thick rope unwound itself as it rose up, then mysteriously descended into an unruly pile on the floor. Unexpected movements of familiar materials characterized the entire exhibition. Nothing was left as a traditional sculpture to simply view. Instead, as the pieces moved, as we moved, as laser lights flashed, shadows appeared and disappeared, and we were constantly caught off guard.

A weather balloon whimsically inflated according to when the international space station passed over particular locations. Near the end of the show, someone accidentally popped it, it hung inert, like a giant used condom. The artists embraced the deflation and did not replace the balloon.

Rocking an oversized magnet back and forth triggered the eerie sound of a humpback whale. Audio signals, the last mating call of the Kaua'i 'ō'ō, an extinct bird from Hawai'i, paired with NASA's Voyager 1 robotic probe, slowly turned a suspended oil pipeline cap. A giant caliper, strung with a single wire, played a note as a propeller rotated, sending a mechanical device to pluck the single string When we entered a windowless room with no way out (sensory deprivation chamber), we heard the sound of our own beating heart. A laser reflected off a water-filled, oversized glass fishing lure, creating light patterns that evoked anything from brain patterns to bone marrow.

A giant top, suspended from the ceiling, spiraled at a crazy angle as it cast mesmerizing shadows on the walls. Made of steel band tracks that held ball bearings, the top was triggered by wave height data from NOAA; as the balls rolled around and around, they created a rhythmic sound like ocean waves breaking on the shore.

Glowing on a large screen in the depths of the chaos, green laser patterns translated the sound of a ringing bell (another oil pipeline cap) by means of transducers (a way to convert a physical quality into electrical impulses) in a hidden pool of water.

As the artists improvised, dynamic representations of invisible forces emerged. They became like musicians conducting new instruments that played themselves, animated by digital data from cyberspace. They connected to our bodies, our lives, our movements, and our feelings. We felt surprise, exhilaration, anxiety, and joy amidst these mysterious, pulsing, glowing objects that conversed with one another and with us. But, finally, as demonstrations of the beautiful complexity and fragility of the planet we live on, "Portfolio of Possibilities," became a cautionary tale. If we are to have a future, we must acknowledge and respect these powerful forces.

(2017)

# Orcas: An Ongoing Tragedy

WE CRIED EVERY DAY AS WE FOLLOWED the tragedy of the Orca mother Tahlequah holding her dead baby for seventeen days. The pod she belongs to has not had a successful birth in several years, and this baby died almost immediately after it was born.

The resident population of this Southern Resident pod is dying for lack of Chinook Salmon. It consists of only seventy-five whales. They are also disrupted by vessel noise (especially cruise ships) and toxins. Solutions are quieting vessel noise, less development in habitat, and breaching the lower Snake River Dam. It is a huge job that requires going beyond token gestures, like not eating Chinook Salmon.

Writer Katie Herzog outlines the pollution problem and the urgency of supporting the superfund clean-up of the Duwamish which is, of course, being rolled back by the current administration. Read her article from the Stranger "slog" online: "To Save the Orcas, We Must Clean up the Duwamish." (Aug 24, 2018)

The Lummi tribe consider the Orcas as family members. They refer to them as "qwel ihol mech ten" or "The People that live under the water."

Before this summer of grief, the Lummi carved a totem dedicated to Tokitae (Sk'aliCh'elh-tenaut), the last survivor of a horrendous capture of baby orcas in 1970, when a third of the population of this same pod of Southern Resident orcas were taken by aquariums for display. Three died during the capture. Tokitae is at the Miami Seaquarium.

She is known as Lolita there and lives in an illegally small tank where she performs tricks for audiences. The aquarium has refused to allow Tokitae to return to her family in the Northwest. When the Lummi' totem reached Miami, ceremonies were held outside the aquarium, but no one was allowed to come in.

At the same time, the Lummi are collaborating with the National Oceanic and Atmospheric Administration (NOAA) to try to feed a wild orca in the same Southern Resident pod, who is starving to death. This is a risky and unprecedented operation, as orcas are extremely intelligent, and could refuse food. The analysis is that she may have worms or an infection of some kind that is preventing her from eating.

Orcas eat about 420 pounds of Chinook Salmon per day.

These magnificent mammals are incredibly bright. During the capture of babies in the 1970s, one of the witnesses spoke of the gathering of the pod around the capture site, their obvious grieving at the loss of their babies, and their loud crying. Once the babies had been removed in a truck, the rest of the pod left the area, never to return.

Does this not sound familiar, as children are ripped from their parents and sent off to captivity? Although no longer in the news, the children are *still* being detained.

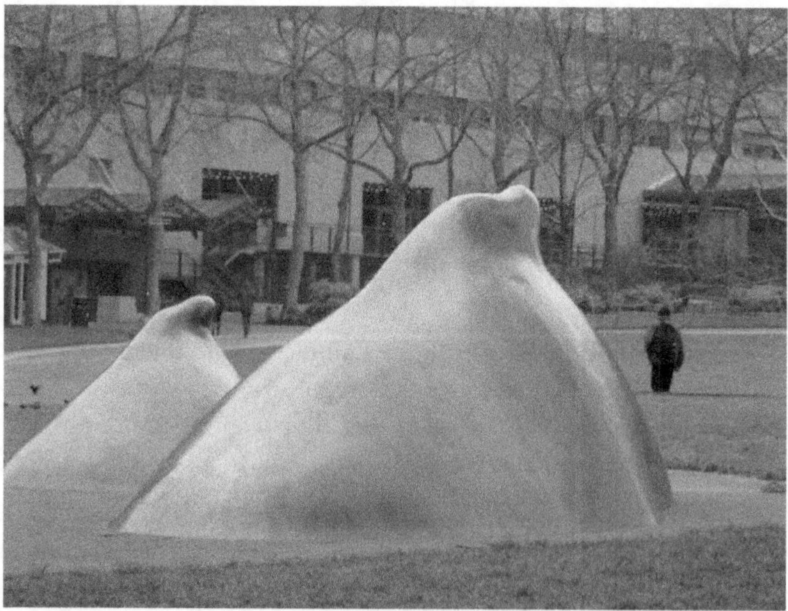

Gloria Bornstein, *Neototems,* Seattle Center, public sculpture, 1995, bronze. "The pod design was based in a nearly forgotten Salish Indian legend of whales swimming from Lake Union to Elliott Bay beneath the Seattle Center."

I want to end with Gloria Bornstein's beautiful *Neototems,* a whale pod in bronze, a public artwork at Seattle Center. We need a lot more beautiful art like this that celebrates these special creatures.

I also acknowledge the incredible reporting by Lynda V. Mapes at *The Seattle Times* on this summer of grief and crisis with our Southern Resident orca pod. (Note: Lynda Mapes has just published an expansion of her articles in the book *Orca,* (Braided River and *Seattle Times,* 2021)

(2018)

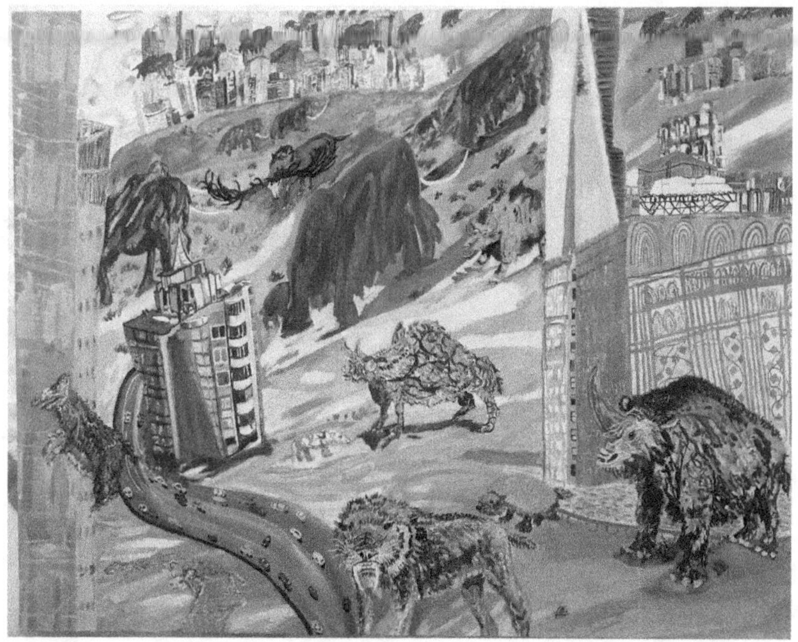

Olive Ayhens, *Critters and the Cathedral*, 2019, oil on linen, 37x49" "All the animals are the extinct ancient mammals. They were in North America before humans."

## Olive Ayhens: Urbanities and Ur-Beasts

OLIVE AYHENS' VIRTUOSO PAINTINGS in watercolor and oil could not be more embedded in our present moment of climate crisis. Yet, the theme of the collision of nature and humans, of the beauty of nature and our power to extinguish it, has been the main focus of Ayhens' work for many decades.

Her love of drawing and color drives Ayhens to include minute details of architecture or landscape in each work. In *From Lori's Window,* painted from a bird's-eye perspective, nature is almost entirely crowded out. At the same time, the artist's acute awareness of the delicate balance of life and death means that nothing is stable or permanent, all is shaking at its foundations, soon to topple. How ironic that the artist had a residency in the World Trade Center, and painted from that elevated viewpoint, represented here by the small watercolor *Slice of Manhattan,* 2000, before it all came down.

Nature invades. Trees and water flow through urban structures and down roads. *Dumbo Dreams*, 2018, based on the view from the artist's studio, shows us the East River and the Brooklyn Bridge from high above the middle of the river. But look again. Nothing is calm here, the floods are rising. In *Downstairs Deluge*, the water fills the hollow frame of a skyscraper, trees invade the lower floors. In *Oceans Rising*, 2017, the sea storms into the city with dramatic, energized waves. *Interior Wilderness,* 2008, comes closer with structures collapsing as rivers flow through them.

But she also gives us the opposite, nature crushed by our structures. In *Hyper Urban*, 2017, nature has almost vanished between intersections, ramps and multiple layers of highways. Another variation is *Flyway Intersection*, 2019, painted in Bavaria as suggested by the intense colors. Here the birds sitting in the pond in the foreground gather together to observe the gaudy urban frenzy, an example of Ayhens' humor.

Ayhens revels in playing with interior/exterior ambiguities as in *Grand Central Inside/Outside,* 2012. We see the amazing constellations painted on the ceiling of the station become actual sky next to the Chrysler building, as traffic flows through the middle of this grand building which the artist clearly enjoyed painting.

Another ongoing theme is her fascination with what the artist calls Ur-beasts—already extinct mammals who roam the earth again. She often combines actual mammals with imaginary details (Ayhens rarely confines herself to simple observation or description, although her ability to do that is staggering). In *Camelid in the City* a mammal extinct for 4.9 million years stands on the edge of the (newly rebuilt) rocky embankment in DUMBO (Down Under Manhattan Bridge Overpass) in New York City and gazes at the turbulent bright green water of the river. In this work, the mammal and the painted rocks and river dominate the work, and the urban landscape is moved to the background. In her recently finished work, the Ur-beasts invade the city itself.

Originally from California, Ayhens moved to New York City in 1996 with a Marie Walsh Sharpe Fellowship that provided studio space. Since then, Ayhens has been awarded a Guggenheim Fellowship, as well as many other awards and residencies that have enabled her to continue to explore many landscapes. They include the scrub desert of Roswell, New Mexico (*Outskirts of Roswell,* 2014), the dry desert of Malta (*Deep Time Malta*, 2009), the prehistoric menhirs in Carnac, France (*Carnac,* 2010), and, most recently, the lush swamps of Florida (*Polluted Swamp,* 2018). But her work follows a consistent theme of both the absurdity and tragedy of our intersections with nature, seen as early as 1992 in *Nature's Sanctuary,* with its power plants and swimming pool, against the background of a dramatic Northwest landscape. A single extinct bird and two amphibians cling to the bank in the foreground.

Some of the earlier works are classics: *Computer Lab,* 2006, the lab of her longtime friend Joe Doyle, immerses us in the tangle of wires of an entire tech world as a living organism. *Amphibian Emergency,* 2009, depicts frogs trapped inside a glass skyscraper. Frogs were already on the endangered species list in 2009, and Ayhens suggests a frightening life for these habitat-deprived amphibians. Outside the window is the wasteland of urban living. As habitat is destroyed, we hear every day of vanishing trees, species, insects, birds, animals. We recently learned that there are more birds in cages in Indonesia, than in the wild.

Olive Ayhens deeply feels the contradiction of our ability to both create and destroy, to build extraordinary structures, and to kill one another. In some of her works that contradiction is clearly depicted, as in *Lamb,* 2006, in which the coffins of the war dead appear in the midst of a luxurious rooftop garden. The lamb reclines almost invisibly on a sofa in the foreground, clearly referencing the sacrificial lamb of biblical traditions.

Ayhens seduces us with line, color, texture, but through wild shifts in scale and perspective, she conveys her deep distress with the current condition of the world. Although she has pursued this vision her entire career, her work is absolutely of our present moment. Her fantasies have become realities in the age of global warming.

(2019)

# 4 Indigenous Resistances

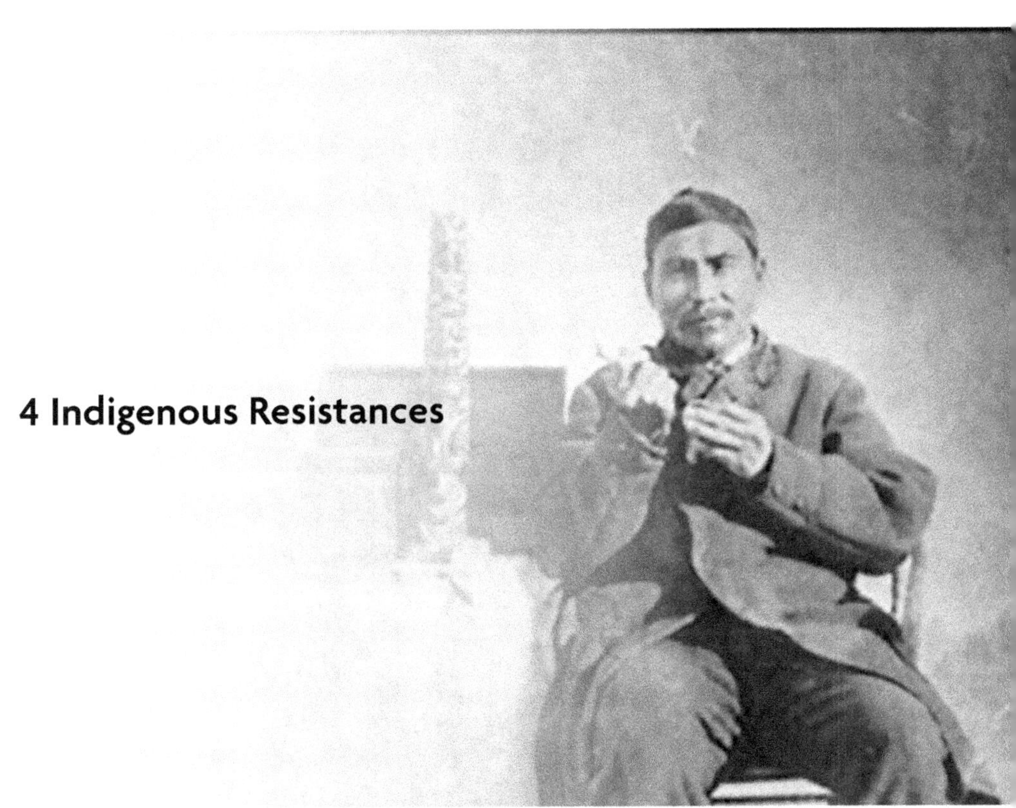

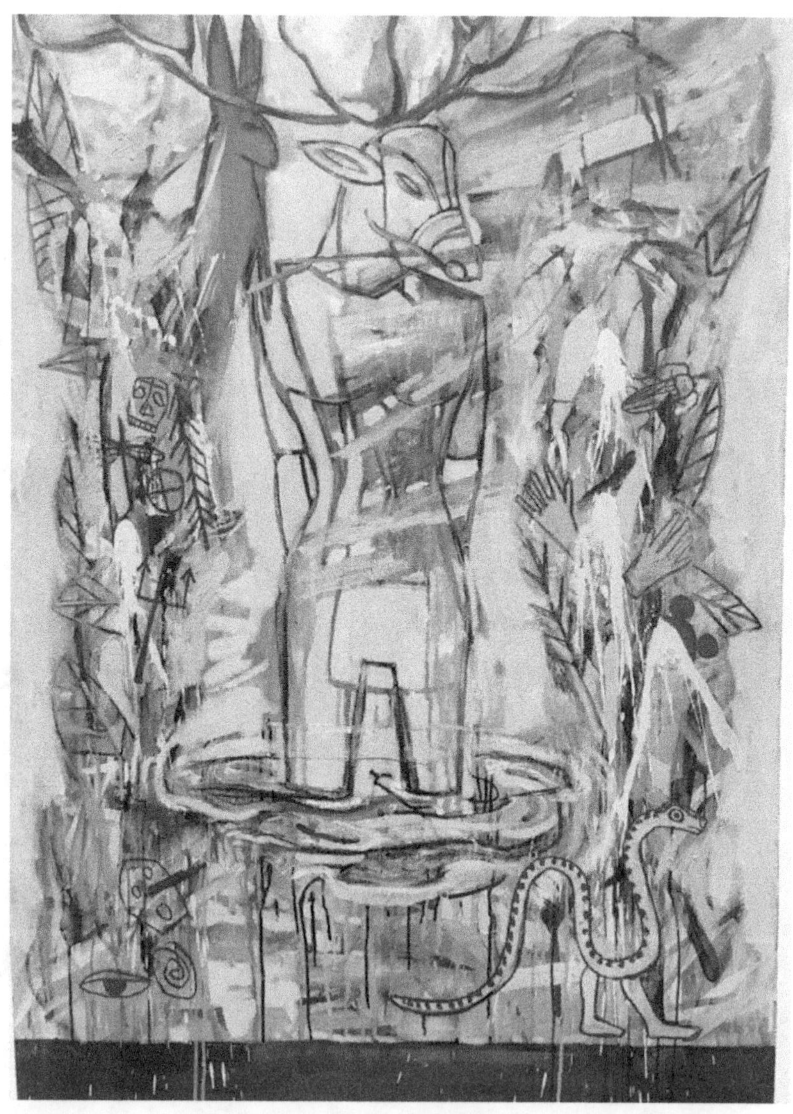

Jaune Quick-to-See Smith (Citizen of Confederated Salish and Kootenai Nation, Montana), *The Swamp*, 2015, oil on canvas, 60 x 40", Courtesy of Jaune Quick-to-See Smith and Garth Greenan Gallery, NYC.

# Jaune Quick-to-See Smith and N. Scott Momaday: Devastation and Survival

"Jaune Quick-to-See Smith: In the Footsteps of my Ancestors," at the Tacoma Art Museum, confronts us immediately with her deep connection to the natural world and what we are doing to it as colonial extractors.

*The Swamp*, 2015, puts the current crisis right in our face in both the styles of White modernism and Native abstractions. The artwork is described as follows:

> A figure both human and animal stands in a swamp, wreathed by symbols of the vivid life one finds in swamps. Humans and animals are caught up in the stew of action, just as none escapes thoughtless decisions that poison the air and water that everyone needs. This painting acknowledges the importance of swamps within our ecosystems, their cleansing waters, and their rich habitat.

In the central figure, Smith stated that she "created an elk anthropomorphic female figure, converted from a male elk love medicine." As we look at it, we feel ever more deeply entangled and disoriented. The central figure is standing knee deep in a pond that looks like a stew. The most distinct creature is a walking snake, in the lower right, that seems to be walking away from the devastation. Embedded in the hot yellows and reds are fragments of masks, feathers, a pair of hands, an "Indian" stereotype profile, yellow face with a single feather headdress. Oops there are the ears of Mickey Mouse (an obvious reference to Disney, here standing in for corporate takeovers)! In the upper left a majestic trickster rabbit (named Nanabozho) oversees the entire disaster.

According to Gail Tremblay's catalog essay, "Nanabozho was sent to earth by Gitche Manitou who assigned him to name all the plants and animals and to create a system of mnemonic mark-making that would help humans remember the order of things in ceremonies and stories."

We feel the spilling of blood, the disruption of the sun, the pallid blue background indicating a vast space on which we have laid spoil to the planet. We can also see the devastation wreaked on Native tribes on this continent in the last 500 years embodied in the paint strokes and the cascading images. Linear outlines suggest pictographs, but not literally, more invented—there is a Mexican mask, a bomb.

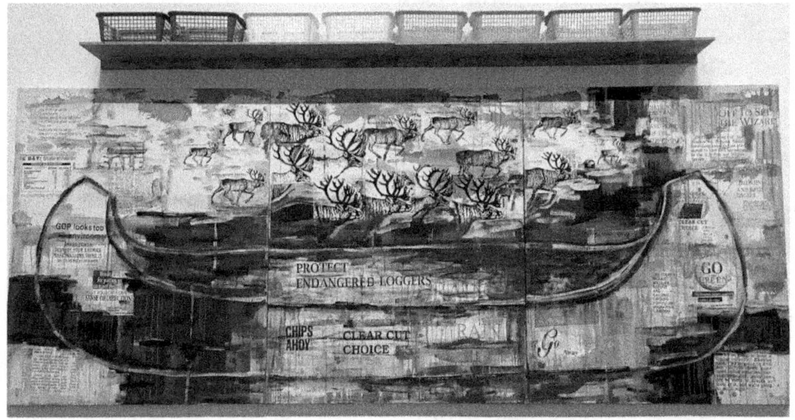


Jaune Quick-to-See Smith (Citizen of Confederated Salish and Kootenai Nation, Montana), *Tongass Trade Canoe*, 1996 triptych, mixed media on canvas, 60 x 150, " Courtesy of Jaune Quick-to-See Smith and Garth Greenan Gallery, NYC

And that is only one painting!

The *Tongass Trade Canoe* is an astounding ecological statement from 1996, and chillingly pertinent to our present catastrophe. It refers to the Tongass National Forest in Alaska, the calving ground for many caribou. You see the caribou marching across the top of the painting. The plastic laundry baskets suggest the trivial products that come from the destruction of the natural environment.

According to the Southeast Alaska Conservation Council

> The Tongass contains nearly one-third of the old-growth temperate rain forest remaining in the world, as well as the largest tracts of old-growth forest left in the United States.

Old-growth temperate rain forests hold more biomass (living stuff) per acre than any other type of ecosystem on the planet, including tropical jungles. The Tongass alone holds 8 percent of all carbon stored in U.S. national forests and is recognized as a globally significant carbon storage reserve.

Surrounding the huge canoe image are references to the devastation being wrought on the environment as a result of greed, exactly our problem today. This huge painting was completed more than twenty years ago.

But there is also humor: "Protect Endangered Loggers," "Chips Ahoy," "Grizzlies and Bald Eagles, Goodbye Clutter," "Clear Cut Choice" (as of 2020 the Tongass is once again under threat of development).

I wrote about Jaune Quick-to-See Smith in my book *Art and Politics Now,* in the ecological chapter which addresses the huge difference of "enlightenment" White European attitudes to nature—that it is separate (and inferior)—and the Indigenous perspective that we are all part of nature. In my book I illustrated "Fear," also in the Tacoma exhibition, a powerful anti-war work, where her excruciating images of war overwhelm us with their detail and specificity.

The U.S. tried very hard to obliterate the Native point of view, the Native peoples, the Native cultures of this country. Thank goodness we White people failed in that endeavor, and we may have only their perspective to save us now.

## Words from a Bear

In the movie recently screened at the Seattle Public Library, *Words from a Bear*, about writer N. Scott Momaday, we were once again confronted with the ongoing strength of the Native American message of our embeddedness in the land, in nature. We learned about the U.S. efforts at genocide: slaughter of buffalo and horses, the banning of religion, especially the Sun Dance, forced marches to reservations far from familiar lands, boarding schools—the effort to make Native children White by removing them at the age of four from their families; allotments which broke up tribal territories. Then, after World War II, there was urbanization which again isolated Natives from their culture and families, and on and on.

But Momaday was lucky. He did not go to a boarding school; his parents were storytellers and writers and painters and teachers; he got a full scholarship to Stanford and received a Ph.D. in 1963. In 1969, he won the Pulitzer Prize for his book *House Made of Dawn.* This astonished him and thrilled the entire Indigenous community. One writer declared that we moved "beyond the ethnographic past."

The main theme of the movie, though, is that he "invested himself in his landscape." He stated, "I am who I am because of the land." His voice is crucial in today's world as we are increasingly alienated from nature. He says we cannot separate from the land. It is that insight that we all need as our culture increasingly is devolved into looking at life through a small screen filled with scarce metals taken from the earth.

(2019)

# John Feodorov's Spiritual Ambiguities

*Souls Awaiting a Future*, from John Feodorov's recent show "Ambiguities" at South Seattle Community College, at first looks straightforward. The "souls" lying on the floor are twelve praying bears on pedastals, amusingly suggesting some in-between state of being. There is a celestial television projection, as well as stars hanging from wires. There seem to be four realities at least at work here: our own (and what we bring to the work in terms of belief systems); the teddy bears, the video of outer space; and the wires hanging from the ceiling with small stars at the ends.

Feodorov questions our assumptions with humor and humility.

He was raised in Whittier, California, as the son of a Jehovah's Witness/Navaho mother. He travelled with his family to the Navajo Reservation to visit his grandparents and relatives. No wonder multiple realities are his focus.

He has a riff in store for New Agers, particularly those who borrow Indian elements for personal spiritual quests. In a video titled "We're Feeding the Gods," dancers perform what appeared to be a type of ritual dance, but they are in a kitchen and other random places, some of them pseudo-beautiful. It is a real dance, but we can see that the context as it changes makes the dance seem pretentious and hollow. Perhaps that is John's attitude to institutionalized religion as well as New Age practices.

Dominating everything are the teddy bears, a theme John has used before. On the ground were empty teddy bears with their stuffing reassembled as a giant teddy-shaped apparition, as though the ghost of all discarded teddy bears is collectively haunting us, and lurking behind that ghost is the real bear—an heroic creature, outraged by this travesty of cuteness that contradicts his grandeur.

[Note: this post is dedicated to the Colville Indians who have just had a devastating loss of timber from this summer's forest fires.]

(2009)

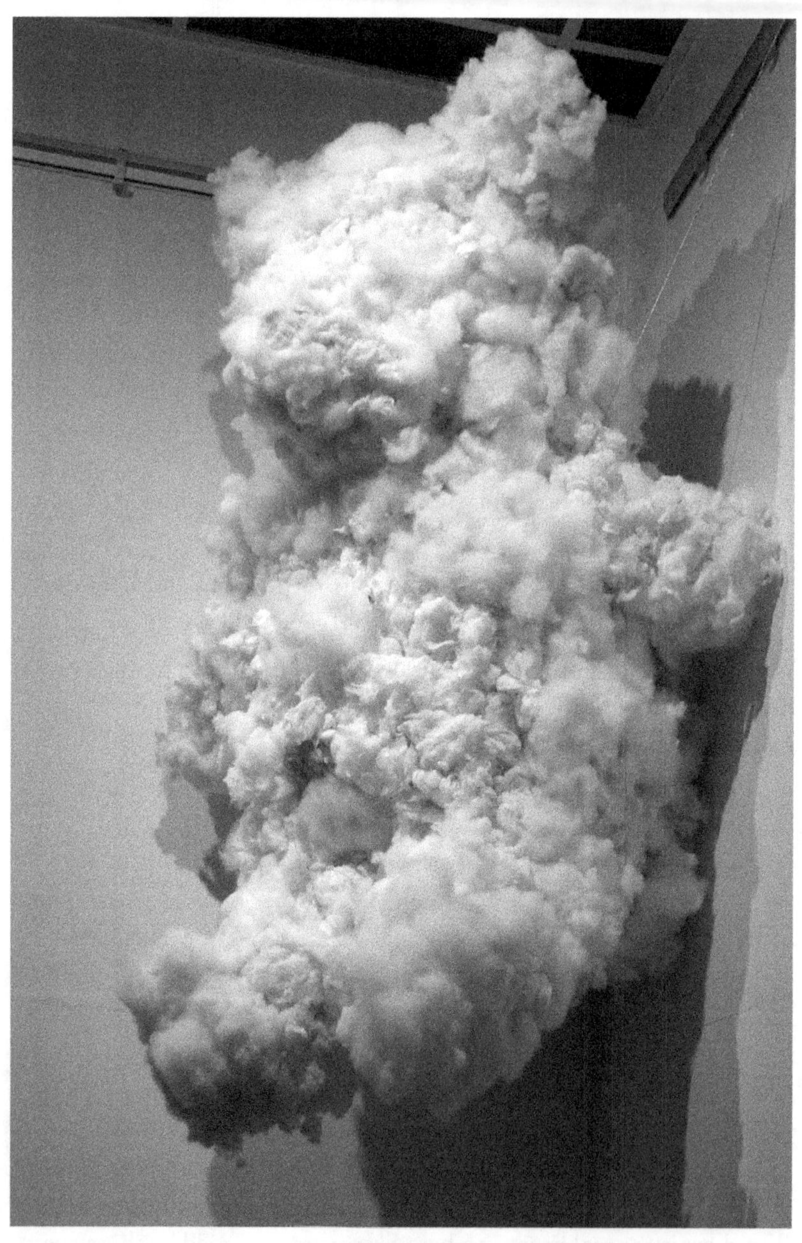

John Feodorov (Diné), "Ambiguities," 2009 installation view, South Seattle
Community College

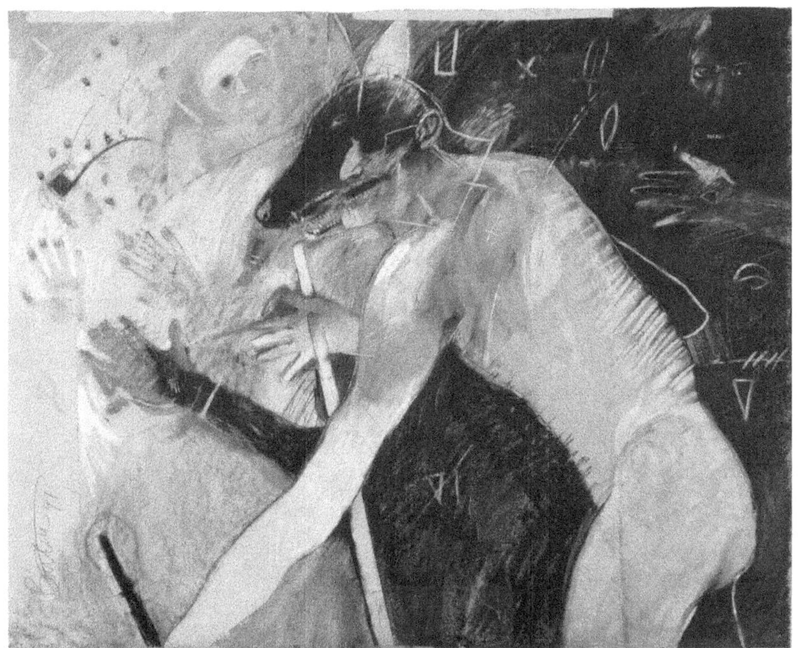

Rick Bartow (Wiyot), *Going as Coyote,* 1991, pastel, charcoal, and graphite on paper, 48 x 60, " Collection of the Hallie Ford Museum of Art, Willamette University, Gift of the artist and Froelick Gallery, Portland, Oregon

# Not Vanishing: Contemporary Expressions in Indigenous Art

THE TITLE "NOT VANISHING: CONTEMPORARY Expressions in Indigenous Art, 1977-2015," curated by Gail Tremblay and Miles R. Miller at the Museum of Northwest Art in La Conner, Washington, obviously turns on its head the cliché about "vanishing races" applied to Native groups from the turn of the 20th century. Edward Curtis embarked on his well known "preservation" photographic project at the time when assimilation and extermination were the ongoing policies of the U.S. government.

This ambitious exhibition includes seventy-eight works of art by forty-nine artists from twenty-three tribes in the Northwest, extending north into Canada and eastward to Idaho and Montana. We are invited to look closely and think carefully about the multiple trajectories of the artwork that point to layers of meaning and interpretation.

Featuring both well known and emerging artists, the exhibition embraces us with many voices. I can only touch on a few artists and ideas here. Rick Bartow's *Going as Coyote,* is carefully described by curator Tremblay in her essay:

> One immediately notices the way the artist divides the picture almost in half, the right side, dark, and the left filled with color and light. To the left of the center, the artist's body leans forward toward the light and seems almost illuminated against the dark half of the drawing. . . . He draws his own face with mouth open and teeth revealed. The top of his head transforms into a dark coyote face, also with teeth bared. The coyote's ears are light and brightly colored.

> The artist portrays himself as a dancer and carries the two dance sticks that define the front legs of an animal when one performs the role of that animal in a ceremony. In this drawing, he portrays the tension of existing in two different realities.

> In front of the artist is the dark shadow of an arm reaching into the light. It does not carry a dance stick but reaches like a third appendage into a space filled with hand and finger prints that as they rise transform into coyote tracks so the human marks of the dancer visibly merges with coyote, as dance and coyote face a space illuminated by all the colors of day. . . .

Tanis S'eiltin's installation, *Territorial Trappings*, 2012, epitomizes the theme of the exhibition: the mixture of Indigenous perspectives and contemporary art, Native values and pressing environmental issues that affect us all. S'eiltin's theme is Native ties to the fur trade that continued right into her childhood.

Fashions such as fur hats made from sea otters, or fur jackets from lynx hides directly benefited the livelihoods of Indigenous peoples, but

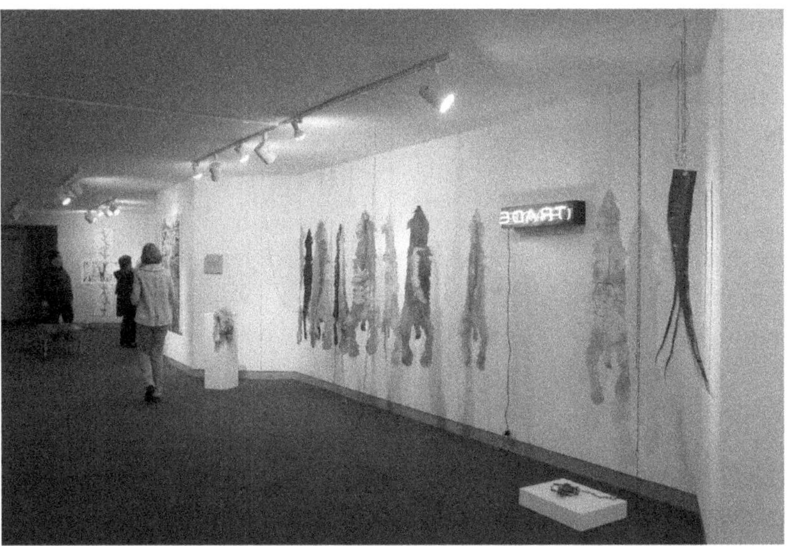

Tanis S'eiltin (Tlingit), *Territorial Trappings*, 2012, lynx pelt, plastic sheeting, acrylic spray paint, neon sign, dimensions variable, installation view "Not Vanishing," Museum of Northwest Art, La Conner, Washington, installation November 2015

also impacted their traditional relationships to the natural world. The ambiguity of this economic trade-off is suggested in the gallery with a neon sign reading "Trade" backwards.

Returning to the work of John Feodorov and his bears, he describes his installation in "Not Vanishing":

*Domi-Nature* is comprised of 12 white-washed Teddy Bears kneeling and praying silently before a projection of the three smoke-stacks from the Navajo Generating Station, a coal-fired power plant located on the Navajo reservation. The bears genuflect as if before a vision from heaven. This is an updated version to an earlier installation I created in 2001, just before the terrorist attacks on 9/11. Since then, this piece has taken on a more serious and tragic association for me, particularly with recent environmental tragedies such as the BP Oil Spill and the nuclear meltdown at Fukushima Japan.

Feodorov and S'eiltin address environmental concerns from sharply contrasting perspectives, but both convey the complexity of the relationships between Natives and the environment. While Indigenous artists and activists are taking a lead in protesting environmental destruction and climate change, others are working for those companies or encouraging and inviting power companies onto their land for desperately needed jobs.

Another artist who is acutely aware of these contradictions is Joe Feddersen. As a member of the Colville Confederated Tribes, in Eastern Washington and Southern Canada, Feddersen brings together stunning technique with subtle, but strong statements. He worked for power companies earlier in his life, and you see in some of his work the geometric abstract form referring to those giant electrical transmission towers. At the same time, those same towers carry energy from the Grand Coulee Dam, which destroyed many fishing grounds of the traditional Colville during its construction and subsequent flooding.

Artist Lawney Reyes narrates a tale from the perspective of his own family in *B Street. How the building of Grand Coulee Dam Changed Forever the Lives of One Indian Family and Devastated an entire tribe.* A "Dreamcatcher" by Reyes is included in "Not Vanishing," and an outstanding example of his work stands at a major street intersection in Seattle as an homage to his sister Luana Reyes, and brother Bernie Whitebear.

The exhibition purposefully includes a wide range of media: from weaving, beadwork, and carved cedar boards (John Hoover's beautiful *Loon Dance*), to non-native traditions of printmaking, acrylics, glass and bronze. Standing guardian figures by Joe David and Preston Singletary are made from blown and sand-carved glass.

Often the works mix traditions and aesthetics, as in the entire room of extraordinary glass work by artists Joe Feddersen, Lillian Pitt, Preston Singletary, Caroline Orr, Susan Point, and others. That room epitomizes the cross-cultural sophistication of these artists, as they work in a non-traditional material but imbue it with Indigenous references and forms, as well as contemporary issues.

For example, Lillian Pitt's extraordinary *Shadow Spirit in the Grass* draws on both Indigenous meaning and contemporary ideas with cast New Zealand lead crystal and metal. Part of a series called "Shadow Spirits," it is, as Tremblay writes, "cast by making a mold around a clay sculpture she created for the purpose." Embedded in the clay are natural materials; here the imprint suggests a navel that "marks the connection between humans and the generations that precede them and make their lives possible."

One of my favorite younger Native artists included in "Not Vanishing" is Wendy Red Star. Her work humorously plays with the clichés about Indians, even while she makes a deeper point. At the time of the Seattle Art Fair this past summer, Red Star installed numerous life-size hunting decoy animals in Volunteer Park, a witty comment on one aspect of our contemporary interaction with nature. In this exhibition, her small car with the long title in two languages—iilaalée = car (goes by itself) + ii = by means of which + dánniiluua = we parade—plays with contemporary perspectives on ceremony and Indigenous identity.

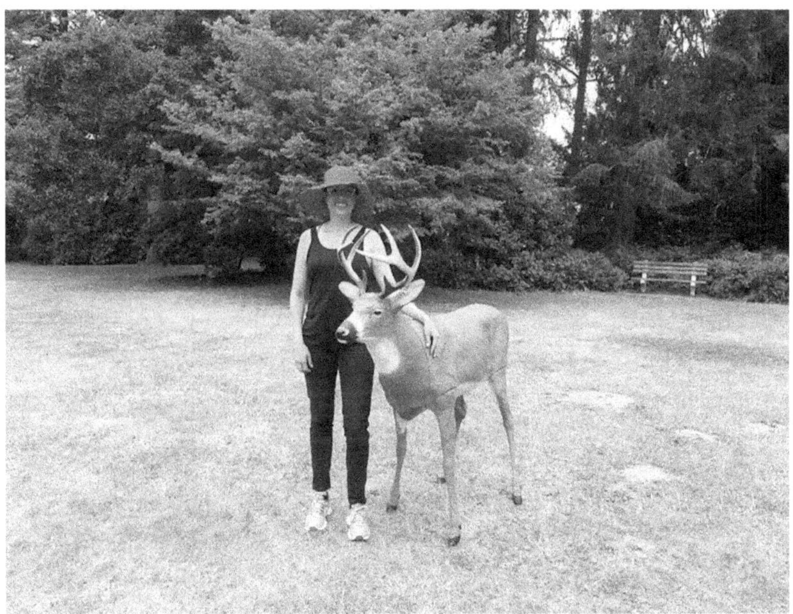

Wendy Red Star (Apsáalooke /Crow) with Decoy in Volunteer Park Seattle, 2015

Gail Tremblay and Miles R. Miller, the curators of the exhibition, fortunately included their own work as well.

Tremblay's *Exploding Star*, created by the painful technique of weaving with metal thread, refers to both environmental issues and mythic traditions. In fact, in her introductory talk, Gail explained the work in terms of historic myths, but in her wall statement she spoke of "materials we have ripped from the Earth who sustains our lives." In other words, she connects the ancient and the contemporary in both the imagery and its significance.

Miller, best known for his beadwork, here contributes two large prints, *The Traditionalists,* that speak of the Lewis and Clark expedition and its absurd misunderstanding of the Native tribes that it met on its way West. He enumerates both their invented place names, as well as the anguish from the Natives' perspective.

"Not Vanishing" can also be analyzed from the perspective of mainstream art history styles: expressionism in drawings and paintings by Rick Bartow, James Lavadour, Jaune Quick-to-See Smith, and Sara Siestreem; affiliations with Robert Rauschenberg in the provocative imagery by Corky Clairmont: *Split War Shield*, made from cash and handmade paper that looks like tire tracks; "pop art" in the tribal masks from automobile parts by Larry Beck; minimalism by Joe Feddersen in his reductive geometry; realism in Larry McNeil's poignant homage to his father and Matika Wilbur's project reimagining Native portraiture. And then, of course, there is the fact that Native artists practiced abstract art for centuries before it was "discovered" in Europe and by the "American Abstract Expressionists."

Erin Genia's *Blood Quantum Countdown* affiliates with conceptual art as it poignantly points to why these artists so urgently sustain their cultural heritage in the midst of their immersion in the contemporary world. She explains:

> Blood quantum originated during a historical period of the U.S. when Native Americans were viewed as a vanishing race. Today, it enjoys widespread use by tribal and federal governments as a legitimate method of determining whether a person can be considered an American Indian. This piece warns that continuing its use inevitably leads to a countdown to our extinction . . . Our survival as a people is based upon a whole spectrum of qualifying factors, from lineal descent to connection to our tribal communities, to protecting, preserving and revitalizing our tribal cultures. It's time to reassess the viability of the blood quantum system.

Indeed, the theme of "Not Vanishing" is exactly that—these artists in many ways are demonstrating the complexity of contemporary Indigenous art. The exhibition provides us with a window into what might be possible if the history of American art could be more truly inclusive. Like the exhibition "Our America" that focused on contemporary Latinx art, this exhibition exposes a rich history of contemporary art that does not surface in the mainstream of art history except for token examples.

Living in the West, in the midst of dozens of tribes, all of them producing contemporary culture, I am acutely aware of this omission. When I go to D.C., a visit to the National Museum of the American Indian, right on the National Mall, is often at the top of my list. But when I speak about that museum to other art historians living there, they have never been there except perhaps to eat. This tells us a lot about marginalization.

Unfortunately, there is no printed catalog of this exhibition. There is a lot of written material which I understand will be posted on the website of the Museum of Northwest Art. Gail Tremblay's essay provides an historical trajectory for both traditional attitudes to Indigenous art (heavily ethnographic), the stimulus of the 1930s Indian Arts and Crafts Act, as well as the Institute of American Indian Art.

The exhibition in La Conner, ought to be at the Seattle Art Museum, or travelling to a major city. The fact that it is in a hard-to-reach museum, and has no published catalog, demonstrates that an inclusive history of contemporary American art and art history has a long way to go.

(2015)

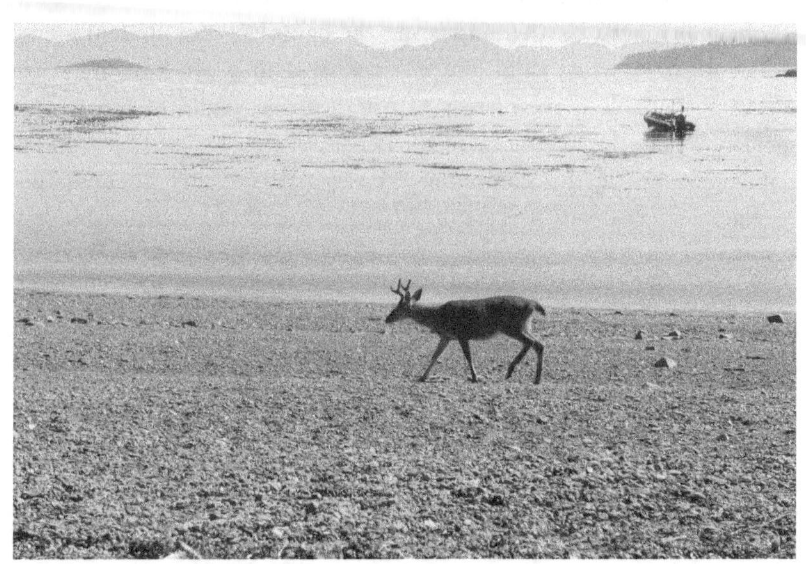

Deer Crossing Beach at Skedans, Haida Gwaii, 2013

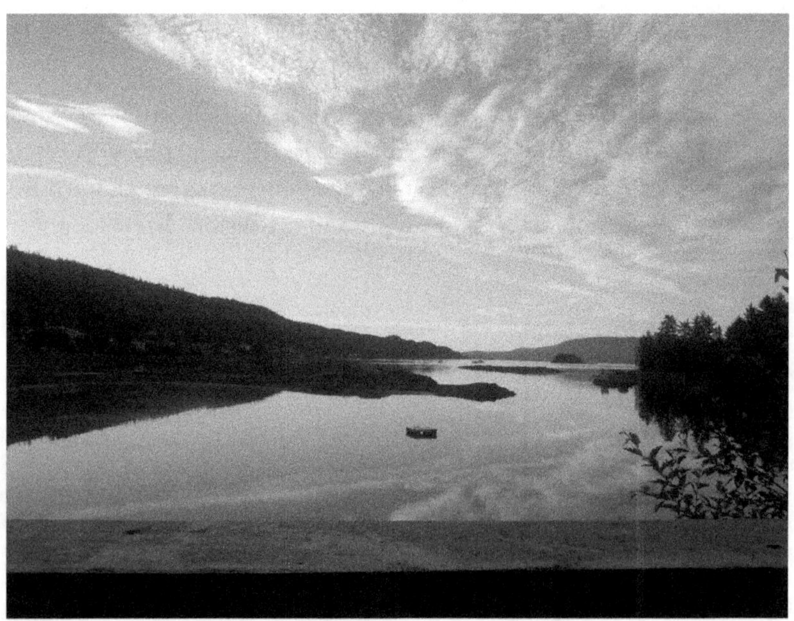

Haida Gwaii, Early Morning from Spruce Point Lodge 2013

# The Magic of Haida Gwaii

## Part I: Tradition Resurrected

When you visit Haida Gwaii you can feel the magic of 10,000 years of continuous history. Haida Gwaii (formerly Queen Charlotte Islands) is the homeland of the Haida. As you approach on the long ferry rides from Vancouver Island and Prince Rupert, B.C., the mountains descend steeply to the sea, covered with uninterrupted forest; the sky expands; the sea stretches; the clouds dance high and low and the fog sometimes hangs below the mountains, enveloping us. The sun breaks through clouds of many grays, waters of many blues, greens and silvers. The rain pours out of distant clouds.

We see the flash of salmon leaping, and the incredible grace of huge whales surfacing as they blow out air and then dive with their tails sweeping upward.

Many eagles fly in the sky, dozens of ravens and crows scavenge on the ground as we arrive.

On the islands we meet people (both First Nation and White) who live off the land—crabbing, fishing (catching the spring salmon or scallops, halibut or cod), catching deer (introduced, of course, along with rats, raccoons, and squirrels), growing vegetables, harvesting berries—just like the ancient Haida.

Along with this basic existence, which is increasingly crucial for survival today, given the expense of living on this remote island, the Haida also have survived by logging, working in canneries, and industrially-linked fishing.

But we feel the closeness of the natural world and the human world portrayed in the Native myths: the people intersect with their animals and birds, and they intersect with each other, help each other, and collaborate to confront emergencies. Raven, the trickster, discovered human beings in a large clamshell on the beach, and because he had just gorged himself on the foods of the sea, he coaxed them out and let them flourish. He then intersected with them playing tricks, causing trouble, bungling his greedy ideas, and generally playing with right and wrong.

Eagle swoops from on high to grab small birds and fish, lands on high perches. He stands above us all. Bear is the caretaker animal, who often is seen on poles protecting people and other creatures. Killer Whale (Orca, actually a dolphin) often is depicted with a human on his back, a woman kidnapped and then later recovered. And of course Raven, the trickster, the most provocative of them all.

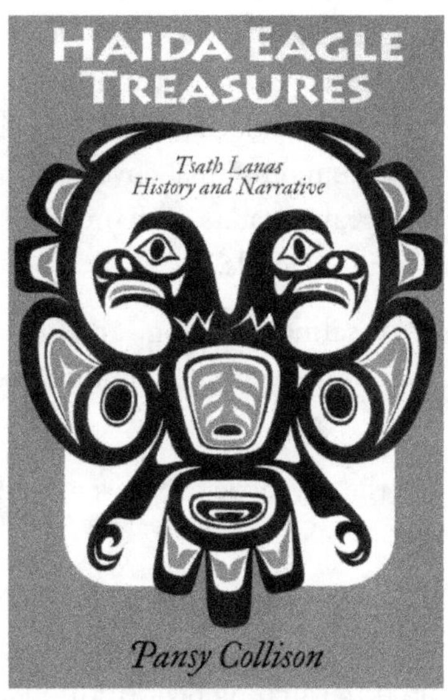


Pansy Collison, *Haida Eagle Treasure: Tsath Lanas, History and Narrative,* Detselig Enterprises, 2010, cover design: James Dangerous

All of the stories are part of an oral tradition that has been passed down for centuries and is still being passed down, although now there is also a written language (and only thirty fluent speakers exist today). Pansy Collison, in her book, *Haida Eagle Treasures: Tsath Lanas History and Narrative* (available to order at the Haida Heritage Center), describes the stories she heard from her grandmother and her mother, as lessons in how to behave. The stories all have a larger theme of understanding the results of our own actions.

Today Haida are closer than ever to their past, their history, as they create a Legacy Pole which is being installed on Windy Bay (Hlk'yah GawGa in the Gwaii Haanas National Park Reserve (also a National Marine Conservation Area Reserve and Haida Heritage Site). Raising a pole takes a long time and a lot of people. There will be a 24-hour live broadcast online.

The Legacy Pole celebrates twenty years of cooperation managing this precious group of islands between the government of British Columbia and the Haida. That agreement was the result of years of Haida resistance actions, starting on Lyell Island in 1985, continuing up to the present. The Legacy Pole is the first pole installed in this southern area of the Islands in 130 years.

During those years, the poles of the seven villages on the island which remained until the late 19th century, were removed to various museums, except for the mortuary poles. Some are in the museum near Skidegate, the Haida Heritage Center. Since 2001, seven poles representing each village, have been raised at the Heritage Center.

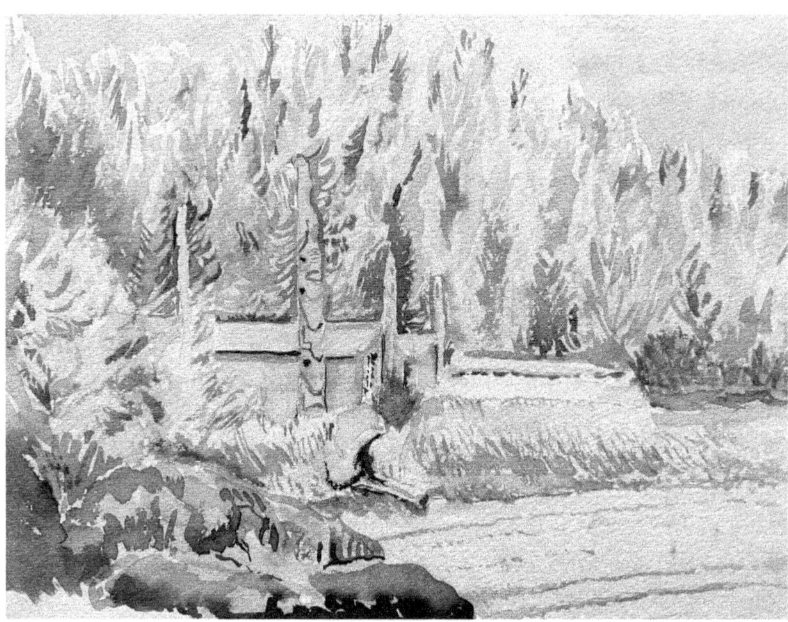

Henry Matthews, *Museum at Haida Heritage Center*, 2013, watercolor

The long-inhabited villages were forced to be abandoned when their populations were decimated by smallpox introduced by European traders (in some cases intentionally). In addition to smallpox, there was also the period of residential schools, when many children were sent away and stripped of their Indigenous identity. Christian missionaries also did a lot of purposeful destruction (the bones of children have been recently found at many boarding school sites), although today many Haida are Christians. Today the descendants of those ancient peoples live in two villages on Haida Gwaii, Skidegate and Old Massett.

Among the historic villages in Gwaii Haanas, we visited Skedans (K'uuna Llnagaay), a site with beaches on both sides of a spit. Its sheltered mooring was full of bull kelp, another source of food. At its peak this village had around thirty longhouses, fifty pieces of monumental sculpture, of which twenty-two were house frontal poles, eighteen single mortuary poles, three double mortuary poles, five memorial poles, and five mortuary figures.

Today we see only a few mortuary poles and indentations in the land where longhouses were once located. The continuity of the history and the earth reclaiming its own is deeply moving.

A watchman guide wearing a traditional cedar hat, and a red jacket with the watchman insignia—which appears on many poles, takes us through the site pointing out a fallen log that is actually a crouching bear; an eye on the side of a fallen pole with a tree growing out of it; a square indentation which is a house where thirty people once slept. We see a tall pole with simple indentations that becomes, when explained, a multilayered potlatch hat, one layer for each potlatch suggesting enormous status; and another pole with salal growing on it that keeps it from falling apart.

The Haida have survived, as have their stories of Raven, Eagle, Bear and Whale; as have their songs, their dances, and their potlatch tradition. Many of their songs actually belonged to specific people who died, but who gifted these traditions. While much has been lost, much is being gained, as these ancient traditions intersect with modern ones. Pole carving is one of those lively traditions that is practiced by several master carvers assisted by many others. Robin K. Wright has published a book on *Northern Haida Master Carvers.*

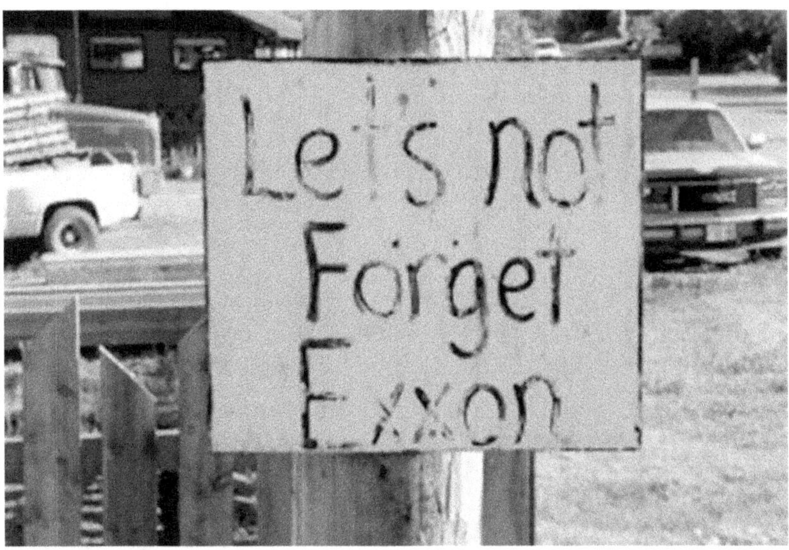


"Let's Not forget Exxon," Haida Gwaii, 2013

## Part II: Haida Gwaii: Thanks, But No Tanks"

Through the windows of the Haida Heritage Center, the beach and sea and sky and birds beckon us to embrace the stunning land that belongs to the Haida people today and for the last ten thousand years.

Although their traditional communities were decimated by smallpox in the late 19th century, and by 1900 the Haida were reduced to only 300 people concentrated in two villages—Old Massett on the northern end of Graham Island and Skidegate on the southeast—these villages today are active centers of Haida culture.

In 1985 Bill C-31 enabled First Nations peoples in Canada to regain their status, and Skidegate welcomed people to return. This summer everyone was thrilled with the raising of the Legacy Pole in honor of twenty years of joint management of the islands, "from the bottom of the sea to the sky," with the British Columbia government.

In the windows of the Haida Heritage Center, curator Nika Collison has placed a succession of quotations from the Joint Review Panel Hearings on Enbridge's Northern Gateway Pipeline project— a proposal to construct twin pipelines, the westbound pipeline to export asphalt/bitumen, heavy tar sands oil diluted by toxic chemicals imported from China, through the eastbound pipeline. The pipelines will travel between Alberta and the coast of British Columbia. The oil will then go by giant tankers through these delicate shorelines and seas. The hearings were held all over British Colombia, as well as on Haida Gwaii, in 2012.

Tribal leaders testified eloquently, pointing out that the project failed to accurately measure the risks: "Northern Gateway does not appear to understand the responsibilities that flow from being inextricably linked with the natural environment" (as quoted in the *Haida Lass*, Newsletter of the Council of the Haida Nation). Enbridge put out propaganda that included "benefits for aboriginals," which gave them a ten percent share!

Collison alternates quotes between tribal leaders and other opponents with the words of the oil company. In this particular setting we can sense the absurdity of the oil companies' perspectives to their fullest. We can understand the deep divergence of the two mind sets, one offering "jobs" and "economic opportunity," the other saying the land, sea and sky's health is more important.

The quotations provide the entrance to "Thanks, But No Tanks": twenty-five striking works of photography, animation, cartoons, paintings, and sculpture by both native and non-native artists that protest the pipelines and tankers.

A young woman named Michaela McGuire was so affected by the hearings that she decided, as an amateur photographer, to make images about the significance of the threat of the tankers to Haida culture. The result was a series of staged photographs (developed in a collaborative workshop) with Haida youth, men and women wearing traditional regalia, standing by the sea or in the forest, with a brief text which brings home the meaning of the destruction of these lands for Haida people.

In addition, McGuire created a potent self portrait of her oil-soaked hand reaching out toward the camera, her screaming face visible through her fingers. (I was unable to get permission to reproduce one of these works.)

As curator Collison told me, "The strength of the photos catalyzed the show."

Another dramatic response to the threat of the tankers came from Janice Tanton who had supported herself comfortably with sales to patrons from the oil community. When she came to Haida Gwaii for a residency, she completely changed her mind, and chose to oppose the Enbridge project.

Tanton's "State of Interdependence: Crossing Over at Alliford Bay," her striking painting of "everyman" gazing out over Alliford Bay, shows the strength of her distress. As she crossed Alliford Bay on a small ferry she was crossing over not only physically, but also emotionally and mentally, to another way of understanding the world. It is easy to believe in this change: these islands exert a magnetic force.

Hanging from the ceiling in one room, is a paper maché head of Canadian Prime Minister Stephen Harper. It is one prop for a multimedia video called "Haida Raid 2: A Message to Stephen Harper." An animated video that includes a rap song performed by JA$E El-Nino that begins:

"I met a Native man that did a span in Afghanistan

He even toked hash with a clan of the Taliban"

The animation by Haidawood includes Raven reprogramming the computer so that the oil is redirected into Stephen Harper's face.

The curator also included a 1977 cartoon book *Tales of Raven, No. 1: No Tankers, T'anks.* Michael Nicoll Yahgulanaas and John Broadhead created it to oppose a previous disastrous project that would have brought oil through Hecate Straits, the body of water between the B.C. mainland and Haida Gwaii, aptly named after the Greek goddess associated with crossroads, entrance-ways, fire, light, the Moon, magic, witchcraft, knowledge of herbs and poisonous plants, necromancy, and sorcery.

That protest successfully moved the Exxon Oil project to Alaska, and we all know what happened next—the Exxon Valdez oil spill that still has not been cleaned up. Leaking tar sands out of old tankers could never be cleaned up at all, so thick is the tar coming from the Alberta fields.

Kayoko Daugert was accustomed to making joyful watercolors of nature, so this dark subject was a challenge for her. *Catching Swarms of Invasive False Promises* is a delicate watercolor that appears to be light-hearted until you look closely and see that the children are picking up globs of tar from the beach.

A multimedia sculpture created collaboratively by eleven artists suggests all the forms of life under the sea: "The forest and ocean conceal little known secrets. While we sleep a symphony of cacophonous life explodes—if we don't hear it, does it exist? Invisible, palpable, ruckus, rich . . . "

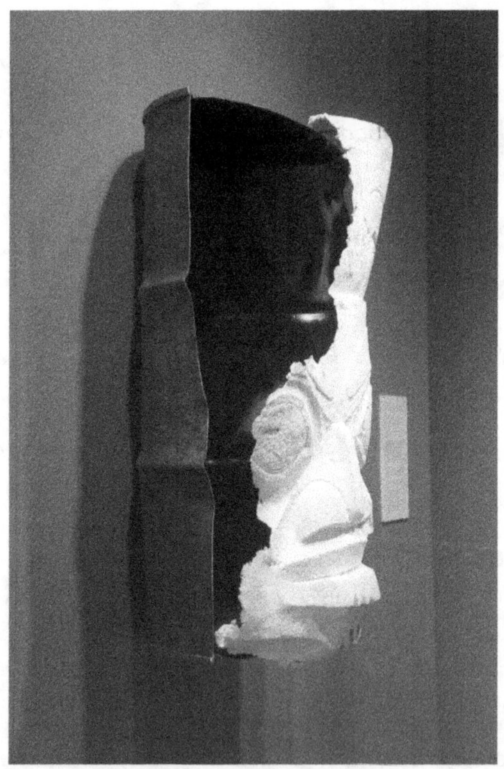

Gwaai Edenshaw, *Hollow Promises: Two Hundred Years of Pain and Exploitation,* 2013, Plaster and rusty oil can, Courtesy of Museum at Kay LLnagaay and the artist

One of the most striking works in the exhibition is by Gwaai Edenshaw. *Hollow Promises: Two Hundred Years of Pain and Exploitation* mounts a fragment of a mask-like face on a rusty oil can. Edenshaw's work addresses the theme of prostitution: oil boom territory leads to a 600% increase in transient workers and transient prostitution. This ragged face exposes those ravages. I also read the piece as a reference to the renewed threat to the Haida from the tar sands tankers. It is accompanied by a short poem:

> A hollow torn form smudged with greasy fingers.
>
> A worn soul under the heel of "away from home"
>
> The price of money . . . we cannot bear it.
>
> The price of oil we will not carry it.

The irony is that at the same time as the exhibition, the Haida were creating the Legacy Pole honoring twenty years of cooperative management protecting Gwaii Haanas from "the bottom of the sea to the top of the sky." Gwaai Edenshaw was an assistant, along with Tyler York, on the Legacy Pole with lead carver Jaalen Edenshaw. At the dedication, the Haida declared their "responsibility to conduct ourselves in a way that honors our ancestors." Since those ancestors have recently offered fierce and successful resistance to the destruction of their land, we know what to expect next if Enbridge continues its project.

The plan is to fight in the courts because the First Nations have never given up their lands in treaties in Canada, and they still have title to their land. But Stephen Harper, as Prime Minister, is doing everything he can to turn back the clock and take away Indigenous rights, while talking as though he is providing economic progress. Raven's action in turning the pipeline programming so that the tar sands squirts right in Harper's face is a great idea. But Haida will be fighting with their bodies, minds and spirits, as will other First Nations groups, alongside U.S.-based tribes and many other groups who are also fighting the tankers and tar sands pipelines across the continent.

Stephen Harper is trying to "reset" the relationships with First Nations, meaning apparently to revoke their rights under cover of providing increased "opportunity." The absurdity of these opportunities, to allow the complete destruction of the land in return for some temporary jobs in a toxic environment, is obvious from the vantage point of Haida Gwaii. (Note: as of 2020, Pierre Trudeau is continuing the project, in spite of continued resistance, but it has still not been built.)

(2013-14)

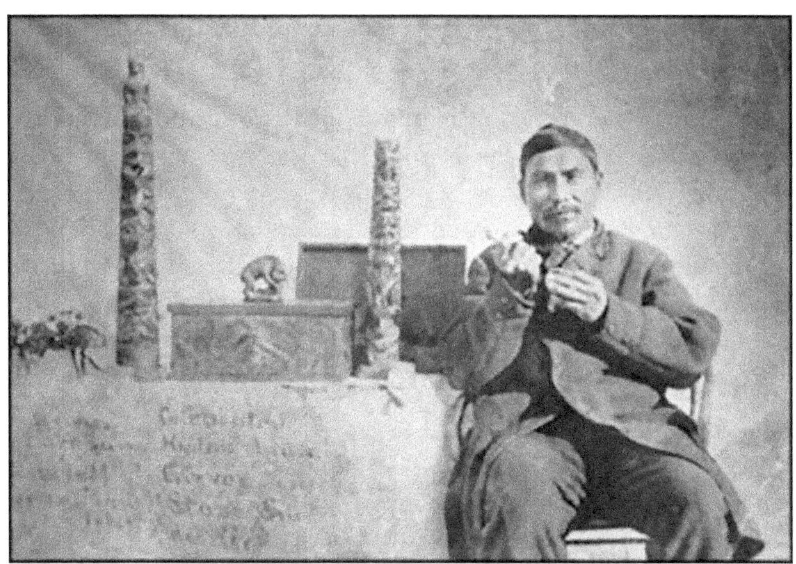

Charles Edenshaw, Anonymous, c. 1880

# Charles Edenshaw: Haida Sculptor in the Era of Assimilation

A RARE OPPORTUNITY APPROACHES THIS FALL. We can see the first major exhibition of one of the founders of twentieth century Haida art at the Vancouver Art Gallery in Vancouver B.C. Robin K. Wright, Director of the Bill Holm Center for the Study of Northwest Coast Art at the Burke Museum and international expert on Haida art, has curated a new exhibition of the work of Charles Edenshaw (1839-1920), a pioneering artist working at a time when Haida and their culture were under great duress.

Haida had no word for art in their language. Art for them was deeply integrated into life. It did not exist as an aesthetic object until after contact with European traders, but Haida art is now a central reference point for creative expression in the Northwest. Along with other Northwest tribes, Tsimshian, Kwakwaka'wakw, and Tlingit, these artists carve, weave, engrave, and paint extraordinary art based on complex design principles.

Since I have just returned from a soul-expanding trip to Haida Gwaii (formerly the Queen Charlotte Islands), I can say unequivocally that this exhibition is not to be missed. We have a small collection of Haida art on view at the Seattle Art Museum that you might want to revisit before you go. You can also prepare yourself by looking more carefully at our many totem poles in Seattle, some of which are Haida; revisiting the Burke Museum and exploring their website which has a wealth of information.

The Haida have maintained their culture for 10,000 years. They reached low ebb around 1900, as smallpox decimated their traditional settlements and forced them to consolidate in just two villages on Graham Island: Old Massett and Skidegate. At the same time, many Haida children were sent off to boarding schools, often to their deaths; potlatch, the celebration that accompanies pole raising, was outlawed (until 1951); Christian missionaries forced rapid changes in all aspects of life; and economic resource exploitation by outsiders led to crushing poverty in the midst of natural plenty.

Yet, these powerful people have survived, and today their culture is strong again. One turning point was the 1985 Repatriation Act, which allowed First Nations peoples to reclaim their rights and to return to their villages. They immediately staged a logging protest on Lyell Island the same year, which stopped indiscriminate old growth logging and led to widespread changes in the logging industry as a whole. It also led in 1993 to a joint management agreement with the government of British Columbia for Gwaii Haanas, the islands in the southern part of Haida Gwaii, which includes seven ancient villages, now abandoned. Their strength is not surprising. Haida Gwaii is a group of hundreds of islands that sit on the very edge of the continental shelf. The seas are filled with a wealth of marine life, from whales to tiny crustaceans. The temperate climate supports edible vegetation year-round on both land and sea, (supplemented today by deer introduced in the 19th century).

The stunning landscape of the Haida has a magnetic appeal: we feel the real depth of nature's power and its dangers; we feel the closeness of animals and birds. In the midst of this wealth of nature, the

Haida have been shaped by it and they are continuous with it, as we see in their many stories preserved through oral traditions.

Throughout this long history they have produced a wealth of art from cedar and spruce roots, from argillite (the only deposit is on Haida Gwaii and only the Haida can have access to it), and from the tall cedar trees. Bill Reid's famous sculpture, *Raven and the First Men*, 1980 helped to revive the Haida traditions. Today many Haida poles represent the distinctive tales of Eagle, Raven, Bear, Whale, Humans and other creatures.

Charles Edenshaw belonged to a family who made art at the turn of the 20th century. In the midst of dominant "vanishing race" perspectives that justified collectors and museums helping themselves to poles and other artifacts, Edenshaw created extraordinary sculptures based on traditional stories, assimilation of traditional styles, and creative reinterpretations based on contact with Europeans. Edenshaw interweaves traditional approaches to design and form, with new interpretations and ideas. For example, an extraordinary argillite box, in the collection of the Vancouver Art Gallery, features a startling three-dimensional lion head (obviously a creature unknown in Haida Gwaii).

The exhibition includes 200 pieces organized in five themes, "Haida Traditions," "Narratives," "Style," "Forms," and "Legacy." "Traditions" includes both work from Charles Edenshaw's family and objects that were commissioned by others to demonstrate the Haida "way of life" to outsiders. "Narratives" includes the artist's original creations in argillite that provide lively interpretation of traditional stories shaped with traditional styles and forms. "Legacy" includes eminent contemporary Haida artists who claim their lineage, as well as their inspiration, from Charles Edenshaw.

When you visit the Charles Edenshaw exhibition, keep in mind how far the Haida have come since this artist began to make art, and how strong is the will to keep the Haida life and spirit alive for another 10,000 years. Charles Edenshaw left his tools to the grandfather of Bill Reid, the well known carver who led the revival of Haida art and culture starting in the 1950s. Bill Reid is the father of Gwaai Edenshaw— mentioned above, who was an assistant on the Legacy Pole and creator of *Hollow Promises, Two Hundred Years of Pain and Exploitation.*

(2013)

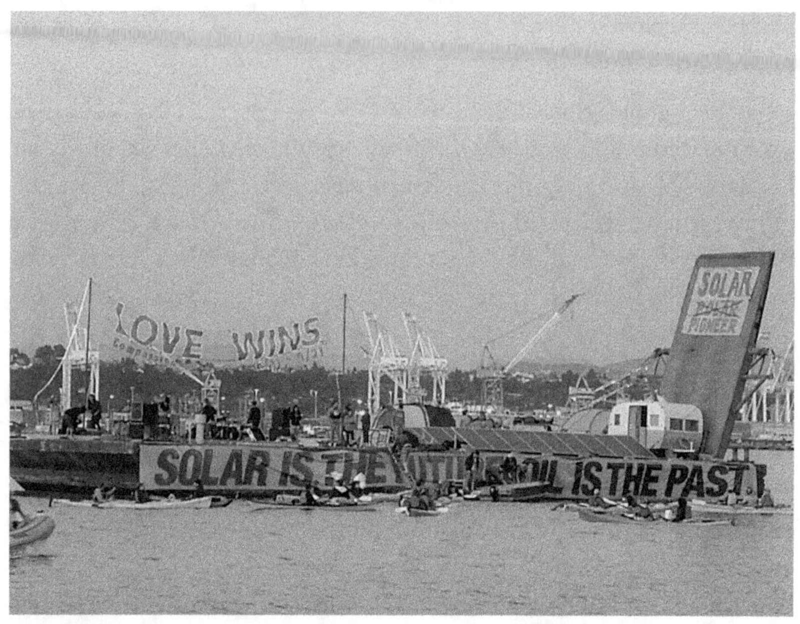


Solar Barge at protest of *Polar Pioneer* and arctic drilling, Seattle 2015

# Native Paddlers and Kayaktivists Protest Drilling in the Arctic

THE WISDOM OF THE ELDERS HAS TAUGHT us many things. Our ancestors had much time to observe and learn from the delicate balances and cycles of nature. With this profound gathering of knowledge and wisdom, they understood the importance of passing on the teachings to future generations. They knew how to learn, respect, acknowledge and share. Our ancient stories tell us that Great Spirit gave us everything we needed to live upon the land without want.

As long as we respected each other and the domain of the tree plant and animal peoples, and returned their bones to their people with gratitude, there would be no war, greed, hatred or destruction of ourselves and our sacred Mother Earth. If we were to forget these teachings, the opposite of paradise would fall upon the land. We believe now is the time for us all to come together and remember this Time of Paradise.

—Paul "Che oke' ten" Wagner

Paul "Che oke' ten" Wagner, Native American flutist and traditional storyteller from the Wsaanich (Saanich) Tribe of southern Vancouver Island, British Columbia, played "Living Freely on the Land" on the solar-powered barge at dusk during resistance to the *Polar Pioneer*. He spoke of his grandmother: "she would talk to the water. I do not come to disturb, I come to cleanse my spirit." About the *Polar Pioneer* he said, "that thing over there doesn't represent respect."

In the Northwest the Indigenous leaders and paddlers give deep resonance to our climate change protests.

When the "Paddle in Seattle" began on Saturday, May 16, it was led by Duwamish, Tlingit, Coast Salish and other canoes filled with tribal paddlers. Then followed 300 kayaks, rowboats, canoes, rubber rafts, and other craft paddling across Elliott Bay to protest new Arctic oil drilling by Shell Oil in the supersensitive Chukchi Sea off the northwest coast of Alaska.

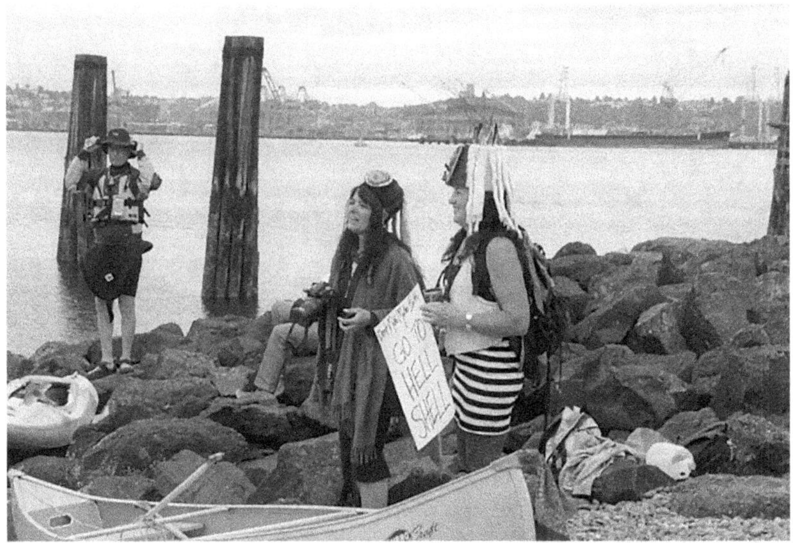


Tlingit paddlers at protest of *Polar Pioneer*, Seattle, 2015

The massive oil platform, the *Polar Pioneer*, is being refurbished in Seattle. It was made by the same Japanese company that more recently made our giant tunnel boring machine, Bertha, that has been broken down for over a year.

When they were physically close to the giant Shell platform parked at Terminal 5 on Harbor Island (it is breaking many laws because of its size and function), the kayakers joined arms and raised massive banners protesting the Shell plan. They also carried individual protest flags attached to light weight bamboo rods. Backbone Campaign, Greenpeace, Rising Tide, 350.org were all represented and led by the Duwamish people, on whose land the entire man-made Harbor Island stands. After the swarm of the water flotilla, "the mosquito fleet," there was a party in Jack Block Park, a tiny green spot attached to Harbor Island, surrounded by high hurricane fences, an "amenity" required of the Port of Seattle.

In front of the massive rig, the small colorful boats collectively made a powerful statement against capitalism and exploitation of the environment.

But the exciting part of this protest is that all ages participated and that the protest took many forms.

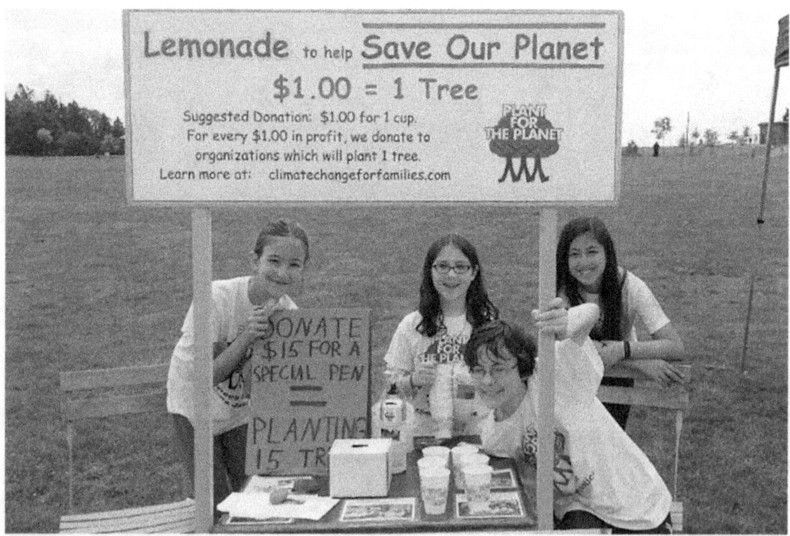


Plant for the Planet Youth Movement Seattle, 2015

The Washington Youth Climate Change Challenge sued Washington State Department of Ecology for dereliction of duty. On Sunday, March 18, the international youth group Plant for the Planet was raising funds to plant trees and go to a climate change conference in Germany to help draft language to convince the G8 (in December of this year in Paris) to make international policy to save Mother Earth from a climate catastrophe. Children were encouraged to draw pictures of salmon.

Over Memorial Day weekend, a college student in Bellingham, Chiara D'Angelo, age twenty, strapped and suspended herself, for an astounding 66 hours, from the anchor chain of a support ship used for Arctic drilling.

Art, song, dance, poetry, puppets, music, chanting are all part of Seattle's art protest traditions. The giant scale of the signs carried by kayakers were on webbed supports so they wouldn't blow the boats away.

The small flags with great logos for individual kayaks had carefully thought-out bamboo holders or were designed to tie on to kayaker's backs.

Denise Henrickson made wind sock salmon that create a fleet of salmon.

The creativity of the imagery reminded me of Occupy, and certainly these protests are directly linked to Occupy in the widespread collaborative outcry against capitalism. Issues are finally interlocking with climate change and anti-capitalism. The protesters represent a wide political spectrum from the Sierra Club, to Rising Tide, and Greenpeace (five Greenpeace activists had attached themselves to the *Polar Pioneer* in the middle of the ocean as it crossed from Asia). But also protesting are city and state governments because of legal violations by Shell.

On Monday, May 18, dance and song and art shut down work at Terminal 5 as police looked on from bicycles, many of them sympathetic. A giant earth parachute created by tireless Lisa Marcus of 350. org was painted with the Arctic at the center. She also made the small kayak flags and much more. The parachute floated around as people held it. There were also seagull costumes, sea turtles, oil rig signs, and many other creative graphics.

The protests have continued in many forms. We had the" luminescent kayaks" at night on June 5, a spiritual event with prayer flags, altars and beautiful music from the solar barge. Individual kayakers carried carefully-designed lanterns.

> "I keep thinking about when the oil is gone? What will the world be like in 2050? What will our Children be Facing?"
>
> —Mikala Woodward

Then on Monday, June 8, there was another port blockage by brave resisters linked together. The conviction is that by causing even some delay Shell will miss the drilling season for the whole summer. Shell seems obliviously determined, though, and still touts the myth of jobs and the need for oil.

Certainly the most dramatic moment came with the five Raging Grannies: sitting in rocking chairs, wearing photographs of their great grandchildren, with their arms connected together by a large sleeve. They were arrested.

On Sunday, June 14, "Idle No More Native Women Rising," held a three-hour event with singing and dancing, poetry and chanting, as well as protest shouts at the rig:

You will not be successful

You will not make it to your destination

You will not harvest oil from mother earth

You will not pollute the ocean

You will not pollute the sky

You will not pollute our lives

I vow that you will not be successful

You will not damage the lives of our future generations

The Pacific Northwest, the Salish Sea from British Columbia to Oregon, is on the front line of stopping Arctic drilling, as well as the coal trains, tar sands, and the rest of the disastrous outdated ideas of these oblivious corporations. Virtually all of these resources are being plundered to ship for use in China. Sightline Institute has provided us with a map of the fact that the Cascades are in the way of this massive export of resources. Already four of six coal ports have been cancelled. The Tar Sands Pipelines are disrupted. Native tribes are successfully winning battles in the courts in Canada.

The *Polar Pioneer* departed for the Arctic on June 15. Kayaktivists delayed it long enough; it ran aground at low tide.

The people can win a future for our planet.

(2015)

# Break Free from Fossil Fuels!

People of all ages, from excited toddlers to sprightly ninety year olds, gathered during the weekend of May 13-15 to protest at the Tesoro and Shell oil refinery sites in Anacortes. Refining oil from the tar sands puts out toxic emissions that we had to breath and smell during our protest right beside the plants. The plants are on non-ceded Swinomish land that was taken from the tribe by Ulysses Grant in 1873 by Executive Order. They have been the site of deaths of workers and health violations for many years.

All of the coverage so far has focused on the small group of people that were arrested after a three-day action to stop the oil trains into the refinery. This was exciting and important, but I want to focus here on the Indigenous Day of Action at March Point in Anacortes, Washington, on May 14. We had over 1,000 people on the march, accompanied by haunting indigenous music, singing and dancing. In addition, hundreds of kayaktivists held up powerful messages from Padilla Bay, both at night and during the day.

The Indigenous leaders spoke to the heart of the crisis in a way that reflected their deep connection to the natural world. They are not on the earth protesting, but of the earth; they are in a continuum with the earth in a cycle of life. This profoundly important relationship has been forgotten by colonizers who, from their first step on the continent, saw only exploitable resources. The Tesoro and Shell refineries stand as a monument to that greed.

Jules James of the Lummi Treaty Sovereignty and Treaty Protection group led the march, by way of honoring the Lummi's recent success in defeating a coal terminal. At the ceremony after the march, Swinomish tribal elder Diana Vendiola spoke of living on the other side of the peninsula, crabbing, digging for clams, with the belief that

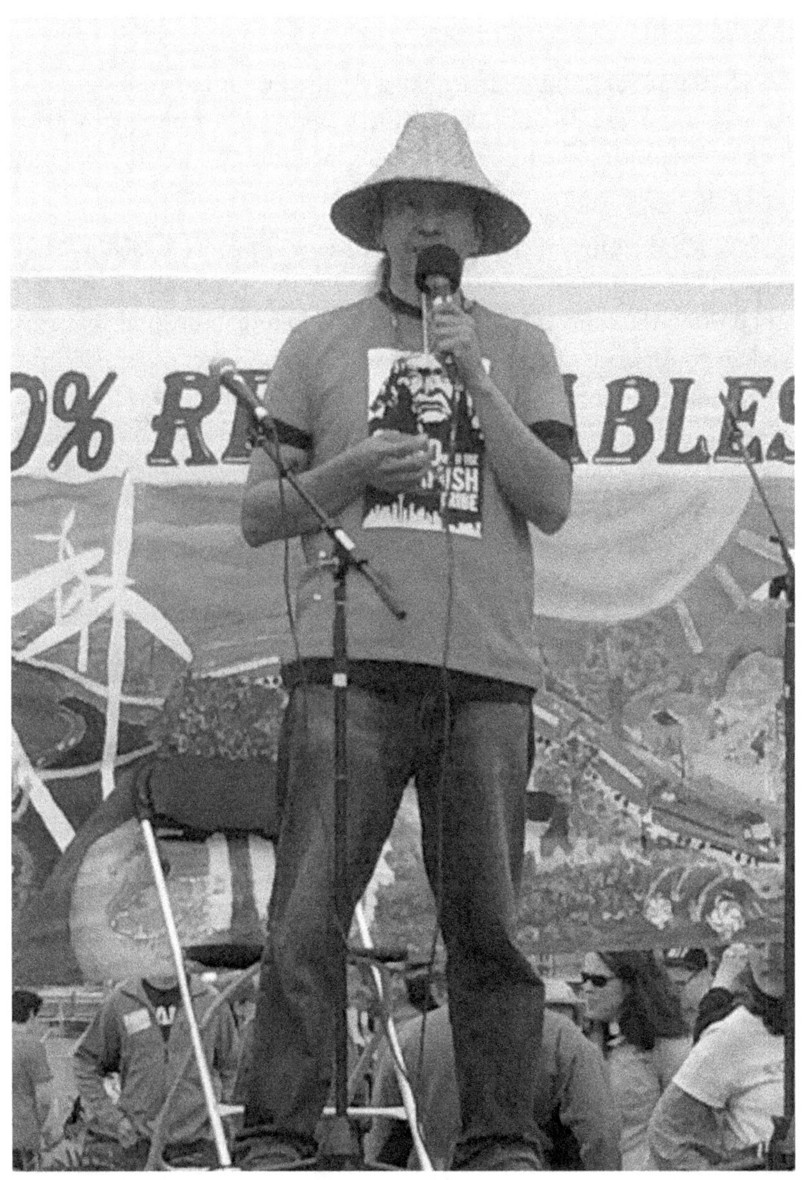


Paul "Che oke' ten" Wagner at "Break Free From Fossil Fuels," Anacortes, May 2016

"water is life" and sacred. Today the fish are toxic, the water is polluted. "How we treat the earth will be our legacy. If earth can't support life, there is no life."

Many tribal groups participated. As the Lummi arrived by canoe, an elder from the Tulalip blessed the water; youth from the Makah spoke of respecting the teachings of our ancestors. We heard other honored elders who asked us to "repay and heal mother earth."

When the Lummi canoe arrived, dozens of people helped to carry it into the center of the ceremony: it set the theme of pulling together and putting the concerns of the community before individual concerns. Makah youth leader Patsy Bane said succinctly, "forget oil, it is killing us." Lummi leader Jules James spoke of building coalitions as the key to winning "the battle to save the earth. They tell us we can't, but we don't live in fear, we love the earth." He has visited the Cheyenne, the Sioux, and other tribal groups who are voting no to energy plants that poison their people. Ruben George, an honored elder from Canada, spoke of the huge Boreal forest fire in the tar sands of Canada: "we must put a stop to this era of destruction."

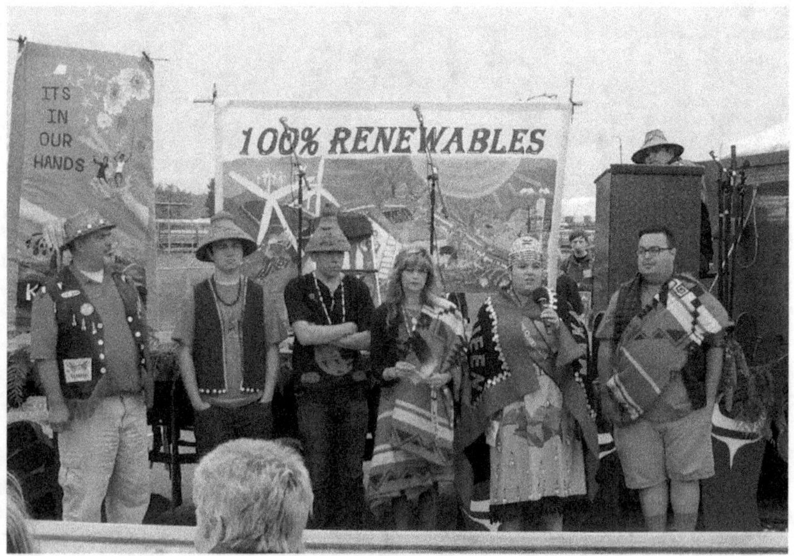


Ceremony with Makah and Quinault at "Break Free From Fossil Fuels," Anacortes, May 2016

Our actions are a part of hundreds of protests around the world during the month of May that are targeting refineries and other polluting industrial sites.

The impassioned and urgent declarations of the Indigenous speakers, as well as the deep commitment of the many activists I met during the planning and throughout the weekend, deeply inspired me to continue to actively work to "Break Free from Fossil Fuels" with the goal of one hundred percent renewables in twenty years or less.

> It was an honor to speak at "In Our Hands" rally to help end the era of fossil fuel catastrophe, my point was that we must step back into the circle of life and learn to honor the gifts our Mother Earth has to offer us, the linear action of the colonial world has a finite end and if our Mother Earth reaches the tipping point, the point of no return for stable climate the human race will reach that end and there will be a great reciprocity or giving back to our Mother Earth but not of our liking. . . . It will be the bones of our grandchildren and their children being given back to our Mother Earth due to our lack of respect for the gifts our Mother.

> —Paul "Che oke' ten" Wagner

(2016)

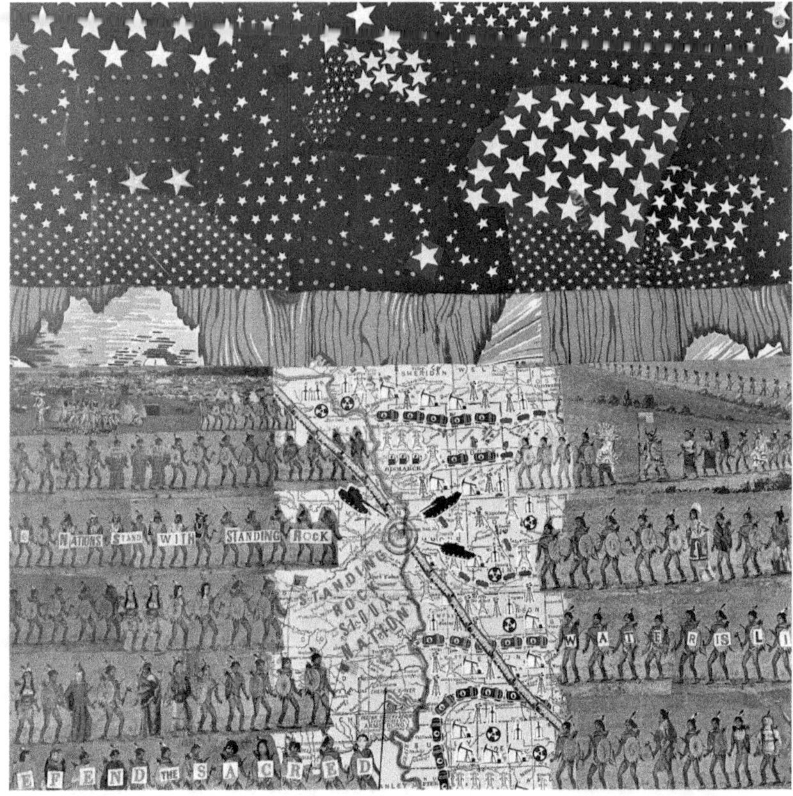

Deborah Faye Lawrence, *Standing Rock Sioux*, collage, 30x30," Collection the author

# The Spirit of Standing Rock

WE HAD JUST TRAVELLED ACROSS THE ENTIRE country by train. On the second night, we passed through Minot, North Dakota. It was minus forty degrees. Minot is about two hundred miles north of the Standing Rock Reservation and the ongoing resistance to the Dakota Access Pipeline (DAPL) continuing in sub zero weather and blizzards.

In Seattle we built eighty winter shelters known as "tarpees," tepee-shaped but covered with heavy duty poly wrap and large enough to hold stoves with a long stove pipe going through the roof. They were designed by Paul Che oke' ten Wagner, the famous flutist who explained his name as "of a feeling to watch over, to care for the people and things that you love for many seasons." Paul has been an inspiring and generous spiritual leader in Seattle at every DAPL march and demonstration. Now he is also an architect. He is combining contemporary materials and traditional structures to create an entirely new type of tepee.

The spirit of Standing Rock is encouraging a surge in contemporary Native art and exhibitions. A fundraiser at the new Sacred Hoop Cooperative Gallery at 55 Bell Street in Seattle included ceramics, posters, beadwork, paintings, masks, drums, jewelry and graphic art. One whole table was filled with writings about Standing Rock and graphic books that dramatically told the story of the conflicts of Whites and Natives over several centuries.

But the fundraiser focused on the stories of those who had been to Standing Rock. It continued for eight hours! While I was there, the story was both personal and mythic. The storyteller, a large man who compared himself to a bear, had just returned from Standing Rock. He told of the spirit of shared purpose there, of shared resources and shared possessions. In spite of the freezing temperatures, he gave away his warm coat and then nearly froze himself. Then he told a mythic tale from the time when "humans had stopped listening" to nature

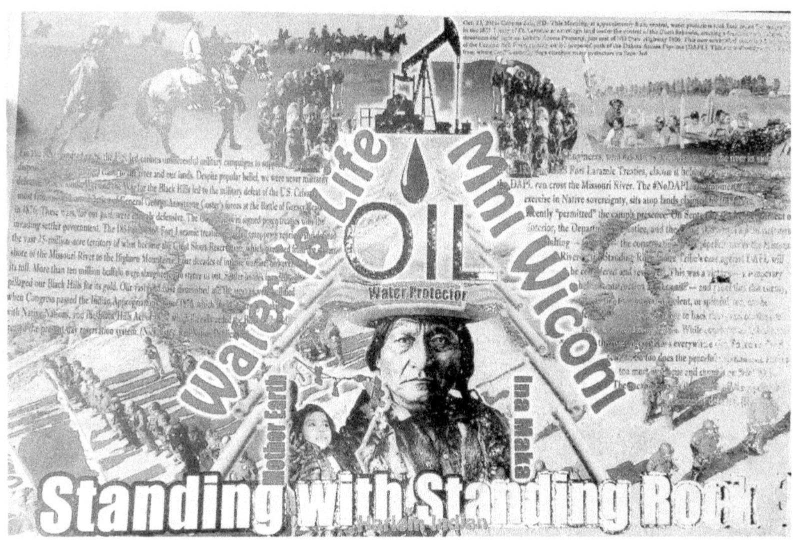


Robert "Running Fisher" Upham, aka "Harlem Indian," *"water is life/Mní Wičoní,* collage and text, 2016

and the animals stopped listening to each other. He punctuated it with powerful drumbeats that were part of the story. They also ensured we were wide awake.

At Sacred Hoop, Robert "Running Fisher" Upham, aka "Harlem Indian," honored the theme of the DAPL resistance, "water is life/ Mní Wičoní," with a large collage that included the early and recent history of the Sioux Indians as text in the background. This artist has also revived the practice of Indian Ledger drawings, the first descriptive images made by Indians in captivity in the 19th century in the margin of ledger books.

The Sacred Hoop Cooperative is the latest addition to native-run gallery/stores in Seattle. Contemporary artist Louis Gong's Eighth Generation in Pike Place Market has received a lot of attention. Sacred Hoop is more low profile. Keep a look out for future events on their Facebook page.

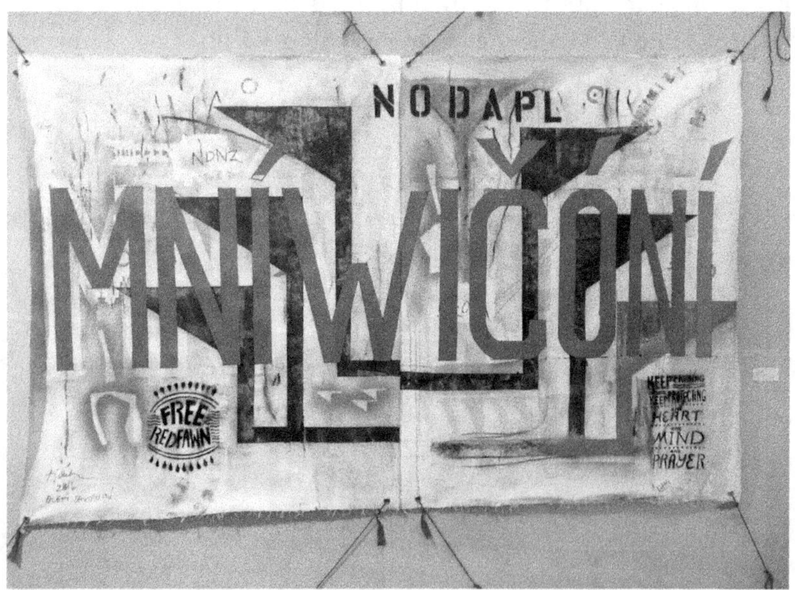


Ka'ila Farrell-Smith (Klamath Modoc), *Mní Wičoní Banner* at the entrance to the exhibition "Protect the Sacred," Tacoma, WA, 2016

"Protect the Sacred," a dramatic and thoughtful exhibition curated by Asia Tale at Spaceworks Gallery in Tacoma. Tail, recently on the staff of the Tacoma Art Museum, chose a cross section of twenty-six well known and young Native artists to participate. She told me that hundreds of tribal affiliations were represented in the Seattle to Portland corridor, from the period of terminations, 1953-68 when the government took over valuable tribal land, and Natives moved to urban areas. She herself is from an Oklahoma tribe.

Tail chose to focus on painting, sculpture, photography and installation. As we entered the door a large banner by Ka'ila Farrell-Smith greeted us. A contrast to "Harlem Indian's" more realistic and text-based homage, Farrell-Smith's *Mní Wičóní Banner* combines references to abstract basket patterns, and a political call to action: "I explore the space that exists in-between the Indigenous and western worlds, examining cultural interpretations of aesthetics, symbols, and place. It is in this space I search for my visual language: violent, beautiful, and complicated marks that express my contemporary Indigenous identity."

This idea permeates the entire exhibition. In work after work we see artists negotiating between Native historical references and styles and contemporary approaches and content.

The photographs of Matika Wilbur, just back from Standing Rock, greet us first. Her subtle imagery resonates with modernism as well as historical and Indigenous references. In *Miss Helen, Last Carrier of the Lovelock Paiute Language*, 2016, we see a moving portrait as well as an homage.

Facing Wilbur's photographs are two realistic watercolors by Yatika Starr Fields. The artist usually paints intensely-colored abstracts, but the impact of joining the protest at Standing Rock led him to record what he was actually seeing and provide a detailed description of the experience.

At the time two tipis were the northernmost structures in the whole Oceti Sakowin encampment. That day the air was alive with anticipation, and the scent of campfire smoke and sounds of all kinds echoed throughout the camp. With the setting sun casting its radiance on the changing colors of

Erin Genia (Sisseton-Wahpeton Oyate/Odawa), *Facing/Not Facing: Toxic Devastation from Oil,* 2016, Glazed terracotta, brass, plaster, wood, acrylic, Courtesy of the artist.

"The piece is presented as a puddle created by an oil leak from a series of broken pipelines. The pipelines delineate the four directions representing the spill reaching out to all corners of the earth. At the center of the crisis is a human face, indicating we are both responsible for the mess and endangered by it. From the U'wa in Colombia to the Ogoni in Nigeria to the Point-au-Chien in Louisiana, in case after case of toxic oil spillage, indigenous people too often face disproportionately deadly consequences.

"The Dakota imagery present in the tiles signals that we are all on native land here in North America, despite current status as contested settler state. Our way of life is tied to the land and being good stewards of our world ensures our survival for generations to come. In 2016, the seven nations, Oceti Sakowin, came together in a historic demonstration of power and prayer at the site where the ironically-named Dakota Access Pipeline meets the Missouri River, to put an end to the wanton destruction of lands and waterways for oil.

"We must face the facts that toxic devastation from the rampant and unceasing burning of fossil fuels has altered the entire world's ecosystem, putting the survival of life as we know it on earth at risk."
—Erin Genia

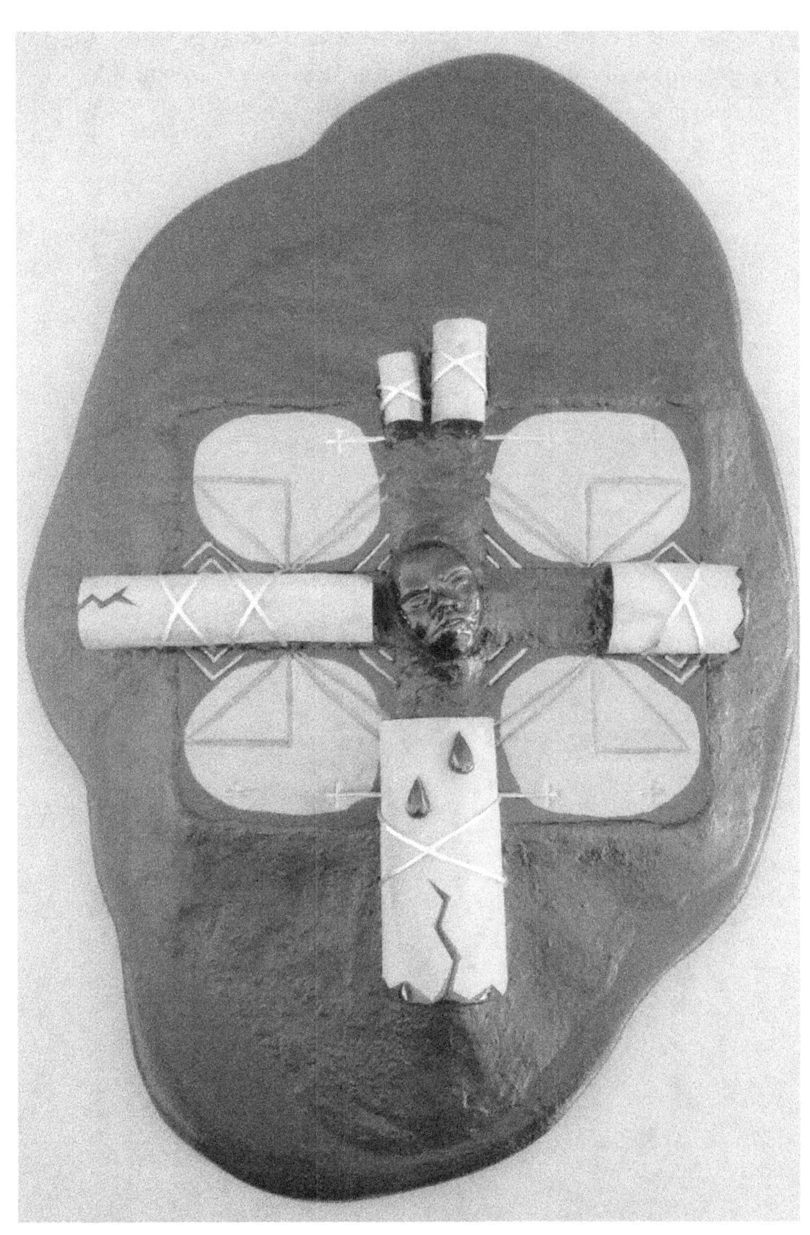

the distant fall trees and surrounding plains, the Missouri river seemingly created its own dominant horizon between past and present. This sacred hill—where burial grounds are present, and where many actions, prayers, and ceremonies take place—has been reclaimed as our own.

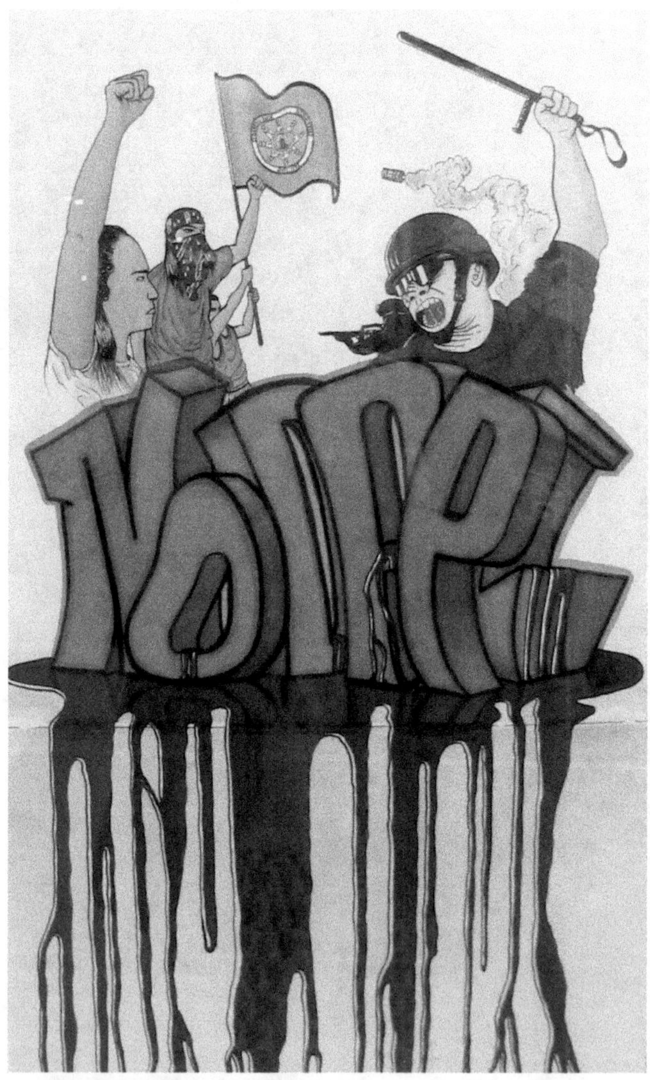

Samuel Genia (Sisseton-Wahpeton Oyate/Odawa), *"No DAPL"*, pen and ink, 2016

Sara Siestreem's conceptual work celebrates rituals of basket weaving with rows of red circles and photographs of her hands in various specific actions.

Erin Genia creates highly original ceramic sculptures with hard core messages like *Facing/Not Facing: Toxic Devastation From Oil, Mobile Spill Response*, and finally *Mní Wičoní: Water is Life Oil is Death*. Next to Genia is the work of Samuel Genia, her fifteen year old son with a bold graphic statement.

RYAN! Feddersen's interactive globe *Micro Spill*, plays on the idea of a snow globe, but when we pick it up we discover it has black magnetic particles that roll around, making a clear point about the despoliation of the land by industry.

I can't enumerate all of the works. Suffice it to say that the exhibition takes time because it encompasses so many styles and ideas. Not all the artists specifically address the issues of extraction or its transportation. But they all tell us that contemporary Native art is flourishing and provocative. All of the works are on sale and a percentage of the sale goes to support the DAPL resistance.

This resistance will continue, as the election of our dreadful new President will only make the need for Standing with Standing Rock, and all other resistance to fossil fuel extraction and transportation, absolutely crucial.

As the storyteller at the Sacred Hoop gallery said: "Stories Heal. Find your standing rock and pull yourself together."

And let us give Winona LaDuke the final word:

We're sitting here. In this world, where there's been no rain in Syria for five years. There's catastrophic storms everywhere. And this pipeline is going to bring about 250,0000 per day tons of carbon into the atmosphere. That's what the Dakota Access pipeline is AND THAT"S WRONG.

(2017)

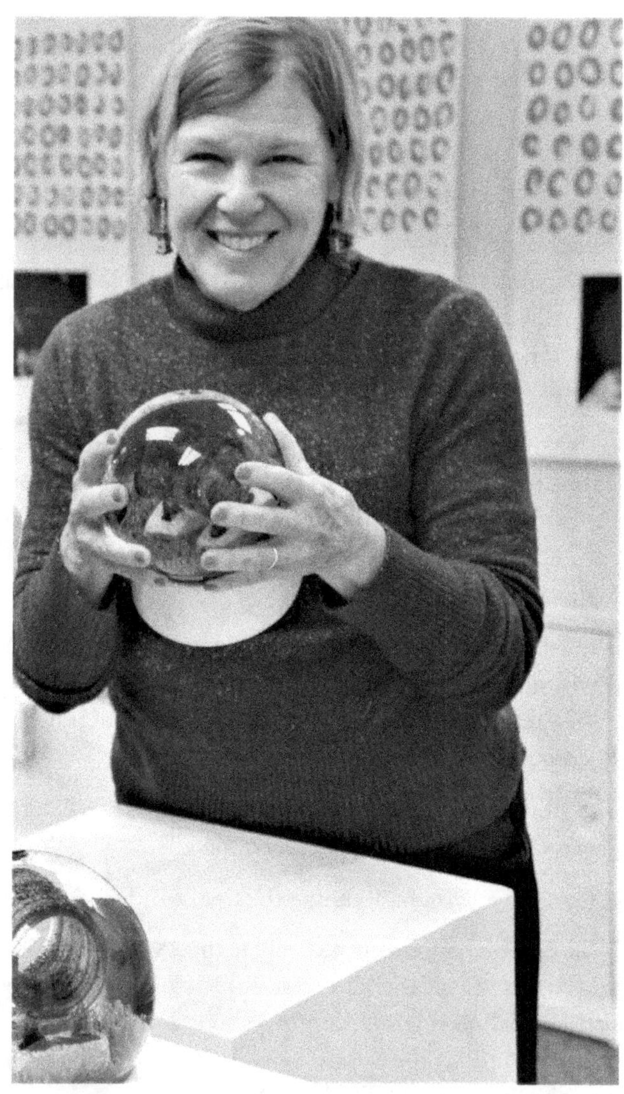

RYAN! Feddersen (Confederated Tribes of the Colville Reservation), *Micro Spill,* 2016,
Acrylic, cement, and astro turf in a snow globe, installation with author

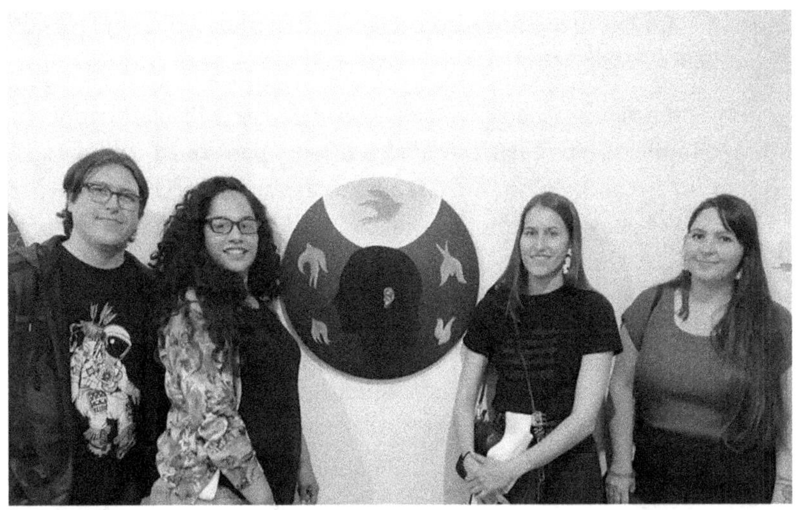

"In Red Ink" artists and curator: Fox Spears, Natalie Ball, Asia Tail (to the right of her work *Bird Heard*, 2017, Oil on Panel), and RYAN! Feddersen

# Red Ink

RYAN! FEDDERSEN REACHES OUT BOTH geographically and conceptually for the intriguing show "In Red Ink" at the Museum of Northwest Art in La Conner. The artists come from as far away as Alaska and Alberta, Canada, and as nearby as Bellingham. While approximately two thirds of the exhibition are familiar artists, RYAN! forces us to expand our thinking and our ideas. She breaks down boundaries of media, chronology, and, above all, clichés.

The most obvious example of exposing clichés is John Feodorov's video collage the "Dance of the Colonizers." Made up of black and white clips taken from the movie *On the Town*, 1949, it exposes the almost unbelievable racism of Hollywood as sailors team up with "girls" at the Museum of Natural History in New York City to mimic "savages." Caricature of caricature frequently appears in this exhibition.

Andrea Carlson, whose affiliation is central Canadian and east coast Anishinaabe/Ojibwe, sends up the absurd cowboy and Indian stereotypes of dramatically leaping horses and men. Her style of pseudo-cartoon, with heavy outlines and brilliant color, underscores her parody of popular culture.

By coincidence, Anishinaabe/Ojibwe is the tribal affiliation of Maria Hupfield and Charlene Vickers, who performed "Jingle and Sounds for Speaking with our Grandparents" at the recent Seattle Art Fair. Their work also combines humor, including self-parody, along with delightful intersections of contemporary performance art and traditional jingles that had migrated off of dresses and onto a giant megaphone.

Placed near the start of the exhibition, Natalie Ball literally cut up clichés in her large collaged artwork that included river rocks, crow feathers, wool and lodge pines—an intentional use of traditional Indigenous materials—along with European-style painting, charcoal and oil stick on canvas. The central figure appears to be an "Indian" collaged and sewn together from mismatched pieces. It has the expressionist directness of a work by Jean-Michel Basquiat.

Also collage-like and humorous, but entirely painted, is the series of works by Ka'ila Farrell-Smith (from the same tribal affiliation as Natalie, Klamath/Modoc), with her three large "bundle" paintings painted on plastic exhibition banners. The "bundle" is amusingly applied to various entities: "Time," "Chief," and "IAIA Students." IAIA stands for Institute of American Indian Arts in Santa Fe, a renowned Indian Art School. The artist drew a bundle of sticks below the photo of the students' caricature historic and tribal references in their dress.

Our familiar Northwest artists Tanis S'eiltin and Joe Feddersen both provide humor with less caricature and more politics—Tanis in *Totem and Tabu*, a Freudian book title. She refers to "tabu" in the installation with pink shoes, a pink suitcase, the book title in flashing neon letters, then adds an old postcard depicting the stolen totem pole that came to Pioneer Square in 1899.

Feddersen's show stopper, *Charmed*, a wall of symbols cast entirely in glass, gives us a delightful mix up of high tension wire towers, petroglyphs, "teepees," and various other "symbols" that can be read as either caricatures or real objects.

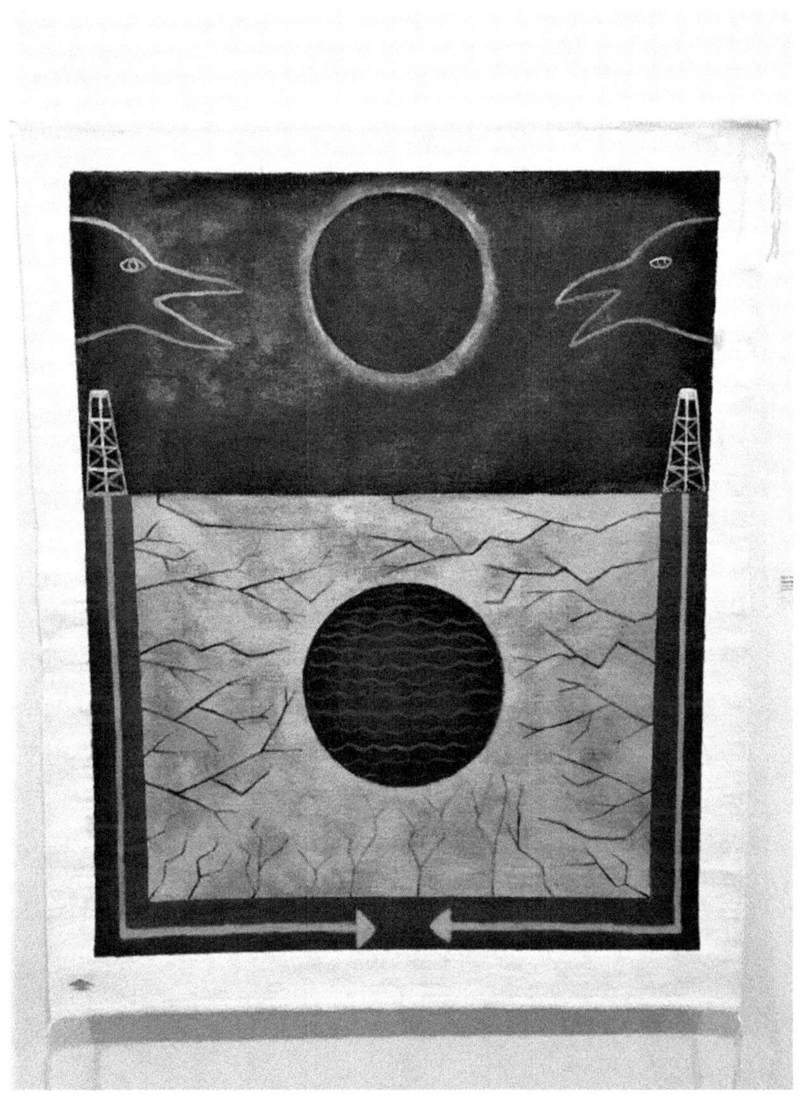

John Feodorov (Diné), *Desecrations 4: Fracking Cracks in the Earth* 2017, 48 x 48",
Painted Navajo rug woven by Tyra Preston, Courtesy of the artist and the Seattle Art
Museum

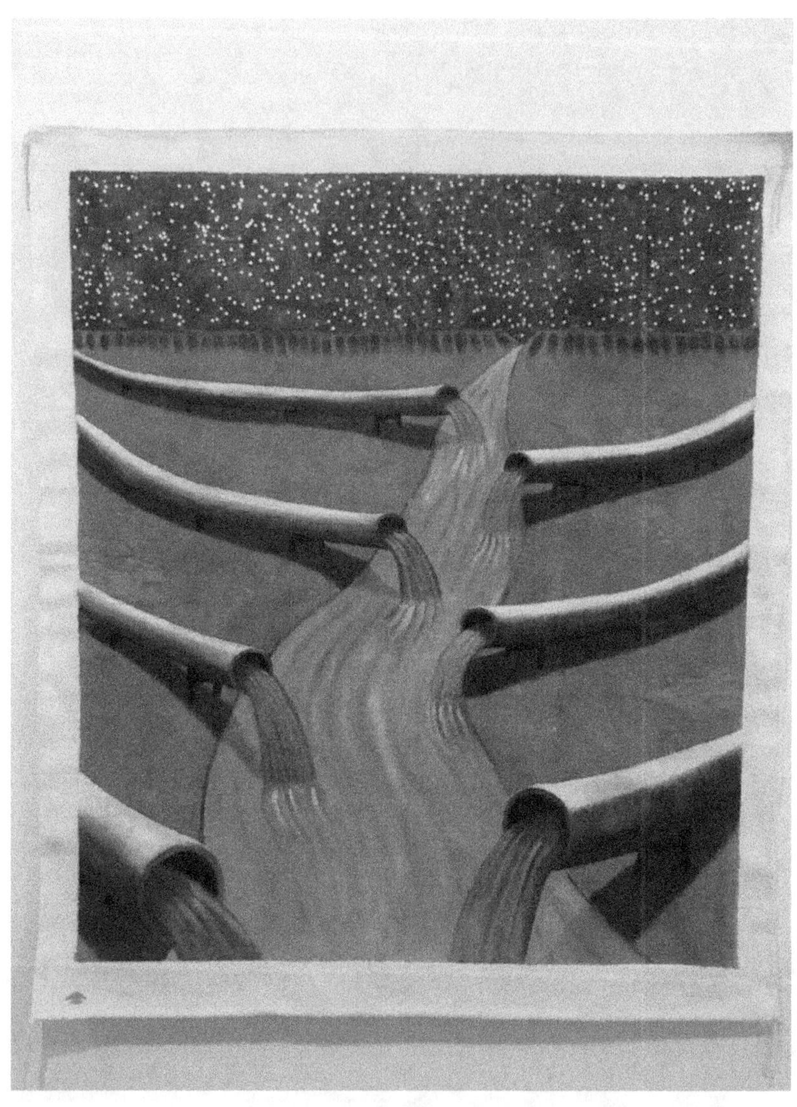

John Feodorov (Diné), *Descecrations 2: the Pipe Lines,* 48x48", Painted Navajo rug woven by Tyra Preston, Courtesy of the artist and the Seattle Art Museum

Feodorov's second group of works reinterpret both medium and content. Master Weaver Tyra Preston created special plain white Navaho rugs for him on which he painted, with some trepidation given the rugs' powerful importance as metaphor of land and culture. The four *Desecrations* refer to pollution on the land: a coal plant, pipe lines, a yellow radiation house and fracking cracks in the earth. Feodorov explained that as he painted on the rugs, he felt he also was committing an act of desecration:

> The series responds to ongoing environmental threats to traditional Diné lands and communities (including toxic pollution caused from uranium mining, coal burning, and fracking), as well as the exploitation and pollution of indigenous land around the world. But, it also refers to my hesitation in painting upon Tyra's beautiful weavings.

> Just as Native lands are under constant threat, so are Native cultures. For me, these rugs act as metaphors for both land and culture. By painting upon them, perhaps I have also desecrated them? My mother taught me that weaving is a sacred art, taught to our Diné people by Spider Woman. So it was with some hesitation and great respect that I decided to undertake this series.

> Understandably, Tyra asked many probing questions of me before agreeing to participate, as well as consulting with a Navajo elder/medicine man from her community. I wish to thank Tyra Preston for weaving these gorgeous rugs, without which this series could not have been realized.

(2018)

# Pollution on Native Lands

Navajo artist Demian DinéYazhi´, in an installation at the Henry Art Gallery, University of Washington, also addresses nuclear pollution on the reservation. The installation includes poetry, sculpture, and video intersecting to create a powerful statement.

It begins with confronting us as viewers with a manifesto presented in segments on a video screen:

"By entering this space you have agreed

To become a lifelong agent

Against humanitarian

And environmental injustice

You have agreed to forfeit your racist misconceptions

of Indigenous identity & respect the sacredness

of Indigenous traditional practices

You are not stepping into the past or staring into a

Picture plane void of Indigenous inhabitants

You are not glorifying western historical inaccuracies

Or romanticizing the cowboys and Indians narrative

By entering this space you agree to never again place

Your hand over your mouth in a mock "war cry"

Or teach your children to be ignorant of the

Indigenous peoples whose land you

Have claimed as your own

From this moment onward you have agreed to learn

The history of the Indigenous ancestral lands

That were stolen & continue to be stolen

Through settler colonial violence

& environmental genocide

By entering this space you have agreed to center

Your politics, social movements & institutions

Of knowledge around the Indigenous peoples

Whose lives & cultures were forever altered

In pursuit of this post-apocalyptic

heteropatriachal colonial nightmare"

The space itself includes more poetry presented in a slide show and reference to a huge uranium spill that occurred at Church Rock, New Mexico, in 1979.

We are so fortunate to have contemporary Native artists who speak to both their heritage and to our contemporary world about the state of the earth and the colonialism that has led us to where we are now.

(2018)

# 5 Upending Expectations

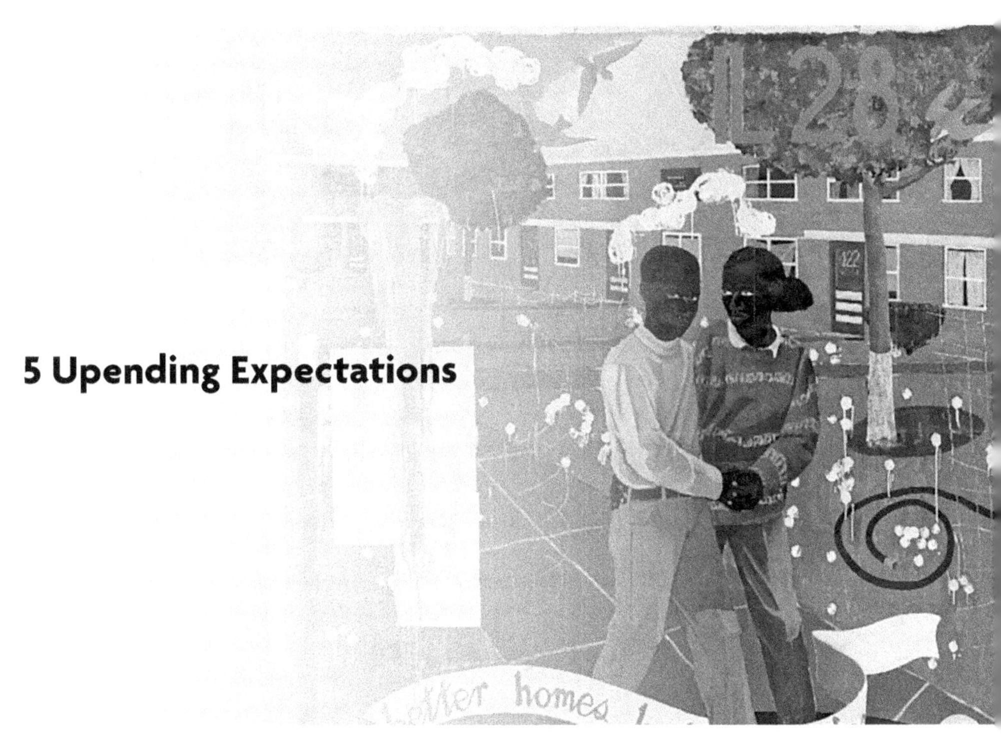

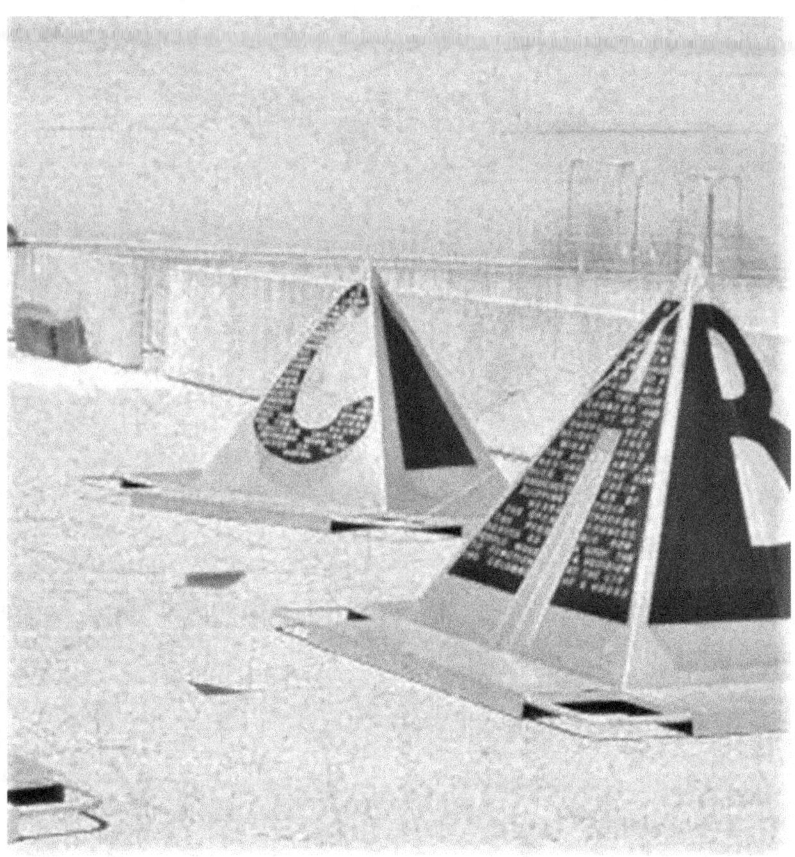

Vito Acconci, *The Portable City*, 1982, installation view, San Francisco Art Institute

# Vito Acconci's Evacuation Plans

Vito Acconci's current installation at the San Francisco Art Institute has two parts: *The Portable City* and *The City that Drops Down from the Sky*. One city forecasts the future, the other recalls the past.

*The Portable City* is composed of three small pyramids, connected by a heavy cable, which are laid out on the roof of the Art Institute. Acconci has given careful instructions on a side of each pyramid on how to store them or use them for emergency shelter:

1 *The Portable City* is stored as a stack of pyramids. The stack can be lifted by the handles at the corners and carried from place to place, wherever the people want to set up the city. When the stack is settled in its temporary site it can be tied in place. Each pyramid then can be lifted up off the other and set in place as far apart as the cable allows.

2 Four people then can grab onto the pyramid at the four corners and lift it up to shoulder height. They might hold the pyramid by resting the handles on their shoulders or by slipping their heads through the open corners. The pyramid now serves as a roof. The people make a decision to function as the living columns of a house.

3 As long as the people keep the roof up another person might step in under it and pull down the two rings on the shade rollers inside bringing down the sides of the house.

This set of suggestions, worded in conditional verbs, rather than a more didactic voice, is placed in three of the twelve letters of the words "portable city," one letter of which is inscribed on each side of a pyramid. Each pyramid has one third of the instructions in the letters P, A and C respectively, a pun on pack, an appropriate reference for a portable city.

The prose is spaced in such a way inside of each letter that only a person who knows English well can put it together to form instructions. Words are split up to conform to the shape of the letters in which they are placed, making a reader strongly aware of the shape of the framing letter, of the nature of words and meaning, and of the arbitrariness of language. The words at the top of the letter p, for example, are divided as follows: THE PORTA BLE CI TY IS STOR ED AS A STA CK. This playing with letters and words relates to Acconci's early poetry in which he worked with words and punctuation positioned on a page. It also recalls his roots in conceptual art and his interest in ideas, which exceeds his interest in aesthetics.

Certainly, the social and political implications of *The Portable City* are far more important than the form of the pieces as a precious object. One issue is the subversion of the normal gallery conventions of looking passively at a work of art that is not to be touched. *The Portable City* cannot even be seen with its shades drawn down unless a minimum of three people cooperate. At least two people (ideally four) have to hold up the pyramid, while another person climbs under it and pulls down the shades. On one level, Acconci's piece is about the artist/object/viewer dynamic. He is not presenting himself as an Oz-like boom from an amplifier. He has removed his powerful, didactic presence, and has only suggested to the viewers how the piece operates.

Thus, the piece cannot simply be viewed; it can only be experienced. Naturally, the way in which the piece is actually lifted and explored often has little to do with Acconci's imagined use. It is apt to be closer to playing with toys. Such a distancing on Acconci's part demonstrates a tremendous commitment to the public. He is willing to let us, in our befuddled and distracted way, make the piece happen. That we must cooperate and interact to do so makes the piece even more challenging.

The idea of cooperation, as opposed to independent, private viewers/people, calls to mind another portable city—the bizarre plans for the evacuation of big cities in the event of nuclear war. The plans call for large populations to move out into the countryside, where they would be hospitably welcomed by small town inhabitants. This plan would be an example of national cooperation to which, perhaps, Acconci's small pyramids make reference. The very awkwardness of the design of the pyramids, requiring four people to sacrifice for every one person who is sheltered, points to the complexity of the idea of shelter, survival and cooperation in the situation of displacement.

Another more immediate portable city is the current evacuation of the Palestine Liberation Organization from Beirut. With guerillas carrying grenades in one hand and suitcases in the other, what could be more timely than a portable city. The Middle Eastern flavor of Acconci's concept is reinforced by the design of the piece—the three pyramids inevitably bring to mind Egypt, and the sides evoke international powers and exotic environments by their swastikas, hammer and sickles and American flag references. One of the pyramids has shades of silver and gold fabric, another is made of imitation tiger skin. These materials and signs correspond to cliché ideas relating to Africa, the Middle East, and global intervention.

Whether *The Portable City* is connected to the art world itself, to evacuation for nuclear war or to the PLA, the main thrust of the piece is the cooperation necessary to make it work. Acconci has transformed the art display into a metaphor for survival.

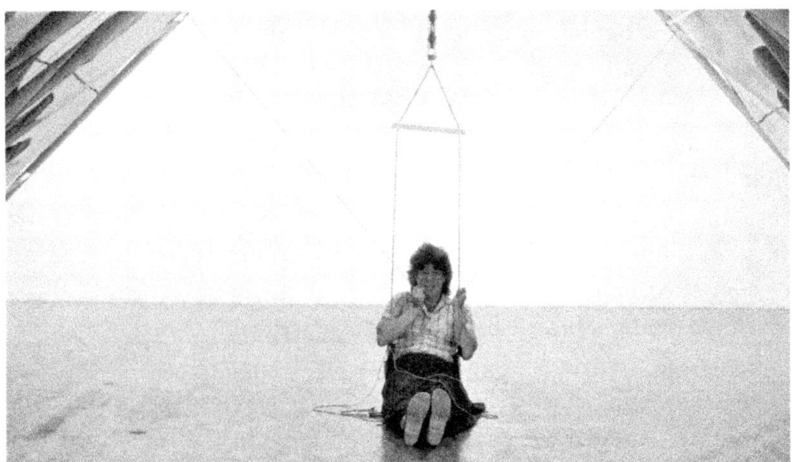

Vito Acconci, *The City that Drops Down from the Sky*, 1982, San Francisco Art Institute, installation with the author

The second part of the installation, *The City that Drops Down from the Sky*, is less coherent in its form and impact, perhaps because the mechanical parts were continually breaking or failing to work smoothly. While *The Portable City* is based on simple principles of lifting and pulling, *The City that Drops Down from the Sky* utilizes pulleys, swings and weights. When they don't work, it dilutes the idea more than the problems of fussy shades affect the pyramids. Both *City* pieces have a toylike character, but the basic functioning elements of *The City that Drops Down from the Sky* are more obviously playthings—specifically shadow plays, swings and sails.

The work is so titled because butterfly-like skeletons that hang from the ceiling of the gallery in the largest of the three pieces, are brought down or "dropped" by someone on a swing in the center. Another person then pulls on the loops that bring up the covers or shades on the wings, an action not dissimilar to raising a sail on a boat. The sails are made of blue sailcloth and dominated by two huge hand signs: a clenched fist with a derogatory upraised finger and the V for Victory symbol. The hands gradually rise up and over the person on the swing as the shades are pulled, giving a sense of the shadowlike advance of a larger-than- life power. When the shades are fully raised, the swing is contained by an inverted tent.

A city dropping from the sky would seem to suggest anxiety or claustrophobia, but the sensation one gets from Acconci's city (there are two other structures, more attached to the ground than the part described above) is that of a gentle shelter, albeit a shelter emanating from larger outside forces of good and evil, emblematically presented in the hand signs. The swing itself also contradicts expectations. A swing suggests a flinging up from earth's gravity into the open sky, a sense of controlled uplift. Acconci's swing is just the opposite. Instead of a rhythmic repeated lift, we can only swing once from up to down on the floor. And as we swing, we are enclosed, rather than released. Somehow neither the swing, the shelter, nor the larger forces come across with conviction. Acconci has put himself too far into the background of this piece. We get tangled in the inadequacies of what we are left to manipulate. Then, once the piece has happened, the city doesn't profoundly affect us.

*The City that Drops Down from the Sky* feels more like an early twentieth century fantasy, comparable in its engineering to something like Tatlin's glider. A fantasy of a city dropping from the sky can hardly be more believable in the 1980s, even if it is butterfly-gentle in its means of functioning or its mode of arrival, as compared to what the movies and NASA offer.

Acconci's pyramids are more effective because of the force of the verbal games and puns, as well as the innate simplicity of the principles implemented. *The Portable City* suggests a primitive state beyond machines and computers, when we will be dependent on simple actions and cooperative good will for the survival of the human race. The choice of a pyramid, the form of an Egyptian tomb, is a resonant form of early history suitable to the future that is still so uncertain.

(1982)

# Nancy Graves: Defying Categories

NANCY GRAVES DEFIES CATEGORIES. Her work is modernist, post-modernist and neither one. She is reverent and irreverent, accessible and incomprehensible. Widely honored since her first years as a professional artist, she has never ceased exploring the edges of what is possible in sculpture and painting. Even as she pursues an apparently modernist agenda of concern with media and form, she uses paradigms and convergent sign systems that suggest post-modern concerns.

Nancy Graves first moved beyond the boundaries of bourgeois artistic acceptability with her *Camels* sculptures. Inspired by the work of Clemente Susini, an eighteenth century Italian anatomist, Graves created twenty-five life-size camels between 1965 and 1969. In these works she turned from her Yale University training as a modernist painter to experimentation with wood, burlap, animal skins, fiberglass, wax, steel, aluminum, marble dust, polyurethane, cotton gauze and acrylic paint. The camels challenged all the acceptable definitions of sculpture and the ban on realism in art. They are Graves's first sculptural exploration in her lengthy pursuit of the immense complexity of both scientific and artistic structural systems, the interconnections of art and nature, and the process of both acknowledging and undermining modernism.

In the late 1960s in New York, Graves interacted with such artists as Yvonne Rainer and Eva Hesse who were challenging the austere boundaries of minimalism with new media and forms. Graves's sculptures, like the *Variability and Repetition of Variable Forms*, 1971 (National Gallery of Canada, Ottawa), paired with her films, were conceptually moving beyond the reductivism of late modernism. *Variability* was far from minimalism and closer to Jackson Pollock's abstract expressionist painting, with its series of vertical poles from which dance an immense variety of airy forms created with steel, latex, gauze, wax, oil and acrylic. Dazzling in its complexity and layers of subtle reference, it cannot be conclusively deciphered, but it evokes the mysteries of art, science, and knowledge all at once. Other early 1970s sculpture

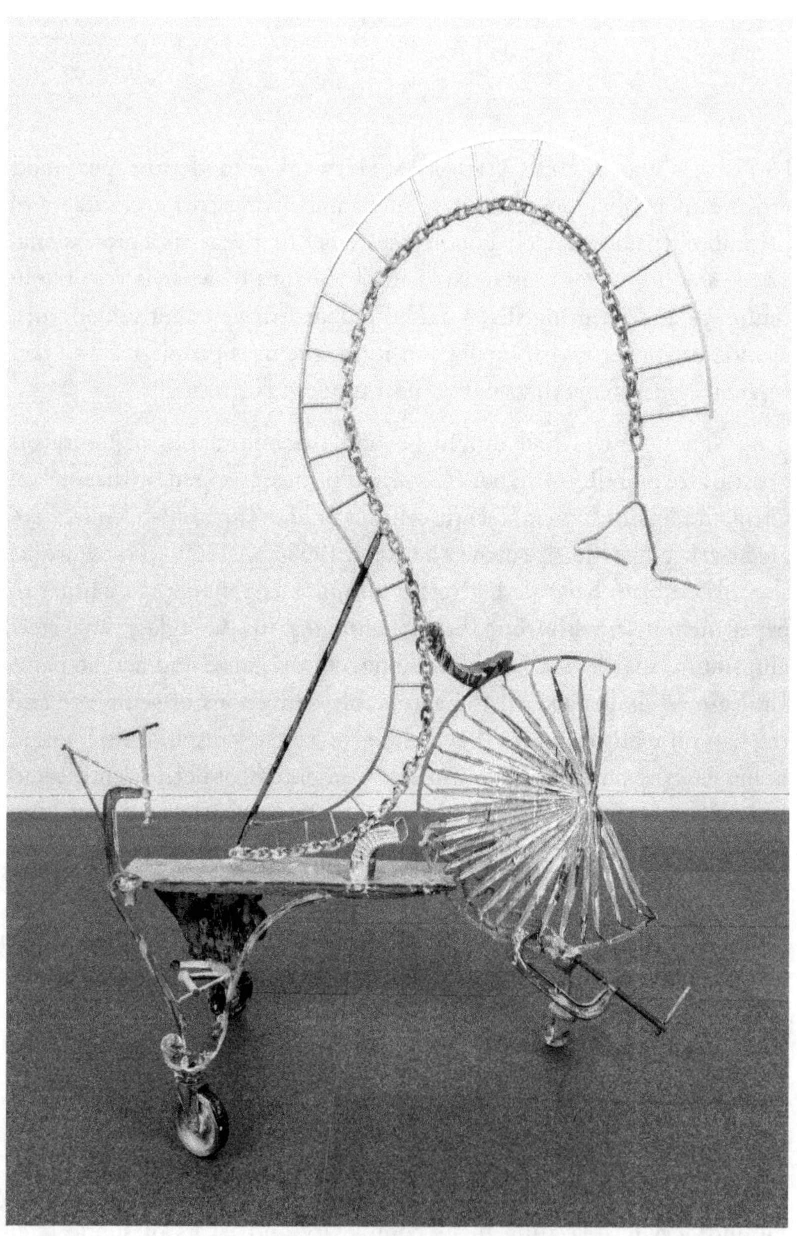

Nancy Graves, *Wheelabout*, 1985, Bronze and stainless steel with polyurethane paint, Overall: 92 3/4 x 70 x 31 1/2", Collection of the Modern Art Museum of Fort Worth, Gift of Anne H. Bass and Sid R. Bass also explore the art/science discourse, by creating fossils in cast bronze, combined with welded metal, and fired and glazed clay.

Graves withdrew from her exploration of three dimensions, and turned to painting during the 1970s. No longer working with galaxies of assistants, she utilized vast conceptual systems including quarry, bathymetric, and topographic maps, phylogenetic charts, submarine, terrestrial and lunar cartography, orbital photographs of Antarctica and paleontography. During a residency at the American Academy in Rome she began to look at archeological maps. On her return to New York, she resumed sculpture with a series that translated archeological site plans into three dimensions.

In the next decade Graves explored the lost wax bronze casting technique to create complex, composite plant forms. While not overpowering as sculptures, as vegetal forms these works suggest bizarre, oversized fossils of exotic species altered by nuclear warfare or climatic adaptation. Structurally, the sculptures look to the work of David Smith in their defiance of gravity, particularly in the use of a "base" that contradicts our expectation of stability. Graves differs from Smith, though, in her emphasis on plants directly cast into bronze and her recasting of found objects. No element of her sculpture is unmanipulated. Her use of sensual, almost cloying, color applied in the tradition of an abstract expressionist-controlled accident argues with, and subverts, the seriousness and complexity of the form and material of bronze as well as the concept of a plant.

One remarkable example is *Wheelabout,*1985. The piece includes bronze cast plant forms (Graves favors tropical and exotic types) incorporated into a cart-like form on wheels, paired with the sweep of a stainless steel halo created by an arcing curve that echoes the shape of the plant form. Bronze castings of C-clamps appear serendipitously, as though the entire construction were jerry-rigged in a backroom shop. Accidents of bronze castings are intentionally incorporated into the piece. Within this panoply of forms the extraordinarily brilliant color—spattered, dripped, and layered—pulls us back from the analysis of structure to the surface, and from three dimensions to two dimensions. It is a Hegelian argument that we witness here, and, ultimately, amazingly, this piece does leave a sense of synthesis, beyond any of its many intricate components.

In the late 1980s Graves again expanded her vocabulary. Her most recent work incorporates subtle references to imagery from famous art works, such as the Empress Theodora as depicted in the mosaic in Ravenna, or the hand of Adam from the Sistine Chapel. In *Canoptic Legerdemain*, 1990, she uses fiberglass to suggest a "waterfall," papyrus plants made of laser-cut stainless steel, a three dimensional metal snake with an aluminum mesh screen "skin," painted references to Egyptian friezes, and the iconic Empress Theodora complete with a suggestion of mosaic and gold ornament. The piece can be read as another level of discourse that is expanding the terms of Graves's original exploration of art/nature/science systems. The "great art" sign system becomes as metamorphosed and re-constituted as the plant forms, the maps, and the camels.

A 1992 sculpture, *Unending Revolution of Venus, Plants, and Pendulum*, includes, for the first time, "literal" time, as opposed to the conceptual time of history or science, or the physical time of making and looking. The sculpture incorporates a "weight-driven deadbeat escapement clock." The weights for the clock are a small, bronze-cast Venus head, a Laocoön head and a horseshoe crab, connected by pulleys and cables. Thus, the miniaturized icons of historic and scientific time literally drive the clock by their weight. The clock in the sculpture actually works on an eight-day cycle (note, not a week) and needs to be wound by a key, already an archeological reference in today's digital world. By including a device that might render the entire piece into a decorative clock frame, Graves takes yet another chance. Rather than a frame, she deconstructs everything and disperses and breaks up the parts.

Graves can be categorized, finally, as a subversive. She affiliates her work with a modernist tradition in its medium of bronze casting, its scale, its play with gravity, its paint application, but subverts that affiliation with eccentric color and a bizarre choice of image. Graves is ironic, but not in a post-modern allegorical, or metaphorical way because, ultimately, her work is still about form, process, and exploration. Even as she demonstrates the arbitrariness of systems of knowledge, she still invests her art with the weight of the tradition of the grand manner. Through her virtuosity, Graves gains a certain power over us, comparable to that of a shaman, but she denies that power and blocks our access to its energy by her trickster-like shifts and layers of meaning. Graves is extraordinary, maddening and phenomenal.

(1993)

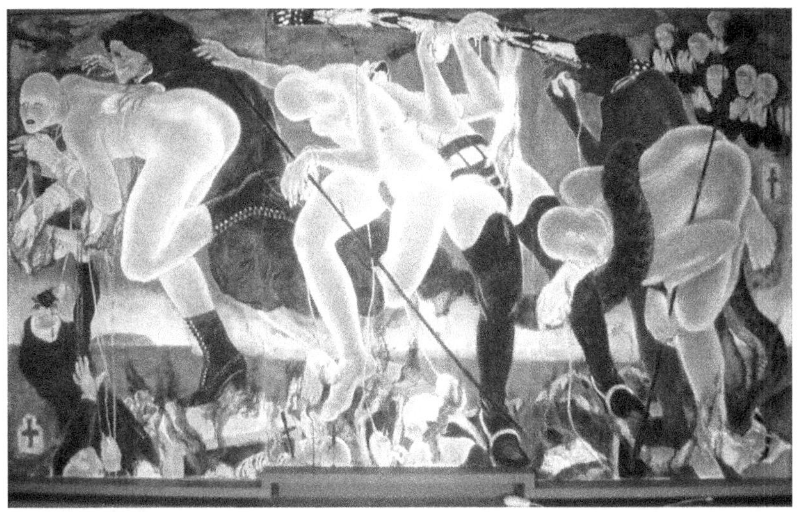

Masami Teraoka, *Garden of E-Mail,* 1996, Oil on canvas, 79 x 129 x 8", Courtesy of the artist and Catharine Clark Gallery, San Francisco

# Masami Teraoka on AIDS and the Internet

IN THESE PAINTINGS TERAOKA MOVES AWAY from his usual adoption of the traditional *ukiyo-e* style. While the artist still works with watercolor (combined on occasion with oil) to create consummate surfaces, the voluminous figures are now more cousin to Botticelli in their illusionism than to the flat colors of the *ukiyo-e*. "The Confessional Series" looks as much to Bosch, Cranach and Ensor, as to Utagawa Kunisada, a garish *ukiyo-e* master that Teraoka prefers to the elegant Hiroshige.

While overtones of the raunchy Kabuki theatre tradition are still obvious, as is the seductive curvilinearity of Japanese art, these new works bridge East and West. But this technical skill is used in the service of a compelling invocation of the contemporary world crises on many levels. The theme is the intersection of the confessional forum of daytime talk shows, in which anyone can parade their traumas to an audience of millions, and the Catholic confessional, in which only the priest hears the lurid dramas of people's lives. Most of the confessional series are tall panels depicting ghastly betrayals of intimacy.

In *Confessional Series, Vampire Bat*, the bats parallel the repulsive, invasive monster priest praying (preying) on the woman's body. Lorena Bobbitt appears in two panels (*Woman with Haunting Mushroom, Woman with Knife*—Lorena Bobbitt, after extensive abuse, cut off her husband's penis while he was sleeping in 1993). The female nudes glow around their edges as though they are radioactive. But these women are more often helpless victim than powerful goddess. The desperate horny men in various guises, Adam, Death, the artist himself, and the priest, fondle and violate them. When I first saw this series I was appalled with the depicted violence and felt it was simply another man acting out his fantasy. But these aggressive travesties of intimacy speak bravely to the horrible betrayals that are the constant fare of news and talk show forums.

Two other paintings in the exhibition demonstrate a radical departure for the artist. While single panels of the confessional series are disturbing, the mural-scaled works, particularly the *Garden of E-mail* and *Uluru Web Site*, both from 1996, overwhelm us. The global themes of the epidemic of AIDS and internet culture become a joined dance of death. The setting is the landscape of the eerie, sacred Ayers Rock and its surrounding desert in Australia. In this huge arena several Eve (or Venus) figures dance on flaming computer monitors held by nuns and priests, partnered or pursued by grasping skeletal figures of death, or other priests bearing more flaming monitors on their backs, and aboriginal men holding sacred staffs. A huge serpent winds through the chaos. The dancers are all caught in a tangle of computer cables and a computer mouse dangles from them like jewelry or fruit garlands. This is a garden of death, with delight as its prelude.

Teraoka sees the internet culture as an addictive plague that parallels AIDS in its intense invasive power over humanity, if not in its certain result in death. Are these paintings simply a variation on the theme of violence against women or are they a protest? Unquestionable, they are intended as a declaration of global plagues in our contemporary society.

At the same time, though, seeing them as a woman, I myself felt clawed and violated, invaded and terrified. In their intensity and confrontation they participate in the culture that they are commenting on, as much as they expose it. They are irrevocably the product of a male eye. Women rarely have any power here, and when they do, that power centers around a penis. Sometimes they are being consumed by flames from the crotch.

The paintings (the *Garden of E-mail* is actually a construction, with a real computer mouse added to connect it to us directly) include a wide range of art historical references and global themes that make them compelling. They are the best work I have ever seen by Teraoka. These works do not exist in an aesthetic place, but in a political place. They are contemporary and historic. They transcend nationality and speak to the world, even as they come out of Teraoka's particular cultural position, as an artist born and trained in Japan and now a naturalized American citizen. He sees crisis from his own experience, even as he sees all of us in it together.

(1997)

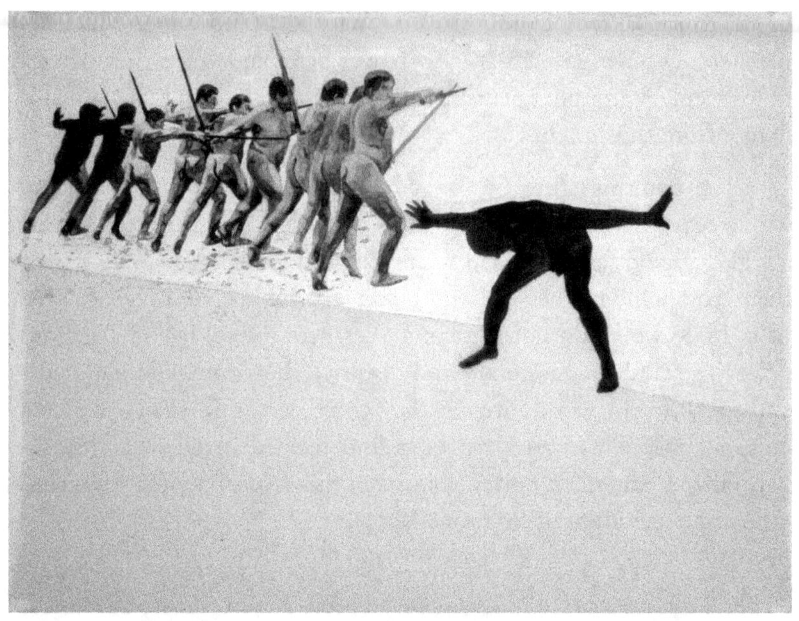

Tatiana Garmendia, *Epic 6,* 2007, pencil, marker, gesso, and ink on mylar, 18x24,"
Collection of the artist, Photograph: Scott Story

# Tatiana Garmendia and the Immorality of War

Water shapes its course according to the ground over which
it flows.

—Sun Tzu, *The Art of War*

TATIANA GARMENDIA'S "EPIC" SERIES, large scale paintings and many
drawings, explores warfare aesthetically, metaphorically, and philosophically. The large paintings are startling: huge nude figures, a seaside
landscape, with a missile erupting or a mortal battle in the background.
A giant fury surrounded by insects hovers over a tank. For Tatiana Garmendia, the ground over which her artwork flows is shaped by her very
unusual experiences and those of her family.

The erupting missile is imaginary: it evokes the fear and anxiety of a child who actually played in missile trenches in Cuba. Garmendia was born just after the Cuban missile crisis, and missiles were buried on beaches near populated areas. In the late 1960s, her father, a doctor who supported the Revolution, fell out of favor with Fidel Castro. When Garmendia was about five, the family was sent to live in a one room apartment at a relocation camp patrolled by armed guards. Children were bused to school, teens worked in sugar cane fields or sorted coffee.

Her father was tortured. Her young brother survived guards randomly shooting at him for sport. The family escaped to Spain because of her mother's Spanish passport. Her mother also was born in the midst of violence—a bombardment during the Spanish Civil War. She was left an orphan. Thus, the family stories behind these paintings are charged with terror, disorientation, and survival. The family moved to Miami, but her father died young. Coming to the United States was a welcome refuge for them.

Thus she has been aware since childhood of the presence of good and the power of evil in the world. At the same time she has been deeply disturbed by the atrocities committed by the United States during the Iraq war. Her art is located in what she calls a "liminal place," a place of ambiguity. She does not present us with easy certainties. She does not have that luxury.

It is telling that one of her reference points is the *Bhagavad Gita*, that ancient Hindu philosophical treatise which is a conversation between Krishna and Prince Arjuna, as he sits poised for battle, but full of the uncertainty of killing his own friends, family, and advisors. The conversation contains the basic principles of Yogic philosophy at the same time that it speaks on the moral responsibilities of a leader who must go to war to oppose evil. Garmendia's exploration of war is, then, not a simple opposition. It is an acknowledgement of the need to counter evil, to survive oppression by strategies and defenses. The "art of war," as conceived by Sun Tzu thousands of years ago, is filled with stratagems for confronting enemies, of offense and defense, of subtlety and secrecy, and, in most detail, the types of terrain on which warfare occurs. Garmendia's dozens of black and white drawings are partially inspired by that text.

As we look at the full sweep of the ink drawings, we see confrontations between mostly nude men drawn in black ink on mylar. White gesso creates opaque frames that suggest terrains or dramatic stages on which armed oppositions take place. Garmendia skillfully shapes figures and outpourings of blood with washes of India ink. These men are the warriors of all cultures: Maori, Aztec, Greek, Spanish, Chinese. They are ancient and they are contemporary. They are actively performing and they are suspended in mid movement. In *Epic 1* two sets of light-skinned men confront a dark-skinned man. All are wielding swords. Between the two groups of three men flows a river of blood. There are facts: the fact of blood loss, as well as the fact of confrontation. But in these drawings there is no victory. There are no heroes. In "Epic 6" one man seems to urgently try to stop the warriors, all of whom are lunging, but perhaps in the wrong direction.

Many seem to be engaged in senseless acts of fighting, as in *Epic 24*, in which forces in futile opposition to one another fill the top half of the drawing, and below a single fighter thrusts a spear forward, spewing

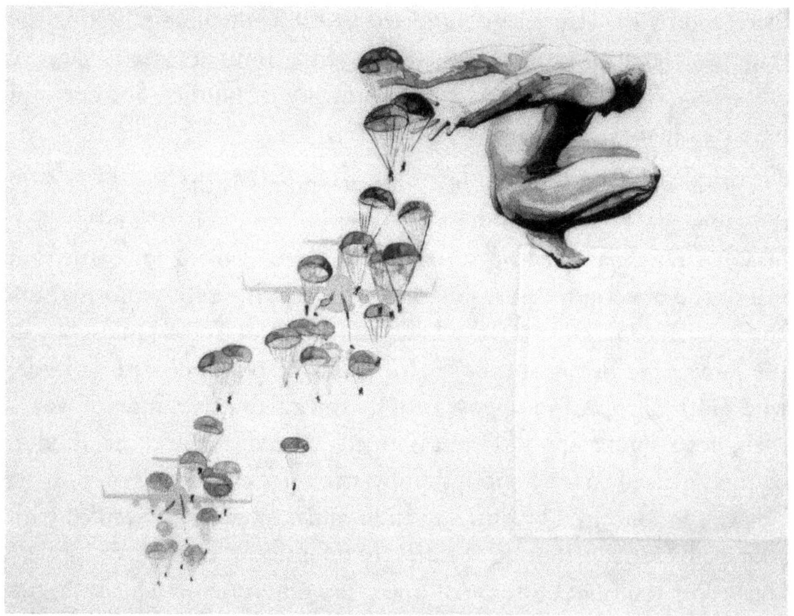

Tatiana Garmendia, *Epic 100*, 2009, pencil, marker, gesso, and ink on mylar, collection of the artist, Photograph: Scott Story

blood, but with no opposition. In *Epic 28*, a warrior faces away from us in a pool of blood. These images are full of classical references: in this case we think of the dying Gaul.

In some cases modernity appears, as in *Epic 100*, in which a man crouches as he drops parachutes behind his back that contain what the artist calls "the terrible seeding of war." Shadowy airplanes seem to be the targets. *Epic 102* includes Tatlin's *Monument to the Third International,* but it seems to be falling apart as people flee, much as the dream of socialism disintegrated in Russia. Other drawings include horses, bringing to mind the age of the crusaders in particular, although horse-mounted warriors are still part of war today. The drawings contain no judgment, no emotion, only the practice of battle; they contain little reference to the impact of war, only the act of confrontation based on orchestrated acts of aggression and defense.

Let us return to the paintings. *In Death at Low Tide*, a large diptych, there are two nude women in the foreground, one observing the men fighting and dying in the background, and one ignoring them, looking at us. We are implicated in the scene by her gaze. *Advancing Storm* brings us back to the missiles. Set in a dark beach landscape, a pregnant woman and a man turn away from the sea in agony and distress, as a missile roars into the sky in the background. Another woman reaches her hands toward the sea, as if trying to prevent the deaths that are coming by pleading with all her energy. Unlike the drawings, the paintings lay out the fear and helplessness of ordinary people caught up in acts of war. Finally, and most dramatically, *Epic Ground Force with Fury*: a voluptuous, aged Fury dances on a small tank as hornets swarm around her. They may be attacking her or part of her power. It is not clear. Does the giant woman represent civilization? Wisdom? Anger? The betrayal of civilization?

Over the last eight years we have seen the disasters of war online and in photographs. Garmendia does not show us that. Instead she explores the peculiar fascination and meaninglessness of war—that can be viewed as an art, simply a slaughter of human beings, or a strategy that allows the powerful to subdue the weak. She does not give us answers. She reminds us that war is a permanent part of human existence in all its contradictions. Rather than references to Iraq and Afghanistan, her drawings and paintings are part of the whole history of warfare.

Sun Tzu says, "Moral Law" causes people to be in complete accord with their ruler.

Obviously, our current practice of warfare entirely lacks "moral law." Garmendia's "Epic" series, in all of its dispassionate exploration, reveals that absence.

(2009)

# Titus Kaphar: Cutting up Myths

Titus Kaphar's exhibition at the Seattle Art Museum responds directly to the mythmaking American art exhibition from Yale University Art Gallery "Life, Liberty and the Pursuit of Happiness." Kaphar literally defeats the conqueror by cutting the conqueror's painted image from a canvas and laying it on the ground, part of a performance in Soho.

*Mother's Solution* is about passing in the African American community, passing for White of course. It is deliberately painted in a pseudo untrained style, as though this bourgeois Black family couldn't afford the more sophisticated technique of a top artist. The cut-out woman is passing for White. Her space is empty, but next to her is her mother obscured by the shreds of her disappeared daughter, hiding behind a sea of canvas tangling her face.

*George George George* is based on the well-known painting *Washington Crossing the Delaware* by Emanuel Leutze. Kaphar excerpts the part of the painting depicting George Washington standing in the bow of the boat as it is rowed across the frozen river on New Year's Day for a famous battle victory. He includes the hand of Prince Whipple, bodyguard and aide to General Washington, and one of the oarsmen rowing the boat, just visible behind Washington in the original painting. (Whipple came to America to be educated, but the captain in charge of transporting him sold him into slavery.) The artist calls attention to the Black hand, the hand of Whipple barely visible in the original painting.

Kaphar states, "George Washington, in his private writings, seemed to struggle with slavery . . . why didn't he do something about it if he had such a problem?" The artist inverts the image of Washington to look like a playing card implying that Washington "gambled with the future of an entire nation." George Washington played some tricks. He had lots of slaves, and he didn't come out against slavery.

This George is no longer commanding.

(2009)

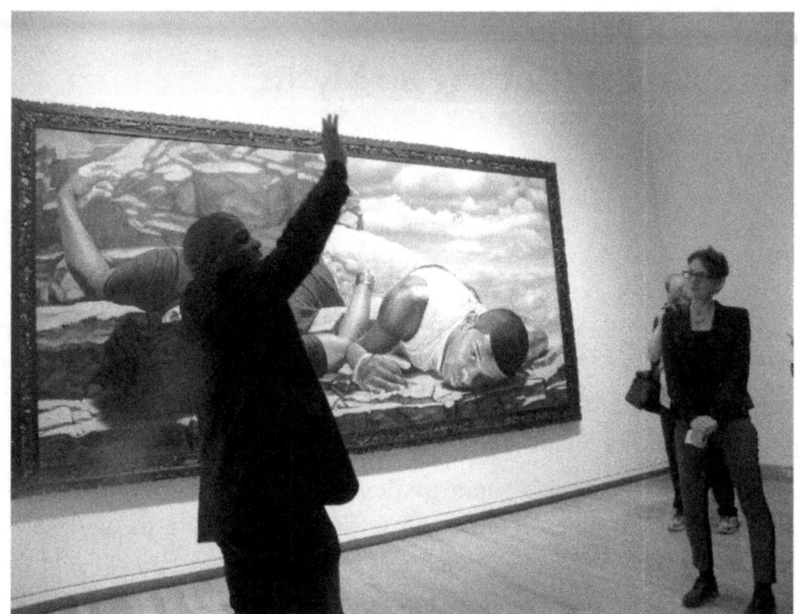

Kehinde Wiley speaking at the Seattle Art Museum, 2016, in front of his painting *Santos Dumont - The Father of Aviation II,* 2009, oil on canvas, 78 x 156," The Minneapolis Institute of Art, Gift of funds from two anonymous donors

# Kehinde Wiley's Heroes and Saints

Michael Jackson looks down at us from his seat on a magnificent stallion in the first gallery of the Seattle Art Museum's stunning exhibition "Kehinde Wiley: A New Republic." Looking closer we see subtle references to Jackson's famously changing color: from rear to head, the horse actually changes color from brown to white and, in the sky, a white and a brown naked child places a garland on his head. Wiley actually met with Jackson and the singer chose the Rubens equestrian portrait of Philip II of Spain as the basis for his portrait (in the original painting the horse is brown and includes voluptuous women with a globe in the sky). Wiley titled his painting *Equestrian Portrait of King Phillip II of Spain (Michael Jackson),* making his provocative purpose clear. The 16th -17th centuries were the height of colonization and the slave trade, so placing Michael Jackson in the seat of power of that period provides an intense contradiction and brilliant upending of history.

Kehinde Wiley characterizes Black masculinity in our contemporary media culture as "structured, manufactured and consumed" to create a "conspicuous fraud." He repositions Black men and women from their traditional role in "grand manner" paintings, often portrayed as slaves or servants or in contemporary media as victims or perpetrators of violence. In Wiley's paintings Black people become heroes and saints. Most of his models are ordinary people, rather than celebrities, making the transformation all the more dramatic and pointed.

He embeds this driving purpose in painting and sculpture that overwhelms us with beauty, scale, and technical virtuosity. As he acknowledges the risk of aesthetics obscuring meaning, he encourages us to look beyond our first glance to the many understated jokes and surprises in the details of the work.

The artist jumps from one historical format to another, keeping us dazzled by his references, but disrupted by his reinterpretations.

Among the portraits, *Mugshot Study* 2006, based on a wanted poster the artist found in the street, stands out as a point of departure and foundation for the more elaborate works. Wiley here simply enhances a traditional mugshot, humanizing the young man with classical chiaroscuro. Under the portrait we see the assigned criminal number of the young man, almost invisible in white on white—a reference to who gave him the number and his status in a society that incarcerates millions of Black men.

A roomful of "Religious Subjects" glow with gold leaf on small private altars, echoing the format of Hans Memling's 15th century portraits of Flemish merchants. But now contemporary young Black men hold emblems of power, their names declaring their identity.

Wiley began his project by finding volunteers in the streets of Harlem, what he calls "street casting," although he presents only beautiful people (he also found models at a casting studio). Unlike, for example, John Ahearn and Rigoberto Torres's plaster portraits of ordinary people in the barrio, Wiley's focus is on physical beauty, even perfection, set in precisely quoted historical formats. If we are going to consume Black men, he suggests, let us consume them as a supremely special experience based on elite status, rather than as criminals or victims or sports stars.

As we are bathed in the transparent colors of a room full of stained-glass windows, beautiful Black men as saints interrupt our expectations of religious clichés. These windows were created by skilled German artisans who had inherited the secrets of the centuries-old techniques of medieval stained-glass windows, a format normally reserved for dead White saints.

Nearby, an alcove of small bronze portraits in the classical Jean-Antoine Houdon style of an idealized head truncated on a pedestal, features African and African Americans. Again interrupting an easy identification with an historical reference, the model for *Cameroon Study* had a shoe on his head. According to the artist, he based it on a shoe seller who balanced a shoe on his head as a way to advertise his wares. Such a surprise is vintage Wiley: a classical format tilts in a new direction.

Michael Jackson's equestrian portrait is part of the theme "Symbols of Power." As a partner to that, Wiley created "An Economy of Grace," portraits of women. Again he found random women to participate, but in this case they were elaborately adorned in Givenchy gowns, with sensational hair arrangements by the celebrity hair stylist Dee TrannyBear. By far my favorite of the women's portraits was *Judith and Holofernes* in which an imposing Black Judith holds the white head of Holofernes (also a woman) against a lush flower background. Wiley's flower backgrounds have a way of wending their way in front of the figure, and most of them have metaphorical significance.

Aside from the triple bronze portrait *Bound*, of three women with huge braided hair intertwined, most of these portraits of women do not critique colonialism and its grand manner presumptions. Black women do not occupy the same oppressed position as Black men in our public media—we have Oprah for example. We think of Black women as powerful, rather than as victims, as bearers of culture and home, as resistors to oppression, as fighters. Celebrity Black fashion models date back several decades and Wiley's insistence on lavish designer gowns and hair seemed to sit in that tradition, although perhaps the exaggeration of the hair and

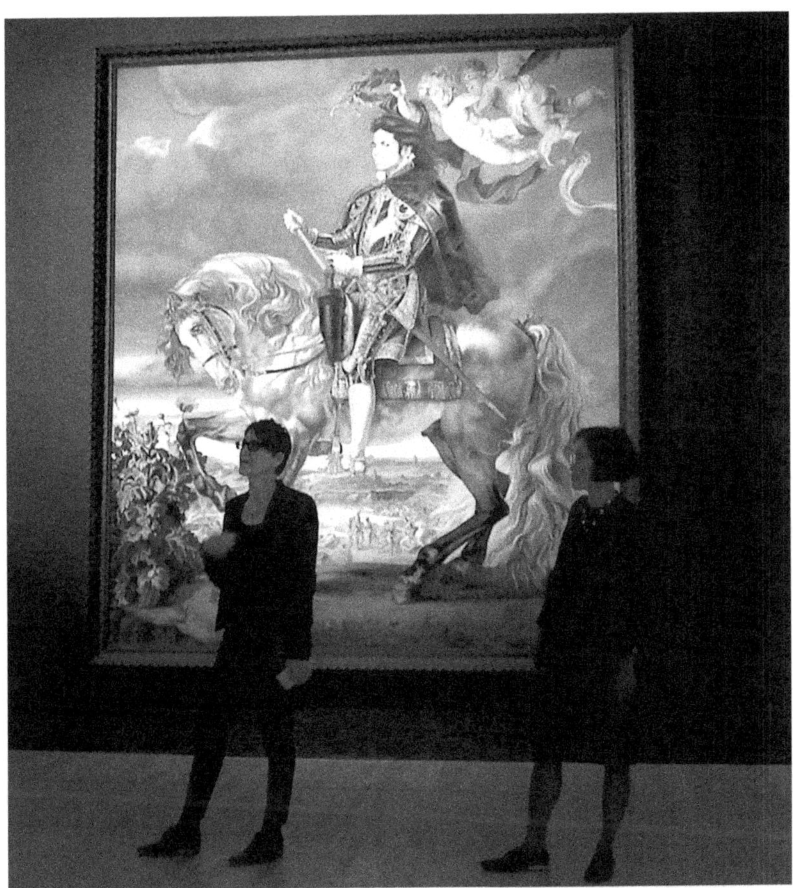

Curators Catharina Manchanda and Chiyo Ishikawa in front of Kehinde Wiley's, *Equestrian Portrait of King Philip II (Michael Jackson)*, 2009, Oil on canvas, 128 x 112", Olbricht Collection

dress is itself a critique because it endowed these women with royalty, not just beauty.

Wiley's painting and sculpture overwhelm us with their scale and meticulous detail (he works with a team in China these days). After flooding us with sensory overload, he provokes us with the unexpected at every turn.

(2016)

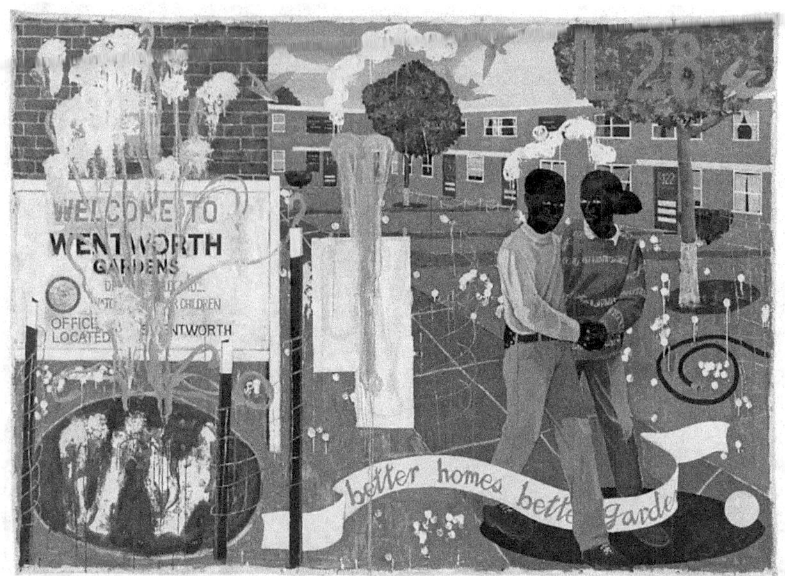


Kerry James Marshall, *Better Homes, Better Gardens*, 1994, painting, collage, acrylic paint and paper collage on canvas, 100 x 142," Denver Art Museum: Funds from Polly and Mark Addison, the Alliance for Contemporary Art, Caroline Morgan, and Colorado Contemporary Collectors: Suzanne Farver, Linda and Ken Heller, Jan and Frederick Mayer, Beverly and Bernard Rosen, Annalee and Wagner Schorr, and anonymous donors, ©Kerry James Marshall, Photograph: courtesy Denver Art Museum

# Kerry James Marshall: Maestro and Shaman

A RETROSPECTIVE EXHIBITION OF WORKS BY Kerry James Marshall at The Met Breuer featured room after room of his magnificent paintings, filled with magnificent people who are very black, blacker than most real African Americans to the point of being confrontationally black for a White museum audience. These Black people are how White people usually see Black people—all one shade of darkness, an absence in the landscape, a trope of fear, a criminal, a threatening presence. Black person coming? Time to cross the street.

But wait. These Black people are simply living their lives: they are living in the housing developments that were built to provide an utopian future for impoverished people. The developments had lawns and playgrounds. The city has public parks to play in. That was enough wasn't it? As in the "Ulysses S Grant" houses, not far from the north end of Central Park in New York City, these were "wonderful communities." So what are these people doing?

They are enjoying life, they are walking hand in hand, they are riding bicycles, they are celebrating Easter. But who are they looking at? Usually, not each other. Or if they do look at each other, their eyes also seem to look outward toward us at the same time, as in the Wentworth Gardens painting, *Better Homes, Better Gardens*. They seem on guard, as though these pastimes are somehow going to be taken away at any moment. They are frozen, not moving, not joyful, not relaxed. They live as if in a dream life: a life free of surveillance, crime, dirt, broken elevators, overflowing washing machines, petty thieves, poverty, gangs, children who die, husbands who vanish or get shot, wives who die. No, none of those aspects of life are depicted here, but they lurk just under the surface. The surface paint patterns, suggesting overgrown flowers or fountains slightly out of control, are more like graffiti or something more generic—simple defacement.

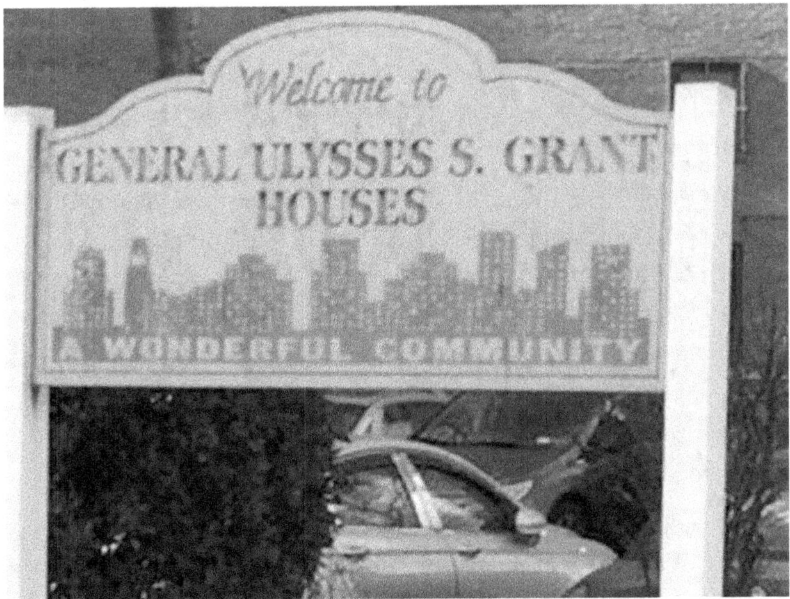


Ulysses S. Grant Houses, New York City

Fathers dig holes—are they graves? The lid of a picnic basket becomes a shield. These people are striving for life, they are taking what is offered as much as they can, but it can disappear at any minute. And the disappearance is because of who these people are staring out at— outsiders, White people, police, drug dealers. Invisible in these paintings, next to these ordinary people trying to live their lives, are all those external threats.

Racism, darkness, fear, death lurks behind every single painting, sometimes obviously, sometimes more subtly. Marshall honors African American as well as White heroes, he memorializes those who have died in the cause of freedom for slaves, or former slaves. He knows his history, and he honors those who died, such as the members of the Stono Rebellion (a little-known slave uprising in 1739), and Nat Turner, much less lionized than White John Brown.

Marshall's painting, *Portrait of Nat Turner with the Head of his Master*, 2011, shakes up some White viewers. We are used to dead "others," or historic long-time-ago dead, but here is a White "master" in the U.S. decapitated by a rebellious slave! Wow.

But Marshall confronts other prejudices. He gives us love. Many White people do not think of African Americans as capable of enjoying love amongst themselves because we are obsessed with their sexuality as a threat to us. The Black/White divide has always "swung" on that fear. Marshall not only shows us loving couples, he gives us eroticism, Black naked women and men; he gives us romance.

Lastly, he gives us art, he gives us art history, he brilliantly quotes some of our most famous historical icons—Winslow Homer, Edward Hopper, Edouard Manet, Diego Velázquez, not to mention more recent artists. He quotes styles, plays with decoration, minimalism, text, staging.

Much is made of his paintings in the catalog for the Breuer exhibition. On and on they write about the paint, the paint, the paint. And the art historical references, the contemporary references—almost always to White artists, as though that will legitimize the work.

But the central theme of Marshall's work is to correct an absence. Absence of the Black body as subject—as human being, as living being, as romantic—in the history of art, in museums, in our lives. And the underlying sea of references includes the celebration of African religions, mysteries, symbolism, on equal footing with all those nice White guy quotes from art. Marshall seeks integration of these two reference systems.

## Part II

It was absolutely amazing to me that all the experts writing repeatedly in the catalog about the importance of *A Portrait of the Artist as a Shadow of His Former Self*, 1980, never mentioned that it quotes White prejudices of Black men: caricature, shadow, teeth, eyes. That is the reason for Marshall's title.

We do not see the person, the humanity, the complexity, the dignity (as suggested in all of Charles White's paintings, Marshall's most important mentor).

*A Portrait of the Artist as a Shadow of His Former Self* is significant not as a portrait, but as a manifesto, an absolute exposé of prejudice. Marshall's black on black paintings of the "invisible man," based on Ralph Ellison's book as he has said repeatedly, emphasize that inability of White people to see Black at all as anything other than one single dark place. But as you look harder into these paintings many details emerge—subtleties, nuances. That is what we White people all need to do: look harder.

The artist is present in the "Untitled" portraits of artists, but again we see the caricature of White prejudice; the traditional portrait format is exaggerated, large torso, direct gaze, holding a giant palette, an irrefutable presence; but behind lurks a paint by numbers canvas. If we cannot see humanity in African Americans, we cannot see the enormous subtlety of their art either.

Marshall is a brilliant trickster. He has duped White viewers into looking at our own fears of darkness. He elevates the humanity of the African American experience with delicious colors, textures and drawings, and a dizzying array of styles. All of these approaches seduce us into actually seeing that African Americans are flesh and blood human beings.

That is why Marshall is unique. Dozens of African American artists have presented African Americans in film, photography, painting, sculpture. One reference point is the 1994-95 Whitney exhibition, "Black Male: Representations of Masculinity in Contemporary American Art," just before Marshall emerged in the late 1990s. The work in that exhibition is sophisticated; in some cases, it is cloaked, as in the work of Lorna Simpson, for example, with all those backs and fragments, and no faces.

But to what extent did White viewers or audiences face their own prejudices in looking at the work in the "Black Male" exhibition? Not at all. In fact, often our expectations were reinforced when we saw criminals or large black sexual organs.

Marshall leads us in through art history. He allows us to wallow in our old fashioned, comfortable modernist references. Look, there is Manet's cat, or there is a skull out of Holbein!!! Flat paint samples play with space!!! But as we wander through these references, we cannot avoid the people, the life, the layers of experiences.

For that reason, certainly, the two paintings of beauty parlors: *De Style,* 1993, and *School of Beauty, School of Culture,* 2012, are the greatest gifts that Marshall has given us. They allow us White people into a place that is almost a sanctuary of Black power, on a par with being in a church (which he does not represent, although spirituality appears often). And as we roam through the paintings visually, we White people suddenly realize we have never been here before, and we actually do not belong here. But we can acknowledge that here is real life, real culture, real people. And it is the White ideal that, in the end, is a mirage, an odd phenomenon, as the small children point out in the foreground of *School of Beauty* as they gaze uncomprehendingly at a distorted image of Walt Disney's *Snow White.* Here people really are living their lives on their own terms. No one looks directly at us.

(2017-18)

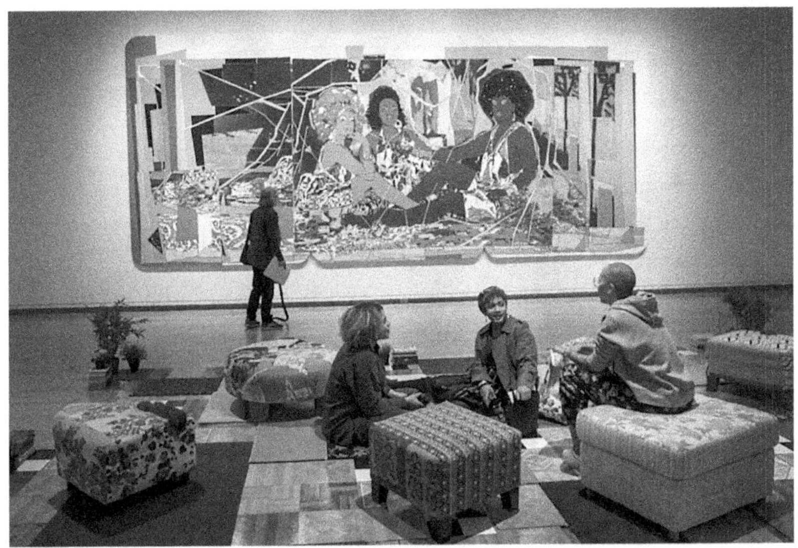

Mickalene Thomas, *Le déjeuner sur l'herbe: les trois femmes noires,* 2010, rhinestones, acrylic, and enamel on panel, 120 x 288" The Rachel and Jean-Pierre Lehmann Collection in the exhibition "Figuring History, Robert Colescott, Kerry James Marshall and Mickalene Thomas," Seattle Art Museum, March 2018, Installation with audience

# In our Face: Robert Colescott, Kerry James Marshall, Mickalene Thomas

IN PROMOTING "FIGURING HISTORY: Robert Colescott, Kerry James Marshall, Mickalene Thomas," the Seattle Art Museum asks these big questions: "Questioning History: Who authors history, who has power, who figures in art history?" Curator Catharina Manchanda selected large paintings by three generations of Black artists to offer us some answers to these big questions.

Robert Colescott is the oldest of the three artists; born in 1925, he died in 2009. Schooled in California, but profoundly shaped by Fernand Léger (with whom he studied), Egypt (where the artist taught), and the Civil Rights Movement, Colescott decided to turn White American history upside down. His iconic work, *George Washington*

*Carver Crossing the Delaware: Page from American History Textbook*, 1975, repopulated the famous painting by Emanuel Leutze with Black face stereotypes led by the famous scientist. It is Colescott's manifesto!

His later paintings continue to redefine both history and art history. The museum has recently acquired *Les Demoiselles d' Alabama: Vestidas (The Young Ladies of Alabama dressed)*, 1985, with its reversal of the original skin colors of the well-known Picasso painting. Picasso's women included prostitutes and a male client on the left; Colescott replaces him with a White woman who may be joining the brothel. Indeed, Colescott's paintings emphasize not only rewriting history, but skin colors. He frequently includes a whole range of tones from white to dark brown as in *Knowledge of the Past Is Key to the Future: Some Afterthoughts on Discovery*, 1986. He features a figure identifiable as Columbus in the lower right, Matthew Hensen (polar explorer with Robert Peary), and a galaxy of people, all with contrasting skin colors. These people never look outward at us. Colescott chose to be more complex in his later works, but his purpose never wavers.

The paintings of Mickalene Thomas dazzle us with their surfaces, scale, and powerhouse representations of women. Thomas, born in 1971, embeds rhinestones on her surfaces that serve to keep us at a distance, even as her huge women take over our space. In her re-imagining of Manet's famous painting, *Le déjeuner sur l'herbe*, as *Le déjeuner sur l'herbe: les trois femmes noires*, three women look at us and beyond us, we are not seen. Thomas's work requires time to explore; she creates landscapes of patterns and styles, mixing photography and painting, combining the geometry of "White male" modernism with decorative fabrics. In fact, just about anything goes in her work; she has no interest in setting any limits on herself or her subjects.

I am sure that the Black Lives Matter Movement had something to do with the framing of the exhibition. Of course, the Seattle Art Museum has shown other Black artists, such as Kehinde Wiley and Nike Cave. In the Jacob Lawrence and Gwen Knight Gallery (subsidized for the showing of Black artists and curated by Sandra Jackson-Dumont, who was the only African American curator at SAM), we saw cutting-edge artists like Titus Kaphar, LaToya Ruby Frazier, Theaster Gates, and Matika Wilbur.

But SAM can answer the question "who has power" by continuing to vigorously integrate its collection, its staff, its audience and its programs. (For starters, admission keeps most people away—the prices are astronomical and special exhibitions are still half price on those free first Thursdays.)


(2018)

# Mickelene Thomas Muse

Mickalene Thomas strategically presented her amazing work to an almost all White press gathering (one Asian person came from Microsoft). "MUSE: Mickalene Thomas Photographs" accompanied by a publication of the same name by the prestigious Aperture Press, features large portraits, small collages, smaller polaroids, and videos along with the work of other artists important to the artist. Thomas spoke of the importance of community. I was impressed by the artist's humility, her respect for other artists, and her understated presentation, in spite of her superstar status.

At the entrance to the exhibition, the artist re-created her living room/studio, including an old tv monitor playing a video about her mother at the center. Indeed, her mother, who died shortly after the video was completed, animated the exhibition as a whole. Thomas carefully outlined her relationship with her mother as well as the making of the video. We have come a long way from Whistler's somber Mother!

Both she and her mother were fashion models, sometimes in partnership. Certainly the artist's sense of presentation, display, color, pattern, and sheer style echoes that perspective. But Thomas takes it much further with subtle layers of meanings and references in every work.

In the "living room" and in the gallery itself we were surrounded by Thomas's bold, frontal head and shoulder portraits of her beautiful Black friends, as well as those of friends and lovers lounging luxuriantly on sofas. But in the press preview she made nary a reference to sex, sexuality, gender, or even blackness. We learned about her techniques, her heroes, her friends. The small scale of the polaroids and collages, the studies for larger works, are the foundation for the huge photo-paintings we saw recently at the Seattle Art Museum, but there are no shiny sequins here.

I was so glad that on the following morning, I went to a second event: a "tête-á-tête," that was billed as a "salon talk" with performance artist Christa Bell and poet Anastacia-Renée. It was described as "designed to be a safe space for an intracommunity conversation among Black women and Black gender non-conforming folks, this will be an outdoor, salon-style gathering. Facilitators will present a family reunion-inspired approach to generate a warm and creatively conducive environment for discussing core themes that emerge in the artwork of Thomas and the tête-á-tête."

In spite of my being a White woman, Christa Bell, a well known performance artist, graciously welcomed me. Instead of discussion, we played hand games, both with a single partner and collectively, then Bell and Anastacia-Renée invited us to lie on patterned quilts on the ground while we ate some snacks—Le dejeuner sur l'herbe! Thomas's iconic work, *Le déjeuner sur l'herbe: les trois femmes noires,* reworks the famous Manet painting, and now we relived it. In MUSE we saw how the artist creates her monumental works through dozens of studies in collage, photographs, and a combination of the two.

However, the main experience of the "salon" was to allow us to actually experience the female solidarity that is central to every work by Thomas. Of course, we know that the artist took hundreds of photographs of each woman, and they had to work hard to look so relaxed, but during the salon luxurious sensuality came to us from within, rather than from outside.

As you go through the exhibition allow yourself to feel it as well as to see it. The lounging women live in their own pattern-filled settings, all created by the artist. But under the artifice, behind the masks, the aloofness, the distant gazes, we know there is a whole world of love and caring.

Mickalene Thomas carefully poses her models in the midst of dizzying colors, textures, and spaces as she presents a private world for public consumption. The density of the patterns amplifies the sensuality even as it blocks our access. That contradiction is her strength. Just as at the press conference she said little about the actual subject of the exhibition, her work exists on many levels according to your perspective. Embedded in every scene are references to Black culture, Black music and personal details. The fabrics themselves tell stories, and in the recreation of her studio many objects connect directly to her mother.

(2018)

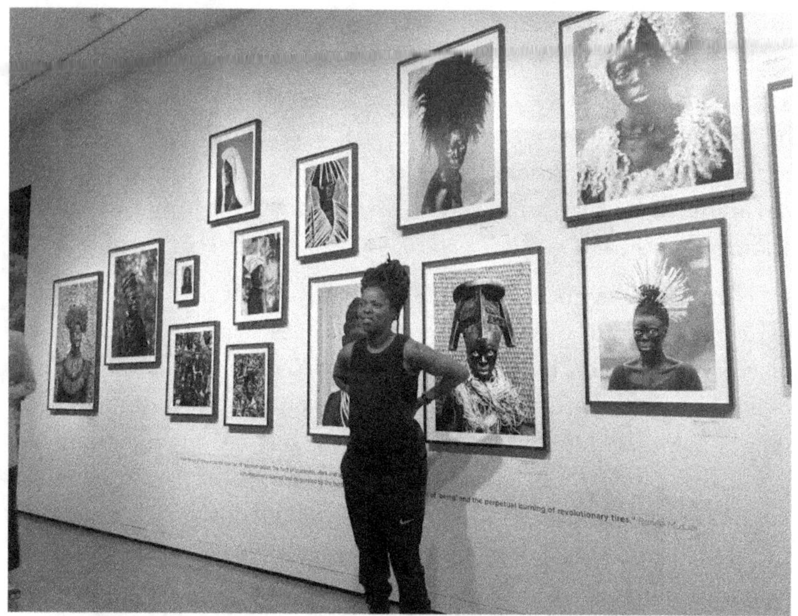

Zanele Muholi speaking in her exhibition, "Somnyama Ngonyama: Hail the Dark Lioness," Seattle Art Museum 2019

# Zanele Muholi "Hail the Black Lioness"

THE OVERSIZE SELF PORTRAIT PHOTOGRAPHS BY South African superstar artist Zanele Muholi (they/them) burst out of the Jacob Lawrence and Gwen Knight corner gallery at the Seattle Art Museum. Their exhibition "Somnyama Ngonyama: Hail the Dark Lioness," spills into four adjoining spaces.

First, a four-foot high self-portrait confronts us in the gallery adjacent to the art of the abstract expressionists (mild White man art by comparison). In the photograph, the artist wears a headdress of sheepskin that takes a lion's mane to the next level of luxuriance. Keeping in mind that it is the male lion that has a mane, this lioness identifies as *they*. They look to the side, focusing beyond us.

Turning around, we see the artist posing in a mural-scaled photograph in what evokes a classical reclining nude posture, until we realize

250

that it contradicts that tradition of exploitation. Lying on their side and holding tightly to multiple plastic pillows that cover all specifically sexual body parts, they displace and occupy the reclining nude tradition constructed for male eyes throughout art history.

Moving into the next space, another four-foot self-portrait evokes the statue of liberty, with the crown replaced by large coils of black foam and the gaze directed skyward. Again, the icon is redefined, reoccupied, remythologized. As "liberty" has become an empty word, this upward gaze expresses that impatience and absurdity.

The oblique gazes accent the whites of the eyes in every image in the show. As we enter the main gallery, painted entirely in black on two walls, we experience these intense looks over and over, trapped as though by pincers on four walls of self-portraits. In each work the artist transforms into a goddess, a miner, a queen, a king, and even a rocky cliff or forest. Muholi collects materials from various places: buying from stores, clothing from friends, items found in hotels or friends' houses. The props enable layers of metaphors and political references that range from historical to contemporary, from personal to public.

For example, in a self-portrait with South African money pinned to their head, a cow's skin pinned on their shoulders, the references can be to the "bride price," the selling of women like cattle, but defiance and resistance embodies the posture and the gaze, even as it seems to suggest surrender.

In another work, an homage to her sister, a gentle and proud Muholi wears a crown and necklace of rubber inner tubes. They confer majesty. Rubber also makes reference to the violent history of rubber in Africa: the Belgian King Leopold ruthlessly killed thousands to satisfy his thirst for that "natural" product. We can draw a straight line to the exploitation in the Congo today to obtain the minerals for our electronic gadgets.

Every single image can be approached with layers of meanings, as brought out by the intense and indispensable series of essays in the exhibition catalog. About the portrait *Kwanele, Parktown, 2016,* a face surrounded by plastic detritus, Ama Josephine Budge writes:

Enough a plastic wrapper for a headdress. Enough chemical spilled oceans. Enough burning of carrier bags. Enough the animal carcass choked with used needles and candy wrappers. Enough electronic waste that will never decompose. Enough acid poisoning that never washes off. Enough villages under sand. Enough sand stolen for cement. Enough salinized cropland. Enough desertification. Enough brown bodies on the shoreline. Enough plastic wrappers forced migration. Enough polyethylene saran-wrapped suitcases—everything I could grab in a moment—abandoned at the immigration center. Enough tear gas in the eyes of protestors. Enough extinct species. Enough plastic-strewn beaches. Enough. Enough. Enough. Enough. Enough. How many times must I say, 'kwanele' it's enough, before what you hear is not more but too much.

The directness of the artist's bold head shots controls us as we look back seeing the steely gaze, the power, the anger, the courage. Muholi speaks of occupying public space, the spaces given to White people. As a South African, Muholi is particularly aware of the segregation of public space and its history in apartheid, but the entire planet is rapidly becoming an apartheid state with migrants imprisoned at militarized borders or drowned at sea.

Started prior to this series, Muholi also continues with an ongoing series of photographs of the LGBTQIA people of South Africa "Faces and Phases." The artist is honoring those murdered and those living amid murders and crimes against their community. Muholi's own studio was ransacked, and unprinted work deliberately destroyed.

Turning the camera back on their own face in these portraits, Muholi allows no objectification of the other, deliberately negating a long tradition of the Black body in ethnography, anthropology, tourist and so called "documentary" photography. The body is Muholi's, the narrative is Muholi's.

The statement is both local and global: the artist has constructed the images all over the world and identified each image by city, and in isiZulu, their native tongue. Working in black and white (albeit with color film) is another political reference to photography as created by White eyes and cameras calibrated in F stops for White skins. Here the subtle tones of black emphasize the many nuances of dark skin colors.

We are caught in the web of these layered metaphors that brilliantly defy the state of our present world. "Hail the Dark Lioness"!

(2019)

# Part 6 Defying Clichés

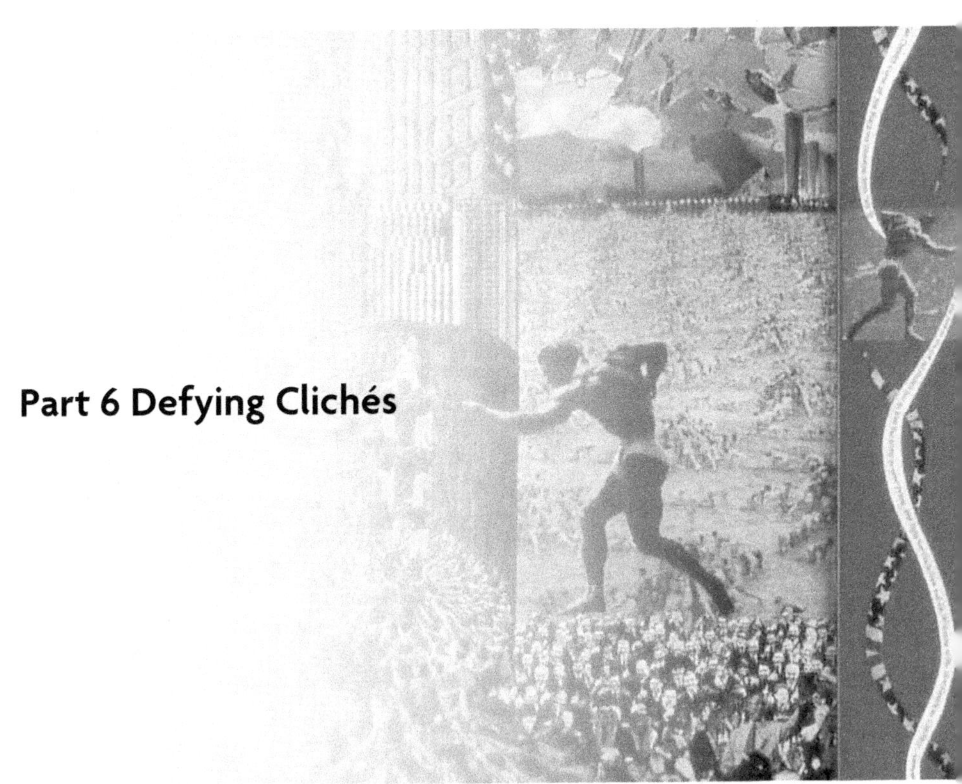

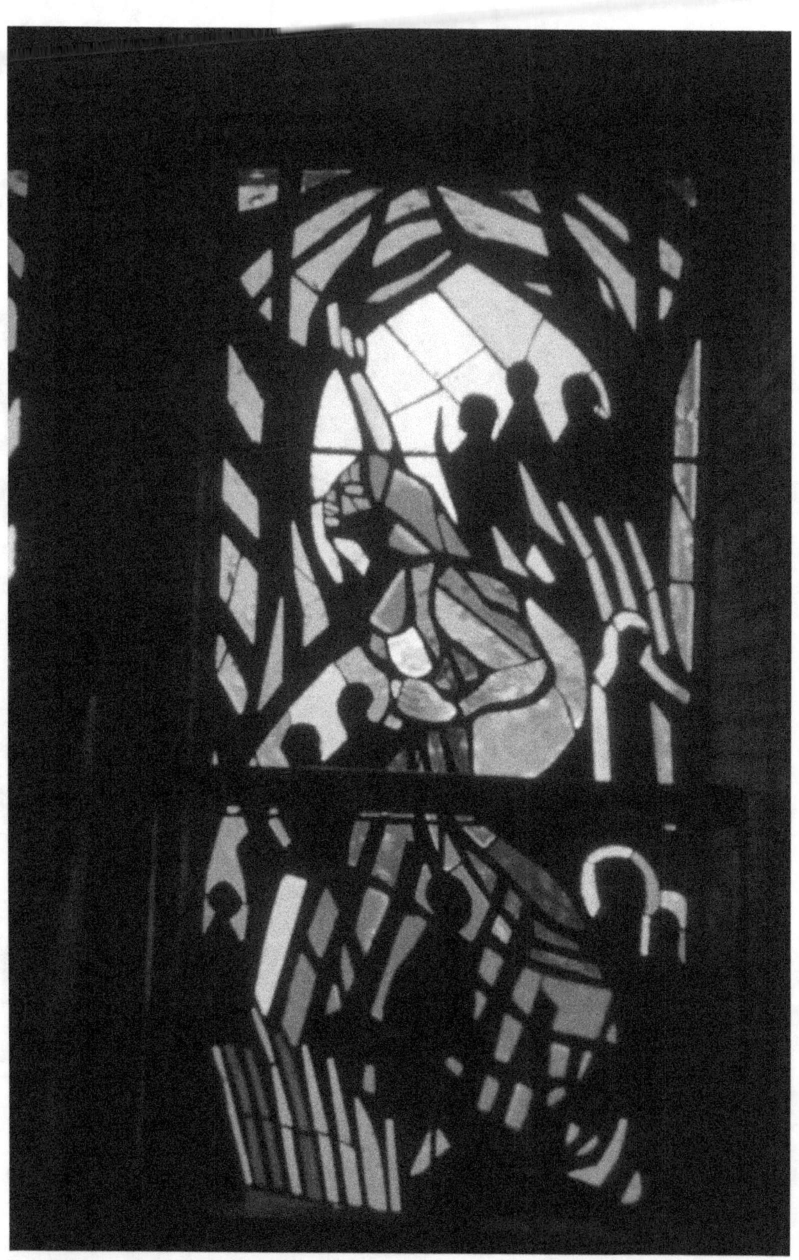

Jean Lacy, *Harriet Tubman,* one of 53 stained glass windows in Saint Luke's Community United Methodist Church, Dallas, Texas, 1996

# Jean Lacy's Stained Glass Windows

I don't think I am radical, I am just in search of truths.

—Jean Lacy

JEAN LACY OPENED HER DISCUSSION about her fifty-three stained glass windows for the sanctuary of Saint Luke Community United Methodist Church in Dallas, Texas, with a letter from Aaron Douglas to Langston Hughes:

Your problem, Langston, my problem, no our problem is to conceive, develop, establish an art era. Not white art painted black. . . . Let's bare our arms and plunge them deep through laughter, through pain, through sorrow, through hope, through disappointment, into the very depths of the souls of our people and drag forth material crude, rough, neglected. Then let's sing it, dance it, write it, paint it. Let's do the impossible. Let's create something transcendentally material, mystically objective, Earthy. Spiritually earthy. Dynamic. (As quoted in Amy Helene Kirschke, *Aaron Douglas, Art, Race, and the Harlem Renaissance,* University of Mississippi, Jackson, 1995)

The stained glass windows for Saint Luke's sanctuary discard traditional and sacrosanct images (what she called the Errol Flynn Jesus). Jean explained: "They present instead the sojourn of black people, the epic religious quest that has come through diaspora. From creation to Migration to Civil Rights, from our ancient past until today." The basis for these connections was partly from a Sunday school curriculum that Lacy developed over many years that made links between the Bible and contemporary events. *The Last Supper* becomes a sit-in at a lunch counter. Christ on the cross is Black and has an Afro.

Lacy was approached by the Reverend Zan W. Holmes Jr., a friend of her ex-husband, to create windows for his new church. She had always worked small, but she decided to take on the challenge. Over the course of a year she talked to many people; she saw Matisse's chapel in France; visited the cathedrals of Europe. She began by paying tribute to the work of some of the writers she admired, such as James Weldon Johnson's *God's Trombones*, illustrated by Aaron Douglas in the 1920s. The "Creation" myth became a starting point, transforming the "Creation" windows into a bird, a spider, snails, a rabbit, a turtle, and an antelope—all from African folk stories of creation.

In the cycle of the "Crucifixion" she includes the lynching of a Black man, at the same time the rope becomes a burial cloth. A boat refers to Egyptian deities, Isis and Osiris, the Holy Family, and a slave ship. Cotton pickers with mask-like faces take the place of shepherds.

Another series shows the emergence from slavery, and includes Harriet Tubman, breaking the chain of slavery, Sojourner Truth, Mary Bethune, and John Wesley, the only White man and founder of the Methodist church. Other references include quilting, the Great Migration, and a birth scene in the inner city.

A third series of images draws on photographs of civil rights marches including Martin Luther King, a lunch counter sit-in, SNCC (Student Nonviolent Coordinating Committee), and Malcolm X.

Robert Foster of Bryant, Texas, fabricated the windows of glass made in West Virginia. The commission from the church gave her complete freedom in terms of color. The result is dazzling.

She succeeded in blending the historical and the educational story of, as she said, "who we are as a people." Her visual narrative, very much in the tradition of the stained glass from the Middle Ages, can be read like a book in terms of symbols and contemporary references.

(1996)

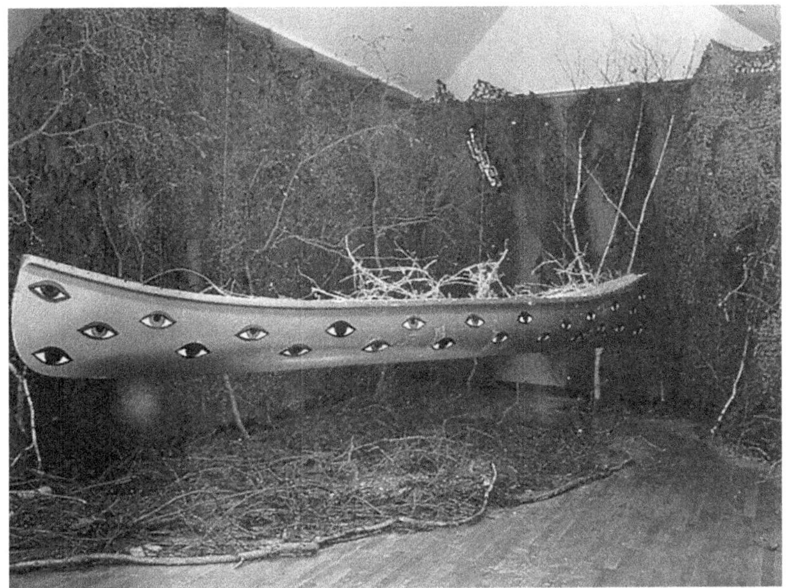

Betye Saar, "A Remembrance of Ritual," installation at the Tacoma Art Museum, 1997, Shell of a collapsible canoe, sand, branches, and oyster shells, masked skeleton

# Icons Now and Then by Betye Saar

ALTARS USUALLY FAIL TO MOVE ME in contemporary art; those tiresome collections of sticks, stones, bones, feathers, and sand sit inertly and without meaning. They seem to be simply the day's accumulation from the beach. In that challenging medium, Betye Saar succeeds in suggesting contemporary spirituality. Her trademark combination is the miniature and monumental, the found object embedded in a large field of paint, using everything from kitsch religious objects to computer components and Polaroids. Saar even invites viewers to make their own contributions.

"Betye Saar: Ritual and Remembrance" comprises several parts assembled from different sources that together create a selected overview of the artist's work. At the entrance to the gallery is a small group of works from Seattle City Light's 1% for Art Portable Works Collection, which include some of Saar's boxes and assemblages of the late

1970s. *Calling Card* is a box that refers directly to the ironies and pain of racism by means of Mammy dolls. The Black Mammy was, of course, the only "calling card" for Black women to enter White middle class houses in the South for many years. The artist's anger over the assassination of Martin Luther King. led to her first constructed boxes, of which *The Liberation of Aunt Jemima*, 1972, is the most famous.

Since the 1980s, Saar's work has been meditative. A show within a show, "Personal Icons," organized by Exhibits USA and curated by Lizzetta LeFalle-Collins, has a separate gallery within the Tacoma exhibition. It includes twenty-six small, mixed-media icons executed between 1988 and 1994, and the installation "Wings of Morning" (1987-1991).

The diminutive personal icons—loaded with Buddhas, eyes, snakes, hands, and other minutiae set in a dense collage of fabrics—could have collapsed into a flea market effect, but didn't, due to Saar's subtle aesthetic sensibility. The viewer can, however, easily sink into the quicksand of occult references. But Saar claims that since her approach is spiritually eclectic, it is not necessary to be familiar with Tantric traditions or Afro Caribbean rituals in order to understand them. That is both true and not true; I find that the small, private altars are incomprehensible if I try to decipher the parts or read them, even as I have the feeling that each one is a specific hieroglyph.

Surrounding the gallery with the icons, the large works of the rest of the exhibition are collectively called "Resurrections." They include the three Spirit Chairs, *Pause Here, Diaspora Spirit*, and *Sanctuary Awaits*, commissioned for the 1996 Olympic Arts Festival in Atlanta, and here shown together as traditional, cast bronze sculptures. (In Atlanta, the "chairs" were in widely separated public spaces.) Although called "chairs," they are far from functional; they signify, for me, the new weighty reputation of Saar. They are imposing contemporary sculptures.

Also part of "Resurrections" is *Mojotech,* 1987, an altar that is well known as the product of Saar's work at MIT, when she began to view computer culture as part of the cultic practice of contemporary society. *Tangled Roots,* 1996, refers to Saar's mixed race background: hands from dummies painted gold, brown, and white stand amidst a tangle of branches and cedar chips.

In the center of the gallery is the installation, "A Remembrance of Ritual," produced for the Tacoma Art Museum exhibition. Above the shell of a collapsible canoe painted with many eyes, Saar suspended branches, and oyster shells. A masked skeleton in the bottom of the boat reflects on the sand underneath and invokes the middle passage as well as the passage from life to death in Native American cultures.

These installations depart radically from the format of altar, icon, and box. Perhaps, because they do not force one to stop and stand still and probe tiny details, then step back to look at a larger picture, they affected me less than the older *Mojotech* installation. The visual and psychic shift from intimate to large scale in *Mojotech* prepared viewers for a larger perspective that has nothing to do with the inside of the gallery. With the recent installations, it is all too easy to just walk by or around them and not actually feel connected.

Why is Saar's work resonant—even in its recent, more simplified, installations—in the midst of the prevailing cool ironies and disbelief of the late 1990s? It may be because she was actually psychic until the age of seven, or because she has a connection to another reality that comes through in her work. She asks us to see beyond the material object, whether in the tiny components of computers or the classical monumentality of bronze. Saar's gentle humility in her difficult commitment to exploring contemporary spirituality is a reassuring contrast to the shallowness of much current installation art.

(1997)

# Marilyn Walgore's Gender Games

Marilyn Waligore's provocative photographs challenge the viewer to re-think cultural constructs about women. Her large format color photographs focus on love and courtship with a sub plot of sex and violence. In a still life format, she plays with such culturally-loaded objects as dolls, clothes, and gravestones to invoke cultural rituals that constrain and confine women. These rituals include such designations as "old maid" and the "biological clock," two phrases that value women only in a reproductive function.

Key to the impact of the photographs is the transformation of the original objects almost beyond recognition by means of color reversal, and the subversion of feminine color to irritating hues of purples and pinks. Waligore adopts disorienting scale shifts and bizarre juxtapositions.

Macabre still life arrangements suggest a cultural masquerade. In one work, a pink-cheeked Cinderella sugar shaker becomes a sorceress with glowing yellow eyes against a background of broken glass and lurid, huge purple shoes. No human figures appear, only cultural simulacra, mediated by social stereotypes.

Waligore revitalizes and transforms the traditional still life. She presents the stasis and imprisonment of gender clichés, a true "still life" instead of the traditional fruits, flowers, and game animals—all of which were often metaphors for male desire. The photographs also combine still life arrangements with text that quotes from clichés, providing another layer of social reference.

Waligore interrupts coherent reading of her images, intervening in a narrative reading with ambiguity and irony. Her images function as hieroglyphs of personal fantasy and memory, rather than clear symbols or metaphors. In seeking material for her still life compositions she

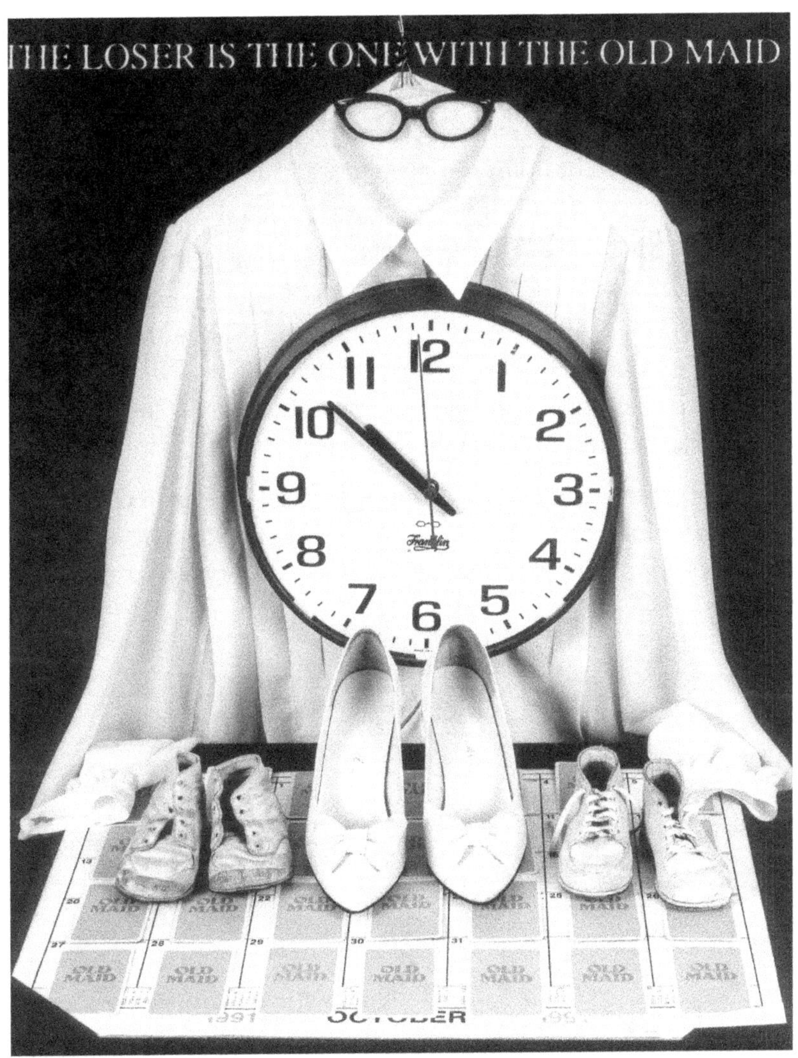


Marilyn Waligore, *Don't Be an Old Maid #2*, 1991, chromogenic print, 30 x 24",
Courtesy of the Artist

avoids already heavily loaded cultural images such as Mickey Mouse or Barbie Doll, finding instead those with less clear baggage based in fairy tales or childhood rhymes.

Kitsch means "gaudy trash" in German. Clement Greenberg set the tone for kitsch as the antithesis of avant-garde art just after World War II and the dismissal continued for many years. But Waligore adopts kitsch as an avant-garde strategy to (re)present cultural constructs invigorated by ironic commentaries and artistic transformations.

In earlier work, created in Wooster, Ohio, Waligore photographed found still life in storefront displays. Since moving to Dallas five years ago, she has found the highly controlled and repetitive imagery of commercial strip malls in suburbia less inspiring, so she has turned to studio still life arrangements. Most recently she has begun to work with historical references, such as imagery and text drawn from encyclopedias as historical markers of our cultural heritage.

Her photographs convey not only the gender issues in our society in general, but also the disjunctive tensions of the modern woman in collision with traditional female roles, an issue that emerges so clearly in Texas.

(1993)

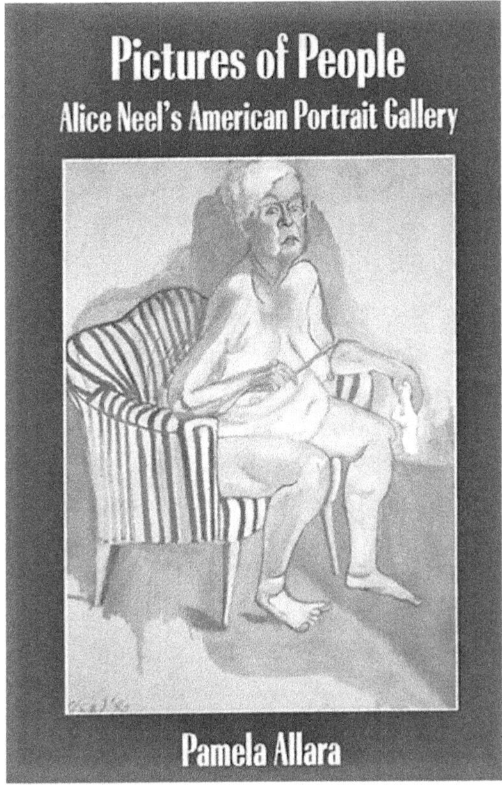

Pamela Allara, *Pictures of People, Alice Neel's American Portrait Gallery*, University Press of New England, 1998, cover art Alice Neel, *Self Portrait*, 1980

## Pamela Allara Faces Alice Neel Head On

PAMELA ALLARA'S STUDY OF ALICE NEEL reads like an exciting novel. At the same time, it is a major work of scholarship. Neel's life covers the entire cultural history of the twentieth century, but this is the twentieth century of the "other."

To begin with, a portrait gallery is an incongruous subject for a political radical, but Allara faces all the contradictions of Neel's career head on. She traces the artist's roots from a privileged background in Philadelphia, where she learned of the Ash Can School of Robert Henri and then married a Cuban artist. Allara next discusses Neel's connection to the Cuban avant-garde In Havana in the mid 1920s, especially the cultural dissonance that Neel experienced. In the 1930s, Neel painted portraits of communist writers and editors, supported by the Works Progress Administration on an hourly wage for the program's entire duration. She moved from Greenwich Village to Spanish Harlem in the 1940s, raised two children alone, and painted portraits of her neighbors.

By the 1950s Neel was again moving in the bohemian circles of Greenwich Village, and she even appeared in the Beat classic film "Pull My Daisy." In the next decade she moved into Andy Warhol's orbit and painted his portrait, after he was shot, as a virtual sacrificial victim of contemporary culture. As Neel turned to serious promotion of her career in the 1970s, she painted dealers, curators, and artists (mostly naked), but continued to break new ground by doing portraits of gay men and gay couples well before that group was "out" in the art world. Neel also painted some of the leaders of the feminist movement in the 1970s, the best-known phase of her career, although as Allara points out, up to that point she was not really a feminist.

Neel's career charts the history of twentieth century culture from the particular places that the artist occupied among marginalized groups and leaders of the time. Allara, adroitly but thoroughly, contextualizes each phase of the artist's career in terms of recent theory, as well as brilliantly analyzing the layers of codes and metaphors in the portraits. In addition, she deconstructs Neel's mythmaking during her celebrity years, without in any sense lessening her stature. In fact, Allara's book reveals a multidimensional woman who is much more complex than she let on. Neel understood that the identity of the artist needed to be salable in the 70s and 80s and therefore she created a marketable persona. Note the outrageous nude self portrait which Allara put on the cover of her book.

For me, the most moving aspect of Neel's work, revealed here clearly for the first time, are the portraits of mothers and children in Spanish Harlem in the 1940s. These women are far from the bourgeois norms of portraiture established by John Singer Sargent, the last major American portrait painter before Neel, and possess a presence that is far more riveting than that of any Boston aristocrat.

(1998)

# Tomur Atagök's Anatolian Goddess Series

Tomur Atagök's "Anatolian Goddess Series" is part of a long preoccupation with representations of women from the ancient Anatolian Mother Goddesses to women in contemporary society. From Cybele to Madonna, Atagök paints women. She includes unknown contemporary women as well as famous icons, but these contemporary women are energetic: they exercise, they dance, and they flamboyantly participate in contemporary life. The ancient goddesses, in contrast, emerge from mythical roots to proclaim their dominance through Atagök's huge enlargement of the small Neolithic statues of these seated matriarchs.

Atagök assertively paints on shiny metal surfaces primarily in pinks and reds. The paintings reflect, both literally and figuratively, the historical power of women in Neolithic times. Dominating this series is the great Anatolian Mother Goddess from Çatalhöyük. That twenty centimeter (eight inch) statuette, excavated from the oldest city in the world, dates from around 5700 BC. The small figure is seated comfortably between subdued leopards as she gives birth. Her breasts, hips and buttocks swell to enormous proportions, representing her supreme importance as she gives birth. Far removed from the slender, even emaciated, ideal for a female body that is now common for some contemporary societies (notably the United States), this goddess proclaims her physical presence and her authority at the same time.

In the paintings by Tomur Atagök, the Mother Goddess joins our world as a life size figure who stands as a guardian. Rather than a fertility symbol, she is now a symbol of women's energy and command. The Goddess wears a type of mechanical diadem/crown in one painting, and sits in front of a golden shower of sun. These goddesses frame a  a third panel representing vertebrae and ovaries. A woman's interior, so often altered today by contemporary medical science, is here protected by the powerful forces of the goddess.

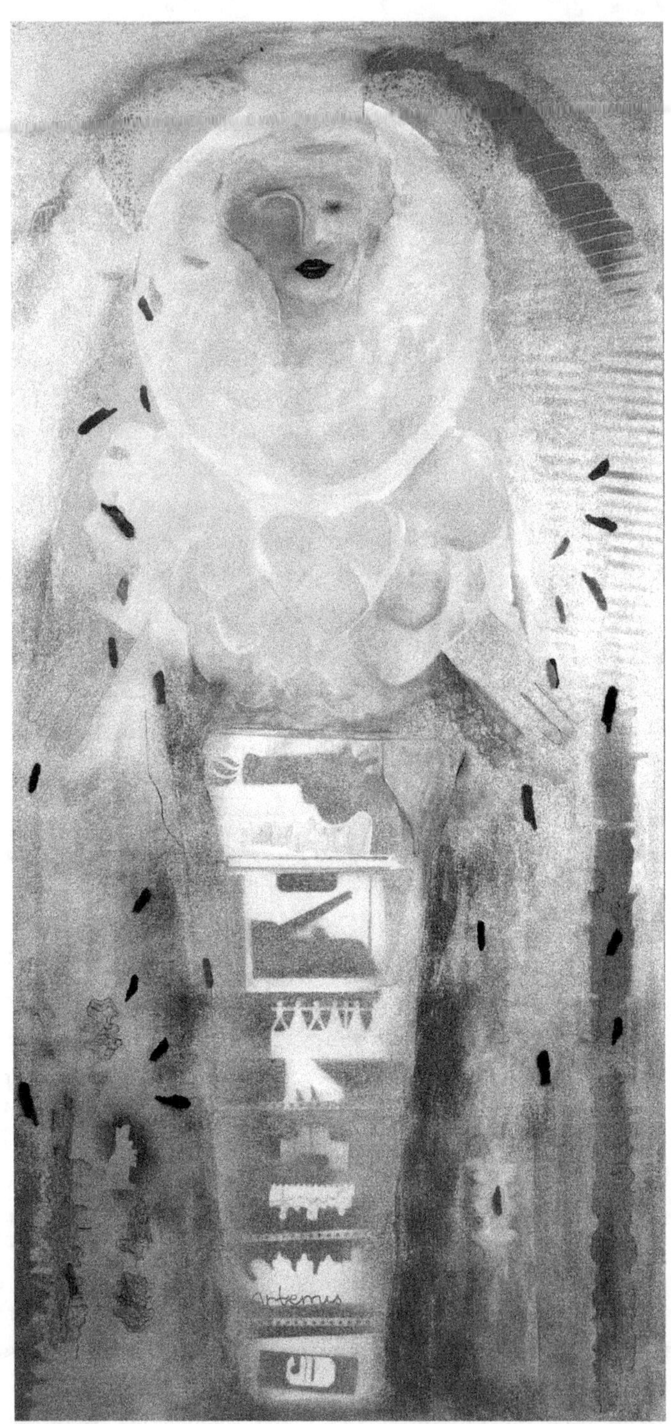

Tomur Atagök, *Artemis of Ephesus* from *The Anatolian Goddess Series*, 1997, oil on canvas, 200 x 100 cm (78 x 40"), Collection of Elgiz Museum, Istanbul, Turkey

Another of these grand paintings is based on Artemis of Ephesus. Artemis, later changed to a slender virgin hunter by the Romans, is here seen in her guise as Cybele, the Anatolian Mother Goddess. Her many breasts carry the power of nurturing and life. In place of the animals under her protection on the traditional statues, this painting has guns, tanks and other references to military warfare. Artemis also has black gloves and a contemporary face with bold red lipstick and blond hair. Atagök created it in response to the violation of sacred lands by military weapons, particularly during the First Gulf War.

The collective presence of these historical goddesses connects contemporary women and historical female power, particularly in western Asia. At the same time, Atagök paints in a style that has roots in abstract expressionism—she trained in the United States from 1960-1973. Tomur Atagök occupies her own major place in contemporary art in Turkey as she embraces the aesthetic focus of modernism, popular culture and feminism. To that she adds her intense political engagement, an understanding of both history and art history, and concern for the state of the planet.

(1999)

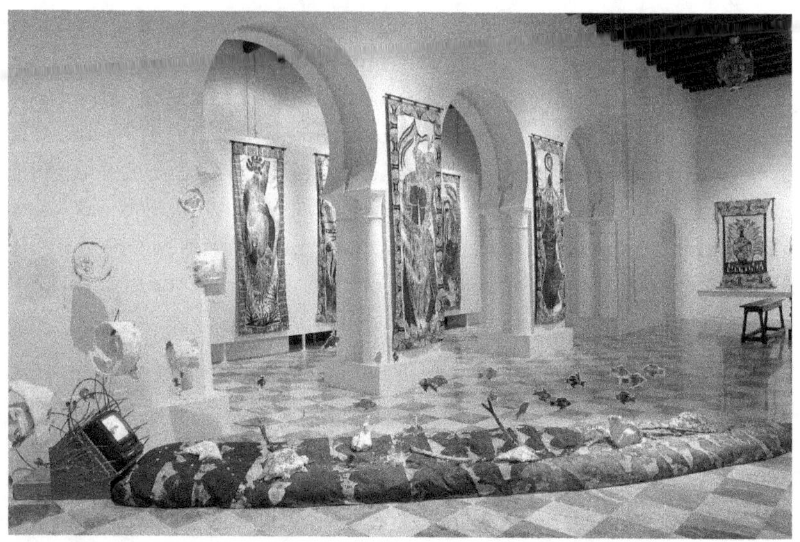

Imna Arroyo, *The many faces of Yemaya*, 2000-2001, floor installation, 7 panels, 93 x 33", site specific installation in exhibition "Imna Arroyo: In Search of My Tracks, A Spiritual Journey," Centro Cultural de Bellas Artes, Guayama, Puerto Rico

# Imna Arroyo:  History, Place, Spirituality

OF AFRICAN, TAINO AND SPANISH HERITAGE, Imna Arroyo is an Afro-Puerto Rican artist deeply committed to acknowledging her multiple heritages and to transforming that heritage into a contemporary artistic statement. Throughout her career she has consistently reached beyond her current work to the next level of creativity, complexity and technical proficiency. She has never settled for a formulaic answer, a single concept, or even a single media. As a result she tells a layered story of her life that resonates with history, place and spirituality.  She frequently turns to the symbolism and language of Yoruba poetry, proverbs, legends, myths and imagery.

As an artist printmaker Arroyo has had an exceptionally rich training, as she constantly explores new techniques. As a young woman in the 1960s she studied with José Alicea in Puerto Rico. After coming to the United States, she earned a BFA from Pratt Institute in 1977 studying with Michael Ponce de Leon and Robert Blackburn. Only

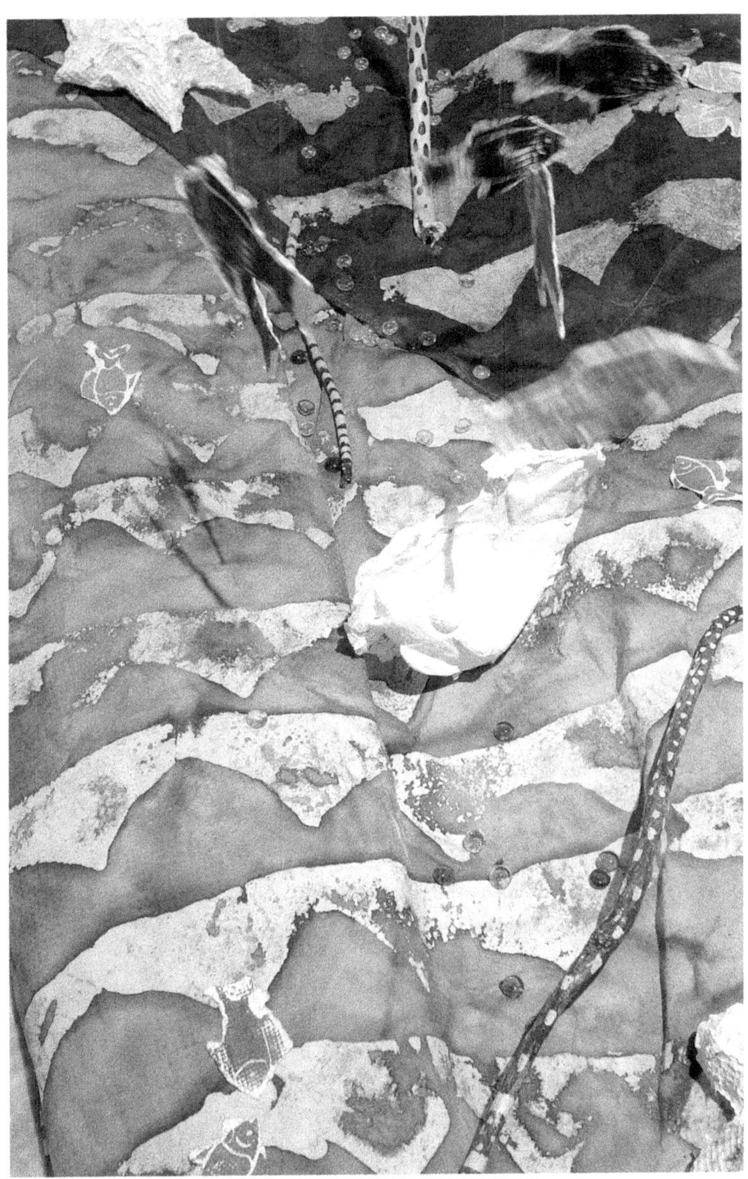

Imna Arroyo, *The many faces of Yemaya,* floor installation, detail two years later she completed an MFA at Yale University. With Gabor Peterdi and Winifred Lutz at Yale and later Krishna Reddy at New York University, she further explored etching, aquatint, and color intaglio techniques. In the 1980's Arroyo learned multi-color Japanese traditional woodcut techniques with Francisco Patlán in Mexico, and aluminum plate printing at Tamarind Institute.

## Part I The Middle Passage

Starting in the late 1500s more than 12 million Africans were transported as slaves from Africa to the Caribbean, then sold for sugar and other raw materials to take back to Europe. The horror of this crime is so great that we are all still processing what it means.

Many artists of African descent address this topic from different perspectives. Imna Arroyo's major installation *Ancestors of the Passage,* 2005-07, focuses on those who did not make it through the three week voyage in unspeakable conditions. Those who were sick or died were simply thrown overboard. *Ancestors* emphasizes the spirits of those who died, making them visible in prints and sculptures. She speaks to their presence in the lives of those who survived in memories and cultural practices.

*Ancestors of the Passage* overwhelms and embraces us with its striking blue satin sea on the floor, the ceramic busts and hands of those lost in the sea, and a series of prints that cover the walls with haunted faces.

Arroyo's awakening to this horrendous act came when she visited the Door of No Return in Ghana: "In 1997 I traveled for the first time to Ghana. It was at the Elmina Castle, standing in front of the Door of No Return that I had an epiphany that we are all part of a spirit continuum. It was an experience that made me aware of the ancestral realm and forever changed my perception of time and space."

Arroyo began exploring Yemaya, Goddess of Water, as a theme in her work in the summer of 2001. It is a logical step from exploring those who drowned in the sea during the Middle Passage to invoking a spiritual presence that both looked over them and looked out for the survivors. "The Many Paths of Yemaya" is a multi-media installation composed of seven panels, woodblock prints, and a floor installation recreating the Atlantic and the Caribbean oceans. It is made of fabric batiked by the artist accompanied by handmade paper sculptures, shells, glass, wood sculptures. The panels are printed on satin and framed with Batik fabric from Ghana.

## Part II Iroko: Tree Of Life

At the same time as these works, Imna created a series based on "Iroko, Tree of Life." It culminated in a multimedia collaborative exhibition in 2017, and it is still going through new iterations. The 2017 exhibition included prints of the *Ceiba, Tree of Life* that depicted its transformation in various cultures.

The artist describes IROKO: TREE OF LIFE:

IROKO was inspired by the sacred Tree of Life, known as Iroko to the Yoruba people of West Africa and those of the African Diaspora, Yaxché to the Maya, Kapok in Southeast Asia, Silk-Cotton Tree to Indigenous North Americans, and La Ceiba in the Caribbean, Central and South America. The tree is of great symbolic, spiritual, mythological, medicinal, magical, commercial, ecological and aesthetic import. Through the exploration of materials old and new, traditional and innovative technologies, this multi-media installation focuses on the mysteries of nature using the Iroko/ Yaxché/ Kapok/ La Ceiba / Silk-Cotton Tree as an anchor to express the power of nature, its continuity and resiliency, which holds the promise for a sustainable future if nurtured and honored.

IROKO addresses the challenge of climate change by exploring the interrelationship between our external ecological situation, our awareness of the sacred in creation, and our internal relationship with the symbolic world of the soul. IROKO's intention is to promote art that expresses that complex, diverse and dynamic intersection, while seeking to connect the intellectual, spiritual and practical components of community building and sustainability.

All quotes from Imna Arroyo based on our email correspondence, August, September 2021.

(1995, 2021)

# Marita Dingus's Acts of Metamorphosis

At a presentation in Edmonds, Marita Dingus revealed some of the secrets of her extraordinary art made entirely of recycled materials. Recycled we already knew, but there is a lot more to it than just reclaiming materials.

She explained in a compelling demonstration that she chose materials that were "worthless," if they have any value at all she takes them to a thrift shop she said, holding a metal ring from a lampshade as an example. Her choice of materials is based on durability as well as the fact that they are judged completely useless in our society. For example, she uses the shiny plastic wrap from Bertolli products, or the spirals from spiral notebooks, or the wire from Boeing airplane construction. Her criteria also includes that the wire needs to be easy to bend–she was making flowers out of Bertolli shiny wrap and wire as she talked.

Her own wardrobe is entirely made of recycled clothes and materials, "things get cut up many many times" she said. When she spent several years in Texas, she packed up all of her belongings in large bags made from recycled fabric. Her purse is based on a Clorox bottle covered in fabric.

Marita is truly living close to the earth as well—she raises chickens, and eats their eggs at her home that she shares with her mother (who also helps with her art) on five acres of old growth woods in Auburn, Washington. Her family moved there in the 1950s. It is next to the cemetery, at that time the only place that African Americans could live in Auburn.

All of the current talk about our carbon footprints, ecology, global warming, living green; Marita has it all figured out.

We don't all have Marita's artistic ability to reclaim useless materials for creating art, but we can think about every single thing we throw away every day and try to cut it in half, reuse it, not use it, or give it to a thrift store. Giving up take outs, plastic bags, and packaged food, even reusing paper napkins as toilet paper, every little bit helps. I've

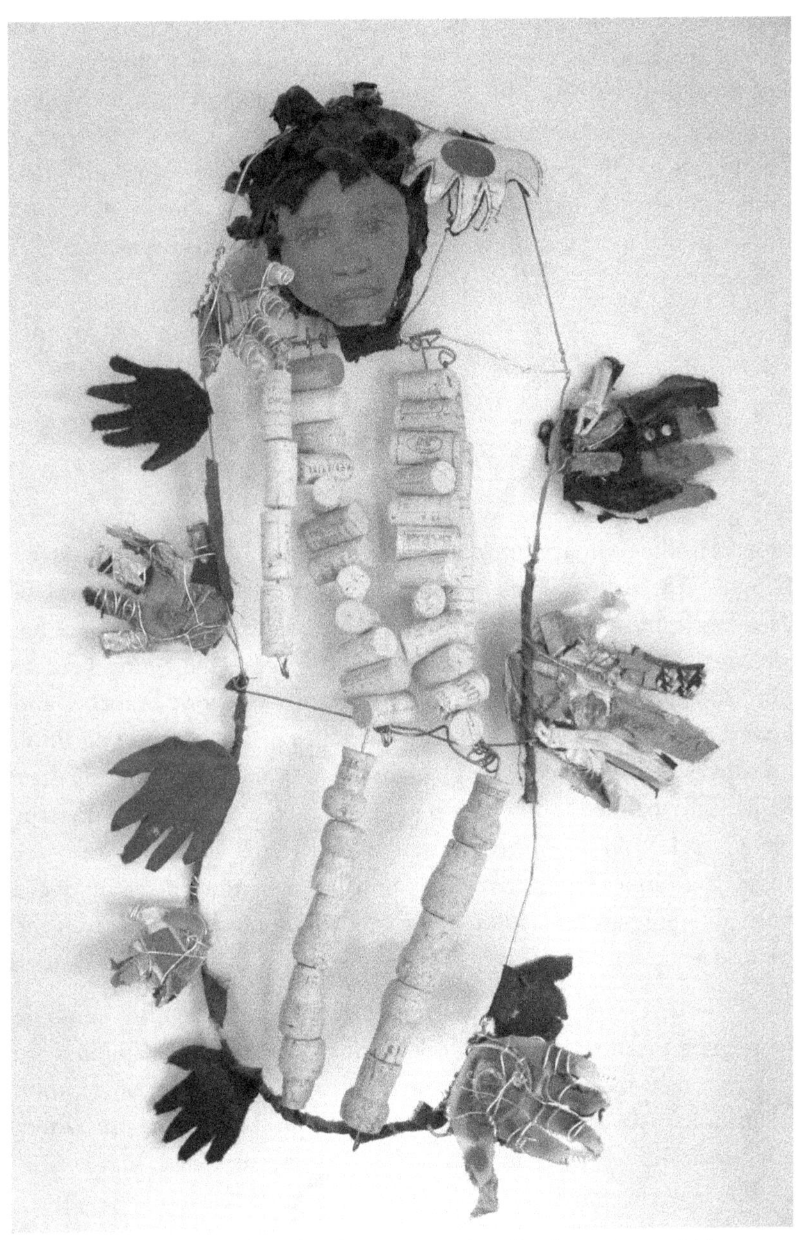

Marita Dingus, *Floating Through Life*, 2002, mixed media, dimensions variable, Collection the author tried to save some useless items, like the plastic tops of take out coffee cups, and let them accumulate, waiting for art to emerge. I had the idea of hanging them on my Christmas tree. It didn't quite happen (family objections), but I looked at the plastic tops and lived with them for a long time, as they piled up, confronting my own waste, instead of flinging them out of sight. Of course the metaphor for Marita is more profound; as an African American she is reclaiming what is considered useless in our society and giving it value as an aesthetic expression.

(2008)

☀

Rarely is one so immediately aware of the particular power of artists to transform the ordinary into the extraordinary as in the work of Marita Dingus. An 18-foot *Woman as Creator,* entirely made from scraps of used fabric and thrown away materials, hovered from the ceiling of her recent exhibition "Talking With the Dead" (Francine Seders Gallery May 2 – June 1). Suspended in a network of wire/fabric branches and leaves, the figure's center of energy is a naturalistic face painted in oil on canvas and oversized, collaged-fabric hands and feet. Dingus pairs a realistically painted face with a body constructed of the rejected scraps of our society in all of her figurative work. This large woman's face suggests an inner focus, her energy flowing from another realm. She is both growing new life and hovering over death, black flowers lie on the ground as delicate green stems reach upward.

The title works of "Talking with the Dead" playfully combine white wire skeletons and flat black fabric phones. These telephones are old, they have buttons that indicate their rotary dials. The conversation amusingly invokes another era: calaveras-type skeletons (those exuberant Mexican escorts) "converse" across cultures as well as across time and beyond the grave.

But the calaveras are simply an amusingly literal reference that underscores the point of the show.

The whole show is a conversation with the dead, more specifically dead African American slaves. Dingus has frequently worked with references to the history of slavery and its brutality as well as to African spirituality. It was specifically depicted in a recent work acquired by the Seattle Art Museum, *400 Men of African Descent* , 1994, in which the artist made 400 12-inch men with no heads as a reference to the 400 men packed into cells before they were shipped off from Ghana as slaves. The artist compresses the references in "Talking with the Dead". The large *Creator* figure generates life and death, but the various other figures bear the strains of a history of physical and spiritual suffering, lack of freedom, or hidden anxieties. These figures are made of pull tabs, corks, test tubes, plastic, wire, fabric—all with painted faces.

The tangled lines of the figures, the compressed organs created with string and wires winding like intestines inside screens at the center of bodies, the blood red figure subtitled "as if it rained blood" that uses a shiny red fabric—all speak of bodily and spiritual pain. *Fabric Figure with Caution Markers* is framed by black and yellow plastic caution tape, the type of tape you can't cross in the street. The metaphor seems clear, this Black man can't cross, he is trapped by the tape. 2-foot figures built up in segments from corks are trapped in frames of hands, helplessly unable to resist invisible forces that have given them only a small space of their own. *Beings Transparent,* figures made of small test tubes are only 1-foot high and suggest people who have reduced themselves to the point of near invisibility. You can see right through them except for their faces and hats. Other figures made only of woven "vines" echo the vines of *Woman as Creator.*

Re-using scraps of fabric is an African American tradition and Dingus taps into ancestral African energy in a way that fills all the works with presence. Her recycled materials become a metaphor for the recovery of the humanity and dignity of African Americans not only in the past but also in the present.

(2003)

❧

The Wa Na Wari cultural SPACE in the Central District focuses on keeping an African American presence in the rapidly gentrifying center of Seattle. Marita Dingus untitled installation felt liberated from the constraints of

White-owned gallery spaces, in which the artist has shown successfully for many years. Here she let loose the frightening energies of oppression, conveyed through black metal junk put together into figures. The blackness of the metal became a force of its own. Knowing that Marita's work can be lighthearted (see the floating copper babies in the Douglass Truth Library), historical (the works owned by the Seattle Art Museum), metaphorical (in her many cork and wire figures), here I saw heaviness, and darkness. Marita always adds painted faces to her figural assemblages: these faces seemed weighed down by their metal bodies.

(2019)

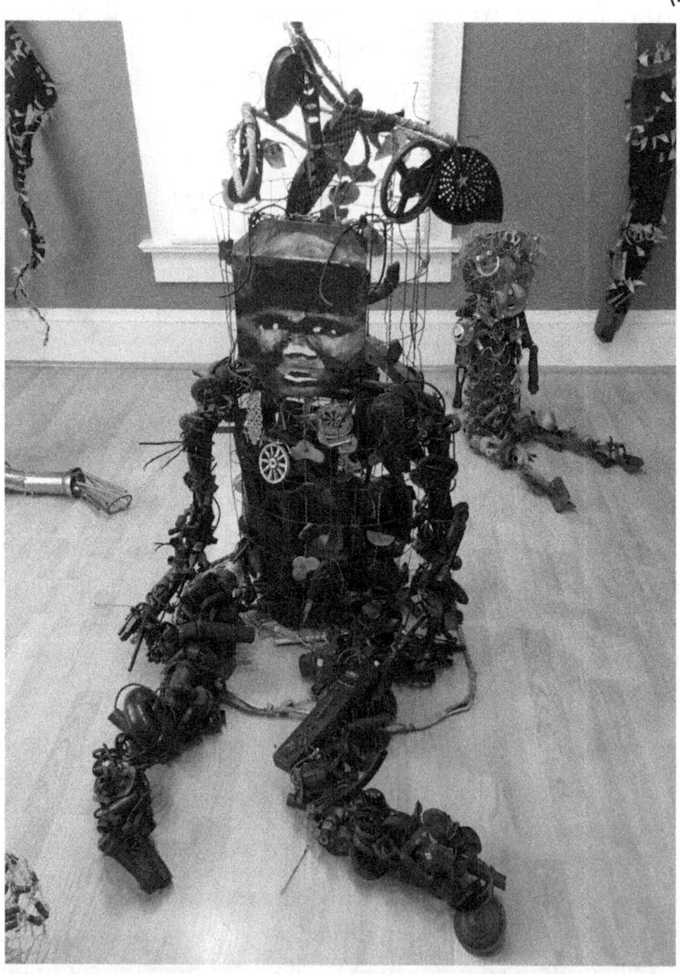

Marita Dingus, *Untitled*, 2019, mixed media, dimensions variable, Collection the artist

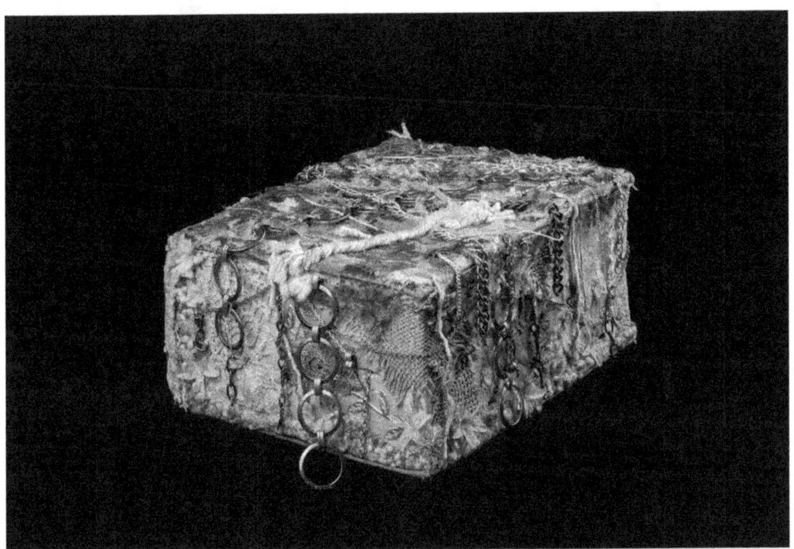

Carletta Carrington Wilson, *book of the bound,* mixed media, 13 x 9 x 6," Photograph: Mark Frey

## Carletta Carrington Wilson's "book of the bound" and "Letter to a Laundress"

The Northwest African American Museum has opened a new gallery with an intimate scale for this special exhibition, "book of the bound." Carrington Wilson is a poet and spoken word performer as well as a visual artist. In this exhibition she has given us twenty-two books, many of them bound shut, with ornate covers of many materials—bone, lace, newspaper, fabrics, string, jewels and much more.

The theme of the exhibition is that slaves were silenced, their narratives lost.

The fabrics of Carrington Wilson's books connect trade, money and the "thread-bare body": the wealth of the traders was based on the bodies of the slaves. As the artist explains in the brochure of the exhibition:

Three vessels, the body, the book, and the ship form an intimate connection in the works of "book of the bound." My work attempts to enter into mysteries binding bodies of flesh to the bodies of land, water, and text that forged and formed the social fabric of our hunger-haunted history.

Her collaged covers become a song to those who could not fill these books with their stories. In some cases the books are opened in a series of pages, accordion pleated, standing, or other formats. Each book has a poetic title, and often also a poem. We see references to those silent slaves who would have been in those pages.

Because European slavers often traded fine fabrics like silk and velvet in exchange for bodies, Wilson believes the stories of their bodies remain in the cloth. She adds another layer as well: merchants could not have sailed ships to Africa without canvas sails.

Carrington Wilson also includes stacks of books whose titles create found poetry. We are invited to do the same thing. This seemingly serendipitous project is revealing. The opportunity for us to create found poetry that points toward issues of the slave trade is empowering.

(2012)

❧

Carletta Carrington Wilson addresses her "letter to a laundress" to her great-great-grandmother, but her profound photo/poem installation currently on view at the Kittredge Gallery in Tacoma honors the work of all those who, in her words, "took in wash."

She found photographs of anonymous laundresses in the archives of the Farm Security Administration, most of them taken in the late 1930s by such well known photographers as Dorothea Lange, Marion Post Wolcott and Russell Lee.

The "letter" is a poem written in blue script on the photographs. It is recited by the artist in a podcast as we view the work.

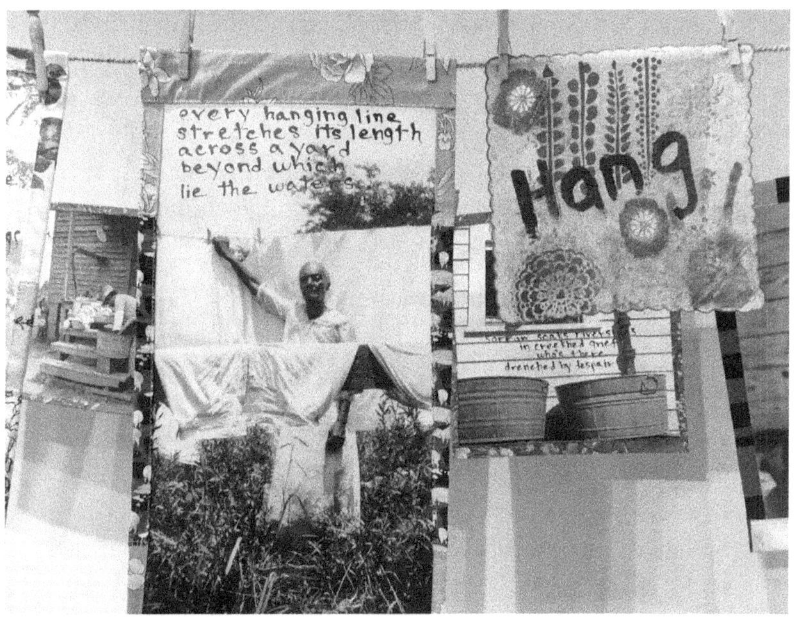


Carletta Carrington Wilson "every hanging line" from the poem "letter to a laundress" by Carletta Carrington Wilson, Installation detail, 2018, Kittredge Gallery, University of Puget Sound, Tacoma; includes Anonymous photograph of Orelia Alexia Franks, ex-slave, Beaumont Texas, July 3, 1937, Library of Congress Prints and Photographs Collection, Courtesy of the Artist

Mounted on fabric, the photographs are pegged to a line, and hang above our heads. As we walk between three lines of closely packed "laundry" the poem unwinds, describing, the many steps of doing laundry before the advent of machines and drip dry fabric.

Carletta has identified ten steps with a single word: Wash Soak Starch Wring Boil Pin Rub Scrub Hang Press.

The photographs are arresting, suggesting the real labor of doing laundry and how it evolved. Some of the photographs are actually from the late 19th century, of early washerwomen stirring laundry in a tub with a washing stick; others have a washboard, that iconic object now seen only as a relic (several are included in the exhibition).

The women rarely look up or out, never at the camera, the photographer. We have all types of women—from those dressed in a muslin shift to elegant women in suits and shoes with heels.

Carletta Carrington Wilson deeply feels words, their meanings, double meanings and symbolism. Thus here, as offered by the artist, is a shift from laundry to something more sinister: "hoist baskets tote tubs lug those loads every bundle extends a line, a line awaiting a line awaiting its hangings." And suddenly as Wilson wrote the poem, she realized the double meaning of hanging as also lynching.

As the artist said in a lecture "The lines of the poem lead the reader away from the mundane duty of washing clothes to a disturbing image of lynching. Thus, we are led into the awful reality that links these women beyond the ordinary task of laundry.

> Post emancipation, in the late 19th and early 20th century there was a rise in the number of lynchings in the South. These mothers, sisters, aunts, grandmothers, cousins and friends knew, were related to, heard of, witnessed and buried someone who had been lynched. They, also, washed the clothes of someone who participated in a lynching. I was just speculating, but this was confirmed by a woman who spoke to me after one of the artist talks.

This exhibition includes other intense works as well: across one wall is a series of fabric works called "field notes," from 2014, with Carletta's trademark layers and meanings hidden in their patterns and textures. You can spend a long time exploring these works, which are, as the artists suggests, like landscapes. One of her themes is the "text of textiles," the steps from cotton into cloth and the metaphors that emerge from fabric.

Then there are simple cut out house shapes, what the artist calls "wordless books," in a series called "knot my name haint my house." They refer to the fact that 90 percent of enslaved people were illiterate. The blue around the doors called "haint blue" was intended to deter ghosts.

On one wall a "knotted line" again has double meaning, the names are (k)not names, but the names given by slave masters, here taken from a plantation inventory. The artist elaborated:

The idea is that once a person becomes enslaved their lines of descent are knotted. Each time a person is sold, with each name change and change of place of bondage the loss of knowledge of familiar ties becomes, increasingly, knotted and unknown.

The artist describes the work "2 resist dying" as referring to both the resist-dye process and, also, that of a man and woman resisting their enslavement. Underneath is a "blood knot, "a tangled pile on the floor invoking the intermixing (knotting) of blood among people involved in the slave trade. The artist specified that ""blood knot" represents the knotted blood lines of Africans, Europeans, Asians and Indians as a result of the global trade networks formed during the transatlantic slave trade."

Carletta Carrington Wilson: poet, collagist, historian, one of the most intriguing creative minds I have known. Here's hoping this exhibition can move to a major museum soon.

(2018)

# Still Life and Concupiscence by Gloria Bornstein

GLORIA BORNSTEIN HAS LIVED IN Seattle for twenty-six years. She taught at Cornish College of the Arts, had an earlier career as a performance artist, and has created several public art works including *Neototems,* a whale pod created in 1995 at Seattle Center. Yet the scope of her layered, witty and subtle intelligence as an artist is not nearly visible enough in this town. Seattle eagerly crowns youthful endeavors, as it did recently in the well-organized and orchestrated LAVA at Noodleworks, an exhibition of the hustling under thirties artists. The theme of lava, energy surging from the earth, worked well with promoting energetic work by young artists. The exhibition even had a professional catalog with solicited solid, art critical essays. But Seattle rarely awards mature artists with substantial catalogs and exhibitions. Gloria Bornstein fares somewhat better than some. In 1994 she had an exhibition at the Henry Art Gallery. Three years ago she had a major retrospective at the Bellevue Art Museum.

Currently (March 16 – October 20, 2002) she is featured at the Seattle Art Museum in "The Poncho Series: Northwest Documents," with an installation that features a work acquired by the museum. I personally would like to see this intelligent work on permanent display.

Gloria Bornstein's two-part installation "Still Life" has a dark side and a light side, a serious message and a humorous pun. The two parts share a self-conscious awareness of the museum installation as installation, of its parameters and conventions, its distortions, and its delights. Instead of making art and putting it into the museum, Bornstein allows the museum to shape the work itself, even as she pokes fun at the museum as a conceptual container for art.

The title "Still Life" is itself art historical: it draws on the tradition of objects on a table that is a characteristic, if peculiar, subject for art.

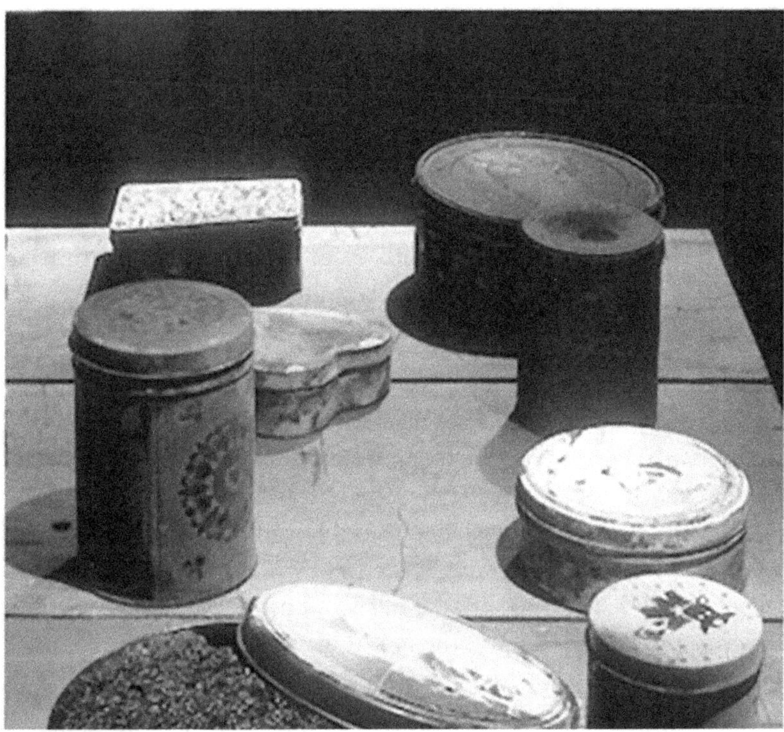

Gloria Bornstein, *Gauging,* 1994, room size: 16' x 16' overall, burned rice, biscuit tins, wood table, video installation on floating film screen. Collection of Seattle Art Museum, Photograph: Rob Vinnedge, ©2017

The Dutch seventeenth century still life, a product of a materialistic mercantile society not unlike our own, consisted of piles of lavish flowers and fruits that refer to the ephemeral nature of life.

Bornstein's still life also piles objects on a table, but these objects suggest historical, biological and conceptual references. The dark part of the installation, *Gauging,* 1994, about thirty tins with charred rice, invokes a child's-size box of burnt rice that the artist saw in the Museum in Nagasaki. The firestorm that followed the dropping of the Atomic bomb on Nagasaki charred the rice. Bornstein's husband's family is Japanese, and this object signifies the ways in which great disasters strike down individuals in the midst of the most ordinary events. The tins full of charred rice are set in a dark room, but they are countered by a video of contemporary rice fields, shot from the window of a moving Japanese train. The video hypnotically shifts perspectives and rhythms. Through the window we see several vistas of lush rice fields and industrial towns close up and far away. On the outside surface of the window rain drags across it in dancing shapes, and on the inside the steamed-up window is only a blur. These shifting views also have art historical resonance; they recall Claude Monet's waterlily paintings, in which we can plunge visually under water, stay on the surface, or see reflections from above.

Reflections and vistas in both cases are metaphors of shifting understanding and perspectives in the midst of mystery. The thriving rice fields are a counterpoint to the burned rice.

Trains for Bornstein also reference the Holocaust in Germany, as the means by which Jews were taken to the concentration camps—a connection she makes as the daughter of Polish Jews who left before World War II, but who lost many friends and family. But of course those trains bore no resemblance to trains with views of green fields; they were closed, crowded freight cars, and we inevitably feel the movement from closed and hopeless to open and positive in the video, even as we also feel its ambiguity; the rain is like tears streaming across the surface.

The Seattle Art Museum acquired *Gauging* in 1999 for its permanent collection through a gift from Helen Gurvich in honor of Anne Gerber. Anne Gerber, who is currently ninety-three years old, established a fund at the museum to acquire art that engages with cultural, social and political issues.

The museum invited Bornstein to create a second piece, *Concupiscense*, to accompany *Gauging* for the "Still Life" exhibition. Set again on a table, in this case a new maple table with a vitrine (glass cover), are a group of shapes rendered in porcelain. These odd shapes, in contradiction to their refined medium, seem to be caricatures, or even pop objects. They are, in fact, hugely enlarged representations based on drawings of invertebrate sexual organs. They include the DNA virus, earthworms, sea urchins, round worms, rotifers, barnacles, flatworms, earthworms and annelids—ancient bisexual life forms. We are looking, then, at a type of cartoon of bisexuality, along with their "sources" in old taxonomy textbooks.

The display parodies the seriousness with which museums show objects that may have an entirely different meaning in real life than they do in the context of art. But in another pun, the title *Concupiscence*, which means sexual lust, is also a reference to the desires of a museum, of a museum curator, of a museum collector, to own work, to pursue work as lovers pursue each other, caught in the grip of their desire. Bornstein actually read the letters of some of the early collectors for the Seattle Art Museum, and this desire, this pursuit, was clearly part of the story.

The brightness of *Concupiscence* makes it appear to be the positive part of the installation, but, in fact, the dark underbelly of desire undercuts its positive character.

Moreover, in today's world as we short circuit the many interlocking ecosystems on the planet in the name of capitalism, these sexual organs may be the only remaining lifeforms in a few more years. The cycle from the deaths in war in Nagasaki and German concentration camps to the current death of the entire planet, as a result of concupiscence, makes the installation as a whole an effort to stay positive in the face of the distortions of nature, science and art, and the perpetuation of those distortions in the context of museum displays.

(2002)

# DeeDee Faces the Abyss, But Still Imagines Utopia: Deborah Faye Lawrence

Hope of a secure and livable world lies with disciplined nonconformists who are dedicated to Justice, Peace and Brotherhood.

—Martin Luther King, *Strength to Love*, 1963

Utopia is racial, gender, sexual, class equality and justice . . .

—John Jota Leaños, 2004

*DEE DEE DOES UTOPIA* SPEAKS TO OUR disrupted and despotic world, offering possibilities for another future. When George W. Bush won a second term as President in 2004, Deborah Faye Lawrence alleviated her despair by sending an email query, "what does utopia look like to you?" Almost one hundred people suggested ideas such as libraries, beaches, well-fed children, happy pets, equality, tolerance, joy, and women's rights.

Paired with these hopes, Lawrence presents the dark realities of neoconservative war mongering and torture.

The artworks incorporate quotes from her email query combined with quotes from utopian and post-utopian thinkers like Thomas More, Jorge Luis Borges, Aldous Huxley and Alfred W. McCoy (who wrote about the history of CIA torture). Words collaged from large individual letters frame some images like ransom notes. In others, words inhabit thought balloons, circles, swags and waves. They encircle and entangle the collages in layers of ideas forcing us to read and think as we look at the imagery.

Subtly composed from thousands of sources, Lawrence's collages include complex compositions, brilliant color, and a wild sense of humor

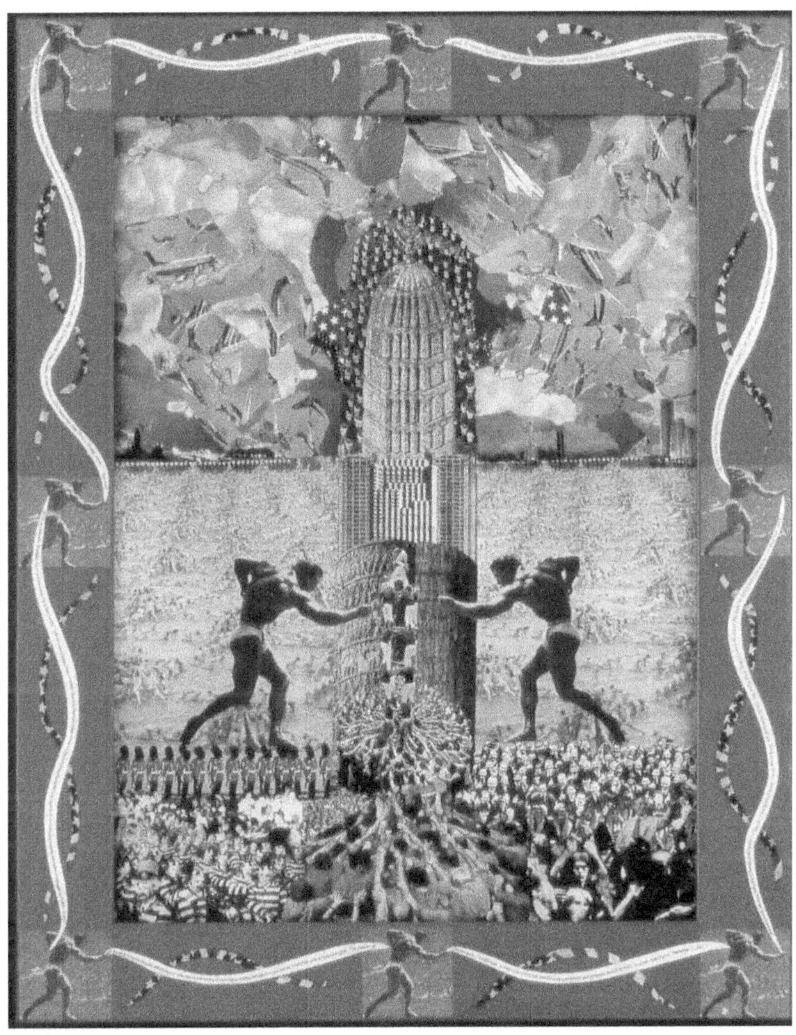

Deborah Faye Lawrence, *Super Macho Jingotopia* ,2005, acrylic collage and varnish on rag paper, 38.75 x 30.5", Collection Ed Marquand

and fantasy (like the Hindu god surfing in *Beachtopia* or the monk watching television in *Bibliotopia*). In addition, there are deadly facts. *Psychotopia* is a hellishly orange work which includes images of Lyndie England at Abu Ghraib, the blindfolded lady of Justice, and details from the nightmarish scenes of Hieronymous Bosch. *Super Macho Jingotopia*, in contrast, declares its hyper-masculine center, reinforced symmetrically by two alpha males against the crowds of mindless syco-phants and the texts of warmongers. For many years, Lawrence has combined political concerns with humor in her sophisticated art. She is a direct descendent of artists like German Dadaists Hannah Höch and John Heartfield. Like them, she cuts up magazines manufactured by capitalists to comment on the ills of society, or to present alternatives. She frequently uses tin television trays as a surface for collage. Their cultural overtones, including passivity and oppression, fit well with her social commentary. Deborah Faye Lawrence uses her power as a visual artist to speak up against injustice and fascism. As she opposes the demonizing language and imagery that dominates our contemporary culture, she offers us a dizzying array of alternatives.

(2007)

# LaToya Ruby Frazier Exposes the Injuries of Capitalism in Braddock, Pennsylvania

We all know about Andrew Carnegie's steel mills and Carnegie libraries for the "ambitious and industrious" public. What we have not heard about are the struggles of African Americans who worked at his mills. The dynamic photographer LaToya Ruby Frazier tells that story in her current exhibition at the Seattle Art Museum.

LaToya Ruby Frazier grew up in what is known as the "Bottoms" of the Monongahela River in Braddock, Pennsylvania, nine miles outside of Pittsburgh. Braddock is the site of the first and the last Andrew Carnegie steel mill, Edgar Thomson Plant. Generations of Frazier's family have worked in that mill since the turn of the century. As African Americans, they were paid less and, over the decades, had many job-related injuries and much illness. But they could not afford to move away from the toxic environment near the plant. LaToya's grandmother, who raised her, was born in the 1940s when the town was prosperous; her mother in the 1960s, and she herself in the 1980s, when the war on drugs decimated her family.

The artist describes a childhood memory: "One night the river flooded. Crossing through miles of man-made manufactures, contaminated soils and debris, it filled the basement and soaked the floors of my childhood home on Washington Avenue . . . if 70 percent of the world is covered with water and more than 50 percent of our bodies is comprised of water, then the properties found in waters that surround our artificial environments reflect not only a physical condition, but a spiritual condition in which we exist." In other words, the toxins in the water are part of the fiber of her body and those of her family. They contaminate not only their bodies, but also their spirits.

Frazier has just received the third Gwendolyn Knight and Jacob Lawrence Prize, awarded biannually for an early career Black artist: she received a cash prize and this exhibition endowed by the Foundation. Seattle Art Museum's Sandra Jackson-Dumont curated this selection of her photographs.

As we approach the Gwendolyn Knight and Jacob Lawrence Gallery on the third floor, we first see a long corridor with selections from Frazier's personal life experience. She took all of these black and white photographs in or near her grandmother's home about a block from the steel mill, where Frazier was raised. Here, as a child, the artist experienced warm love and a special world that her grandmother created inside this house surrounded by toxins, illness, and deterioration. It is that world of love that LaToya celebrates. In the intimate photographs we see her grandmother cradle two dolls from her extraordinary collection of dolls, her hands hold a cigarette and she wears a wedding ring. In one image, the artist, now a young adult, sits on the floor with her grandmother, with a recreated hairdo like those her grandmother lovingly wove for her as a child.

In *Landscape of the Body, Epilepsy Test,* her mother sits in a hospital gown with her exposed back to us, many wires attached. The other half of the frame shows the destruction of the community hospital in Braddock. The wires in her mother's body and the dangling wires of the hospital echo one another.

One color photograph at the end of the corridor, a timely (as we think of Charleston, West Virginia) image of industrial degradation along the Monongahela River with a big sign that says "Clairton Works, Continues Improvement to the Environment."

As we enter the Gwendolyn Knight and Jacob Lawrence Gallery, large format color photographs taken from a helicopter give us the context for the issues that Frazier wants us to understand.

We see the blue Edgar Thomson Steel Mill, still operating, and the lines of railroad cars that carry the steel. Nearby are just a few houses and trees. That is Frazier's neighborhood. But Frazier focuses on the empty hole left by the destruction of the community hospital, and the nearby home of Isaac Bunn surrounded by rolls of white rubber dumped all around it.

Isaac Bunn came to the opening and I talked to him. He wanted to buy more land around his house, but his paperwork was lost, and the owners of the land invited a company to dump rubber wrapped in white plastic there. They look like a snowstorm gone wrong. Inside the house live four generations of Bunn's family.

Bunn is now director of the Inclusion Project. As Braddock has acquired the status of poster child for redevelopment of Rust Belt cities, partly because of its flamboyant mayor, these long-time working-class residents feel left out of the process. Bunn wants them to be part of the conversation. So far, as documented in the photographs, we mainly see the march of the usual condos. In addition, according to both Bunn and Frazier, "social practice" artists from outside the community are creating projects that have no real connection to its history, especially its African American working-class history.

A riveting speaker and personality, Frazier interspersed her narrative of work, illness (the most common ills are cancer and lupus, from which the artist herself suffers), toxins, poverty, racism, community and love, with frequent references to art history and major artists who have been important to her work—ranging from Louis Hines and Jacob Riis, pioneering social documentary photographers, to Laszlo Moholy-Nagy, the avant-garde abstract photographer.

She commented on New Deal photography as "top down," asking us how many knew the name of the woman in the famous *Migrant Mother* photograph by Dorothea Lange. She has studied with Carrie Mae Weems and other contemporary socially-engaged photographers. The intersection of economic and political forces that create and destroy life, community, and environment come across clearly in her art work. She is precisely aware of how she fits into the larger context of social documentary as well as photography in general. Her work perfectly balances aesthetics and content.

On the digital display in the gallery, look for Frazier's sardonic performance that protests Levi ads set in Braddock with the slogan "Go Forth." "Go Forth where?" she asks, if you have no money, and you are dying of cancer and the only hospital in the community has been closed. The digital display includes Frazier's work shown recently at the Brooklyn Museum and elsewhere.

LaToya Ruby Frazier's highly-focused mission to tell the story of working class African Americans counters the narrative constructed by outsiders who have no idea about the life that continues in this ravaged place. Her work belongs to the people who can't afford to leave. She wants them not just to be remembered, but honored.

(2014)

# Martha Rosler: "Housing is a Human Right"

In November 2015, the Seattle-based The New Foundation boldly initiated a $100,000 biennial prize which they awarded to Martha Rosler, in honor of what they described as "her exemplary artistic achievements and enduring commitment to her practice and in recognition of women artists whose work has shown a commitment to social justice." Rosler's purpose in her work in general is "to think through the role of art in the activation of communities." The plan was to have a full year of programming on the subject of "Housing Is a Human Right" following the collaborative model of the original 1989 Dia Art Foundation project in New York City in which Rosler networked with dozens of groups, organizations, activists and artists.

The location of The New Foundation, in Pioneer Square, at a place of intersection between an historical district, art galleries, and many services for the homeless, matched the subject perfectly. Suggesting the gap between the elite art world and daily reality of living precariously that the installation sought to convey, a gallery staff member told me that they had to learn about local services when people came in from the street thinking The New Foundation was a social service agency because of the title of the exhibition. Conversely, they opened the gallery all night during the "One Night Count" (of people sleeping outside in January) but no one came.

Rosler followed the same three-part concept as in her 1989 project. The first installation emphasizes "Home Front:" people's efforts to save their homes;" the second, "Homeless: The Street and Other Venues," critiques and documents efforts to address the problem, both successful and unsuccessful, by a wide range of community activists. The third part is "City: Visions and Revisions."

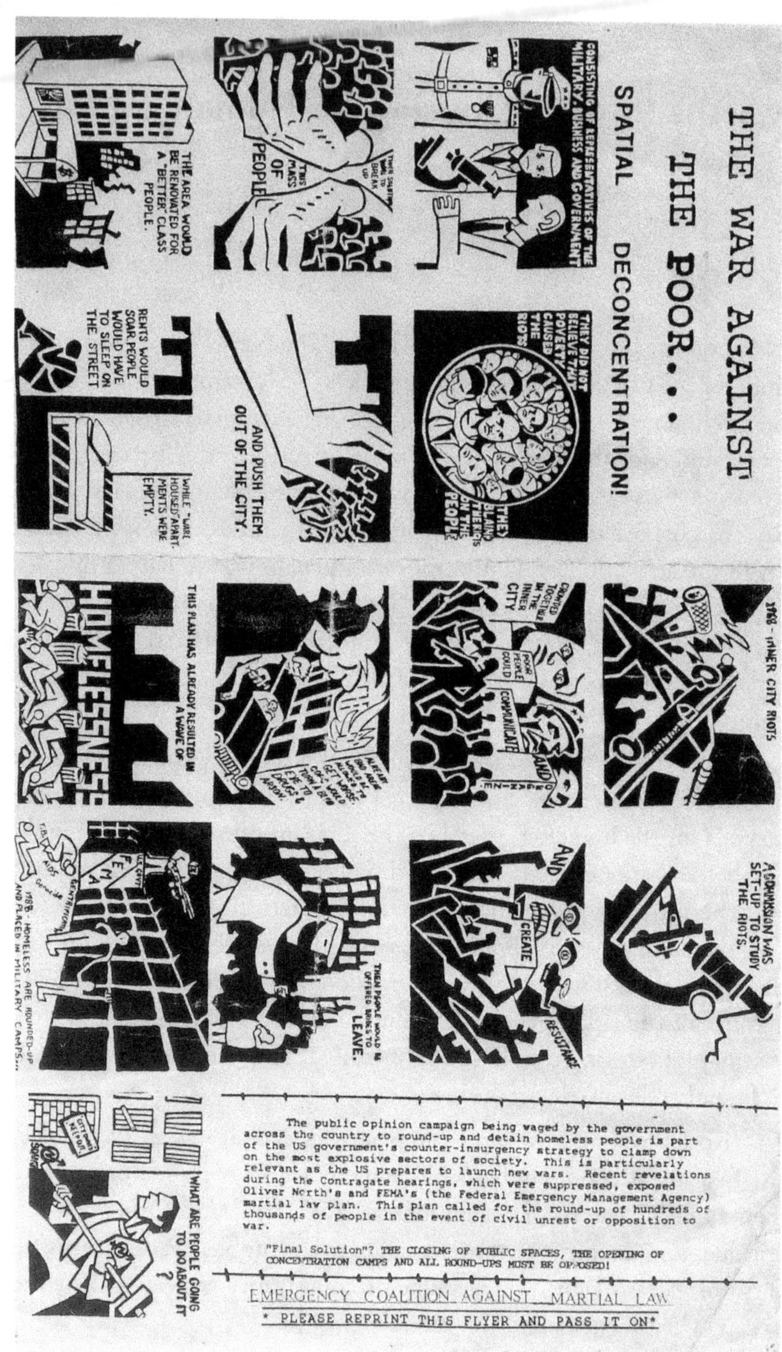


Seth Tobocman, "The War Against the Poor . . . Spatial Deconcentration," in "Martha Rosler's: Housing Is a Human Right" at The New Foundation, Seattle, 2016. Courtesy of Martha Rosler

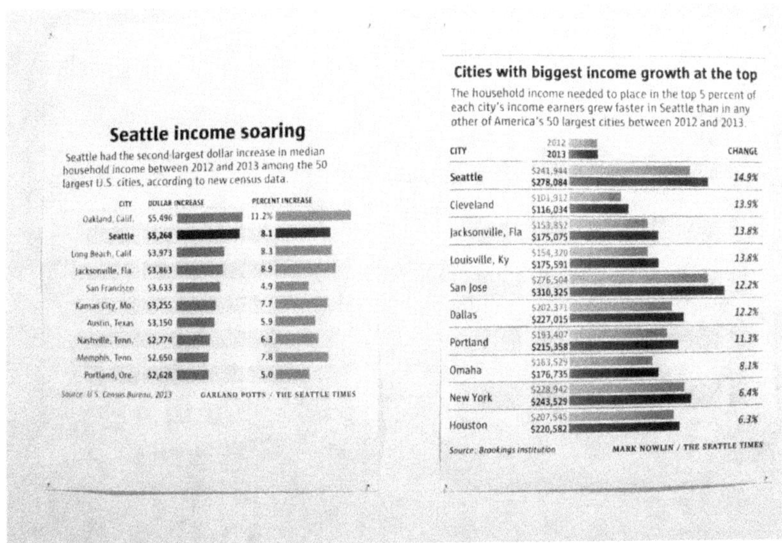


Charts from *The Seattle Times* ("Seattle income soaring" by Garland Potts and "Cities with biggest income growth at the top" by Mark Nowlin), in Martha Rosler, "Housing Is a Human Right" at The New Foundation, Seattle, 2016, Courtesy of Martha Rosler

The installations at The New Foundation included archival documents from the Dia exhibition as well as many subsequent venues, but Rosler added information specific to Seattle.

She dramatizes the rapid escalation of inequality by extending a 1986 graph right onto the wall with an ever-expanding disparity between rich and poor. She added charts about the local tax structure, which massively favors the wealthy (we have no income tax, only regressive sales taxes). All the documents repeatedly pointed to the distance between the mainstream discourse on housing (often *The New York Times*), and the realities of people's lives.

Those realities came through most clearly in the many videos, filmed by grassroots groups, of evictions, gentrification, and the destruction of neighborhoods. We saw activists protesting through every means possible: occupations, marches, legal channels. One historical video film by Edgar Anstey, entitled *Housing Problems*, made under the auspices of the British government, showed "cleaning up slums" during the 1930s.

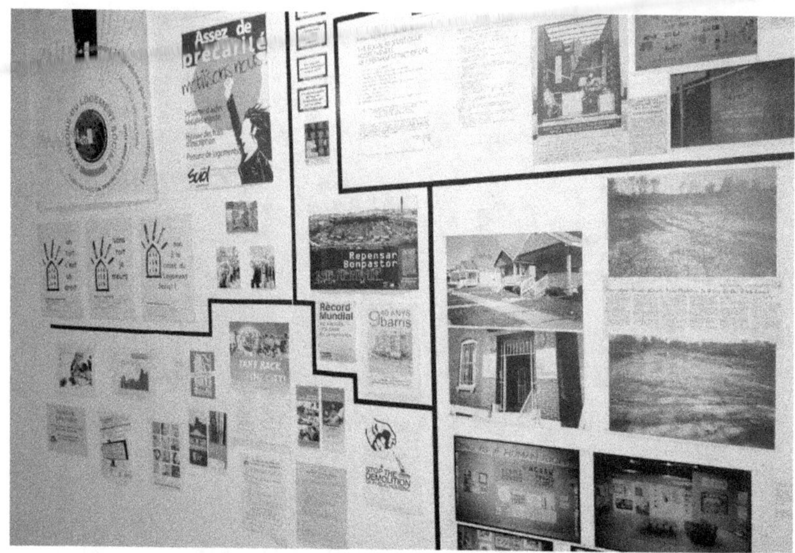

Installation view of Martha Rosler, "Housing Is a Human Right" at The New Foundation, Seattle, 2016. Photograph: Coley Mixan, Courtesy of Martha Rosler

Rosler very carefully arranged photographs, posters, protest signs, paintings, comics, and newspapers, as well as videos, into contrasting relationships with the viewer—vertical, horizontal, diagonal, high, low. The videos could be viewed in a large projection from a sofa, or through headphones at a computer. The artifacts of protest thus suggested the many possibilities for resistance through community collaboration.

The New Foundation, from its beginning in 2014, has consistently diversified its programs beyond traditional visual art exhibitions to include experimental writing, fashion and films. It has sponsored conversations, poetry readings, artists in residence, and performances. It assembled a library with current art magazines. For this project, the library included Rosler's books and files on homelessness, as well as her research materials on Seattle collected in 1991 for a public art project here.

In Seattle's 1991 landmark project, "In Public," several artists addressed homelessness directly. Daniel J. Martinez hung banners through the shopping district with questions like, "Do you have a trust fund account or a savings account?' "Do you have a place to live?" "Do you have a beach house or a mountain house?" "Do you live in a ghetto?" The city quickly removed the banners.

Cheyenne, Arapaho artist Edgar Heap of Birds created two bilingual (Salish/English) panels, "Day Night," covered with dollar signs, crosses and leaves that spoke directly of the condition of local Natives: "Far Away Brothers and Sisters We Still Remember You," and "Chief Seattle Now the Streets are our Home." The work is permanently placed in former Duwamish territory, now called Pioneer Square, where homeless Natives still gather.

Rosler sought out local natives and listened to their concerns. "Hidden Histories" features eleven one-minute spots by several Indigenous speakers, (formatted as PSAs on local radio and television). They include Vi Hilbert, a linguist who saved her Lutshootseed language from extinction; Roger Fernandes, Alcohol and Drug Prevention Coordinator at the Seattle Indian Health Board; and Cecile Maxwell (now Hansen), Chairwoman of the Duwamish Tribal Council. In 1991 Rosler was a pioneer in recording Native tribal speakers as they spoke about what was important to them, the survival of Native language, drug addiction, youth programs, and the trauma of Indian boarding schools.

"Hidden Histories" (now in the collection of the Museum of Modern Art) was first screened in Seattle in 2016 as part of "Housing Is a Human Right." We viewed it in "The Waterfront Space," the project showroom for the upcoming Seattle waterfront promenade made possible by the project of replacing a crumbling two story highway with a tunnel. The beautiful drawings and models presented a clean, safe, sanitized place. The topics included in these "Hidden Histories" remain buried under the new waterfront.

On the panel following the screening, Roger Fernandes, one of the original participants, bluntly talked about the destruction "militarily, religiously, and politically" of the Duwamish tribe, the original, and still unrecognized, tribe of the Seattle Puget Sound area. Qwalsius-Shaun Peterson, a Coast Salish artist, spoke of honoring the voices of ancestors through storytelling and of reframing lost history in contemporary media. Peterson has been invited to create a welcoming figure for the new waterfront. It will be a 24-foot woman with a cedar hat, her arms in a gesture of welcome. Peterson's sculpture, important as it is, positions Natives again at the beginning of the story of White colonization. Perhaps more Native voices and participation are planned.

"Housing Is a Human Right" included two "community conversations" at the downtown Seattle Public Library. Rosler began by presenting details of the installations with an emphasis on the many models for intersections between artists and housing activism. Alison Eisinger, Executive Director of the Seattle/King County Coalition on Homelessness, described the escalating number of people sleeping outside based on the annual "One Night Count."

Finally, a grass roots advocate, Mary Flowers, eloquently exposed the ways that those without homes are dehumanized and categorized rather than empowered. A second panel, presented by homeless and formerly homeless speakers, provided a more in depth understanding of what people do to survive and emerge from the iniquitous structures of racism, classism, sexism, and poverty, that hold them down.

The project also stimulated elite venues to collaborate. The Seattle Art Museum exhibited Rosler's "Below the Surface," 1967-72, and "Bringing the War Home," 2003-8, as well as three earlier videos that acerbically addressed food, fashion and war. In a formal lecture at the museum, Rosler provided an overview of her career (artists turned out in force for this event, although not at the public library or the waterfront).

At the Henry Art Gallery, University of Washington, "Gift City" by Keller Easterling called attention to the benefits to corporations for building their tech campuses in the center of a city—a potent issue here. In Seattle we have Amazon, Expedia, Facebook, Google, and so many others. Amazon is building a city within a city of gargantuan proportions.

The partner to rampant development here, still the same as in Rosler's project grounded in the 1980s, is the loss of housing for low income, minimum wage workers. The term "public housing," still in use in the 1980s, has been replaced with the far different concept of "affordable housing," and the city is currently bulldozing landmark public housing projects.

"Housing Is a Human Right," reached out to several activist art organizations such as Path With Art, which encourages creative expression in all media for adults in recovery. Rosler held two sessions with their students at the Seattle Art Museum. They organized the art exhibit "We Are All Here" in the highly visible City Hall Lobby as well as sponsoring "The Role of the Arts in Civic Problem Solving," a panel that exactly corresponds to Rosler's larger purpose. The New Foundation also connected to the socially-engaged Northwest Film Forum whose film camps for youth create "Citizen Minutes," some of which look at homelessness.

All of these collaborations began to realize Rosler's larger purpose of stimulating art that activates the community around the urgent issue of "Housing Is Human Right."

Halfway through Rosler's yearlong program, Shari Behnke, the benefactor of The New Foundation, unexpectedly canceled the rest of the project at the New Foundation space, and closed it. Two fall exhibitions disappeared, as well as part three "City: Visions and Revisions." Ironically, the segment of the exhibition that pointed to solutions disappeared, so we are left with what we already have, many well-meaning organizations at the top and bottom of the economic scale, pursuing different agendas. Rosler's project held up hope for building connections between artists, community activists, and power brokers in Seattle.

I know of one project that will continue, a partnership with Creative Justice, a county-funded program providing opportunities for youth in the justice system to create art and poetry as an alternative to incarceration. The New Foundation will support their summer program focusing on structural injustice with Rosler's work as a point of departure.

A full year of programming would certainly have had more impact. But, Seattle is a challenging city in which to build connections among artists across class, race, and economic status. As in other cities, there is an almost unbridgeable divide between our active grass roots community and elite visual artists. Our local "art world" reflects the city's demographics. We are a city of White elites juxtaposed to a city of dozens of different communities of people of color, of impoverished families, of struggling unemployed, most of them being pushed further and further south and into the suburbs by rising rents. Artists of color and social justice artists exist on those same margins (with a few token exceptions of course).

In spite of declaring a "Homeless State of Emergency," King County and the City of Seattle continue to sweep encampments in parks and other public spaces; the County is defunding a crucial group that provides a radical model of homeless self-governance because it does not fund paid social workers. That same group, WHEEL (Women's Empowerment and Education), reached out to visual artists to create a city-wide public art project. (Note: in 2021 the City is still sweeping homeless encampments).

Everyone agrees that housing is a human right, but, on the ground, administrators do not support the funding to make it happen. The Rosler project offers a model, a strategy, a possible way forward to a different way of thinking—holistically, inclusively, without judgement and demonizing.

Perhaps a seed has been planted. For those who participated in any part of "Housing Is a Human Right," particularly artists, it may have sparked a commitment to social justice as well as the crucial importance of strategy, analysis, collaboration, and engagement. As Rosler stated, "Art does not make a revolution. People as citizens make revolution."

(2016)

# You Mist, Again (Rattle) and ReRun by Natalie Ball

The Betty Bowen Award winner Natalie Ball (Modoc, Klamath) has installed a provocative pair of works in the Seattle Art Museum. Ball is descended from the famous leader of the late nineteenth century Modoc resistance, Captain Jack. That heritage of warrior defiance is obvious here.

*You Mist, again (Rattle)* and *Re-Run* make up the installation "Twinkle, Twinkle, Little Snake." The artist transforms the comfort of the familiar nursery rhyme into a different feeling entirely, part threatening, part magical. Ball explores the collision of Indigenous and White cultures, as well as African American, also part of her heritage.

One of the unintended juxtapositions of the installation is the view of the Marsden Hartley painting in the next gallery. Hartley's work suggests his affinity with Native American patterns, although he did not move to New Mexico until later in his career. Scholars traditionally focus on the references to Berlin in his symbolism, but seeing his work next to Ball's the connection to Native designs is unmistakable.

*You Mist, again (Rattle)* combines mysterious references and startling juxtapositions. Ball's work frequently suggests collage with extremely disparate elements. She purposefully mixes pop, elite, folk, mystical, and humor, along with her sophisticated command of color and composition, to keep us guessing. Looking closely we see crazy pink hair at the top, what she describes as hair for braiding, as well as deer and porcupine hair. In that detail alone, the cross referencing of the natural world and the cultural world suggests her willingness to defy any accepted parameters. Even the overall idea of the rattle, here on a huge scale, is in our face, and somewhat frightening.

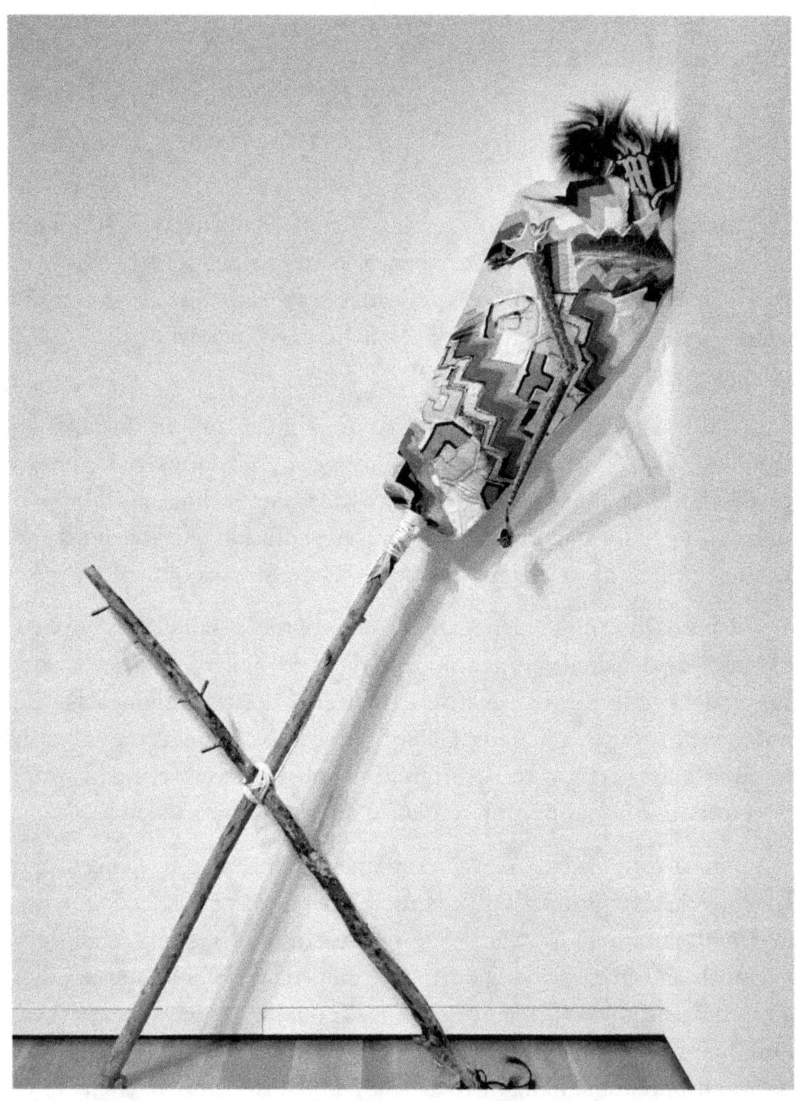

Natalie Ball (Klamath/Modoc), *You Mist, Again (Rattle)*, 2019,Cotton, crystals, pine, polyester, rattle snake, deer and porcupine hair, braiding hair, Converse shoe, acrylic, beads, bullet shells, and deer raw hide, Collection of Seattle Art Museum

Bullet shells embedded in a stick support the giant rattle. And what about that crazy unlaced shoe and the beaded blue rose hanging from the end of the snakeskin? Trickster humor is juxtaposed here with celebrating Indigenous vitality and perhaps some crazy sarcasm.

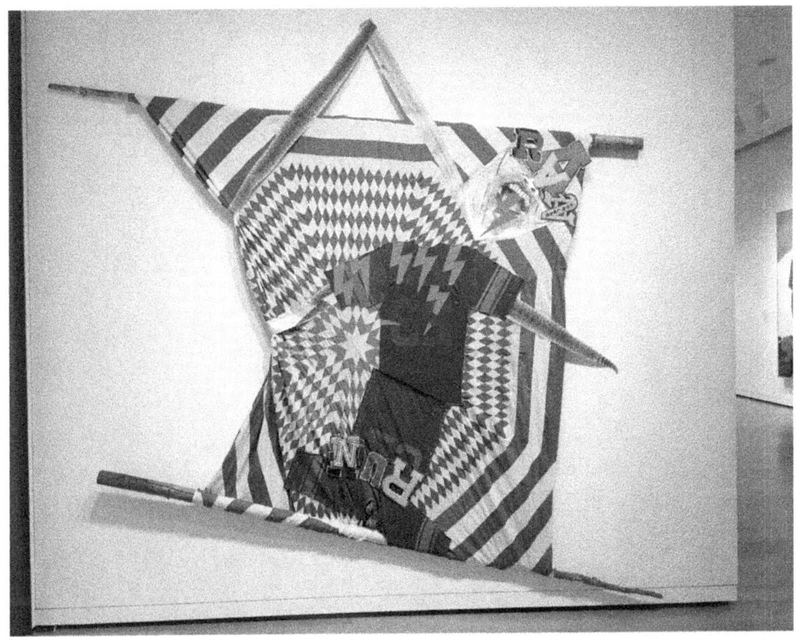

Natalie Ball (Klamath/Modoc), *Re-Run,* 2019, Cotton, crystals, pine, chenille, polyester, rattle snake, canvas, acrylic, and leather, Collection of Seattle Art Museum

The second work *Re-Run*, is a tilted construction created from a diamond patterned quilt. That pattern is joyful, but the words "Run" and "Ran" formed from overlapped sports letters and mascot imagery suggest a different mood entirely and violently interrupt any easy reading. But the larger figure at the center of *Re-Run* suggests a tricky, but successful balancing act, that can refer to life in general. There are so many possibilities here for metaphors, that I suggest that you take a good long look and think about it.

Rattlesnake skin appears as part of both works (although significantly identified simply as rattlesnake). A snakeskin, shed after it regrows a new one, suggests the survival abilities of Indigenous peoples, in spite of White man's best efforts to obliterate them.

The quilt filled with diamonds suggests joy but it is rudely interrupted by the words "Run" and "Ran." The violently cut up sports jerseys and letters in both of these pieces deny any possible cliché of Native or African American culture, giving us instead a proud declaration of survival and humanity.

(2019)

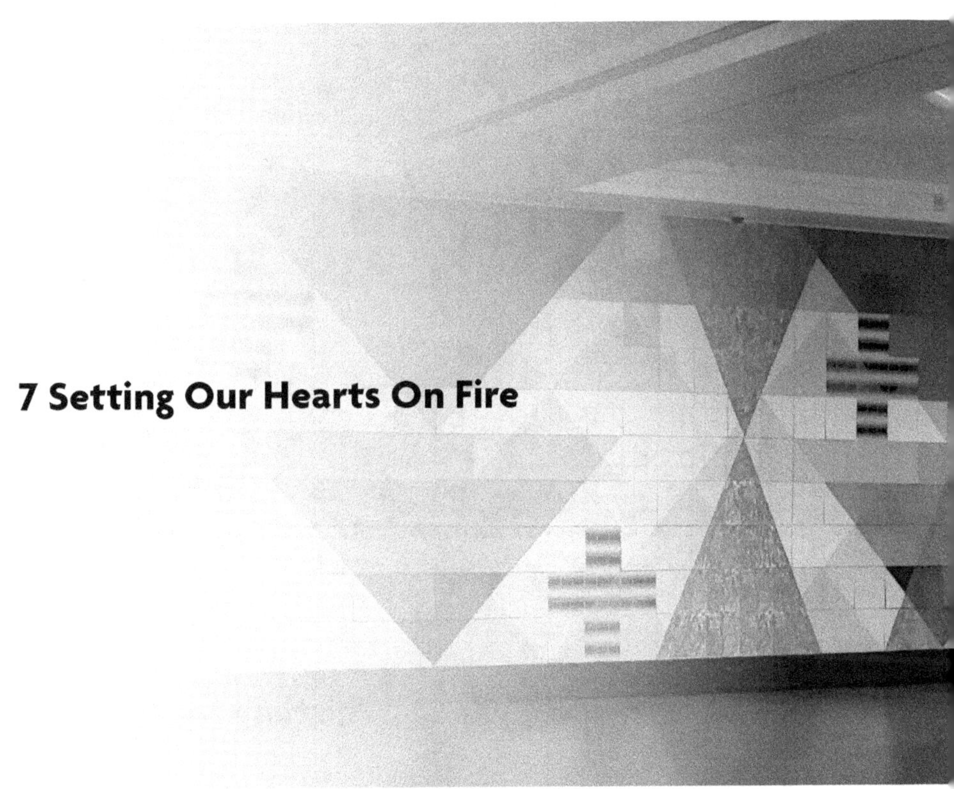

# 7 Setting Our Hearts On Fire

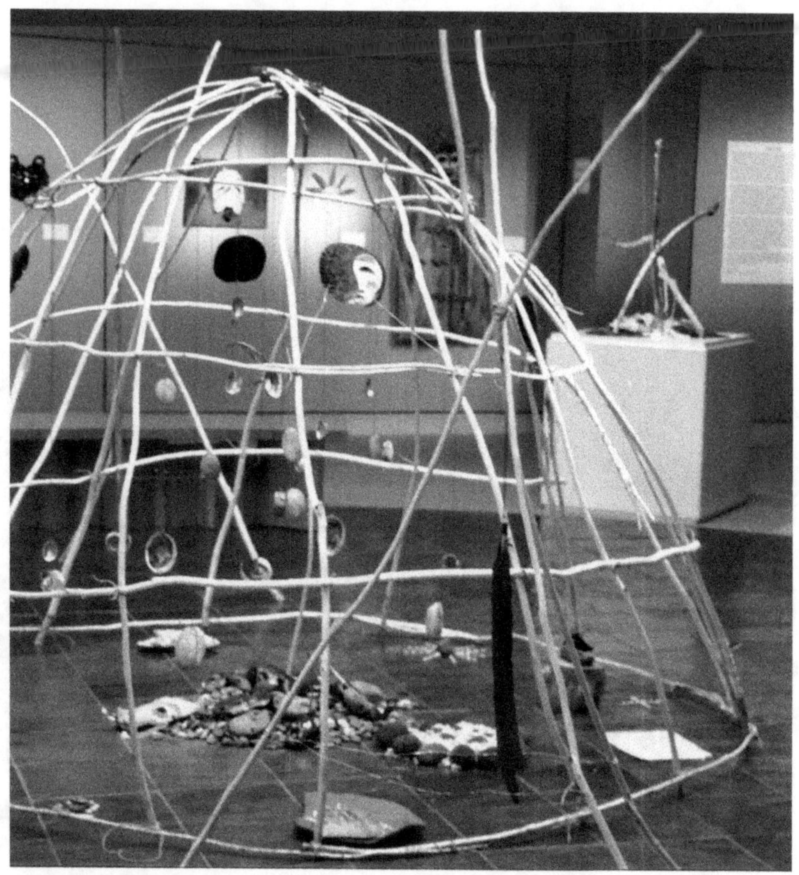

Lillian Pitt (WarmSprings/Wasco/Yakima), *From the Earth,* 1999, Installation, Museum at Warm Springs, The Confederated Tribes of Warm Springs, Oregon

## Lillian Pitt: Spirits Keep Whistling Me Home

From the perspective of mainstream American White culture, the journey to the Warm Springs Reservation in central Oregon is a long one. We pass from the hectic impersonality of freeway driving, through the resource-greedy suburbs and strip malls, past polluted rivers and ruthless clear cutting of the forests, to finally come into a sense of quiet and calm in the center of Oregon, where the woods are intelligently harvested and the people who live there exist in harmony with the 600,000 acres of high desert.

But this is not a throwback to a prehistoric culture or a Garden of Eden. The Confederated Tribes of Warm Springs—an arbitrary group of disparate natives who were thrown together by the U.S. government in the 1850s in the hopes that they would kill each other off—today work collaboratively to provide jobs and income for their members: they have a resort and industries such as clothing manufacturing and lumbering. Visitors have the choice of staying in a teepee, a camper, a tent or a 4 star resort. They can swim, canoe, or gamble.

At the heart of the reservation is the Museum at Warm Springs, a stunning structure that combines contemporary architectural concepts with the community values and forms of the tribes who care for the surrounding land. Using native stone, timber, brick and glass, it invokes a traditional encampment along a creek. Unlike the gargantuan structures of recent museums, the Museum at Warm Springs creates an intimate experience. Its permanent display lays out in simple, but sophisticated terms, the beauty and the pain of the history of these tribes.

This summer the museum featured a major retrospective by Warm Springs/Wasco/Yakama native Lillian Pitt, with the evocative title "Spirits Keep Whistling Me Home." The exhibition, which will be traveling for five years following its debut in Warm Springs, was in perfect harmony with its setting, not only because the artist grew up on the reservation and still considers it her spiritual home, but also because her work brings together contemporary emotional and psychological concerns, international technical and formal references, and traditions and tales from her own complex heritage.

Lillian Pitt discovered as an adult that her grandmother came, not from the Warm Springs Reservation in Oregon, but from the Washington side of the Columbia River Gorge, a region where ten-thousand-year-old petroglyphs survive to the present. The knowledge of her ancient roots transformed her life.

Yet, one of Pitt's most enduring forms, the clay mask, is not part of the artistic traditions of her particular tribal heritage. When she became interested in working in clay and began to make masks, she found herself inspired by Mexican and Northwest Coast traditions. In order to make the masks more personal, she reconnected with the spiritual stories of her early years in the Basin Plateau. At the same time, she learned of ancient firing techniques from Japan, such as anagama and raku.

In the "Stick Indian" series which spans from 1982 to the present, we see these intersecting concerns. The masks invoke the Stick Indian, a spirit who lived in the hills and would whistle you home if you were a good person, but lose you further in the desert or the woods if you were not. These Stick Indian masks are in bronze, raku or mixed media, all with intricate surfaces that give them various personalities. They are, of

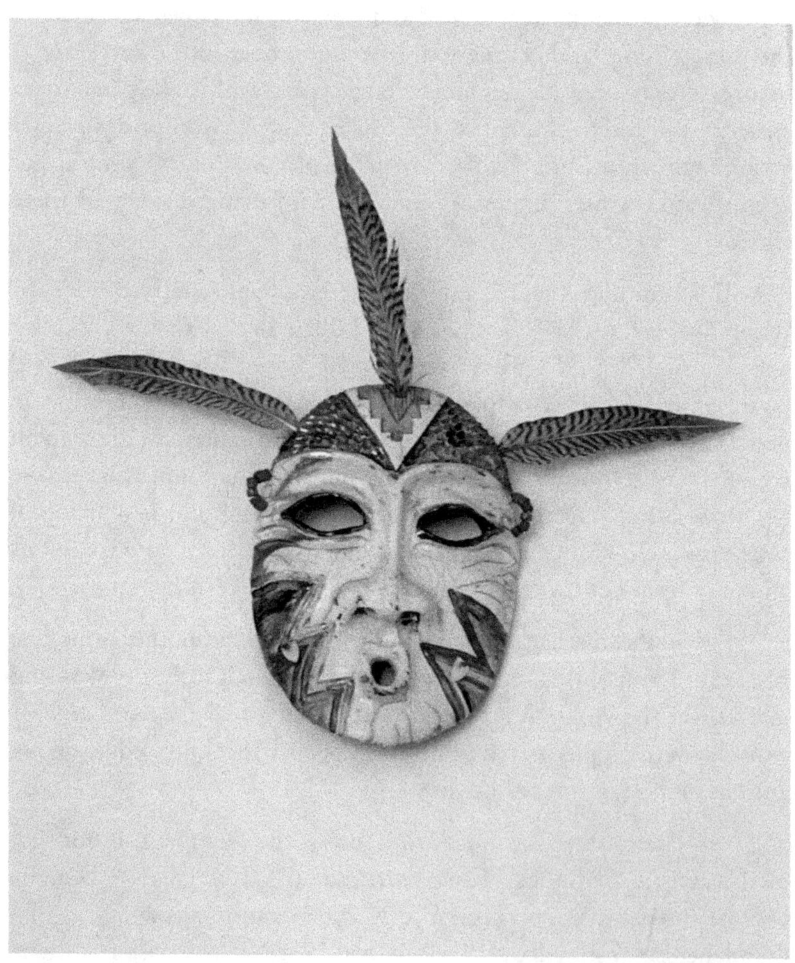

Lillian Pitt (WarmSprings/Wasco/Yakima), *Klatsop Stick Indian* Ceramic and mixed media, Collection of the author

course, the theme of the exhibition as Pitt herself is whistled home by them from her geographical home in Portland. At the same time, she is herself a whistling spirit who speaks to those who are in touch with her values.

In the 1990s Pitt began a series called "In Conflict" in which the mask format is altered to a more personal statement that departs further from the predictable configuration of the face in order to suggest the physical and spiritual changes that the artist was experiencing.

Recently Pitt has also taken the mask form and incorporated it into full length figures on wooden boards. These totems create a powerful sense of protection, at the same time that they feel somewhat dismembered. In *Coyote Musing on His Immortality* or *The Forest is My Secret Home,* the artist has used clay to suggest ribcages, a motif from ancient Wishxam designs, along with beads, sticks chewed by beavers, shells and metal scraps. The startling results suggest the survival of these spirits, even as their homes are interrupted, disturbed or destroyed.

Recently, Pitt moved into three-dimensional installations: simple figures set on pedestals or on a flat piece of wood or ceramic that create an environment. These sculptures still invoke spirits, with titles like *Shadow Spirit Walking Between Fire and Ice* or *Amid a Million Untold Stories Raven Remains,* but they also connect to a more abstract sense of space and form that is distilled from Pitt's deepening integration of material and content.

The collective presence of masks, totems, and installations is intensely spiritual. The journey to Warm Springs, which is actually a different country legally and politically, is also a journey to a nurturing sense of harmony and hope that there is another way of thinking in contemporary America. Native traditions have metamorphosed in the work of Lillian Pitt—as well as in the lives and art of many contemporary Native artists—in response to the new globalism, new technologies, and late twentieth century culture, but Pitt still chooses to connect to a spirituality that reaches back into prehistoric time. This is a profoundly different worldview from that of capitalism, and were it more visible, more widely cultivated, could perhaps save us and the extraordinary planet on which we live. Its persistence and metamorphosis, in spite of the ongoing efforts to obliterate it, is inspiring.

(1999)

# Joe Feddersen's Abstractions as Politics

JOE FEDDERSEN'S EXHIBITION "VITAL SIGNS" celebrates ancient history as well as the contemporary environment of today. The landscape of the Okanagan, shown in this detail of his wall mural of 500 separate pieces, is open and rugged. He refers to contemporary landscape destructions, like clear-cutting, suggested in the brown triangles, and to geometric towers for the high tension wires that gallop across the open land in the center of Washington State. The Okanagan is, for those who are driving to Spokane on the interstate freeway, a desolate, empty landscape, made more desolate by the Grand Coulee Dam which was completed just after World War II. That dam destroyed the ancestral fishing streams of the Colville Indians, the Spokane Indians, and other tribes. There were no fish ladders at that time, the fish were unable to return to their spawning grounds.

Joe Feddersen is a Colville Indian. He comes from that land; it is part of him and his ancestors. After the dam was built, he worked for the power companies, a common occurrence with Indians, whose only choice for a livelihood is the use of energy based on exploitation of their lands. He knows those electrical towers, so when he includes them in a painting they are personal.

He has taught at Evergreen State College for the last twenty years. His work draws on a sophisticated contemporary aesthetic, and materials—like the shining orange fish traps in glass, or the large vessels with reflective paint on which he has sandblasted the contemporary designs of parking lots and tire treads. In the exhibition he has also included some traditionally-scaled woven baskets with tire track designs. He is commenting out of a deep silence and reverence; he accepts the present, but reminds us of where we come from, and suggests where we are now. He does not predict the future.

The exhibition has a curiously calming effect, as though we have gone into the landscape to meditate. I could feel his energy flowing through the room as the various media, scale, colors, and geometries interacted. Feddersen combines the skills of a master printmaker, a weaver, and an artist of sandblasted glass. His connection to time immemorial moves through every work. These are objects for sale now, but they speak of their former identity as functional objects. Since Natives see our relationship to nature, to history, to prehistory, to each other, to animals, as all part of a continuous non-hierarchical flow of energy, these paintings and other objects suggest that idea as well. Abstract modernism has been re-energized with its real sources of power in ancient abstractions.

(2010)

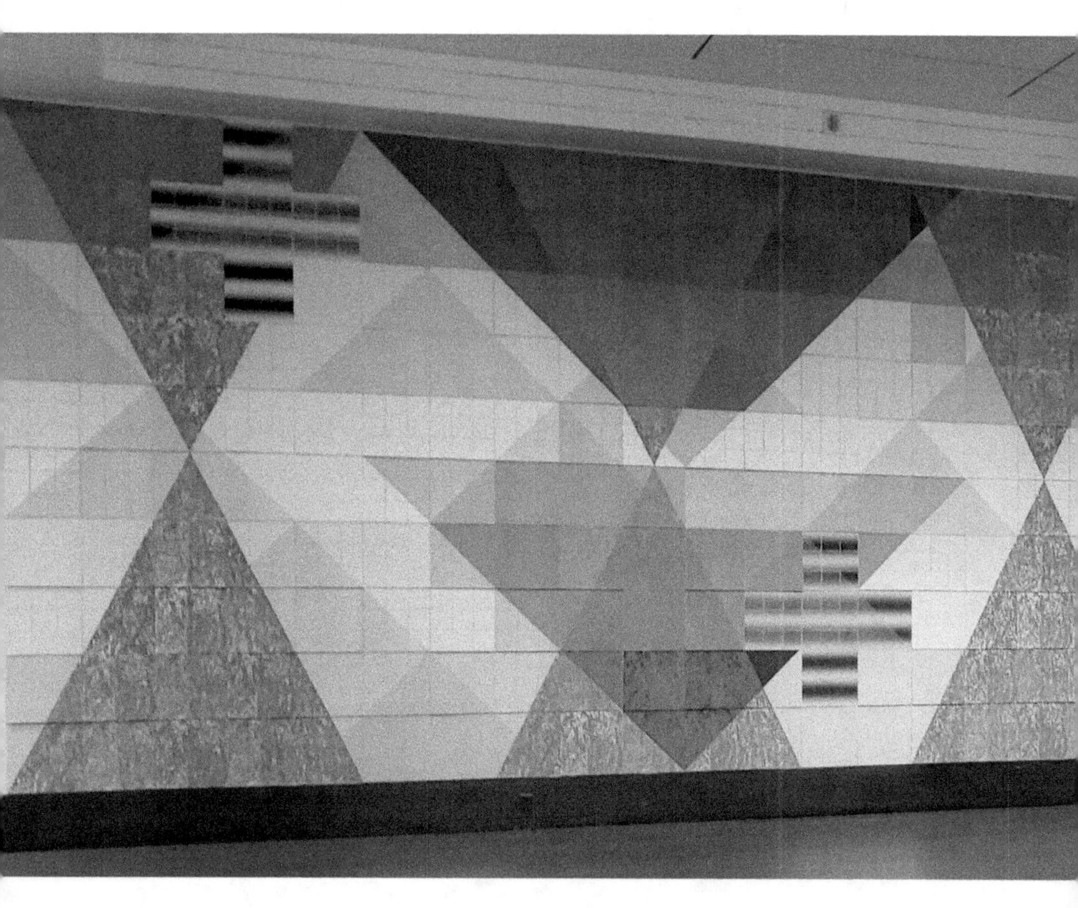

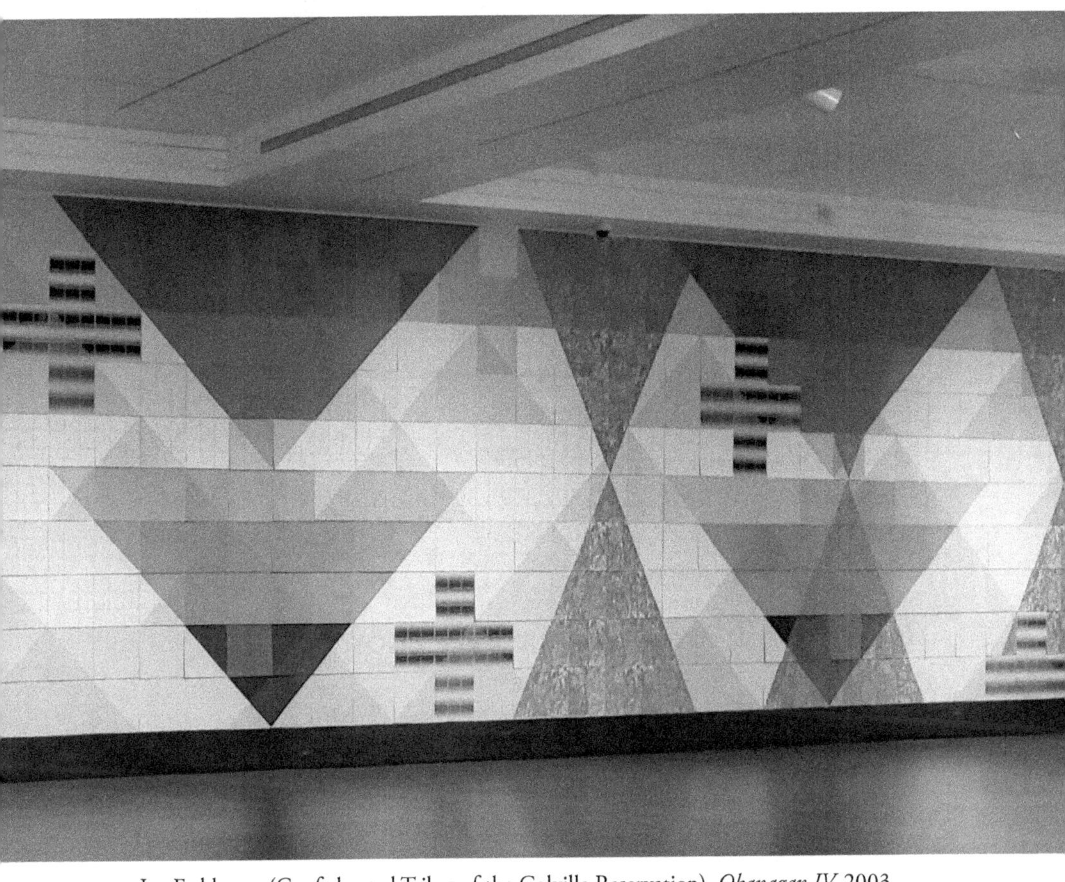

Joe Feddersen (Confederated Tribes of the Colville Reservation), *Okanagan IV,* 2003, siligraph, relief stencil, 144 x 696", Collection of the Eiteljorg Museum of American Indians and Western Art, Indianapolis, Indiana, Courtesy of the artist.

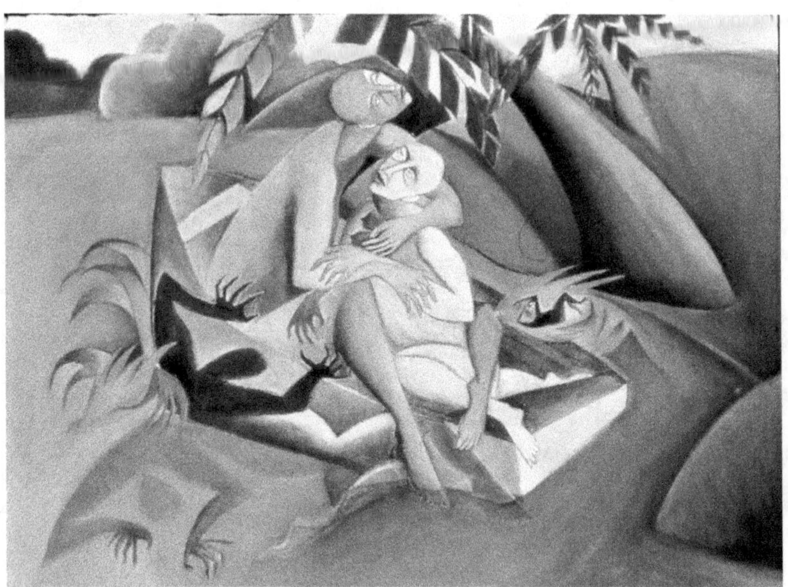

Barbara Earl Thomas, *The Boat*, 1988, 15 x 18", egg tempera on paper, Collection of the artist

# Heaven on Fire: Barbara Earl Thomas

Wedged between our first and last breath, life narrates itself, a play with acts in no particular order—how we treat each other determines the quality of our joy and depth of our suffering.

—Barbara Earl Thomas

AT THE OUTSET OF HER EXHIBITION, "Heaven on Fire," Barbara Earl Thomas immerses us in an installation of shimmering paper cutouts. The carefully lighted patterns, collectively called "The Illuminated Story," shape three separate altar-like settings, each with a text: "Catechism," "White Noise," and "If they were all like you we'd like them." But as we enjoy the decorative beauty of the cutouts and the subtle suggestion of shrine-like settings (which she refers to as lightboxes), at the same time we are jolted by the texts that lay out a few of her personal racist experiences. Moreover, as we look more closely at the patterns, imagery slowly emerges: flames, snakes, houses floating away.

Beginning "Heaven on Fire" with this installation immediately tells us that, like a musician, Thomas develops variations on underlying themes. We can trace a straight line from her first mature work of the 1980s to the present. Over and over, in different media, we see ordinary people trying to protect each other as they are threatened by the forces of nature, particularly fire and water.

Barbara Thomas's art is factual, personal, even intimate, with references to history, mythology, and the spiritual realm—embedded within her own memories. For example, the powerful cock that appears so often refers to the frightening phrase, "before the cock crows three times," predicting betrayal, the biblical story her mother told her as a child. But even as Thomas makes personal references, her life experiences resonate with those of the larger world, particularly the world of African Americans in the last half century.

Her family's fishing trips to catch the bony bottom fish helped them survive but, from the first, turbulent skies and rough water threatened those fishing trips. And then her parents actually did drown while out fishing, eerily predicted in *The Boat*, 1988, a painting Thomas had created eight months earlier in which two figures huddle together in a boat as a frightening shadowy figure rises from the lake and reaches for them.

Many of her paintings in the 1980s and 1990s, both before and after this calamity, confront the turbulence that lurks just beyond the safety of day-to-day life. In the Bainbridge Museum exhibition we see a careful selection from those years. One of my favorites is the early *Untitled* (from "For Women Who Sleep with Crocodiles") of 1982. A woman peacefully sleeps as small crocodiles climb around her, already depicting Thomas's double vision of ordinary life and encroaching danger. In *Reunions, My Mother* and *Dreams of Fish*, a powerful woman protects another as fish swarm about them. *Luna Rescue at Daybreak*, suggests one person (Thomas's people are usually sexually neutral) saving another from drowning, while other figures float helplessly in the foreground and background. *In My Father's House There Are Many Roomers*, a family at the center cling together, as other figures float, flail, and fall around them.

The linocut print series "Story Line" from 2006-2014 allows the chaotic to invade the zone of figures protecting one another with so much intensity that it threatens to take over completely.

In the technique of linocuts, the artist cuts the lines into the surface that will be black when printed; white lines are what is left behind. Similar to woodcut, but without grain, linocuts allow for more detail. Thomas takes full advantage of the medium, allowing the complexity of the prints to soar like an elaborate cantata. All those people in floating houses, also evoke for me the scenes from Katrina, the 2005 catastrophe in New Orleans that hit the African American community so hard, just before Thomas began this series.

That theme of the overwhelming energy of unleashed forces of fire and water continues to the present, metamorphosed in glass vases, a new medium for the artist. Flames gush from the top, lightening, snakes, storms, and more flames fill the sides of the vase-like forms.

From cutting linoleum to cutting paper seems like a short step, but Thomas took her biggest leap into the unknown with the three large white cutouts *Blood Catcher, Blood Letting* and *Blood Taking* that depict the murders of Black men. The very new and very old subject continues her earlier representations of people struggling in the midst of forces beyond their control, but the large scale of the work as well as the medium of white paper with cutout red paper to specifically depict flowing blood, confronts us in a new way with the dangers that threaten Black people as they simply live their lives.

Thomas also fervently believes in the beauty of the details of life. She seduces us into sharing that belief with her varied media and subtle compositions. Never has it been truer than today, that we must immerse ourselves in the beauty at hand, at the same time that we acknowledge the omnipresent dangers of both the forces of nature increasingly out of control in the age of climate change, and the violence stimulated by ignorance, fear, hate, and mass hysteria.

"Between grief and lamentation, is the joy of life's sweet briefness."

—Barbara Earl Thomas

(2016)

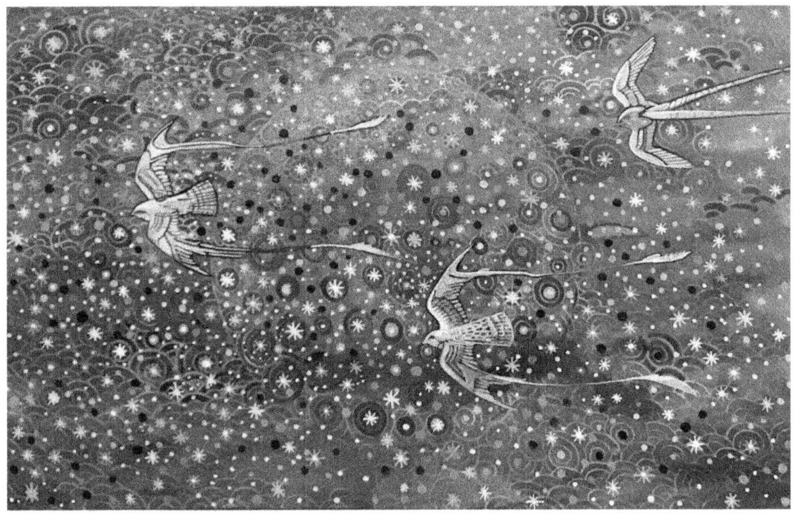

Alfredo Arreguín, *Twilight,* 2019, oil on canvas, 30 x 48', Courtesy of the artist

# Alfredo Arreguín Grieves and Celebrates

In these dark depths of December, and in our equally dark political climate, the Alfredo Arreguín exhibition at the Bainbridge Island Museum of Art will brighten your day, lift your spirits, and sooth your soul. It may also inspire you to activism as well as introduce you to Mexican mythology and spirituality.

Alfredo Arreguín's paintings immerse us in a wonderland of jungle and seascape, populated by animals, fish, insects, and birds. But the jungle and its creatures are more than the sum of their parts, they represent *nagual,* a guardian creature of the spirit world who can transform and lead us to alternative views of the world.

The artist embedded in this wonderland (sometimes almost invisibly), the faces of well known political activists, writers, poets, friends, and, occasionally, the artist himself. The faces deeply disguised within the vast details of the paintings, point to Arreguín's belief in the harmony of nature, the balance of life, and the crucial place that we have within it, rather than outside it. His work has never been more timely or important, as we all despair with the election of a president in Brazil intent on destroying the entire rain forest there for economic profit. Nothing less than the lungs of the planet are at stake.

So plunge into one of his paintings and look at it for a long time, and still come back for more. Explore the dazzling overall intricacy, the detailed patterns, the accomplished linear relationships, the subtle command of color that changes in each work. Then, as you visually wander through the paintings, join the butterflies, the birds, and the animals in the depths of the jungle.

Arreguín's themes—nature, Madonnas, and portraiture—overlap and intersect. In every detail of these intricate works, he contradicts the angry rhetoric of racists creating arbitrary divisions in our beautiful world.

Leaping salmon and whales remind us that the survival of the Southern Resident pod of orca is hanging in the balance. As the whales dwindle in response to environmental degradation, and the salmon fail to complete their migration upstream because of dams, Arreguín's paintings celebrate natural processes and inspire us to protect our Salish Sea.

Arreguín's life story is unusual. Born in Morelia, Michoacán, Mexico, as an illegitimate child, he was passed from one relative to another. On a few occasions, he had the opportunity to be immersed in the jungle, experiences that made a deep and permanent impression on him. He also had enough educational opportunities to learn art as he moved from Morelia to Mexico City. But by extraordinary serendipity he was invited to live in Seattle by a family he met when they were lost as tourists in Chapultepec Park. As a result, he came to the U.S. in January 1956, and gained citizenship with their sponsorship. After serving in the army, he attended the University of Washington, earning two degrees.

Almost immediately, he began to appear in major exhibitions. The National Museum of American Art acquired his work in the early 1990s. One has to ask why, as yet, the Seattle Art Museum has not given him an exhibition and does not even own his work. This exhibition includes works from BIMA's permanent collection, promised gifts, loans from private collections and the artist himself, for a total of almost fifty works for this 50-year retrospective.

Arreguín began honoring Frida Kahlo even in his early work, many years before she became a pop icon. They share a love of folk art, peasant expressions, nature, music, and the sensuality of life. Arreguín includes folk art patterns and their motifs in one layer of his dense jungle tapestries, but more than that, both Frida and Arreguín, embrace traditional spiritual beliefs in Mexico, beliefs that survive, transformed, to this day.

Likewise, Arreguín's love of literature and language pervades his paintings, sometimes literally in his homages to his friends Raymond Carver and Tess Gallagher. At other times more subtly as in his homage to Pablo Neruda. Also look for his portraits of indigenous environmentalists, well known activists, and historical revolutionaries.

(2018)

# Susan Lytle and Alfredo Arreguín Look Closely at Nature

APPROPRIATELY, A TANGLE OF IVY HID the doorbell, but I knew I was in the right place because of the small, pale red ceramic pig on the porch. As soon I entered the simple brick home of Alfredo Arreguín and Susan Lytle in North Seattle, I was immersed in a wonderland that echoed the jungles in Arreguín's paintings. First, Susan introduced me to the delicate Queen of the Night flower, a type of cactus with a flower that blooms for only one night with an exotic blossom. They are one subject of her paintings. (I, of course, immediately thought of Mozart's Queen of the Night in the *Magic Flute*, and her extraordinary impossible aria, like a one night exotic blossoming itself). Nearby on a table was a Jewel Orchid, a lush jungle plant with delicate flowers.

Carved wooden sculpture and ceramics, that included rabbits, elephants, dogs, turtles, and composite beasts (those wonderful carvings from Oaxaca), were arranged in careful ensembles throughout the living room and dining room. Small ceramic figures filled a shelf. I photographed a wall of masks to give a sense of the eclecticism and range of these collections. The unity among many cultures and the universality of the creative impulse is a theme of the house and of the art created there.

One anonymous Mexican painting caught my eye: it was a kitchen scene of a long brick stove with square openings that needed to be fed sticks of wood. Arreguín said it reminded him of his childhood; he used to tend a stove like that when he lived with his grandmother. His riveting life story, from poverty to where he is today, has been told many times, and in many ways. He shared a few anecdotes with me. His stepfather was a dreadful person. As Alfredo tried to flee from him on his bike, he fell off, and his stepfather ran over his bike.

But then his luck changed, he discovered a wealthy father in Mexico City who funded his first art schooling and allowed him to live with him and his family in a large house. But then, once again, his fortunes reversed as his father forced him out of the house on an accusation from his stepmother. And on it went, abrupt changes of fortune, incredible good luck, incredible bad luck. The story of his serendipitous arrival in Seattle at the invitation of a family he met in Chapultepec Park is well known.

As we spoke in the dining room I was facing an early painting, *Tehuanas,* from 1982, in which two female dancers face one another, their white dresses forming two separated sides of a semi-circle, the space between them charged with energy. Arreguín explained that this was an early example of his use of pattern when it took him hours to create the repeated geometric shapes. Now, he says, it just flows from his fingers. Arreguín placed the dancers, static and stately, into the ground in a seamless single flat layer, filled with at least ten shades of red, orange, pink and lilac, creating a festive spirit.

This painting underscored the surprising fact about visiting the house. I experienced the fabric of his life with Susan Lytle. In the house I could feel the interweaving of two spirits who are dancing together through art and life. I was amazed when I went to the simple basement studio and saw that they shared a single long room. There was a slight demarcation created by a pile of Alfredo's paint tubes and Susan's easel, but they have worked like this for over forty years!

On Alfredo's easel was a large painting of leaping orcas called *Twilight.* As we looked at the painting he now and then added a white dot to the surface while we were talking. Arreguín's many paintings of wildlife in jungles and the sea speak to his great sense of the loss of our rich biodiversity. As he stated, "We are the most dangerous animals on the planet." The mighty orca killer whale in our Southern Resident pod, about which Lynda Mapes has written so eloquently in the last two years in *The Seattle Times*, numbers only about seventy-three today, and they are starving for lack of the chinook salmon they need to survive. The salmon, like the orca, are dying out, both threatened by environmental challenges from pollution to noise.

I felt deep sorrow permeating the painting, reinforced by its gentle lighting between day and night. The leaping orcas were celebrating the birth of a new baby, but I felt the threat hanging over the joy. Only last summer, a male baby orca calf born to our Southern Resident pod, lived for less than an hour, and then was carried for seventeen days by its mother, Tahlequah (J-35), in a tragic epic journey.

In the other end of the studio, several of Susan Lytle's completed paintings of the Queen of the Night flower hung on the wall, and a work in progress was on her easel. Seeing these paintings at the end of my visit, fit perfectly with my introduction to the one-night emergence bloom and death of each flower as I entered their house. Lytle carefully explores the rapid transformations and intricacies of these briefly surviving blooms in sequences of small paintings.

As I left, I looked again at Arreguín's *Birds of Paradise,* hung directly opposite the front door. The multicolored birds fly and perch on branches against a background suggesting a sea and sky that clearly speaks of the Asian influence in his works from his visits to Japan while he was in the army in Korea. These birds fly joyfully in counterpoint to the leaping of the huge orcas who seem weighted with sadness. Arreguín said this painting has just been purchased by 4Culture for the Children and Family Justice Center. He wanted to bring a feeling of freedom into a dark place. Here is his narrative:

> Birds have flown the skies since time immemorial. These beautiful creatures have inspired artists for centuries, not only with their graceful flight, but also with their song and plumage. As an artist, I am no exception. I have been fascinated with these flying miracles most of my life, and they appear in my paintings as memories of my childhood, of my travels and my daily walks and communion with Nature. This painting, *Birds of Paradise*, is an attempt to describe my amazement and delight upon discovering these flying jewels from Indonesia and Australia. As an artist, I would never try to compete with Nature's creations. So, in Picasso's words, I paint the lie that makes us see the truth.

So on this visit, I experienced Arreguín, the man, who sorrows for the loss of the connected intersecting web of life on our planet, and Arreguín, the painter, who celebrates life in all its forms. His partner of many years, Susan Lytle, introduced me to the exotic habits and intricate beauty of the Queen of the Night. Together they sing a song that goes straight into the heart.

(2019)

# Preston Singletary's Raven and the Box of Daylight

PRESTON SINGLETARY (TLINGIT, AMERICAN) had a dazzling exhibition in Tacoma at the Museum of Glass called "Raven and the Box of Daylight." The sculptures told the famous Raven story step by step, with some full-on installation and special effects added in. The story flowed through us with each successive episode:

Before here was here, Raven was only named Yéil.

He was a white bird and the world was in Darkness. Raven decides he will try and do something about the darkness, for himself and for the world. As he follows the Nass River, he encounters the Fishermen of the Night. . . . They tell Yéil that Naas Shaak Aankáawu (the Nobleman at the Head of the Nass River), has many treasures in his Naa Kanidi (Clan House) including beautifully carved boxes that house the light.

*Yéil* (Raven) knows he will not be welcome in his raven form and devises a plan to transform himself to a tiny speck of dirt. His plan is to float down the river, as a hemlock needle, into the drinking ladle of the daughter of Naas Shaak Aankáawu. That is how he will sneak into the Naa Kanidi (Clan House).

*Yéil* turns himself into a hemlock needle and falls into the water. He floats into the ladle of Naas Shaak Aankaawu du Seek' (daughter of the Nobleman at the Head of the Nass River) as she dips it into the river for a drink....is ingested by her and she becomes pregnant.

*Yéil* grows into a precocious and precious human boy.

At the center of the exhibition stood a recreation of a clan house with its prized possessions—the stars, the moon and the daylight.

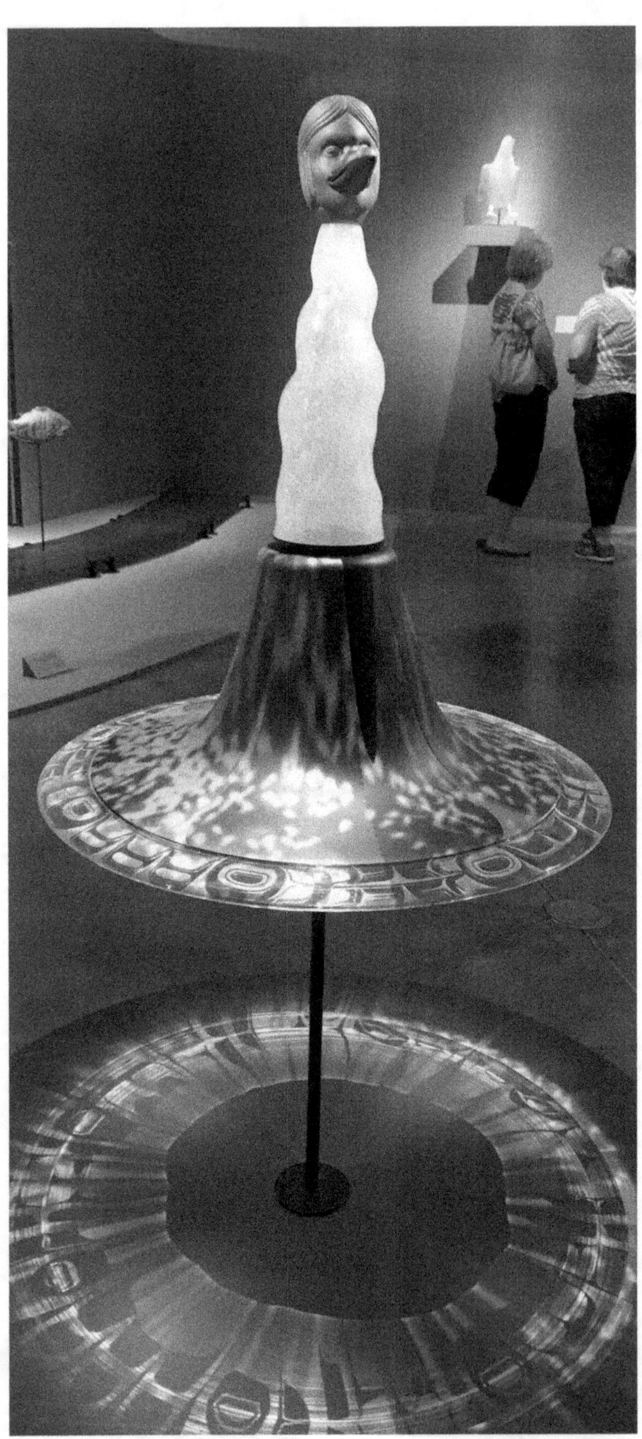

Preston Singletary (Tlingit), "Raven and the Box of Daylight," installation detail, Museum of Glass, Tacoma, Washington, 2018-19

Through pleading with his grandfather, who adores him, Raven is able to liberate the box containing the stars, moon and daylight.

> As the stars fill the sky and as the moon takes its place, light begins to fill the earth. When the sun takes its place in the sky, bringing daylight to the world, it is frightening to all those who have been in darkness. The people are able to see the world around them for the first time and are startled. Those wearing animal regalia run to the woods and become animal people, Those wearing bird regalia jump in the sky and become The Winged People. Those wearing water animal regalia become the Water People. Those who remained strong (and stubborn) became the Human People.
>
> *Yéil* decides it is time to leave and transforms back into bird form. Naas Shaak Aankáawu is devastated that his treasures have been released into the sky. He is so angry that he gathers all the pitch in the Naa Kanidi (Clan House) in a bentwood box and throws it into the fire. He catches *Yéil* as he tries to escape out of the smoke hole and holds onto his feet. *Yéil* is covered in the soot and smoke of the fire. He is transformed from a spiritual being into the black bird we know today. His color marks his sacrifice. His physical form is forever changed for bringing light into the world.

At the same time as this exhibition, we enjoyed musical performance by both traditional Alaskan Tlingit Kuteeyaa and Preston Singletary's band Khu.éex'.

Stonington Gallery is showing Preston's work as well as that of Raven Skyriver and his mentor Joe David. Raven Skyriver and Preston spoke at a panel this summer at the Museum of Glass where they explained the importance of the hot shop there for expanding the possibilities of their work in glass. Skyriver, born and raised on Lopez Island, compared fluid glass to the marine environment. He sees himself as "perpetuating culture in glass." Historically, house leaders commissioned art. It has to be commercial now. His work represents endangered sea creatures. threatened by acidification, overfishing, and pollution.

Preston spoke of beginning his glass work only ten years ago. He spent years studying form line design in order to create glass in the Tlingit tradition with some of the great artists of contemporary Native Art. We all know how stunning his work has been in that medium. His glass work has transformed my point of view on glass sculpture. Last summer, he and Skyriver collaborated on work for the first time. And this exhibition is in honor of that collaboration.

(2019)

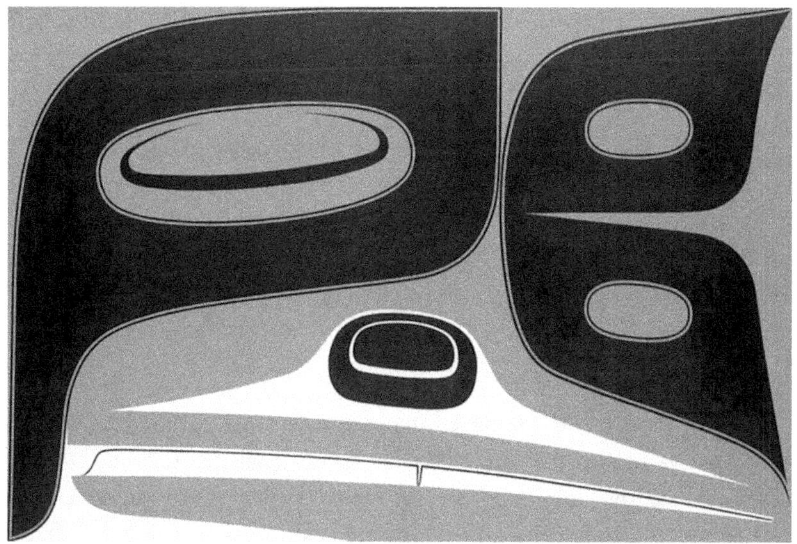

Robert Davidson (Haida), *Oyster Catcher,* 2008 acrylic on canvas, 30 x 40", Cutshall Collection, Courtesy of the Artist, Photograph: Kenji Nagai by permission

# Setting Our Hearts on Fire: Robert Davidson

THE BRILLIANTLY-COLORED PAINTINGS and sculptures of Haida Artist Robert Davidson, at the Seattle Art Museum, warm our bodies and actually set our hearts on fire during these short winter days. There couldn't be a better time to see this radical exhibition of highly-saturated red, black and white paintings and carved, painted wooden sculptures.

I have included above my articles on the Haida and their fight for survival, as well as an exhibition on Charles Edenshaw (1839-1920) at the Vancouver Art Gallery curated by Burke Museum Curator Robin Wright. Charles Edenshaw preserved, resurrected, and transformed traditional Haida art forms, that were mainly for sale to tourists and ethnographic and natural history museums, at a time when the practice of his culture was banned in his homeland. More specifically, from 1884-1951 the Canadian government banned the potlatch, the communal gift-giving ceremony that honored special events such as pole raising with singing, storytelling and exchange of wealth. That action devastated cultural practices among First Nations people and Native tribes in the Northwest.

Finally, in the 1950s, Bill Reid, a White artist who had befriended the Haida, began to resurrect and recreate Haida carving and imagery. A decade later, he mentored the young Robert Davidson. As Edenshaw's great grandson, Robert Davidson is now himself transforming Haida art. He does so from the foundation of a deep knowledge of traditional Haida media, imagery, and art principles.

His career began in 1969 when, at age twenty-two, he carved the first totem pole to be raised on Haida Gwaii in almost a century. Davidson wanted to fill the cultural vacuum that he experienced as a child and young man in Masset (formerly Massett), on Haida Gwaii (then Queen Charlotte Islands). He spent months learning the traditional stories, making tools, and teaching himself carving techniques. The communal celebration that accompanied the pole raising inspired grandparents to sing and dance based on ancient memories preserved in secret and in their souls. The ritual celebration brought the community back alive. That pole raising has galvanized Davidson to this day.

Davidson's bold transformations of tradition, like his decision to carve that first pole, is possible only because of his life-long engagement with traditional culture. As we are overwhelmed by the beauty of his artworks, we also can learn about their roots in realism and myth.

"Abstract Impulse" is a carefully considered title and the labels for each work are respectfully detailed in order for us to understand that this abstract impulse is not related to mid-century abstract painting in the U.S. (e.g., Mark Tobey, Jackson Pollock, et al.). It is in fact the other way around—those White artists ignorantly took abstract motifs from Native art. In Davidson's work, though, the abstraction is based on deep connections to abstract principles coming from Haida design itself. He transforms and enlarges, he gives us a fragment of a whole, he creates an interior space in a traditional totem design.

Traditional references to the whale, the bear, the raven, the human, are integral to the brilliantly saturated colors, the contemporary media, the suggestion of shapes, even the reduction to a single line; we are embraced and even enveloped by the art and its underlying stories.

Robert Davidson reminds us of our deep connections to the natural world. Davidson and the Haida represent respect for land, sea and sky, and for all the creatures of the earth as interdependent equals. This understanding refutes the "enlightenment" hierarchy that places humans as superior beings, a world view that justifies ferocious extraction and destruction of the earth's precious resources.

What a perfect celebration and inspiration Davidson provides for a time in which we must continue to stand up for our planet's survival. If we can carry the warmth of these paintings, based in passion and love for a ten-thousand-year-old history, we will also be inspired to help in their continued preservation and transformation as a legacy for our own grandchildren.

(2014)

All essays not listed below are from my blog
www.artandpoliticsnow.com

"In Memoriam: Jay DeFeo 1929-1989," unpublished, written in 1989 • "Selma Waldman: The Pornography of War"—*Selma Waldman/Naked/Aggression: Profile of the Armed Perpetrator: 1998-2003*, exhibition brochure • *Pornography of Power: The Anti-War Art of Selma Waldman*, Rosetta M. Hunter Gallery at Seattle Central Community College, September 21-October 24, 2008, exhibition brochure • "Jacob Lawrence: History Painter from Harlem to Hiroshima"—*Making a Life, Creating a World, Jacob Lawrence and James W. Washington, Jr.*, Northwest African American Museum, catalog essay, 2008-2009 • "Jacob Lawrence" *Art Access* May-June 2021 • "James W. Washington Jr.: Painter, Activist, Sculptor"—*Columbia Magazine*, Winter 2011 • "Bauhaus in the Northwest: The Art of Mary Henry"—"Mary Henry's Abstract Paintings," Bryan Ohno Gallery, Seattle July 5-28, *Art Papers*, November 2002 • "Designed Obsolescence"—"Lubbock: Designed Obsolescence/Third Floor," *Art Lies*, Spring 2005 • "The Performing Black Body"—"rAdIcAl prEsEncE: Black Performance in Contemporary Art," *Raven Chronicles*, Fall 2013 • "Gloria Anzaldúa: Beyond Binaries"—*Gloria Anzaldúa, Light in the Dark/Luz en lo Oscuro: Rewriting Identity, Spirituality, Reality*, ed. by AnaLouise Keating, Duke University Press, 2015, *Raven Chronicles*, Vol 22, Summer 2016 • "Paradigms and Paradoxes Nature Morality and Art in America"—*Art Journal*, summer 1992 • "Maya Lin: Extinctions and Confluences"—"The State of the Planet: Two Projects by Maya Lin," *The New Earthwork, Art Action Agency*, ed. by Twylene Moyer and Glenn Harper, International Sculpture Center, 2011 • "Water Cycles and Water Treatment"—"Visualizing the Water Cycle: Buster Simpson Jann Rosen-Queralt, and Ellen Sollod at Brightwater Treatment System," *The New Earthwork, Art Action Agency*, ed. by Twylene Moyer and Glenn Harper, International Sculpture Center, 2011 • "A Cautionary Tale of Nature's Forces: Amie McNeel, Mark Zirpel and Sam Stubblefield"—"Amie McNeel, Mark Zirpel, and Sam Stubblefield at MadArt: Portfolio of Possibilities," *Sculpture Magazine*, January/February 2017 • "Olive Ayhens: Urbanities and Ur-Beasts"—*Olive Ayhens: Urbanities and Ur-Beasts*, Lori Bookstein Projects, catalog essay, October 2019 • "The Magic of Haida Gwaii"—"Haida Gwaii," *Raven Chronicles*, volume 19, Fall 2013 • *Charles Edenshaw: Haida Sculptor in the Era of Assimilation*—"Haida Gwaii: Charles Edenshaw," October 26, 2013 – February 2, 2014, Vancouver Art Gallery, *Leschi News Culture Column*, September and October, 2013 • "Red Ink"—"In Red Ink," Museum of Northwest Art, July 7-September 23, 2018, *Art Access*, September 2018 • "Vito Acconci's Evacuation Plans"—"Vito Acconci: The Sheltering City,"

*Artweek*, September 1982 • "Nancy Graves Defying Categories"—"Nancy Graves," *Women's Caucus for Art, National Honorees Catalog*, 1993 • "Masami Teraoka on AIDS and the Internet"—"Masami Teraoka: The Culture of the Apocalypse," *Art Papers*, January/February 1997 • "Tatiana Garmendia and the Immorality of War"—"Tatiana Garmendia's Epics," Patricia Cameron Gallery, catalog essay, 2009 • "Kehinde Wiley's Heroes and Saints"—"Kehinde Wiley: A New Republic," *Art Access*, March 2016 • "Kelly James Marshall: Maestro and Shaman"—"Kerry James Marshall: Maestro and Shaman," *Leschi News Culture Column*, March 2018 • "In our Face: Robert Colescott, Kerry James Marshall, Mickalene Thomas"— *Leschi News Culture Column*, March 2018 • "Mickelene Thomas Muse"—"MUSE: Mickalene Thomas Photographs' and 'tête á tête,'" *Leschi News Culture Column*, September 2018 • "Somnyama Ngonyama: Hail the Dark Lioness"—*Leschi News Culture Column*, September, 2019 • "Jean Lacy's Stained Glass Windows"—"Jean Lacy," *Women's Caucus for Art Newsletter*, Dallas, 1996 • "Icons Now and Then by Betye Saar"—"Betye Saar," Tacoma Art Museum, April 19-June 29, 1997, *Art Papers*, September/October 1997 • "Marilyn Walgore's Gender Games"— "Marilyn Waligore: Gender Games," catalog essay 1993 • "Pamela Allara Faces Alice Neel Head On"—"Pamela Allara, Pictures of People, Alice Neel's American Portrait Gallery," University Press of New England, 1998 *Women Artists News*, 1998, Book Review • "Tomur Atagök's Anatolian Goddess Series"—*Tomur Atagök : Anatolian Goddess Series*," Çirağan Kempinksi, November 21-24, 1999 • "Imna Arroyo:  History, Place, Spiritualty"—"Bridging Traditions," *Imna Arroyo: In Search of My Tracks, A Spiritual Journey*, catalog essay, January 1995 • "Marita Dingus's Acts of Metamorphosis 1-3"—*Art Papers*, September/October, 2003, and *Leschi News Culture Column*, October 2019 • "Still Life and Concupiscence by Gloria Bornstein"—"Gloria Bornstein: 'Still Life' at the Seattle Art Museum," *artdish.com*, 2002 • "DeeDee Faces the Abyss, But Still Imagines Utopia – Deborah Faye Lawrence"—*DeeDee Does Utopia, Deborah Faye Lawrence*, Marquand Books, catalog essay, 2007 • "LaToya Ruby Frazier Exposes the Injuries of Capitalism in Braddock, Pennsylvania"—"LaToya Ruby Frazier: Born by a River," *Leschi News Culture Column*, September 2014 • "Martha Rosler 'Housing is a Human Right'"—"Martha Rosler: 'Housing Is a Human Right' in Seattle," *Art Papers*, July/ August 2016 • "Lillian Pitt: Spirits Keep Whistling Me Home"—"Warm Springs Oregon: Lillian Pitt 'Spirits Keep Whistling Me Home,'" *Art Papers*, October 1999 • "Heaven on Fire: Barbara Earl Thomas"—"Barbara Earl Thomas: 'Heaven on Fire,'" Bainbridge Island Museum of Art, *Art Access*, September-October 2016 • "Alfredo Arreguín Grieves and Celebrates"—"Alfredo Arreguín: Life Patterns," Bainbridge Island Museum of Art,  *Leschi News Culture Column*, December 2018 • "Setting Our Hearts on Fire: Robert Davidson"—"Setting Our Hearts on Fire: Robert Davidson," *Leschi News Culture Column*, January 2014.

A native of New York City, SUSAN NOYES PLATT is currently a freelance art historian and art critic based in Seattle, Washington. She has published four books on art and criticism, *Modernism in the 1920s* (1985), *Art and Politics in the 1930s* (1999), *Art and Politics Now* (2010), and *Breaking Ground: Art Modernisms 1920-1950* (2020). She was an assistant professor of Art History at Mills College, and a tenured professor at Washington State University and The University of North Texas. In 1999-2000 she taught at Yıldız Technical University, Istanbul, Turkey supported by a Fulbright Fellowship. As a critic she has written for numerous publications both national and international, as well as locally in a monthly newspaper column and bimonthly art magazine. She also writes a blog on her website www.artandpoliticsnow.com.

www.ingramcontent.com/pod-product-compliance
Lightning Source LLC
Chambersburg PA
CBHW051754050726
47598CB00006B/2279